*The I.R.S. and the Freedom of
Information and Privacy Acts of 1974*

The I.R.S.
and the Freedom
of Information and
Privacy Acts of 1974

*The Disclosure Policies
of the Internal Revenue Service
and How to Obtain
Documents from Them*

by

Marcus Farbenblum

McFarland & Company, Inc., Publishers
Jefferson, North Carolina, and London

This book is intended to provide the public with the knowledge, experience, interpretations, and opinions garnered by the author during thirty years of employment with the Internal Revenue Service. It is not intended as legal or other professional advice. Taxpayers encountering difficulties with the Internal Revenue Service are strongly advised to obtain the assistance of an attorney, certified public accountant, enrolled agent, or other competent professional. The author and publisher disclaim any responsibility for any liability, loss, or other adverse consequence resulting directly or indirectly from any person's choosing to act or rely upon any statement presented herein.

British Library Cataloguing-in-Publication data are available

Library of Congress Cataloguing-in-Publication Data

Farbenblum, Marcus, 1934–
    The I.R.S. and the Freedom of Information and Privacy Acts of 1974 :
the disclosure policies of the Internal Revenue Service and how to
obtain documents from them / Marcus Farbenblum.
        p. cm.
    Includes index.
    ISBN 0-89950-640-2 (lib. bdg. : 50# alk. paper) ∞
    1. United States. Internal Revenue Service.   I. Title.
II. Title: IRS and the Freedom of Information and Privacy Acts of
1974.
KF6301.F37   1991
343.7305′2 – dc20
[347.30352]   91-52755
                                                                                              CIP

Manufactured in the United States of America

McFarland & Company, Inc., Publishers
  Box 611, Jefferson, North Carolina 28640

Table of Contents

Introduction

This is the story of how the Internal Revenue Service makes its records available to the public. It is also the story of how the Internal Revenue Service withholds its records from the public, sometimes in compliance with laws which require confidentiality to protect the public interest and sometimes in flagrant disregard of laws which require disclosure.

And this is a practical guide on how to make the Internal Revenue Service tell you everything you have a right to know, whether it concerns the contents of your own investigatory files, the procedures under which the Service operates, or any other record maintained at public expense.

The Congress has provided the American people with three powerful laws designed to guarantee public access to the Internal Revenue Service's records: the Freedom of Information Act, the Privacy Act of 1974, and the disclosure provisions of the Internal Revenue Code.

The operation of these laws should have resulted in an Internal Revenue Service open to public scrutiny and responsive to the needs and desires of the public it is intended to serve. Instead, the Internal Revenue Service remains shrouded in mystery, carrying out its duties in ways that are incomprehensible to most taxpayers.

Few taxpayers are aware that laws which require the public disclosure of government records exist, and few appreciate the tremendous benefits to be derived from their use. Fewer still know how to use these laws effectively. Nor is the Service interested in spreading this knowledge. On the contrary, the Internal Revenue Service often seems intent upon discouraging inquiry and offers the taxpayer in search of information as little cooperation as possible.

I know. For more than 15 years, I served as the Internal Revenue Service's leading expert on the administration of the Freedom of Information Act and the Privacy Act of 1974. As chief of the Freedom of Information Branch in the National Office of the Internal Revenue Service, I was responsible for designing, initiating, and implementing the procedures necessary to make records available to members of the public. Specialists under my supervision prepared the responses to requests for National Office records, staffed the Freedom of Information Reading Room, and provided guidance to the disclosure officers who served the public in our field offices.

We did what we could to bring the Internal Revenue Service into full compliance with the disclosure laws. It seemed, however, that the very officials who assigned these responsibilities to us were often intent upon preventing us from

1

carrying them out. Our efforts to encourage the liberal release of records to which the public was entitled were seldom completely successful. Records had to be pried loose from officials determined to protect their programs. Behind the official policy of open government lurked a culture based upon the belief that the best information policy for an investigatory agency was to take everything and give nothing.

The public, far from insisting upon their rights, often seemed to conspire in their exclusion from open government by inactivity and a willingness to take no for an answer. Over the years, far more people told me that they understood why we had to deny their requests than demanded to know what earthly reason could justify our withholding the requested information.

In 1986 the Internal Revenue Service processed 188 million tax returns, 85 million of which were individual income tax returns. The Examination Division audited more than 1 million returns, two-thirds of which resulted in additional assessments. The Collection Division took enforcement action against 2.5 million deliquent taxpayers. The Criminal Investigation Division completed 6,000 investigations, obtaining almost 2,500 convictions, most of which resulted in prison sentences.

Despite this very extensive activity, there were only 10,820 Freedom of Information Act requests and a few dozen Privacy Act requests in 1986! That works out to one Freedom of Information act request for every 17,365 tax returns filed, or one for every 7,855 individual taxpayers.

Of these 10,820 requests, 2,749 were so poorly constructed that they could be denied as "imperfect" without having to locate or evaluate a record for release. More than a quarter of all the requests received had failed to provide an adequate description of the records sought or had failed to state the requester's agreement to pay the rather minimal fees which would have resulted from the release of records. A further 1,224 requests asked for records which did not exist. Another 640 requesters asked for records concerning themselves but failed to establish their identity. A few requesters neglected to provide their name or address.

As a result of these careless errors, almost half of all the requests made in 1986 could be disposed of without any consideration of whether a record should be released. Only 5,845 requesters received a response which actually said either yes, you may have these records, or no, you may not!

When compared to the almost 4 million taxpayers facing Examination, Collection, or Criminal Investigation activity during the year, the number of persistent Freedom of Information requesters was ludicrous. The overwhelming majority of taxpayers appear to be perfectly willing to face serious adverse action without bothering to make any significant effort to learn what the agency knows about them or how they came to be in that situation. In fact, even subjects of major criminal investigations seldom bother to make such inquiries, apparently being willing to face trial and risk imprisonment without writing a simple letter which could produce information which could literally save their freedom.

The majority of Freedom of Information requesters are not taxpayers who face serious difficulties. Nor are they scholarly researchers, news reporters, attorneys, accountants, or businessmen. Judging by the thousands of requests I have personally reviewed, the great majority of requesters appear to be rather ordinary people who somehow have come in conflict with the agency and are desperately trying to find out why. They seem to have exhausted all other remedies known to them and are pursuing access to records as a last resort. Typically, they seem to believe that they are being singled out for unreasonable and unfair treatment. They appear to believe that the answer to their problem can be found somewhere in their records or in the procedures they believe govern their treatment. They may or may not be right; their problems may be the fault of the Service, or they may be of their own making.

Since most requesters probably found themselves in need of help precisely because they were ill prepared to deal with the demands of the bureaucracy, it should not be surprising that few are successful in seeking access to their records, especially since the Service generally prefers to reject their requests as imperfect rather than attempt to identify and resolve the underlying problem.

Of the 5,845 requesters who were able to secure a yes or no response based upon an actual analysis of the desired records, 1,996 received either a full or a partial denial.

Only 3,849, or slightly over one-third of the requesters, actually received everything they asked for, if we assume responses which claim to have located and released all the requested records are entirely accurate. In reality, there is a tendency to make a minimal interpretation of a request so as to simplify the task of responding, a sort of "give them something and they'll be happy" approach to Freedom of Information processing.

The Freedom of Information Reading Room, which dispenses only the most innocuous, routinely available printed matters, known as "shelf materials," was responsible for more than half of these full grants. As a result, the 3-to-1 odds against a fully successful request are considerably overstated. The odds against extracting from the Service a new record not previously released would have to be a least 5 to 1.

For those requesters who are not satisfied with the response, and these statistics would seem to indicate that there is little ground for satisfaction, the Information Act provides for an appeal. During 1986, the Service received 802 appeals, which would indicate that about seven out of every eight less than fully successful requesters were nevertheless satisfied with their response. In fact, almost two out of every three requesters who received absolutely nothing accept that result without further action, even though the Service's response carefully explained the availability of appeal rights!

One reason for the minimal use of appeals may be the belief that the agency, having once denied a request, is unlikely to reverse itself. That belief could be justified, since the 802 appeals produced only 21 full grants. There were, however, 65 appeals which resulted in an additional partial release of records, although many of these did not involve a significant release of new material.

Finally, if both an initial request and an appeal have failed to produce the desired result, the Freedom of Information Act (Information Act) provides for a challenge in the Federal courts. There were 48 such suits in 1986. Every

Internal Revenue Service official who contemplates denying a record to a Freedom of Information requester is aware that his decision may result in litigation in which he will have to defend his decision. The odds against such a denial being taken to court in 1986 were 145 to 1.

It is obvious, therefore, that few taxpayers requesting records will receive what they are looking for. Many may receive some innocuous document that will justify moving their request into the grant column for the sake of compiling attractive statistics, but few will receive anything worthwhile. And hardly any will bother to do anything about it, thereby encouraging further intransigence by officials who already have little inclination to comply with the disclosure laws.

But how valuable to the requester are the records which have been released? How valuable are the records which should have been released? There is, of course, no reliable measure by which to answer these questions.

No taxpayer has ever called me to say, "Thanks, you saved me a fortune." Certainly none has ever called to say, "Thanks, you kept me out of prison."

I am convinced that no release of records pursuant to the Information Act has ever interfered with the law enforcement responsibilities of the Internal Revenue Service. No guilty person has ever escaped punishment based upon information received in a release of records. Not one penny of tax has ever gone uncollected because of a legitimate release of information. Moreover, I am also convinced that the vast majority of records withheld from taxpayers could have been released without the least likelihood of any harm to any government activity.

Many taxpayers who did receive information could have experienced considerable benefits, well-deserved benefits, from the information received had they understood its nature and its significance and known how to make adequate use of it. The great misfortune which overshadows the disclosure process is that government activities are so complex, that persons receiving information are usually unable to understand it. Not knowing what to do with information is not, however, a valid reason for not seeking it. On the contrary, it is reason to seek even more information or to seek guidance on its use and evaluation.

Finally, I am overwhelmingly convinced that the greatest beneficiary of an active, knowledgeable public effectively demanding their rights of access to records would be the Internal Revenue Service itself. My experience of 30 years in the Internal Revenue Service has repeatedly demonstrated to me that there is a remarkable consistency of belief among Internal Revenue Service officials. There exists within the Service a pattern of accommodation which leads management to cooperate in the achievement of organizational goals based upon shared beliefs which may not be true; in fact, many of them may be patently ridiculous. Closed societies are remarkably comfortable and effective until the moment of their collapse.

The American people need to know more about the Internal Revenue Service. The Internal Revenue Service needs the American people to know more about the Internal Revenue Service.

The objectives of this book are to help Internal Revenue Service officials overcome their reticence to release information to the public, to make the public aware of their rights to access Internal Revenue Service records, to help the public understand and use the information they receive, and to turn the Internal Revenue Service into an open society capable of benefitting from candid and honest interaction with the public it exists to serve.

I was unable to achieve these goals in the Service. Now you and I are going to achieve them outside the Service.

Chapter One

The Code of Confidentiality

The laws which require that taxpayers file returns and pay taxes and the laws which authorize the Internal Revenue Service to process those returns, collect taxes, issue refunds, perform investigations, and assess additional taxes and penalties are contained in what is known as the Internal Revenue Code (Code) or more specifically, Title 26 of the United States Code (U.S.C.).

The Code, as it is referred to by Service personnel, is more than a simple compilation of the laws which define and authorize just about everything the Internal Revenue Service does; it is the soul of the Service. Revenuers think, act, and live by the Code. Every problem has its resolution somewhere within the Code; all other legal requirements are perceived to have relevance to tax matters only as the Code permits.

Much like the religious texts which guide other societies, the Code deals with everything. It should be no surprise, then, to find that the Code contains several sections which provide very specific guidance on the disclosure of tax records. The most important of those sections, section 6103, Confidentiality and Disclosure of Returns and Return Information, provides 27 pages of detailed instructions on what is to be released and what is not to be released, to whom it should be released, under what circumstances, and for what purposes. As its title makes immediately apparent, the overall thrust of the Code is confidentiality.

Section 6103, in the form in which it now appears, was established in 1976, two years after the amendment of the Freedom of Information Act and the passage of the Privacy Act of 1974. It was no accident that these three great laws were to appear during the same period, for they have a common genesis in society's concern over how government's information practices are to affect citizens' lives. The detailed disclosure requirements in section 6103 represented a response to Congress' concerns that existing protections of taxpayer confidentiality were inadequate in the light of perceived violations during the Watergate era. Moreover, both the timing and the greater detail indicate that the special provisions governing the disclosure of tax information were necessary to perfect the disclosure scheme established by the Information Act and the Privacy Act. Both the Internal Revenue Service and the courts consider section 6103 to take precedence over the other acts, although not operating independently of them.

The new law primarily reinforced existing concepts of confidentiality by including requirements which were previously embodied in regulations. The concept that the information a taxpayer reports to the government ought to be confidential has been a part of our system for generations.

To the Internal Revenue Service, the confidentiality of tax returns is more than a legal requirement. It is the rock upon which all disclosure practices are based. It provides far better protection than the Privacy Act affords to the records of other agencies. It takes precedence over the Information Act. It expresses the will and the expectations of the American people.

Should an Internal Revenue Service employee be revealed to have violated section 6103 by making an unauthorized disclosure, as may at times occur, other revenuers view his actions with shock and dismay. There is no sympathy for violating this statute; it is something we live by, something we believe in. And it is a good statute, a statute which contributes to the success of voluntary compliance with the tax laws and protects the American taxpayers' rights of privacy.

There are times, however, when the confidentiality of tax information can be overdone. Old disclosure hands tell a story which illustrates what the bureaucracy can do to a perfectly appropriate principle. It may be an apocryphal tale, for I have no personal knowledge of its truth, but many of my friends claim that it really happened. It seems that many years ago, a special agent in the Criminal Investigation Division was using an informant on an organized crime case. Paid informants are always hard put to come up with enough information to earn their keep; the agents who use them constantly demand some return of the government's investment. As a result, the informant will disgorge a great deal of bad information along with the good—half-truths, rumors, distortions, even complete inventions. Having little understanding of the functions of government and the separation of powers amongst federal, state and local authorities, informants will frequently report information to the wrong agency. In this case, the informant reported information that had little relevance to tax administration. He reported that a murder was being planned, and he provided enough information to prevent the crime being committed. The special agent was shocked. Something had to be done, but was this information which could legally be shared with local law enforcement agencies, or was he legally bound to keep it confidential?

The special agent asked his supervisor for guidance, and the question was referred, through appropriate channels, to the National Office. In the National Office it was assigned to a disclosure specialist for response. The specialist studied his reference materials but could find no clear precedent. The question was referred in turn to counsel for a legal opinion. Counsel studied the matter but could offer no immediate opinion. After a time someone asked whether this was a hypothetical question or a live case; the specialist called the field for more information. The response was yes, it had been a live case, but there was no longer any need for an answer, for neither the question nor the victim was now "live." The murder had been committed while the National Office was considering whether authority existed to tell anyone about it.

Not all bureaucratic aberrations of the confidentiality principle involve matters as dramatic or as irreversible as murder. The confidentiality principle does, however, color the way Service personnel feel about the release of records. It can easily be misapplied, and it can lead to some very strange results. Consequently, we must take a very careful look at what section 6103 says and how it defines the matters it covers before we can consider the effects of the Information Act and the Privacy Act on the availability of Service records.

Tax Returns

Section 6103 refers to two very distinct types of records—tax returns and return information. The distinction between these two types of records will determine the kind of protection they will receive and the circumstances under which they may be disclosed.

Almost everyone believes that he knows what a tax return is. For disclosure purposes, however, his knowledge may not be precise enough to be of much help. The Code defines a *return* as

> any tax or information return, declaration of estimated tax, or claim for refund required by, or provided for or permitted under, the provisions of this title (i.e. Title 26 of the United States Code or the Internal Revenue Code itself) which is filed with the Secretary (i.e. the Department of the Treasury, including the Internal Revenue Service) by, on behalf of, or with respect to any person, and any amendment or supplement thereto, including supporting schedules, attachments, or lists which are supplemental to, or part of, the return so filed.

Careful consideration of this definition will show that it consists of five separate parts, each of which has some potential for creating disclosure problems if it is not fully understood.

The first part indicates that the return may be a tax or information return, a declaration of estimated tax, or a claim for refund. Consequently, a Form W-2, Wage and Tax Statement, filed by your employer, or a Form 1099-INT, Report of Interest Income, filed by your bank or credit union, would be a return.

The second part indicates that the item must be required by, provided for, or permitted under the Internal Revenue Code. If it is not in the Code, the guide which governs everything that the Service does, it is not a return and does not warrant protection as a return.

The third part indicates that it must actually be filed with the Secretary; the Internal Revenue Service or some other component of the Department of the Treasury must receive it. If you prepare a return and lose it on the way to the post office, the finders may do what they like with it. There is no protection for what has not been filed; it is simply not a *return* under the Code. Nor is there any protection under the Code for a copy of a return which you gave to a finance company or to a real estate office to document your level of income. Such revelations are entirely your own concern. The Code does, however, contain provisions to ensure that states which require copies of federal returns to be attached to state returns protect the confidentiality of such federal returns.

The fourth part indicates that it must be filed by, on behalf of, or with respect to a person. In other words, you do not have to file a document personally for it to be your return. It may have been filed by someone else, either for you or about you.

The fifth part indicates that a return includes supporting schedules, attachments, or lists which are supplemental to, or a part of, the return. This means that something which your wildest imagination would not have identified as a return might very well be a *return* if it was filed with a return. Or something may be filed after, or even before, a return is filed and nevertheless be a part of a return if it meets the balance of the definition. Sometimes this concept will lead to some very strange results. For instance, an article in a newspaper describing an artifact on display in a museum, or an article telling of the damage done by a recent storm, would be publicly available information. But if you were to attach either of them to your tax return to document the value of your donation to that museum or to support the damage done to your home by that storm, such news clippings become part of your return and deserve all the protection afforded by the Code.

The definition of a *return* makes no mention of any form. We all know that a Form 1040 is a tax return. The number 1040 is probably the best-known number in the world, but it is irrelevant to the definition of a return. A return need not be on a form; it need only meet the requirements of the definition as outlined above. Claims for refund, for instance, are frequently submitted as correspondence without using any form.

It should be obvious, therefore, that many things which are not filed on return forms, which may have become separated from returns, or which may never have been associated with returns are in fact returns. It sometimes requires careful consideration to determine what might be a return, but the Service may not always give that consideration. The reason for that is quite simple. According to the Code, a taxpayer is always entitled to receive a copy of his return. It cannot be denied to him. Other information may, however, be denied.

Whenever a conflict arises concerning the release of information to a taxpayer, it is in the Service's interest to define a return as narrowly as possible and thereby provide a basis for denying access to a record. It is in the taxpayer's interest to define a return as broadly as possible and thereby establish a right of access. When you reach the point where you are struggling to obtain records concerning yourself, remember the definition of a return; it may serve as the lever which pries loose the documents you need.

Return Information

The second category protected by section 6103 is *return information*. Return information receives about the same protection afforded the return itself. The major difference is that return information may be withheld from the taxpayer to whom it pertains. The Code states that "return information shall not be disclosed to such person or persons if the Secretary determines that such disclosure would seriously impair Federal tax administration."

The Internal Revenue Service will therefore try to define as much information about you as possible as return information. Keeping this distinction in mind, let us look very carefully at how the code defines return information. The term *return information* means

> a taxpayer's identity, the nature, source, or amount of his income, payments, receipts, deductions, exemptions, credits, assets, liabilities, net worth, tax liability, tax withheld, deficiencies, overassessments, or tax payments, whether the taxpayer's return was, is being, or will be examined or subject to other investigation or processing, or any other data, received by, recorded by, prepared by, furnished to, or collected by the Secretary with respect to a return or with respect to the determination of the existence, or possible existence, of liability (or the amount thereof) of any person under this title for any tax, penalty, interest, fine, forfeiture, or other imposition, or offense.

In other words, virtually all information which the Service receives or creates in the administration of your tax affairs is your return information. Everything you are likely to seek in connection with your treatment by the Service, which in fact pertains to you, is almost certain to be your return information. And all this information must be made available to you unless its release would seriously impair federal tax administration. No exemption in the Information Act or in the Privacy Act which might appear to authorize withholding a record from you can be effective against you unless its release would seriously impair tax administration in accordance with section 6103.

The Service does not always recognize that grand fact, and it will at times seek to withhold records on what would appear to be legally available exemptions without considering whether those records might be return information whose release would not cause the requisite serious impairment of tax administration!

Often, the opposite mistake will be made, and records which are entitled to no exemption will be withheld because their release would seriously impair tax administration, even though they are not return information. Using the broadest possible definition for return information can pay because it can make available an exemption that is unlikely to be challenged by anyone who has been denied the opportunity to examine and evaluate the records.

Some thought has to be given to what "seriously impair tax administration" means. The *Disclosure of Official Information Handbook* states that "return information should be denied . . . only if disclosure will impair an imminent or ongoing tax administration function in some significant way, or have an adverse impact on the Service's ability to administer the tax laws. An example of impairment is disclosure of information which would reveal the nature, scope, limit or direction of the Service's examination or investigation. Another example is disclosure of the identity of confidential informants or prospective witnesses."

That instruction limits *impairment* to some imminent or ongoing activity. You cannot be denied information which might impair some action which might sometime take place. It has to be imminent, that is, something which can reasonably be expected to take place in the immediate future. Nor is it possible to impair something that has already taken place. The Service will frequently ignore these distinctions and withhold records which pertain to an action which is completed and may or may not relate to some future activity which may never take place. The law does not permit such withholding of return information.

The impairment must be "significant." There does not appear to be a definition of what is significant, but it would seem reasonable to assume that the intent is that in order to warrant withholding information, its release would have to preclude the successful conclusion of some legally required activity, not merely subject the Service to a little additional effort or some administrative burden.

There appears to be a great deal of opportunity for challenging the withholding of return information on the basis of serious impairment of tax administration, but so far there do not appear to have been any meaningful efforts to overturn such determinations. Most people, judges included, seem to accept impairment denials without question.

Now that we have defined *return information* and seen why it is important to know what is and what is not return information, let me add that it can sometimes be very difficult to identify return information since both the content of records and their location must be considered in making that distinction. For example, let us analyze a series of memoranda.

The first memorandum discusses the treatment of a class of taxpayers, without mentioning any specific taxpayer. It is not return information and it may or may not be disclosed based upon other considerations.

A copy of the first memorandum is placed in your case file. That copy has now become your return information. Any copy which has not been in your case file may still be disclosed without mention of you, but the copy which is in your file cannot be removed and disclosed to anyone else.

The same memorandum, prior to being placed in your file, has your name written at the top in pencil so that it may be associated with your other records. That copy has also become your return information. Your name cannot be removed from that copy in order to permit its release, for once it has become your return information, it must forever remain so. The identifying facts cannot be removed from return information to permit its release.

A second memorandum discusses only your tax matters and mentions you by name. Copies may exist in various places. The memorandum is your return information, regardless of its location. Your name usually cannot be deleted, and the memorandum cannot be released to anyone else.

A revenue agent reads the second memorandum and decides that this is very worthwhile information equally applicable to another case he has, so he includes the memorandum in another taxpayer's case file. Now the memorandum has become the other taxpayer's return information. It is still your return information, but you are not entitled to know that it has a separate existence elsewhere. The other taxpayer would be entitled to receive the memorandum as his return information, but for this purpose, your name would be deleted. No matter how large this club of involved taxpayers becomes, none is entitled to know of the others, each retains the right to access the memorandum as his return information, and no other party will ever develop a right to learn of the memoranda's existence.

A third memorandum is written. It has two paragraphs. The first deals generally with the treatment of a class of taxpayers without identifying any of them. The second names several taxpayers to whom this information is applicable. In this case, the first paragraph is not return information. The second paragraph is the return information of all the taxpayers mentioned, but none may learn of the existence of the others. When placed within the case file of any taxpayer, the entire memorandum, including the first paragraph, is the return information of that taxpayer.

There is, of course, no limit to the number of paragraphs in a memorandum, a report, or any other document. The return information need not be neatly contained in one or more paragraphs, but may be mixed into the same paragraph with nonreturn information. Any of the foregoing situations or any almost unlimited variety of other situations may occur. A request for records which include but do not exclusively consist of return information may therefore represent a tremendous sorting and analysis task.

There are no formal procedures for accomplishing this task. In fact, there are no procedures whatsoever for releasing return information upon the demand of the taxpayer. The Service has proceeded upon the assumption that its procedures for tax administration will be adequate for handling any return-information-release situations that might occur. The taxpayer will receive everything that he needs, everything that he has a right to obtain, without ever having to ask for anything. The Service knows what is best for the taxpayer.

As a result, any demand for return information that is unrelated to some other tax administration activity and any appeal of the denial of return information must be processed through the use of Information Act procedures. Section 6103 requirements for the release of return information to the taxpayer on demand have, as a practical matter, no independent existence outside the Information Act.

The Service is fond of claiming that requests for return information should be processed exclusively under section 6103 without recourse to the Information Act. It does so because such exclusive processing would give it every advantage while stripping the taxpayer of his rights of access and appeal. The Service has never taken section 6103 access requirements seriously enough to create the procedures necessary to make it work. The taxpayer seeking his own return information must make his request under the Information Act, as failing to do so means permitting the Service to play using their ball, on their court, by their rules.

Chapter Two

Internal Revenue Service Attitudes

On July 4, 1967, the Freedom of Information Act became the first law which required that federal executive agencies release their records to any requester in accordance with specific standards established by law and subject to enforcement by the courts upon complaint by any person whose request had been denied.

Supporters of the new law emphasized that it had developed from doctrines of open government inherent in our democratic heritage. The constitutionally guaranteed rights of free speech and a free press were meaningless without being complemented by a right to know. The control of the government by the people was impossible if the people were ignorant of the government's actions. Information held by the government was in reality the property of the people, who had a right to access it, subject only to minor limitations necessary to avoid undesirable consequences recognized by the law. Government records were viewed as a natural resource to be available for public use in pursuit of the public good.

Despite these claims of a traditional, perhaps even constitutional basis for the public right to know, the new law met with almost universal rejection and derision by career government officials. These men and women, who shared the very same heritage upon which the Information Act was based, saw it as an ill-conceived threat to the public welfare which could destroy the nation and lead to anarchy.

In the Service I frequently heard that the Information Act was proof that the Congress did not undertand what it was doing and had no appreciation of the consequences of its irresponsible actions. The act was bad law and had no redeeming features at all. It would permit dishonest taxpayers to learn how to cheat without being detected and would drastically increase the tax burdens of the honest majority. One official claimed that the Information Act would "open Pandora's box, expose Medusa's head and unleash the dogs of hell."

How could the same law which promised to open up a new age of government responsibility and public involvement be so universally despised and feared by the very people who would have the responsibility for enforcing it? One reason was that the claims of a basis in our traditional heritage were mere puffery. The Information Act was a logical development of our democratic heritage, consistent with our shared ideals, but there was nothing "traditional" about it. It was revolutionary, and it ran counter to the trend of modern history.

13

For the first century and a half of American history, there was no meaningful concern about access to government records because government had little or no effect upon the average citizen. The federal government built forts along our coasts, kept a fleet at sea, expanded our western frontier, and kept watch over the Indians. There were no income taxes except during the Civil War and World War I. Government was supported primarily by customs duties collected at ports or at sea by the Revenue Cutter Service. Most Americans had no contact with any federal agency, except to receive or mail a letter at the post office. Those letters and most government records were likely to have been written by hand, using a quill sharpened with a penknife and dipped in ink made of lampblack. The Information Act, as it ultimately developed, would have been technologically impossible prior to the development and widespread availability of photocopying machines.

Neither the need for a Freedom of Information Act nor the means to carry it out existed until modern times. The vast expansion of government services — which began with the creation and growth of regulatory agencies under President Franklin Delano Roosevelt's New Deal and continued with President Harry S Truman's Fair Deal, President John F. Kennedy's New Frontier, and President Lyndon Johnson's Great Society — created both the bulk of the government's records and the need for the public to access them.

The Public Information Section

For 180 years the way our government kept its records was based upon "housekeeping" statutes which officials take the actions necessary for the operation of their agencies. The first change to the concept that heads of agencies were to decide what to do with their records came in 1946 with the enactment of the Public Information section of the Administrative Procedure Act.

The Public Information section provided that "except to the extent that there is involved (1) any function of the United States requiring secrecy in the public interest or (2) any matter relating solely to the internal management of an agency — Every agency shall make available to the public...Public Records — Save as otherwise required by statute, matters of official record shall in accordance with published rule be made available to persons properly and directly concerned except information held confidential for good cause found."

For 21 years, the Public Information section was the governing statute. And it contained six ways to withhold information from the public:

1. The function involved might require secrecy in the public interest.
2. The matter might relate solely to the internal management of the agency.
3. Withholding might be required by statute.
4. The release might not be in accordance with published rule.
5. The requester might not be a person properly and directly concerned.
6. The information might be held confidential for good cause found.

Who was to decide what might require secrecy in the public interest or who was properly and directly concerned or what was good cause found? Why, it was the responsible official who maintained the records, acting under delegation from the head of the agency! Thus, the rather free and easy authority of the "housekeeping" statutes was augmented in 1946 by a Public Information section which in effect drastically reduced what was to be public and seemed to stress the need for secrecy.

It was this law, in effect during a time when government record keeping was growing rapidly, which created the public perception that a wall of darkness was descending upon the federal government and ultimately made the Freedom of Information Act necessary.

Government officials were, of course, very comfortable with the Public Information section, which made it easier to justify withholding records than to grapple with the risks of releasing them. Officials who resisted the requirements of the Information Act were doing nothing more than clinging obstinately to the provisions of prior law.

In the Service the period in which the Public Information section governed the release of records was not necessarily a time of secrecy. A great many records were released to the public; that is, they were released to those members of the public who were properly and directly concerned.

One of the great accomplishments of the Information Act is claimed to be the release of the previously secret *Internal Revenue Manual*. But the *Internal Revenue Manual* was not secret! The Service provided a complete copy of the manual, with current updates mailed when issued, to the library of a major university. Thus, the manual was available to the good people who could be relied upon to use it responsibly, while being denied to everyone else.

Unfortunately, even if the logic of differentiating between responsible users and the general public were valid, the Service lacked the judgment necessary to effect such a distinction. A former dean of the very law school which received the manual was convicted of fraudulent failure to file tax returns without any resulting change in the subscription arrangements for providing the manual.

On the other hand, the bad people to whom access to the manual was denied included members of Congress performing properly authorized oversight investigations. In 1959, Representative John E. Moss, Democrat of California, chairman of a House subcommittee investigating the withholding of government information accused the Service of making a secret even of its authority to impose secrecy. The committee wanted access to certain public comments upon which the Service was basing a newly issued rule. The Service refused to provide the information, basing its refusal upon the *Internal Revenue Manual*, but then refused to allow the committee access to these manual provisions, claiming that it was a confidential document. Congressman Moss commented, "It appears that I.R.S. regulations not only permit secrecy to cover public comments on which the agency's actions will be based but even the regulation permitting secrecy is secret."

Once the Information Act went into effect, with its egalitarian concepts of equal release to all requesters, the Service reviewed its policy. In order to be fair, special releases such as that which provided the manual to the university were ended. The concept that what was released to one could be released to all eluded the Service; instead, it decided that what was denied to one should be denied to all. It made for an easier defense.

Shared Experiences

The officials who resisted the Information Act were motivated by more than a desire to cling to the comforts of old ways of doing things. Their behavior was prompted by emotions and attitudes of which they were probably unaware.

Most persons who had risen to positions of authority in the Internal Revenue Service by 1967 had shared experiences which inevitably influenced them in favor of excessive secrecy. They were likely to have grown up during the hard times of the Great Depression and to have served in the Second World War, two events which encouraged people to look for security and avoid taking risks.

No one could ever forget the wartime posters of Uncle Sam in full red, white, and blue costume, with a finger pressed to his lips, saying "Shhh!" Nor is it possible not to have been affected by the poster which showed a Liberty Ship, its stern sinking beneath a dark sea, its bow spewing smoke and flame against a sky inscribed with the message "Loose lips sink ships!" In a lighter vein, a popular advertisement of the time showed a smiling serviceman with the message "Don't talk chum, chew Topps Gum." It was no accident that the Public Information section, which stressed secrecy, was enacted in 1946, and that the leaders of government felt comfortable with it for 20 years.

The Great Purge of the Internal Revenue Bureau

The red scares and the great spy trials of the early cold-war period served to emphasize the need for secrecy which had become common among government employees. Most people have at least some awareness of incidents of repression during what became known as the McCarthy era. Usually, they will immediately think of the Hollywood blacklist of writers accused of having Communist sympathies. Few, however, will recall that the postwar age of repression also involved the great purge of the Internal Revenue Bureau and that the modern Internal Revenue Service was born of the painful death of its predecessor.

The Internal Revenue Bureau was a small organization which had little contact with most Americans before the Second World War. The need to finance the war and its aftermath resulted in an increase in tax collections from $5 billion in 1940 to $50 billion in 1951. The number of tax returns filed rose from 19 million to 85 million. In order to accomplish this extraordinary task, the Internal Revenue Bureau expanded from 22,000 to 57,000 employees. It was believed to be a temporary expansion, and many organizational decisions were hurriedly made. The nation, however, never returned to prewar conditions, and temporary growth turned permanent. The agency was badly in need of reorganization within a few years of the end of the war.

The great patriotic task of collecting wartime taxes was accomplished by men who were too old or too infirm to perform military service. They were hired at a time of great labor shortages when anyone capable of doing anything at all was in great demand. They were often ill prepared for the tasks demanded of them, and some were totally incompetent. A few were corrupt. They were also political appointees.

The White House and the Congress came under Democratic control in 1933 and were to remain under Democratic control for the next 18 years. All Internal Revenue Bureau collectors were politically appointed on the recommendation of local Democratic party bosses. The system was probably no worse than any other which might have been used, and the Democratic party was probably no worse than any other party might have been. President Franklin Delano Roosevelt died in 1945. Soon the war ended, and the need for his depression-inspired New Deal disappeared in the face of postwar prosperity. A newly conservative America was ready to dismantle the existing order. Everyone closely associated with the New Deal, whether "left wing" Hollywood writers or "incompetent" tax collectors, was about to get burned.

The great purge of the Internal Revenue Bureau began as a drive to improve the efficiency of the hastily expanded agency. A House subcommittee investigating government personnel practices reported, "There is no control exercised in Washington over the various 2,338 Internal Revenue Bureau field offices separately administered by 11 different regional offices."

In 1950, Senator John J. Williams, Republican, Delaware, became the prime mover in a drive to use the congressional investigatory powers to clean up the Internal Revenue Bureau. What began as a Republican attempt to embarrass President Harry S Truman's Democratic administration soon hit pay dirt as numerous improprieties and illegalities were uncovered. Many Internal Revenue collectors testified that they were untrained and unqualified for their jobs, that they were incapable of performing them, or that they had never believed that there actually were duties that they were required to perform. Others told of turning their paychecks over to the Democratic party and living on the "proceeds of their efforts."

In the three years during which the great purge ran rampant over the bureau, 380 employees were dismissed for 16 types of offenses, including accepting bribes, embezzlement, failure to pay taxes, falsification of records, and unauthorized outside activity. There were, however, only about 100 criminal convictions, although these included some very high-ranking officials. It was a terrible scandal, but few people noticed that the ousters involved only about 1 out of every 150 employees, and the criminal convictions involved less than 1 out of every 500 employees.

The Internal Revenue Bureau was reorganized as the "Internal Revenue Service." In order to keep the staff honest, it was announced that every employee's tax return was to be audited every year. Hundreds of employees resigned. It was assumed that these resignations involved dishonest employees trying to avoid getting caught, although it would seem eminently sensible for the most honest person to resign rather than face an annual tax audit. No one noticed that some who resigned were low-paid female clerical employees who may have wished to spare their husbands (who had no involvement with the agency) an annual audit of their joint returns.

Soon after the reorganization, which ended the system of political appointments and brought the agency under Civil Service rules, a classification survey examined the jobs of about 9,000 of the 54,000 Internal Revenue Service employees. Some 2,400 employees were upgraded as a result. But about 700 employees were downgraded and faced dismissal. The official reason for these adverse actions was that "they were downgraded for not producing in accordance with their salary bracket," creating forever the impression among Internal Revenue Service employees that failure to meet quotas could cost them their jobs.

The great purge of the Internal Revenue Bureau created a distrust of Congress and the political system and a sense of fear which was to last for years, perhaps decades. It also created a belief in the need for secrecy, a common symptom among victims of similar repression in totalitarian states. Many of the officials responsible for implementing the Freedom of Information Act years later were survivors of the great purge; others were the spiritual heirs whose careers had been sponsored by survivors of the great purge. One, perhaps the most secretive of the lot, once said to me, "You just can't imagine what it was like around here." When I asked him to explain what it was like, he refused to say anything further.

Executive Privilege

In 1954, another incident occurred which was to have a lasting effect upon Internal Revenue Service attitudes of secrecy. Senator Joseph R. McCarthy, Republican, Wisconsin, was investigating the Department of the Army under the Eisenhower administration. There were charges and countercharges, involving such obscure issues as whether McCarthy's subcommittee was attempting improperly to use its powers to obtain preferential treatment for a certain army private and whether the army had promoted a dentist despite an alleged record of being a "subversive." Somehow, these odd issues impinged upon a claim that the Fort Monmouth Missile Research Center was honeycombed with "Reds."

All of this would seem to have nothing to do with the Internal Revenue Service. There arose, however, a dispute as to whether certain government officials could be required to testify before the subcommittee concerning their conversation about the case. In order to resolve this dispute, President Eisenhower, on May 17, 1954, issued a letter to the Secretary of Defense. The key paragraph:

> Because it is essential to efficient and effective administration that
> employees of the Executive Branch be in a position to be completely

candid in advising with each other on official matters, and because it is not in the public interest that any of their conversations or communications, or documents or reproductions, concerning such advice be disclosed, you will instruct employees of your Department that in all of their appearances before the Subcommittee of the Senate Committee on Government Operations regarding the inquiry now before it they are not to testify to any such conversations or communications or to produce any such documents or reproductions. This principle must be maintained regardless of who would be benefited by such disclosures.

The doctrine was known as *executive privilege*. It immediately became apparent to observers in the Internal Revenue Service, that had President Truman issued a similar letter to the Secretary of the Treasury when Senator Williams was investigating the Internal Revenue Bureau, the great purge could never have happened, and the extensive suffering which it caused, much of it directed to persons who were completely innocent of any wrongdoing, could have been avoided. Thereafter, the doctrine of executive privilege was to become enshrined in the hearts of Internal Revenue Service officials as a patriotic justification for secrecy.

In the years during which I attempted to encourage compliance with the Information Act, I was repeatedly told that the doctrine of executive privilege provided a legal basis for withholding records from the public, on the theory that what could be denied to Congress could surely be withheld from the public. Actually, although executive privilege became one of the ingredients of one of the exemptions to the act, it was not relevant to the Information Act in the sense that managers were trying to apply it.

In order to counter these arguments in favor of withholding records, I researched the concept of executive privilege. I found that the position so broadly applied by President Eisenhower in 1954 had been severely restricted by President Kennedy in 1962, who stated that executive privilege could be invoked only by the President and then only in very specific instances.

Virtually every Internal Revenue Service official with whom I discussed the issue over a period of many years was familiar with the broad position on executive privilege taken by President Eisenhower but denied any knowledge of the restrictions asserted by President Kennedy. Apparently, they remembered only the positions which favored their tendency to withhold information. In one conversation, when I mentioned that President Kennedy had been strongly in favor of open government, I was told, "Of course he was, but look how he ended up!"

Lie Detector Tests

Senator Williams continued his campaign to expose wrongdoing in the Service with occasional success. In 1960, he capped his investigations by revealing that the Service had assigned its own investigators to learn the source of the senator's information. In a frightening internal witch-hunt, Service officials were being required to undergo lie detector tests seeking to find out if they had cooperated with the senator's legal, if uncomfortable, inquiries into the Service's illegal activities!

One official was revealed to have been fired from his Civil Service position for having refused to take the lie detector test. Moreover, the dismissed individual had not been one of the senator's informants. A review of the man's personnel records revealed that he had an exemplary record and had recently been recommended for meritorious recognition. He was dismissed, according to Senator Williams, on "trumped up charges of insubordination."

The message to all, a message which was to last for decades, was simply that loyal or disloyal, public-spirited or purely self-interested, you could screw up your career by not playing the game close to your vest.

Thus, in every disclosure determination, all who were involved had to function on the presumption that self-preservation demanded the defense of secrecy as a demonstration of loyalty.

This message is reinforced by regulations which provide that no Service employee may testify about anything involving his official duties without first obtaining written permission. The process for obtaining such permission is administered by the same disclosure personnel who have responsibility for responding to Freedom of Information requests for records.

The Insider Mentality

There are few benefits to the Civil Service other than a sense of job security, the certainty of an ultimate pension, and the continuity of pursuing objectives which seldom change. For managers and executives there are no rewards proportionate to their responsibilities and none of the perquisites which private industry heaps upon its leaders. But government service does provide a sense of being an insider, knowing what is happening, influencing what may someday become history. Requiring the release of information to any requester diminishes the value of knowledge and detracts from the satisfaction of being knowledgeable. It threatens the identity of the insider, who might now just as well be an outsider.

The release of records and an increase in public involvement in government loosens the bonds which hold the agency together as a functioning society. And such release threatens to destroy continuity and bring change.

Change is not only uncomfortable; it could mean the end of a program. There is nothing, other than his paycheck and his pension, to which a bureaucrat is more devoted than the continued existence of his program.

The Law Enforcement Illusion

If that program happens to involve law enforcement efforts, special disclosure problems are certain to exist. The great secret which lurks behind every law enforcement program is simply that such programs cannot be successfully carried out. There has never been a law enforcement program in any democratic society which has been adequately staffed and funded to be successful. It makes no difference whether the program be the prohibition of alcoholic beverages, drug control, or some effort to ban handguns. Law enforcement cannot succeed without such excessive effort as to make it unpalatable to a free people. Consequently, law enforcement agencies commonly resort to the creation of a mystique of infallibility, supported by an occasional example of some exceptional success. The intent is to make every little crook believe that he has not got a chance and thereby discourage crime as much as possible. Unfortunately, the release of too much information makes it increasingly difficult to maintain the illusion.

It has been a long time since the Service established its image by putting racketeer and bootlegger Al Capone into prison, but the Service still attempts to take advantage of that achievement. To this very day, recruiting posters announce that it took an accountant to bring the mobster to justice. The Service loves to promote itself as the great police power which eclipses the FBI in its accomplishments.

Many Americans, too young to remember the Chicago mobster, are not impressed by his conviction. Nor are they impressed by news articles, published just before tax returns are due, announcing the tax fraud convictions of a show business personality, a judge, an athlete, or a locally prominent businessman.

TCMP and DIF

If taxpayers were not impressed by the misfortunes of those who had been apprehended, they would be impressed by learning that the Service has computers which are able to analyze their tax returns to determine with almost perfect precision whether those returns should be subjected to audit. That analysis depends upon the use of statistical data and the application of a formula of predictability. The statistical data is known as the Taxpayer Compliance Measurement Program, or TCMP. The formula is known as Discriminant Function, or DIF.

TCMP consists of a series of extremely intensive audits of carefully and scientifically selected returns. The objective of TCMP is to have a perfect random selection of returns and thereby know the exact dollar range within which all items of income and all deductions will fall.

DIF is the mathematical technique used to classify income tax returns to determine examination potential. The objective is to avoid wasting resources examining returns which do not require adjustment and to focus on those returns most in need of attention. Mathematical formulas are developed using TCMP data and are programmed into the computer to identify returns by assigning weights to certain return characteristics. These weights are added together to obtain a total score for each return processed. The returns are then ranked in accordance with these scores. The higher-scored returns have the greatest potential for significant tax changes.

The problem with the entire TCMP and DIF process is that it must be kept secret. If anyone were to learn the TCMP data, she could construct reasonably accurate DIF formulas, assuming she had the necessary mathematical skills. If anyone were to learn or reconstruct the DIF formula, she could score her own return. If anyone were to learn enough DIF scores, she could simulate the ranking of returns for selection for audit. A person could then reverse the process the Service uses to identify returns for examination and create returns which would report the least possible taxes while having the least likelihood of being examined. This is the great fear of the Internal Revenue Service.

In 1981, Congress amended the Internal Revenue Code to provide protection for return information or statistical data derived from return information which involved the standards used for the selection of returns for examination. Thereafter, TCMP and DIF were safe from disclosure. But for almost 15 years prior to that finding ways to defend TCMP and DIF from Freedom of Information requesters required a considerable level of legal dexterity and some very creative effort. Unfortunately, this effort was often misguided. TCMP and DIF are highly technical applications, and their details are kept secret from all but a handful of Service employees. The officials who tried to defend TCMP and DIF frequently were not technically familiar with those materials and often misunderstood the records they were denying requesters. Officials who try to defend information which is beyond their technical competence tend to cast a broad net that catches all sorts of innocuous materials that bear only the slightest relevance to the subject requiring protection. The defense of TCMP and DIF became a defense of every variety of statistic, formula, code, or mathematical process.

The Defense of Trivia

The secrecy provisions of the Public Information section, the shared experiences of many Service officials, and concern for the protection of the law enforcement process combined to create a state of mind that made it almost impossible to comply with the Information Act. These attitudes were reinforced by the confidentiality provisions of the Internal Revenue Code. One further characteristic of life in the Service came into play: The Service functions through the consensus of its managers. No one can afford to give the appearance of differing from his peers, least of all his superiors. Every manager will try to guess the direction the Service is proceeding and then recommend to his superiors precisely what they expect to hear. As a result, records requested by the public were carefully analyzed in the light of the legal provisions requiring their release and frequently withheld in complete disregard of that analysis.

Even the most trivial information could seem to warrant a vigorous defense. Consider the case of the *Quarterly Statistical Reports*.

In 1972, I was assigned a Freedom of Information request for certain statistical tables identified only by their National Office report symbol. I located the tables in an office of the Audit Division and was briefed on them by the audit analyst who was responsible for receiving and analyzing them.

The tables consisted of nothing more than a compilation of returns which had been examined in various district offices, broken down into categories of type of tax, size of income reported, and the amount of additional tax proposed for assessment. Nothing in the tables could identify any taxpayer or even suggest anything about any class of taxpayers. These were totals, generally based upon many returns.

It was immediately apparent that there was little difference between this information and tables routinely published in the Commissioner's Annual Report. I suggested that we could give this information out; there was no reason for any concern. No so, the audit analyst advised me. This data was far more detailed than what was published; this was monthly data with quarterly subtotals, whereas the information in the Commissioner's report consisted of annual totals. Moreover, these tables had far more line items and much more detail than the tables which were released.

All that the audit analyst said was true, but it also seemed irrelevant to whether the tables could be released. The audit analyst advised me that these tables had never been released and that his division felt very strongly that we should protect this information, at least on the first go-around. If the Service were to release it, such release should be made on appeal, when the decision would be made by the Commissioner.

I asked the audit analyst to discuss the matter with his manager and let me know the result. I did not quite understand the need to withhold these records, but I would prepare whatever response the Audit Division preferred since the records were their responsibility.

Meanwhile, I received a request for similar records prepared in the Collection Division. The Collection Division, however, had no objection to the release of their statistics. They seemed to feel that their statistics demonstrated that they were doing a fine job, and they were pleased to release them. I prepared a response releasing the collection statistics and submitted it to the Assistant Commissioner (Compliance) for signature.

A few days later the audit analyst advised me that his managers were aghast at the thought that we might release their statistics and expressed the belief that such a release would signififantly interfere with tax administration. Based upon this position, I prepared a response denying access to the records and submitted it to the assistant commissioner.

Both proposed responses came back to me with a note stressing the need for consistency; the release of the Collection Division records might undercut our defense of the Audit Division records. It was of course a totally illogical position to take. I discussed the matter with analysts in the Collection Division, who graciously agreed to deny access to their records in order to maintain a united front and support the Audit Division position. We therefore denied access to two sets of records because we believed that one of them should not be released.

About six weeks later, I was called to the office of the Assistant to the Commissioner. The denial had been appealed, and the assistant was looking into the matter in order to make a recommendation to the Commissioner. The audit analyst was also at this meeting. It was quickly agreed that the Collection Division would concur with anything that was agreeable to the Audit Division. I immediately explained that I too was solely interested in supporting the needs of the Audit Division. That left the ball entirely in Audit's court.

Much to my satisfaction, the Assistant to the Commissioner grilled the audit analyst mercilessly on the need to withhold these statistics. The conversation, paraphrased to the best of my recollection, proceeded as follows:

"Why do these statistics have to be protected?"

"Because disreputable taxpayers could abuse them and avoid paying taxes," replied the analyst.

"How?" asked the assistant.

"I'm not quite sure," replied the analyst.

"You're not quite sure?"

"Well, I mean, sir, I don't know, but my management insists that they must be protected, they feel very strongly about that."

"How long have you been with the service? You are an audit analyst, aren't you? How long have you been working with these statistics? Who knows more about them than you do?"

The analyst admitted that he had been with the Service for about 20 years, had been in charge of these or similar statistics for at least 5 years, and there was no one who knew them as well as he.

"Well, then if you don't know how to abuse these statistics, what makes you think that someone else could do it?"

The analyst explained that he did not think in terms of deviousness, that one could never know what the requester might be able to do with the records, that taxpayers were unpredictable, that the situation far too serious to warrant taking chances.

The assistant seemed totally dismayed at the lack of serious argument to support withholding the records. Finally he suggested that the audit analyst and I each take some of these tables and spend a week "thinking like thieves" in order to try to find some logical sequence of events that might warrant withholding the records.

The week went by quickly. Careful study of the tables convinced me that there was nothing that anyone could do with them. In fact, I wondered why the Audit Division maintained them in the first place.

At the second meeting, the audit analyst announced that he could explain how these records could be abused. The tables showed that some districts examined fewer returns of certain classes than did other districts. And some districts were less successful in making additional assessments or made much smaller assessments than were made in other offices. A taxpayer could study these tables, identify the district least likely to do much with his return, and mail it to that location. If enough taxpayers had such information, they could swamp our least efficient districts with returns, overloading their capacities, while our most efficient districts would be forced to waste their resources working less worthwhile cases.

The assistant stared at the analyst for a long time with an expression that

I can only describe as complete disbelief, not so much disbelief of the explanation but disbelief that anyone would offer such an explanation.

"I thought returns were mailed to service centers, not to district offices. I thought we parcel them out to the districts. Couldn't we send them wherever we liked to be worked? Couldn't I detail revenue agents to other offices if I wanted to? Couldn't we let taxpayers know that anyone playing that sort of game would be selected for certain examination? Couldn't we think of a hundred ways to solve that problem while we're sitting here? Couldn't your division think of a hundred more solutions if I asked them to?"

The audit analyst agreed that we could indeed do any of those things. But he explained that his division did not think we should have to. It believed that the best solution was to prevent the problem by protecting the records, and consider other alternatives only if the attempt to protect failed.

I left the meeting convinced that the statistical tables would be released. A few days later I was told that a decision had been made. The Audit and the Collection statistical tables were to be denied on appeal. No one ever told me why.

Some weeks later, I received a telephone call from an attorney in the Office of Chief Counsel. The attorney told me that he had just learned that some books which were related to the statistical tables we had withheld were on the shelf at the Department of the Treasury library and that members of the public, including some recognized as frequent requesters of Service records, had probably made use of them. He had requested that the librarian remove the books and send them to me for study.

When the books arrived at my office, I quickly determined that they were not only related to the materials which had been withheld but were exact copies of the same reports. The only difference was that the printouts of tables had been reduced to normal page size, the identifying report symbols had been replaced with document numbers, the pages were marked "Official Use Only," and the books were titled *Quarterly Statistical Report*, a title I had not previously seen associated with the tables.

When confronted with this situation, the audit analyst admitted that he had known that the statistical tables had been reduced and bound as books for use within the Service. He had not mentioned it previously because we had not asked him about it. In fact, we had specifically asked for the information by National Office report symbol and not by document number, leading him to believe that that was what we wanted. He had a set of printed copies, but whenever we discussed the reports, he had shown me only the cumbersome computer printouts. He knew that a copy of each *Quarterly Statistical Report* was sent to a Treasury official, but he did not know that they were being placed in the library and had been available for public use.

The attorney made further inquiries at Treasury and learned that the official who received the reports reviewed them and then sent them to the library simply because that is what is done with books. He never thought about the information being confidential.

The designation "Official Use Only" which had been added to the books was defined by Treasury as meaning that a preliminary determination had been

made prior to printing that the material was at that time considered exempt
from release under the Freedom of Information Act; it would be reconsidered
in the event of some future request. We found, however, that this definition
was not contained in the *Internal Revenue Manual* or any other Service reference material. The individual who had classified the books had done so without
any clear understanding of what the classification meant in the hope that whoever saw it would understand what his intention was! Unfortunately, when the
books arrived at Treasury, which did have an issuance which defined "Official
Use Only," neither the receiving official nor the librarian noticed or complied
with the classification.

The most surprising aspect of this sequence of events was that examination
of the approximately 30 volumes involved revealed markings which established
that some of this material had been on the library shelves and available for
public inspection for years. Nobody had noticed it, or nobody had cared to use
it, or nobody could figure out what to do with it. The entire rationale for withholding the statistical tables had been defeated by these events. Not only was
release likely to be harmless; we now knew that actual release had indeed been
harmless.

The attorney passed all this information on to the Commissioner's office
and informed me of what was to be done next. Presumably these instructions
came from the Commissioner or his assistant.

The 30 volumes were not to be returned to the Treasury library since they
did not belong there. We had no intention of withdrawing information from
public availability, even though the original release was inadvertent. I was to
place the books in the Internal Revenue Service Freedom of Information Reading Room. I was to keep an eye on them, to form a rough opinion of how much
they were used. But I was not to release any further statistical reports. We were
taking the position that the release of these statistics was harmless because they
were out of date when they were first noticed by the public. The release of current statistics would presumably cause the types of harm envisioned by the Audit
Division. Any future request for current statistics was to be evaluated separately
based upon the age of the information at the time requested, without reference
to these events.

Shortly thereafter I was advised that the bound volumes of the *Quarterly
Statistical Reports* would no longer be produced.

The reports were on the reading room shelf for a year or two. Reading
room personnel reported that an occasional visitor glanced at a volume, but no
one made any extensive use of the material. Then one day I returned to my
office after a week's absence to find the complete collection of *Quarterly
Statistical Reports* neatly stacked upon a vacant desk. I was told that our director had brought them in. I went to the director and asked why.

The new Commissioner, the director explained, had made a tour of the
reading room. He had picked up a volume of the reports, glanced at a few
pages, and remarked, "Something like this could give the taxpayers a road
map."

I asked if the Commissioner had known about how the reports had come
to be in the reading room. Had he known that they were previously in the

Treasury library? Had he known that his predecessor had made the decision to place them on the shelves? And what had the Commissioner meant by his remark? Did he actually say to remove the reports? Did we make any attempt to explain the circumstances, to question his intent or offer any advice? Shouldn't we send him a memorandum outlining the background and seeking clarification?

"Oh, I wouldn't think so," came the response. "This Commissioner is pretty sharp. He really gets into something when he is interested. You know, he knows a lot more than we think he does. I wouldn't want to tell him anything he hasn't asked for. We better keep this stuff here for a while. Then we can always put it back when the time is right. No one will look for it anyhow."

A few weeks later the collection of *Quarterly Statistical Reports* disappeared from the desk. I did not bother to ask what had happened to them. I never saw them again.

For the next few years, whenever anyone asked for statistical information of any consequence, discussions of what to do concluded with someone remarking, "Something like this could give the taxpayers a road map." That statement provided us with a sort of sense of direction; it told us what was wanted.

Ultimately, statistical information was again made available to the public, but not without litigation to pry it loose. The end result was what we had known it would be from the beginning. But when you live in the land of Oz, you have to travel along the yellow brick road.

Chapter 3

Siege Mentality

The Internal Revenue Service suffers from a siege mentality. It affects everything the Service does. And it is a major determinant of Service behavior in observing the requirements of the Freedom of Information Act and the Privacy Act of 1974.

In 1966, as a management trainee, I was assigned to perform a study of why revenue officers in the Manhattan and Brooklyn districts were leaving the Service at the height of their careers. Personnel provided me with the names, addresses, and resignation papers of perhaps three dozen revenue officers who had left during the current year. Each had at least one year but not more than three years' service. All had therefore completed both the classroom and on-the-job phases of their training and had enough field experience to be considered fully qualified journeymen. Each had been hired on the basis of a good record in college, high scores on the Federal Service Entrance Examination, and an appropriate performance on his selection interview. Each was the recipient of satisfactory or better ratings from his supervisors during his short career. In other words, these were the sort of employees upon which organizations build their future. Yet each had precipitously left his occupation at a time when he could expect to be singled out for better things.

The resignation forms showed that a majority claimed that they had left to accept positions offering a better income. A few explained that they were seeking further education. One had said that he was relocating to another area for personal reasons. I found that none of the statements given as explanations for their resignations were true.

The individual who said he was relocating I found at his mother's house. Those who were going to graduate school were doing it part-time and did not have to give up their employment for that purpose. Those who left for better pay quoted salaries that were a little higher, a little lower, or just about the same as those they had given up.

It was obvious that the real reasons for leaving the Service had not been cited. But why not? What reasons could three dozen young men who may never have met one another be trying to conceal?

In probing for an explanation, I found that these young men were very much alike in many ways. They were all loyal to the Service. They were all concerned about the welfare of comrades left behind. They all had enjoyed being revenue officers. They all believed that collecting unpaid taxes from recalcitrant taxpayers was important and honorable work. They all had good relationships

28

with their supervisors. Each was willing to talk about great adventures and the good old days on the job. But not a single one could face another day on that job.

The revenue officer who had claimed to relocate told me that the truth was that he had to quit because riding the subway to work made him ill. He had taken pills, but he could not overcome his motion sickness. Even thinking about riding the subway made him ill. He excused himself for a moment, and while he was gone, his mother told me that for weeks before he resigned he had been so ill that every morning, between leaving the subway and walking a block or two to the Internal Revenue Service district headquarters, he had to stop to throw up.

When he returned, I asked if he also became ill upon returning home. No, he replied, his motion sickness did not bother him in the afternoon or evening. He just could not ride the subway in the morning!

None of the others had such drastic symptoms, but they did admit that their jobs had become absolutely unbearable. Each attributed the problem to one or more of three basic reasons cited repeatedly.

First, management always demanded more. The slow man was compared to the average. The average man was compared to the best. The best man was compared to his highest month. The best man's highest month was compared to some mythical revenue officer who had done far more. No accomplishment ever seemed to serve any purpose other than to raise the performance curve and create ever-greater expectations. Everyone knew that there were no quotas; no one had ever heard of a revenue officer promoted for exceeding quotas; no one had ever heard of a revenue officer disciplined for failing to meet quotas. But everything was counted, and today's count was never quite enough.

Imagine frenzied supervisors running up and down an aisle shouting, "How many have you got, how many closings, how many seizures, how many levies, what have you got for me today, dig down in your bag, it's almost the end of the month, who's holding out, never mind yesterday, what've you done for me today, we're short, we're not even up to last month, the guys in group two are way ahead, you're making me look bad! It's after nine o'clock, everybody out in the field! Out, out, out, and seize, seize, seize!"

That was the way they told it, and that was the way I had known it to be for the six years I spent as a revenue officer. And that was only the first of the three reasons.

The second reason for leaving was that most of these young men had developed a considerable sense of sympathy for the taxpayers against whom they were required to enforce collection. Revenue officers must daily face human beings who cannot resolve their problems. True, the problems may have been of their own making; the hardships now faced may have been well deserved; nothing more is expected of these taxpayers than is expected of us all. But still, they are human beings who cannot resolve their problems. The application of force that is statistically motivated against human beings whom we have no cause to hate is a tremendous burden to carry.

The third reason for leaving was the most important. The Service seems not to have any loyalty to its employees. In the face of the tremendous pressure to perform and the tremendous burden of carrying out enforcement actions which often seem cruel and unfair, even to the men assigned to the task, the Service seems to do nothing to support its employees. The Service, or its upper management, seem to be totally oblivious to the fact that employees are often called upon to perform impossible tasks.

One man explained that his supervisor had directed him to take certain actions against his own best judgment, but when complaints were received, the supervisor explained that the revenue officer was overzealous.

Another told of being put in charge of a group that specialized in seizing businesses. When congressional complaints were received, an investigation was undertaken of his behavior. When it was over, he was told that the investigation had uncovered no evidence of wrongdoing on his part. He was not satisfied with a letter that said no evidence of wrongdoing had been uncovered; he wanted a letter which said that he had done nothing wrong. He did not get one. He quit.

Several explained that when they followed manual instructions to the letter and things did not work out, it was their fault. When similar situations recurred and they questioned the manual, they were told, "Last time was different. Go by the book." And when things did not work out again, it was their fault again.

Basically, the consensus was that these three dozen revenue officers had resigned because working for the Internal Revenue Service was a damned-if-you-do, damned-if-you-don't occupation.

I submitted my findings and made some suitable recommendations. I was told that my report was well received, but I never saw any evidence that anything was done to alleviate the problems identified.

In 1987, more than 20 years after my little study was submitted, revenue officers testified before a congressional committee that abusive enforcement actions were taken against taxpayers because they were required by a quota system which stressed the need for seizures! The Service responded that there was no quota system but that erroneous perceptions has resulted from the ill-conceived actions of overzealous supervisors!

What the Service did not mention was that there had recently been a study by an outside consultant which had compared stress in the revenue officer occupation with other high-stress positions, such as policeman, air traffic controller, train dispatcher, and fireman. The Service is not likely to release that study to an Information Act requester. The reason is that it contains something that the Service does not want you to know. The Service does not want you to know that a scientific researcher found that revenue officers do indeed experience a high level of stress, and a major reason for that stress is their very considerable sympathy for the taxpayers against whom they must take enforcement actions.

In 1986 and 1987, a study was performed to "develop and implement a plan to improve overall conditions under which managers and executives operate." Twelve highly respected managers, supported by an outside firm of professional consultants, sought the input of the Service's 9,322 managers. A total of 8,884 managers elected to take part by submitting completed survey forms.

A sample of these (including myself) was subsequently interviewed by the consultants to develop further information.

The results of this study were published as *The Treatment of IRS Managers—ERR-6 Task Force Report*, Internal Revenue Document 7173. This document was printed without being classified "Official Use Only" and is therefore available to the public upon request.

Amazingly, the report states that 25 percent of all Service managers are suffering from poor morale. Despite their poor morale, managers are extremely loyal to the Service, dedicated to their jobs, and eager to report every conceivable kind of positive attitude toward accomplishing their responsibilities. The following passage is especially relevant:

> Managers believe that the system for matching workload with resources does not work well ("We are always asked to do more with less.... if we did 100% last year, we can surely do 105% this year, and 110% next year, when does it stop?"). *An equation exists which balances resource needs with the amount of work at a given level of quality.* If the workload increases, or resources are reduced, either productivity must increase or the level of quality must decline. *Managers frequently find themselves in situations where they believe the equation is out of balance.* They feel that the Service does not give them any guidance in correcting the situation ("They're blind, or they pretend they're blind, to the problem.") and because of emphasis on numeric (quantitative) goals, quality is likely to be sacrificed.

Thus, at the very time that the Service was telling Congress that there are no quotas and that abuses committed by Service employees result from overzealous attitudes, managers were complaining about operating conditions that could be described only as quotas!

When was the last time that you called any government agency seeking any kind of service and received assistance from an overzealous employee? The Service's compliance functions seem to have a unique capacity for hiring overzealous employees who consistently, over a period of many decades, take enforcement actions which go far beyond the duties assigned to them!

The first time that a Treasury Department spokesman testified that he believed that there had once been a quota system but it was no longer in effect was in 1924. Sixty-four years later, Service spokesmen were using the same excuse: "Although we used to do that, we don't do it anymore."

If the disclaimers are true, and I believe that they are, why should the belief in the existence of a quota system persevere, both inside and outside the agency, over several generations? One reason is that the Service methodically denies public access to the documents which would demonstrate the truth! For instance, the National Treasury Employees Union, which testified before congressional hearings in 1987 that they believed there was a quota system, was repeatedly denied access to key portions of the Senior Executives' Performance Objectives and Expectations, Form 6419, which would have shed considerable light on the subject of quotas. The Service continues to believe that it can hide information without creating the impression that it has something to hide!

Actually, the claim that there are no quotas is not a lie. The simple truth is that over many years of institutional adaptation, the Service has developed a system of shadow quotas, invisible but pervasive. There are neither official quotas nor informal quotas. But everything is counted. Everything is evaluated on the basis of these counts. Future operations are planned on the basis of extending or improving upon past performance. Everyone is evaluated upon the basis of performance and attitudes and expectations. Awards and promotions are based upon evaluations. Awards must be justified. Justification must be based upon facts. Facts are frequently derived from numbers. So while there are no quotas, there is considerable pressure to exceed them, although it may never be quite clear what they are. Success in the Service depends upon the ability to demonstrate an acceptable level of competence in chasing rainbows.

The managers responding to the study of their morale also had comments to make upon their working conditions:

> *There was a consistent feeling among managers that the Service says it wants people oriented managers but rewards the opposite managerial behavior....* The Service is generally viewed as too authoritarian ("military style," "dictatorial," "yellers and screamers," "rulers"), production oriented at the expense of people ... too dependent upon statistics ("rewards those who deliver the plan no matter who or what"), unable to recognize and deal with failure whether involving programs, new ideas, or people ("operates from fear," "very defensive"), operating with short-term goals, too conservative, and too demanding of conformity ("don't make waves"). Managers feel that these tendencies are rewarded and therefore tend to be more prevalent at higher levels. ("The 'macho manager' is the one who gets the rewards." "Executives are purely task-oriented and that is why we have the moral problems we do ... the unit managers deal directly with people; they care about their employees. The IRS mission comes first but they are also people-oriented, whereas IRS executives aren't.")

Finally, the report stated, "There is a belief among many managers that the Service's commitment to them is only 'lip service,' and doubt that this Initiative will have any impact."

There you have it, a description of an institutional culture which has remained virtually unchanged over several decades; a culture which makes impossible demands of workers and managers alike, and fails to provide the necessary support to those who struggle to achieve their assigned tasks.

That, I believe, leads to a siege mentality. It works like this: Congress assigns to the Service the virtually impossible task of collecting huge amounts of revenue. It provides drastic powers that would permit the draconian enforcement of law but insists that these powers be exercised with sensitivity, compassion, and restraint, so as to appear consistent with American ideals of fair play.

The Service, lacking the resources necessary to carry this burden, invents myths of cooperation, invincibility, and success. The American system of taxation is described as a system of voluntary compliance, but little mention is made of the fate which will inevitably befall those who fail to volunteer an adequate amount in a timely fashion. The Service is the most efficient government agency in the world; therefore, a lack of resources is not really relevant to the accomplishment of an impossible task. The Service can and does successfully carry out its mission. It is the envy of the civilized world, and quite probably of the uncivilized world.

All this is accomplished by making ever-increasing demands upon the Service's managers and employees, in a hot-house atmosphere which differs from a nineteenth-century sweatshop only in that it has computers. The official answer to a lack of resources is to buy bigger, faster, and fancier machines. But no consideration is given to the fact that while these machines can accomplish extensive tasks, they do not help the field personnel who have to face the taxpayers. In fact, they compound the problem because they rapidly produce more work that requires individual enforcement efforts to resolve than would otherwise exist. The simple reason is that under a manual system, you may have identified 5 tax cheats but had time to pursue only 3 of them. With a simple computerized operation, you could surely identify 10 tax cheats; with a more sophisticated system you might be able to identify 100 cheats. But you still only have time to pursue 3 of them. Computerization results in a tremendous increase in the Service's ability to perform, but the job keeps getting harder for the field employee who has to go out and face the taxpayers.

More and more pressure is placed upon the employees and their managers, and they receive less and less support. The basic system is very effective. It has been used for centuries by military and religious organizations. Press your members to pursue an impossible goal, whether victory over the enemy, finding the Holy Grail, achieving a sense of oneness with the Creator, or reducing the revenue gap. Some may quit and some may fail, but most will make sacrifices in hopes of attaining the goal. Each sacrifice justifies further sacrifice; everything you have been through becomes an investment which makes accomplishing the goal more and more important to you as an individual. The goal becomes a part of your sense of personal identity. The result is an extreme loyalty to the organization — a pride in its achievements, a belief in the rightness of its cause, and a trust in its mission.

But someone is responsible for the immense pain suffered in carrying the impossible burden. Who is causing this constant stress? Why it is them, not us. We are a part of the Service; we can do no wrong. They are at fault; they are the taxpayers. The first thing that any recruit to the Service learns is that the world consists of the Service and the taxpayers. The Service is us, and the taxpayers are everybody else. Taxpayers may or may not pay taxes. They may or may not owe tax. Their tax status is not the important thing. The important thing is that they are the outsiders; they are different from us. They are the enemy.

Commissioners may stress public service and may undertake campaigns to refer to taxpayers as customers in the hope that they will be treated accordingly. Unfortunately, this inverts the problem and can never be successful. Taxpayers are not abused because they are called taxpayers and seen as outsiders. On the contrary, the system requires the abuse of taxpayers because all enforcement activities, whether objectively justified or not, are inherently abusive. But you cannot abuse "customers," "fellow citizens," or "neighbors." In order to support the activities your job demands of you, you must view your victim as a creature who warrants no sympathy and deserves whatever penalties befall him.

The more impossible the demands placed upon enforcement personnel and their managers, the less likely they are to retain a sense of fair play and an identity with the public. If the employee lacks the performance skills necessary to cope with those demands, the ability to successfully play the numbers game, or the personal resilience necessary to cope with a sort of split personality which offers one set of behavior to management and another to the public, he becomes overzealous in a frantic effort to comply with the perceived demands of his superiors.

There are no self-made monsters. For every Frankenstein monster, there is a Dr. Frankenstein. When the Service tells Congress that abuses were committed by overzealous employees or were prompted by overzealous supervisors, it is simply saying, "I didn't do it; my creature did it." But Congress will believe the Service and accept its excuse because the Service is the creature of Congress, which assigned the impossible tasks in the first place and ravenously insists upon greater efficiency and more and more revenue.

Beyond abused employee, abusive employee, and overzealous employee, there remains a final step on the road to the siege mentality. Years spent in pursuit of the unachievable goal and the unknown quota produce a sense of frustration which is expressed in the belief that the Service has inadequate powers and that there are too many restraints upon the Service. In fact, we *require* protection. The taxpayers are out to get us. We are the victims. It is not the Service which abuses the taxpayers; it is the taxpayers who abuse the Service. They lie, they cheat, they steal. They are out to get us.

Try to imagine that you are a longtime Service employee. Through diligent application, hard work, and great personal sacrifice, you have risen to a position of power and responsibility in the Service. You have adapted to the cultural environment of the Service so skillfully that you are no longer aware that there is a cultural environment. You have internalized all the values and objectives of the Service; you are in complete harmony with your fellow managers; and you can act in consensus with their wishes without being aware that they are not your own. You can treat your subordinates exactly the way you have always been treated and never question the propriety of your actions. You know how to deal with taxpayers; you know how they have to be dealt with.

Now you receive a Freedom of Information request. Someone wants to know something about how the Service operates. You may not fully understand what he wants or why he wants it. But you know what he will probably do with it if he gets it. After all, you know what They are like. You know They are out there. And you know that They want to get you. Would you give him what he asked for?

You may find it difficult to believe that a siege mentality can exist in a manager who is responsible for administering an important government program. You may doubt that such a person's behavior could be influenced by an emotional state of which he is totally unaware. And you may find it totally incredible that records could therefore be withheld from an Information Act requester who is legally entitled to receive them. But what you do not know is that the siege is real. Consider the activities of the Church of Scientology and of the tax protest movement.

Chapter Four

The Church of Scientology

In the early to mid–1970s the Internal Revenue Service was encountering increasing pressure to release records which had heretofore been withheld from the public. During this time of turmoil, the attention of the Service was diverted from the proper implementation of the Information Act to the machinations of the Church of Scientology.

Almost invariably, when a requester sought access to apparently sensitive records, the managers having control of the material would ask me whether the requester might not be acting for the Church of Scientology or whether the records might not in some way relate to or be of use to the church. The subsequent analysis of the records focused less upon whether they should be available to the general pubic and more upon what the church might or might not be able to make of them.

The tax-exempt status of the Washington Church of Scientology had been revoked in 1967, and an adversarial relationship between the Service and one or another of Scientology's various component organizations seemed to continue for years thereafter. But the records which gave rise to questions about the church's involvement never seemed to have anything to do with the church, nor did the managers who raised those questions have any interest in or responsibility for any of the church's tax affairs. In fact, they seemed to know little about the church and clearly had neither favorable nor unfavorable feelings about its teachings and activities. They just worried that the church might be trying to get at our records.

I knew that the organizer of the church had also tried to estabilsh a political party, the Constitutional Administration party, in an attempt to exercise control over government activity, including the activitiy of the Internal Revenue Service. I also knew that Scientologists were sometimes stationed outside the entrances to the Service's national headquarters distributing copies of their newspaper, *Freedom*. And I knew that that newspaper sometimes attacked the Service and seemed to try to lump it into a coterie of imagined Scientology enemies which included psychologists, Interpol (the international police organization), and Nazi Germany.

On one occasion our office had received several hundred almost identical Information Act requests within a period of about two weeks. Each request originated from an address on or close to the campuses of two or three West Coast colleges. Each request asked for copies of a handful of entries in the *Special Agents' Handbook*, our criminal investigators' manual, which had seemingly enticing titles. One item which almost every requester asked for was "Protecting the President." This instruction merely explained that protecting the President and certain other persons was the responsibility of the Secret Service, that at certain times, such as during presidential election campaigns, the Secret Service might not have enough personnel to carry out all its duties, and that special agents might then be temporarily assigned to the Secret Service to help out. The content was much less intriguing than the title. Nevertheless, someone had manipulated several hundred college students to write to the Service demanding copies of these instructions. Just three or four out of several hundred requesters mentioned in their letters that their requests were based upon suggestions made by representatives of the Church of Scientology.

Despite these incidents, there seemed to be little reason for the concern being shown for the safety of our sensitive records. When I asked why people felt that the Church of Scientology was after our information, I was told that Scientologists were involved in spying, burglary, and the theft of records throughout the world. In Europe, police had stopped a car driven by two Scientologists in a routine traffic check. The young men acted so suspiciously that the police searched their vehicle and discovered files concerning the Church of Scientology which had been stolen from a mental health center in Utrecht in the Netherlands. In the United Kingdom, there were similar reports of thefts from hospitals.

When a broken window was discovered in one of our offices in which Information requests were processed, I suggested that it had probably been done by kids throwing rocks and could not possibly be related to the type of work we did there. I was asked whether the office contained any records that might be of interest to the Church of Scientology.

When a door to our office was discovered forced open during the night, I pointed out that the lock was old and worn and that a replacement had been requested weeks before. I suggested that the guard might have pushed a bit too hard when trying the door and the lock had probably given way under the pressure. I was asked whether the office contained records of interest to the Church of Scientology.

When our photocopying machine broke, I was asked if the damage might not have been done by some unauthorized person who was unfamiliar with the machine's operation and who might have broken it while surreptitiously copying records for the Church of Scientology.

Who were these Scientologists, and why did so many people believe that they were a threat to the integrity of our records?

The Church of Scientology was founded by a science-fiction writer named L. Ron Hubbard. The original form of what was to become the church's doctrine was published as "Dianetics: The Evolution of a Science," in the May 1950 edition of *Astounding Science Fiction* magazine. The material in the article appeared to be a pastiche of pop psychology and bits of pseudoscience borrowed from various occult doctrines popular during the past century. A later explanation of Dianetics was published as "Dianetics: The Modern Science of Mental Health."

Whatever the merits of Scientology, its beginnings as a "science" published by a fiction writer in a science-fiction magazine, and its claim to be a modern science of mental health discovered and developed by a person without any relevant professional standing were certain to invite opposition. In its early years, the Church of Scientology encountered active resistance from members of the medical and psychology professions and from the government organizations responsible for protecting the public from pseudoscientific hokum.

In 1955 Scientology practitioners were arrested for teaching medicine without a license.

In 1958, the Food and Drug Administration seized and destroyed a large supply of a drug called Dianazene, which was being marketed by an organization related to Scientology as a cure and preventive for radiation sickness.

In 1963, the Food and Drug Administration raided the premises of the Founding Church of Scientology in Washington, D.C., and seized some electronic devices known as E-meters, little boxes with gauges and wires leading to handgrips. They were used in a process called auditing in which a Scientology practitioner would ask a subject questions the answers which presumably led the subject to better mental health. The E-meter acted somewhat like a miniature lie detector, identifying physical reactions which would assist the auditor to recognize those questions which were emotionally significant to the subject.

The Food and Drug Administration viewed the E-meters as devices designed for the practice of medical quackery. The Church of Scientology viewed them as devices employed in the pursuit of the church's ministry. Aside from the basic disagreement as to the nature of the devices being seized, the raid was especially offensive because it seemed to have been staged as a media circus designed to discredit the church. A federal judge subsequently ruled both parties correct by ordering that the meters not be used for secular purposes but for religious counselling so long as it was clear that they were not used in pursuit of a cure for a medical condition.

These experiences seemed to convince the Church of Scientology hierarchy that they were being persecuted and were justified in using virtually any means to defend themselves from their enemies.

Between 1963 and 1967, the Church of Scientology and its associated organizations were under investigation or subject to restrictions in Australia, New Zealand, the United Kingdom, and the Republic of South Africa.

By the time the church began having problems with the Internal Revenue Service, it seemed to have become a secretive bureaucracy, frequently abusive of both its members and the public, suffering a bad press, convinced of its innocence, and fearful of harassment and persecution. The Service, however, was also a secretive bureaucracy, frequently abusive of both its employees and the public, suffering a bad press, convinced of its innocence, and fearful of harassment and prejudice. The two adversaries looked at each other and were fascinated by what they saw.

Thus, when Internal Revenue Service managers felt threatened by the imminent release of their records pursuant to the Information Act, they reacted by blaming their dilemma upon a villain. The most likely villain around was the Church of Scientology. But this villain was not merely a scapegoat. This was a villain who was not only convenient and convincing; this was a villain who was guilty!

In August 1978, eight Scientologists, including some of the highest leaders of the church, were indicted on criminal charges involving the theft of government records. On October 26, 1979, seven persons were convicted of conspiracy to obstruct justice and one person was convicted of the slightly lesser charge of conspiracy to obtain government documents illegally.

It was ultimately revealed that Scientologists had indeed infiltrated the Internal Revenue Service. The church had amassed a collection of 15,000 Service records — a collection which at that time could not have been put together by any legally available means. On November 1, 1974, an electronic bug had been placed in the conference room in the National Office of the Service. Moreover, the Scientologists were attempting to contrive an incident in which a psychotic staff member in the Service would mail out the Service's files to persons or groups, thereby creating a pretense justifying the church's access to its records.

These incidents served to introduce or emphasize four assumptions which were to poison the atmosphere of Information Act processing for years to come, if not forever.

First, it was thereafter assumed that a requester might not be simply seeking records for his own use but might be acting as a surrogate for some other person or group. Rather than focus upon whether a record should be available to the general public, sensitive records were analyzed in the belief that their ultimate recipient was to be the person least entitled to them and most likely to make the most devious use of them. For the most part, this assumption was a red herring since any analysis of the availability of records to the general public would necessarily include consideration of the worst possible result. This assumption made it more difficult to analyze records, wasted time, and increased the likelihood that records would be withheld. Psychologically, it was easier to deny records when imagining their receipt by an enemy than by the general public.

Second, it was thereafter assumed that the analysis of whether records could be released was to consider not only the records immediately at hand but whatever additional records the ultimate recipient might already possess. This concept made it especially difficult when considering the release of records after deleting portions which could be withheld. How could anyone know whether the information proposed for deletion might not have already been released in some previous grant?

Third, it was thereafter assumed that the records a recipient already possessed would not be limited to those items legitimately obtained. A recipient could reconstruct the deleted portions of a record through the use of knowledge gained from stolen records. Those 15,000 documents amassed by the Church of Scientology were difficult to dismiss.

Fourth, it was thereafter assumed that a requester might have secret allies within the agency ready to assist him in his quest. The very disclosure experts who were recommending the release of records might be part of the conspiracy. Truly sensitive records were withheld from the experts trained to analyze them and denied by proxy, based upon the biases of the officials who had the most to lose from their release.

In the final analysis, the greatest damage resulting from the Church of Scientology's infiltration of the Service was that it served to legitimize any fantasy which might be raised to justify the withholding of records which should have been legitimately available to the public.

Operation ACE

On the other hand, the Service's reaction to the Church of Scientology might have resulted less from the improper access of records than from the church's custom of publicizing what it had learned. It was the church which in 1980 embarrassed the Service by announcing to the news media a 1973–1974 project referred to as Operation ACE.

Only three categories of professionals are authorized to represent taxpayers by appearing before the Internal Revenue Service. This right to practice is limited to attorneys, certified public accountants, and "enrolled agents." The first initials of these three professions produced the acronym ACE.

The documents released showed that in 1972 an official in the Southwest claimed that "convictions for willful failure to file among attorneys exceed other professional groups." It was suggested that simultaneous indictment of 200 or more attorneys nationwide would lead to a dramatic improvement in compliance. Bad ideas often seem to have a sort of bandwagon effect, and soon the regional project had grown into a national program and had been expanded to include certified public accountants and enrolled agents.

Although a National Office reviewer cautioned that "the Service would be laying itself open to the charge of indicting a whole profession because of the isolated failures of a few individual members," a national project was approved. But oddly, the original thrust of obtaining a dramatic improvement in compliance was abandoned in favor of a case-by-case approach, and it was stressed that "no reference should be made to the national scope of the project." Thus, the project was not abandoned because of the risk of adverse public response; it was merely made less apparent.

The Service collected the names of 201,000 lawyers and 58,000 accountants. Of these, a sample of 15,000 lawyers and 10,000 accountants was drawn for investigation. Ultimately, the project led to the conviction of 137 persons and the assessment of $5,530,146 in taxes, penalties, and interest. The important thing is not whether picking up approximately $221 for each person investigated represented an effective use of resources but whether this sort of industry-intensive scheme is fair to the many innocent persons identified for investigation on the basis of professional association. The Service traditionally prefers to investigate persons whose individual notoriety will contribute to the newsworthiness of their conviction. Consequently, the original finding that the convictions of attorneys exceeded those of other professionals need not reflect anything more than reinforcement of prejudices resulting from the Service's case-selection preferences.

Paranoia breeds paranoia. As a result of the revelation of Operation ACE, attorneys and accountants began to claim that the true purpose of the project was to discourage tax practitioners from dedication to the interests of their clients since being overly successful in the adversarial relationship with the Service might result in their own returns being examined. Later, when the Service was setting up a computerized file based upon powers of attorney issued by taxpayers authorizing attorneys, CPAs and enrolled agents to represent them before the Service, many practitioners expressed the fear that this innocuous administrative tool for ensuring the proper delivery of correspondence was in reality a devious method to determine the extent of their practices and thereby subject the most successful to unwarranted personal audits.

The Saint Anthony Raid

The Church of Scientology also revealed to the public in 1980 that in the early 1970s the Service was pursuing a policy in Idaho of collecting taxes by publicly embarrassing citizens who had failed to pay. Attorneys' offices were padlocked, automobiles were chained to telephone polls, and other dramatic incidents were staged in response to a memorandum which stated, "A proven method of preventing delinquencies has been through embarrassment to certain taxpayers. . . . It has been my experience that seizures which result in 'sensationalism' tend to remain fixed in the public's mind and are a great deterrent of delinquency."

A National Office spokesman stated that the memorandum "is rife with errors in judgement."

The very same individual who as district director was responsible for the policy of public embarrassment also authorized the armed raid on the small town of Saint Anthony. The district director had become "excited about protesters." He wanted an operation that would "educate" taxpayers and create a sense of "respect" for the Internal Revenue Service. The 3,000 residents of the town were believed to include numerous tax protesters. The obvious way to deal with this hotbed of noncompliance was to send armed special agents from door to door demanding evidence that tax returns had been filed or that taxes had been paid. The fallacy behind the program, apparently overlooked by the responsible officials, was that there is no legal requirement that anyone maintain and display records evidencing their compliance with the law.

There were not sufficient special agents available to canvass the entire town, so a mixed force including unarmed revenue officers was put together. As a result, the revenue officers became concerned for their personal safety and complained to their union and to their congressman. They reasoned that the decision to send armed special agents showed that management considered this a dangerous assignment. Quite possibly the special agents would provoke the local residents to irrational acts, acts which would be directed at the unarmed members of the task force.

Upon receiving congressional inquiries, the Service canceled the armed raid on Saint Anthony. Subsequent inquiries showed that a list of proposed targets for these visits included primarily persons who were under no obligation to file tax returns. Most of the residents of Saint Anthony were law-abiding citizens, and none were known to be tax protesters.

In a perverse demonstration of insensitivity to the principle behind the Information Act and the rights to taxpayers, the district director responsible for these ill-advised programs was transferred to the National Office and appointed director of the Disclosure Operations Division, where he not only controlled the release of documents concerning his own activities in Idaho but also exercised extensive influence over the success of the continuing Freedom of Information campaign by the Church of Scientology and others who had exposed those activities.

Chapter 5

The Tax Protest Movement

The greatest single factor to affect the way the Internal Revenue Service reacts to Information Act and Privacy Act requests for access to records has been the tax protest movement.

Tax and *protest*; the words go together well. What could be a more natural reaction to being taxed than to protest? It is what we would all like to do.

What red-blooded American has not sometime in his life spent a moment imagining himself as a patriot disguised in Indian war paint throwing bales of British tea into Boston harbor, whooping "No taxation without representation"? Or, if a more recent example is needed, how many of us refused to pay the telephone tax because we believed the proceeds supported an unpopular war? And how many of us sympathized with the few who withheld from their income tax payment an amount equal to the percentage of the budgetary pie which they knew would pay for past, present, and future wars?

Let us forget these memories right now. They have nothing to do with the tax protest movement as the Service has experienced it in recent years. There are no patriots and no pacifists in the tax protest movement. There are only misguided victims, cruelly hoaxed by dishonest and violent leaders, who have somehow tricked the gullible into believing that theirs is a perfect system which permits its followers to cheat the government out of legally established taxes in the firm conviction that it is they who are being cheated by the government's attempts to collect those taxes.

Or is that too harsh an accusation? After all, no one knows exactly what a tax protester is or just what constitutes the tax protest movement. What we do know is that tax protesters seem to jump up, wave their arms, and shout, "Here I am!" The Service then has no choice but to enforce the law and apply whatever penalties may be appropriate.

Officially, at least as far as the *Internal Revenue Manual* is concerned, a tax protester is a person who advocates or engages in illegal acts designed to result in the nonpayment of taxes. Generally, protesters can be identified by about a dozen tax schemes in which they engage.

Typical Protester Schemes

Protesters may simply not file a tax return. Or they may file a return but refuse to pay any tax. The most common schemes, however, seem to involve filing returns which omit all or most of the relevant data or alter the form so that no tax can be computed. Instead, entries are made which explain or supposedly justify the protester's action by referring to various constitutional arguments.

The chief of the constitutional arguments, and probably the heart and soul of the protester movement, is that the Sixteenth Amendment, which established the income tax, was not properly ratified and is illegal. The argument is based upon the premise that Ohio ratified the amendment before Ohio was actually a state, and therefore its ratification is a nullity. Actually two more states ratified the amendment after Ohio, so there were quite enough ratifications whether you count Ohio or not. Not so, respond the protesters. The proclamation announcing ratification in 1913 came after Ohio acted but before the other two states did. The protester argument seems to be that Ohio acted too soon, the other two states acted too late, the proclamation was too early, no further proclamation was made, and therefore no one need pay any income tax!

If this argument has not convinced you that the income tax is illegal, the protesters will tell you that because documents were copied by hand at the time, errors crept in, and as a result no two states ratified precisely the same document. Since each ratified something different, none of the ratifications are valid! The protesters have carefully documented and can prove this claim. Of course they can. Discrepancies in handwritten documents are commonplace and usually insignificant. They certainly do not invalidate amendments to the Constitution!

Other constitutional arguments include the contention that filing a tax return violates the First Amendment because the taxpayer has religious or moral objections to some or all government programs paid for by taxation. Filing a tax return is claimed to violate the Fifth Amendment right against self-incrimination. The Internal Revenue laws are alleged to violate the First Amendment due-process clause. The Federal Reserve System is said to be unconstitutional because currency is not backed by gold or silver. The Internal Revenue laws are claimed to violate the Thirteenth Amendment because various bookkeeping and records-maintenance requirements constitute involuntary servitude. And the Tax Court is supposed to be unconstitutional because it does not provide trial by jury!

In addition to these arguments, tax protesters are able to find every variety of defect in the passage and codification of most tax statutes. The qualifications, appointment, and oaths of office of most government officials are claimed to be illegal. The design, approval, and distribution of tax forms are challenged as improper. The placement and functioning of the Service's offices is claimed to violate some technicality. And the performance of virtually every activity engaged in by the Service is denounced as violating some principle established by the Old Testament, the New Testament, Magna Carta, English common-law, the Declaration of Independence, the Articles of Confederation, the Constitution, or any other source the protesters choose from their own version of history, literature, and philosophy.

One of the favorite arguments advanced by protesters is the claim that Federal Reserve notes do not constitute income since they are not redeemable in gold or silver. They will explain that Federal Reserve notes are not real money; only gold and silver may be constitutionally taxed. Federal Reserve notes, they will explain, are actually accounts receivable and are not reportable as income until paid in gold or silver. Some protesters will file a return in which the income has been reduced to reflect the declining value of the dollar resulting from inflation, claiming that their income was in 50-cent dollars or 20-cent dollars, or whatever value they consider appropriate. Some will file otherwise proper returns but state that no tax can be paid because no legal currency with which to pay it exists. Still others will arrange their affairs in accordance with various barter schemes in hopes of permitting them to enjoy the fruits of their labor without appearing to earn any income.

Many protesters, and not a few taxpayers who simply wish to avoid paying taxes without espousing any philosophy, submit withholding certificates claiming excessive exemptions and thereby attempt to preclude their employers from withholding an adequate tax.

Other protesters will file returns which employ elaborate schemes involving vows of poverty or family trusts in an attempt to shift income to a nontaxable entity which then pays all their expenses. Aside from the expenses of creating the sham organization, all the benefits of the donated property and income return to the perpetrator. Since the perpetrator receives back everything given, the state of poverty is easily endured and if the scheme is successful in avoiding the payment of taxes, can become quite comfortable!

What all of these schemes have in common is that they are all fairly transparent, seldom escape detection, and have virtually no prospect of prevailing in litigation. The repeated use of previously unsuccessful schemes is the result of these schemes being promoted by ruthless leaders whose vision of tax protest permits them to seduce converts into performing acts the leaders know will cause their followers to be caught and punished. The naive convert thinks he is being sold a scheme which will permit him to avoid paying taxes. In reality, he is being sold a scheme designed to trap him into conflict with the Service. The objective of the movement is not to avoid taxes for its members but to create conflict with the Service and thereby ultimately destroy the system. Thus, the individual tax protester is always a dupe, easily caught and punished but completely expendable to the movement. It is unfortunate that leaders have to sacrifice their followers to reshape society in the mold of their own concepts of justice and morality, but what else are great men to do?

The Organizations

New members are usually introduced to the movement by being brought to a meeting by a friend or neighbor. They will hear that money really belongs to the person who has earned it, that when the government takes it by taxation, it is stealing because taxation is illegal. They will be told that government can function quite well without being funded by taxes. If necessary, they will be told that the movement is not just about money but about saving our heritage, establishing our freedom, rescuing our country from the bureaucracy. And they will spend some money, pick up some literature, meet some new friends, and begin to become involved. They will find that there is a great deal of truth in much of what is said. They will probably also find that there are enough unexplained but provocative theories to make them feel compelled to attend another meeting, just to find out more about the movement. After a few meetings, it will all begin to make sense, and they will probably join.

The Service has identified many such organizations, including the Tax Free Foundation, Your Heritage Protection Association, the Citizens Law Enforcement Research Committee, Americans for Constitutional Government, United Tax Action Patriots, the Little People's Tax Advisory Committee, National Tax Strike, the U.S. Taxpayer's Union, and the most militant of all, The Posse Commitatus, also known as the Sherriff's Posse Commitatus or the Citizen's Posse Commitatus.

New adherents appear to join the less radical groups initially and then pass on to the more violent groups if their involvement merits such progress. They will find, however, by the time they become involved with the Posse Commitatus, that tax protest is no longer the sole or even the main interest of the group. Literature distributed by the Posse shows that it is basically a racist organization whose views parallel many of those of American Nazis and the Ku Klux Klan. They are involved with survivalist activities, stockpile arms, and preach violent rebellion. They appear to be opposed to the existing institutions of federal and state government, most financial establishments, environmentalist concerns, any restrictions upon individuals, and any limits to their doing just about anything that they want to do. Their literature seems to indicate that they hate Jews, blacks, Hispanics, city dwellers, white-collar workers, liberals, Communists, social workers, judges, lawyers, law enforcement officers, government employees, and news reporters. They probably hate you too, whoever you may be!

The ultimate fantasy envisioned by tax protesters seems to involve an Arab oil embargo leading to an extreme fuel shortage which in turn causes famine. Farmers will be able to feed only their own families and will refuse to sell food because there is no silver or gold in circulation and paper money, "greenies," is worthless. Hordes of starving city dwellers, mostly blacks and Hispanics led by radical Jews, will then attack the farms, ravishing white women and killing cows. Naturally, they have to accumulate all the gold and silver and stockpile all the weapons and ammunition they can so that they will be prepared for the inevitable battle.

The true identities and the real objectives of the tax protest movement are secret. But there have been rumors that the movement has received financing from Muammar Qaddafi's Socialist People's Libyan Arab Republic.

As secret as the leadership and its objectives may be, the local activities of these groups tend to be very vocal and highly visible. Their intention would seem to be to draw as much attention to themselves as possible, presumably to recruit new members. They produce a great deal of literature and distribute it prolifically. Frequently they will mail these materials to the Internal Revenue Service since their objectives are not only to arouse the public against the tax system but to rouse the Service against the public.

This process requires not only that their followers file protester type returns and get caught at it but take part in confrontations with the Service.

Confrontation

The revenue agent or revenue officer who encountered a tax protester when away from the office and alone might well find himself subject to verbal abuse, threats of violence, or physical assault. When protesters appeared at Service offices they would frequently be accompanied by a coterie of fellow fanatics, shouting slogans, distributing literature, accosting other taxpayers, and generally attempting to disrupt the procedure and delay resolution of tax issues. The presence of these associates would be justified by the claim that they were witnesses. To the Service, witnesses are persons who have knowledge of a taxpayer's tax affairs and appear to offer testimony; they are therefore permitted to take an appropriate part in the proceedings. To the protester, however, witnesses are there not to contribute to the event but to observe it and to bear witness to the protester's faith in the movement.

Usually, the witnesses will carry tape recorders, cameras, or video equipment. The Service will permit a sound recording of its proceedings but will not allow any form of picture taking. The reason is simple: Photographs of Service employees have appeared in protester literature, identified by name and address and designated as "Patriot's Enemy." The accompanying text would contain statements such as "We don't recommend ordering all kind of merchandise sent to his home on a 'Bill me' basis, nor do we recommend calling him Collect at 3:00 AM, nor do we recommend any other kind of action against this vulture who preys on Patriotic Lovers of Freedom, who believe they have a God-given right to keep what is theirs! Keep an eye out for this vulture!"

Revenue officers who visit protesters to serve legal demands may find what the property is posted with a warning: "Notice to all officers of the law. No trespassing, whether Internal Revenue and Treasury Agents, Federal, State, County or City Agents.... Any officer ... will be treated as any other trespasser or lawless intruder would be when attempting to break and enter an inhabited dwelling when warned not to do so. Survivors will be prosecuted."

Some protester literature has carried the names of judges who have presided over protester trials, with the suggestion that they not be hanged from the nearest large oak tree. Meanwhile, many protesters can be identified by the small gold hangman's noose they wear in their lapels. Others wear small ruby crosses, originally manufactured for the Ku Klux Klan more than half a century ago but still readily available at gun shows and swap meets throughout the country.

The protester bag of dirty tricks goes beyond threats and insinuations of bodily harm. Late-night telephone calls are a favorite device for harassing employees. Sometimes young women will call an employee's home and tell his wife, "Gee, I never guessed he was married. I would never have become involved

with him had I known." Other times racial slurs will be used to upset the
employee. After having signed letters addressed to known protesters, I personally received phone calls that repeated a taped message: "Hi. I just called
to wish you a happy Yom Kippur. How are your parents? Are they dead? Were
they killed in the Holocaust? Too bad. Well, better luck next time. Next time
we'll get all of you."

Some employees have received unsolicited mail, merchandise, or magazines, either with payments due on delivery or bills to cover the costs. Not infrequently, pornographic materials are sent to the home. There have been incidents in which truckloads of manure were dumped on employees' lawns, lawns
which did not need the additional fertilizer.

Unwarranted lawsuits have been filed against Service employees. Fictional
reports have been filed with credit bureaus. Liens attempting to record imaginary debts have been filed with local authorities.

Whatever effect the tax protesters may have had in mind when they engaged
in these tactics, the major result has been that thousands of Service employees
have become convinced that tax protesters are not merely a special category of
taxpayers in an adversarial relationship with the agency but personal enemies
who must be fought and defeated. And it is generally accepted in the Service
that in this struggle, this personal and immediate struggle, protesters do not
deserve the slightest consideration, not even when they make Information Act
requests.

Questions, Questionnaires, and Requests

There seem never to have been placed upon this earth any group of people
so curious about the operation of the Internal Revenue Service, so eager to ask
questions, and so willing to make pests of themselves as tax protesters.

Most Service personnel who have had any experience with the protesters'
seemingly insatiable and contentious demands for information believe that
they are motivated solely by a desire to harass the Service and force it to waste
its resources in useless attempts to respond. When a protester makes an Information request, he is just dumping manure on our lawn!

I doubt it. I believe that tax protesters are unable to distinguish between
records and reality. The accumulation of information is not intended to harass
but to control. The acquisition of records provides a sense of power. They all
ask for the same things, so obviously they do not seek to discover anything not
already known. But they individually experience some sort of satisfaction at
possessing a copy of a record whose content is already known to them! I have
provided some of them with the most worthless records imaginable, and they
have called to thank me for sending them. This interpretation of protester
behavior is consistent with their behavior when in court. They simply ignore
reality in order to repeat oft-defeated arguments based on irrelevant or misinterpreted documentation, and they seem incapable of understanding why
they always lose in spite of their wonderful collection of historical documents!
In fact, protesters frequently alter the documents they receive, create forgeries,

and invent imaginary records which they joyfully sell to each other, totally oblivious to the fact that what they have is absolutely worthless and useless except for whatever emotional satisfaction they get from it. In other words, tax protesters are sick people. For lack of any better terminology, we can call them records freaks.

When a tax protester receives an appointment letter advising him that his return is under examination, he is likely to respond with a letter that asks 30 questions and ends by stating, "Upon receiving answers to the aforementioned questions, an examination date can be determined."

By the simple device of sending in 30 questions, the protester has reversed roles with the revenue agent, and it is now the protester who plans to schedule the examination! Well, why not? These questions are good enough to repeat for you. I know you will love them as much as every revenue agent who has ever received them does.

1. Please state the authority (specific section of the Internal Revenue Code) for the solicitation of the information you desire.

2. Please state whether disclosure of such information is mandatory or voluntary. If mandatory, what penalties will result from noncompliance?

3. Please state the principal and specific purpose or purposes for which the information is to be used in any capacity.

4. Please state the routine uses which may be made of the information or any other use of the information.

5. Please state the effects on the taxpayer if not provided the information requested.

6. Please explain and show that the investigation is of the kind authorized by federal statute.

7. Please explain why and how the demand for information is not too vague and broad in scope.

8. Please explain and show that information sought is relevant or material to a lawful subject of inquiry.

9. Please explain how and why the investigation is pursuant to a legitimate purpose.

10. Please explain how and why the inquiry for information may be relevant to the purpose.

11. Please show and prove that the information is not already in your possession or cannot be obtained from other sources.

12. Please show and prove that the Secretary or his delegate has determined that further examination is necessary.

13. Please show and prove that the other administrative steps required by the Internal Revenue Code have been followed to the letter of the law.

14. Please show and prove that after initial investigation, the Secretary or his delegate has determined further examination is necessary and warranted.

15. Please show and prove that the taxpayer has been properly notified that further examination is necessary.

16. Please state the exact reason or reasons for the examination of each year requested in detail.

17. Please state whether there is a misconception and/or mistake on the tax return for each year.

18. Please specify exactly wherein the mistake lies, or if in fact one exists.

19. Please specify exactly which item of income or expense is in question on the tax return, if any.

20. Please state why this specific income or expense is in question or is being examined.

21. Please explain why and what issue, in law or in fact is questioned, if any.

22. Please state the name, address, and phone number of any person or persons informing you of any question or concern involved in any item on any tax return or any activity of the taxpayer.

23. Please state exactly what was said, either oral or written, concerning any item, tax return or activity of the taxpayer by any person or persons in #22 informing or directing you to conduct an examination directly or indirectly.

24. Please state and prove that taxpayer is not being subjected to an examination based on or for any political, ideological, harassment, pressure tactic, or bad faith purpose, and is not being singled out for prosecution as an example to other taxpayers for any reason.

25. Please state and explain why the examination cannot and will not amount to an inquisition or arbitrary inquiry on the part of the tax examiner.

26. Please state and explain why IR Code Section 7605(b) does not apply to any examination of taxpayer where "No taxpayer shall be subjected to unnecessary examination or investigations."

27. Please state the exact methods used past or present to gather information concerning taxpayer and whether information was gathered through use of surveillance, phone tapping, mail coverage, interviews, illegal entry, informers, spy, or other.

28. Please state whether verification of specific deductions would be the limited scope of the examination.

29. Please state and explain any objections to the use of electronic recorders during the examination.

30. Please state whether examiner would be prejudiced against a taxpayer who arranges his affairs to minimize his taxes as the law permits. Why?

The first few of these 30 questions bear recognizable resemblance to information the Privacy Act requires the Service to make available. But the information required to be available has already been supplied to the taxpayer, so the questions are really redundant. But beyond the first few, the rest seem to mimic points taken from here, there, and everywhere, and have no relevance to anything at hand. These questions do not constitute a Privacy Act request. They do not constitute an Information Act request. And they do not constitute a request pursuant to any section of the Internal Revenue Code. In fact, they do not constitute anything but another load of manure dumped on our lawn.

The Service does not answer these 30 questions. These letters are either dropped into the examination file or, in many offices, simply trashed. But nothing happens as a result of not answering them. The protesters apparently do not expect them to be answered. They are simply sent in, usually by certified or registered mail, to be disregarded by the recipient. Of course, they are not totally disregarded; they do let the revenue agent know that the taxpayer is trying to get away with something.

Why, then, do protesters send these letters to the Service? I believe that there are two reasons. First, if you are going to have a movement, you have to be able to sell your followers something. And second, they serve to reinforce the tax protester's delusions about the tax system and the protesters movement.

If the meeting takes place, the protester will attempt to take immediate control by producing a *Public Servants Questionnaire*, another set of questions which can be purchased at any protester meeting. The questionnaire is handed to the revenue agent, or the protester will attempt to read the questions. The first few questions ask for details about the identity, home address, and job assignment of the employee. The rest of the questions are increasingly denigrating and quickly assume a "when did you stop beating your wife" attitude.

Among the more interesting items on the questionnaire:

- Is the name given by the public servant his right name?
- Has public servant ever employed an alias or assumed name?
- Has public servant ever served time in prison for a misdemeanor? A felony? A crime? Give reason for public servant's incarceration.
- Has he ever been employed outside of government or outside of tax-supported agency such as a welfare bureau, a government school, etc.?
- What are his qualifications for conducting this investigation?
- Has the public servant been courteous and cooperative?
- Has he made any threats?
- What is the nature of his threats?

The questionnaire ends by providing for the "public servant" to swear or affirm that his answers are "complete and correct in every particular," and calling for the document to be witnessed by two people. Its final statement is "Taxpayer may administer an oath if he so desires."

This questionnaire, of course, has no legal validity. It has no status under the Privacy Act or the Freedom of Information Act. There is no requirement that it be answered or entertained in any way. What, then, is its purpose? I believe that it serves to embolden the protester. By attempting to reverse roles and make the protester the interrogator and the revenue agent the subject, it provides the protester with a sense of power and gives him the courage to disrupt a procedure in which most taxpayers feel helpless and apprehensive. The *Public Servants Questionnaire* is a magic bullet, sold to the gullible protester to help get him into trouble. The movement's leaders, who must be aware of its ineffectiveness, use it as a device to manipulate their followers.

Like most people who become trapped in immoral movements, protesters

have to be slowly sucked in and tricked along the path set out for them. Each
little act increases their involvement. Each error and every moral lapse increases their culpability until they become totally committed to a movement
whose objective they are unable to imagine. I believe that the tax protester
movement, which attempts to give the appearance of being committed to
American traditions, individual freedoms, and constitutional guarantees, exists for the purpose of overthrowing the government of the United States and
establishing a Fascist dictatorship.

In order to achieve its ultimate goal, it needs an enemy, the Internal Revenue Service, and a struggle, the abolition of the income tax, to serve as tools
to enslave its followers. In helping to achieve this objective, the *Public Servants
Questionnaire* is very successful. It not only encourages the protester to get
himself into trouble, but its use is frustrating to the revenue agent, who frequently feels impotent when confronted with such questionnaires. There is
only one way law enforcement officials can react to feelings of frustration and
impotence, and that is to turn the screws on the son of a bitch who makes them
feel that way. And that too contributes to the struggle and helps fulfill the plans
of the leaders of the movement.

The third line of attack pursued by the protesters is to file Information Act
requests for records which identify Service employees, such as telephone directories and staff rosters, and for records which pertain to individual employees,
such as copies of the certificate attesting to the employee's oath of office. Such
records are generally available to requesters without any problems, but obtaining them seems to serve no practical purpose. Employees make their identity
known to taxpayers with whom they have dealings; thus a list of the employees
in an office makes nothing further known. Every employee takes an oath of
office. Unless a certificate has been lost, every personnel folder contains the
same form attesting to the same oath. Even if an occasional employee somehow entered duty without having taken an oath, it would make no difference
in validity of his official actions. Why, then, did hundreds of protesters throughout the country ask for these records? And why is there no evidence that the
recipients ever did anything with the records they received? An obvious answer
would be that this was just another instance of harassment. But these records
are easy to locate, require no extensive review or processing, and can usually
be supplied in short order. If this is harassment, it is the most minimal harassment available.

The truth was something else entirely, something far more sinister. Every
request specifically directed toward a record relating to a particular employee
was intended as a threat, a statement that "we know who you are, and we are
going to get you." Every request for a roster of employees was intended as a
statement that the protesters' hit list was not limited to the enforcement personnel who had handled their cases but was to include everyone employed by the
agency, down to the lowest-graded clerk. That was how these requests were intended, and that was how they were perceived. Everyone felt uneasy, but the
clerks, the least powerful people in the agency, felt the most threatened of
all.

The next line of attack consisted of Information Act requests for various documents which related neither to the employees nor the protesters. Some of these made obvious sense, such as requests for *Internal Revenue Manual* sections which dealt with the tax protest movement. Others were more difficult to understand. For instance, there were numerous requests for applications to publish Forms W-4, Employee's Withholding Allowance Certificates, in the *Federal Register*, but there is no requirement for such publication, and consequently no such requests exist. We were also asked for copies of our application to the Office of Management and Budget for approval of Form W-4 pursuant to the Paperwork Reduction Act and for copies of the resultant Notice of Office of Management and Budget Action. We sent out copies of these dullest of all bureaucratic forms, but we were never able to understand what anyone could do with them or even what anyone might have imagined they could do with them, unless, of course, these requests were simply the protesters' way of saying, "Don't forget, we are still here, and we can make you jump whenever we want to!"

Finally, individual protesters would ask for their own Examination or Criminal Investigation case files. The protesters produced their own request forms for these records and even assigned form numbers to them. From time to time they would revise the forms and either assign a new form number or show a revision date in imitation of Internal Revenue Service forms in an attempted role reversal. These requests, correctly submitted and perfectly proper under the law, served the eminently logical purpose of keeping protesters informed of how our investigations were progressing. But they also served to expand their collection of documentation, to give them something to show and discuss with their fellow protesters, and to provide them with a sense of power as a result of having made the agency act in response to their commands. The records released in response to these requests were generally quite innocuous, but most Internal Revenue Service employees did everything they could to reject, delay, mislay, or ignore these requests. It was not unusual for those lower-graded generally powerless clerical employees repeatedly to move tax protester correspondence to the bottom of their pile of typing assignments.

As a result of the strange behavior of the tax protesters, large numbers of Service employees in those districts in which the protesters were most active felt that they were engaged in a personal struggle with a gang of dangerous lunatics. Others did not consider the protesters a threat but found their antics amusing. One experienced, and respected disclosure specialist told me that there was no need to worry—the protesters were "good old boys" whose activities were not unlike getting drunk on a Saturday night and raising a little hell. Monday morning they would pay the two dollars and go back to being respected members of the community!

Run, Gordon, Run

On February 13, 1983, 63-year-old Gordon Kahl and several other persons were in an automobile leaving a church meeting in Medina, North Dakota.

Several men attempting to stop the automobile were surprised by sudden bursts of automatic gunfire. A moment later, two U.S. marshals were dead, and three other law enforcement officers lay wounded in the roadway.

Gordon Kahl was a fanatic tax protester who had been convicted in June 1977 of failure to file federal tax returns. The meeting at the church was held "to discuss religion, the United States Constitution, the Federal Reserve, purported unconstitutional acts by the Internal Revenue Service and establishment of an alternative form of government for townships after the United States Government collapses." This particular meeting, and others Gordon Kahl had previously attended, constituted violations of the terms of his probation on the tax-fraud conviction.

The law officers who had been gunned down in cold blood were attempting to serve warrants as a result of these probation violations. Gordon Kahl, however, was not a man who easily accepted interference in anything he felt like doing. He drove a car without a driver's license, ignored the tax laws, violated the terms of his probation, and did not hesitate to kill without warning. After the shootings, Kahl fled into the Dakota hills and managed to escape capture by stealing a police car whose radio enabled him to monitor the directions intended to guide his pursuers.

That same day, Kahl's son was arrested at a local hospital after seeking treatment for gunshot wounds. His mother was arrested when she appeared at the hospital to inquire about the young man's condition. Shortly thereafter, two more men were arrested for taking part in the killings.

Kahl was described as a man who "didn't believe in nothing, only what he wanted to do." It was reported that he had sworn that he would never be taken alive. A federal assault team arrived to take part in the chase, which proved to be one of the most extensive manhunts the area had ever known. Kahl, who had survivalist training, had disappeared without a trace.

A $25,000 reward was offered with no immediate success. Kahl was believed to have the assistance of members of the Posse Commitatus and other organizations active in the area, including the Farmers' Liberation Army, the National Freedom Movement, and the United Tax Action Patriots. Authorities stated that they believed Kahl's flight had involved many other people and that there were probably numerous persons who knew his whereabouts but were afraid to come forward because of the Posse's local reputation for violence and vengeance.

A search of Kahl's home uncovered 30 rifles and more than 20,000 rounds of ammunition.

On May 28, 1983, Kahl's son and one companion were each convicted on six counts of assault and two counts of second-degree murder. They were sentenced to life plus 15 years. Another individual was convicted of harboring a fugitive and conspiracy. Mrs. Kahl was acquitted of all charges. Gordon Kahl was still at large.

Negotiations were under way with a leader of the tax protest movement for terms of surrender, but Kahl did not come forward. More information became available about the Posse Commitatus. It was reported to have chapters in every state except Hawaii. It routinely engaged in paramilitary training exercises, often jointly with Ku Klux Klan and Minutemen units. Kahl was rumored to be in hiding among the Posse's 2,000 members in Wisconsin. Other rumors stated that he was being passed from house to house and state to state, as a sort of honored trophy among Posse chapters.

On June 3, 1983, acting on a tip, law enforcement officials advanced on an Arkansas home. They were immediately fired upon, and a two-hour gun battle ensued. A local sheriff was killed before tear-gas cannisters fired into the bunkerlike structure set fire to a huge cache of ammunition and dynamite. A body found in the ruins was later identified as Gordon Kahl, who had kept his promise not to be taken alive. Four more protesters were subsequently convicted of harboring the fugitive.

To the tax protesters Gordon Kahl became a hero. Protester literature claims that Gordon Kahl was murdered by the government because he was trying to tell the people that the U.S. government is under the control of a conspiracy of Jews and Masons. The protesters even had a song about Gordon Kahl:

> You'll be worthy of a statue,
> By the time they ever catch you,
> Keep on runnin' for our freedom,
> Gordon Kahl.

Gordon Kahl provided the Service with a villain. The Service did not get a song. No one will ever again suggest that the tax protesters are "good old boys."

Effects of the Protest Movement

The tax protest movement's use of the Freedom of Information Act added to the evidence which convinced many officials that the act merely served to harass the agency and waste its resources. Prior to the appearance of the protesters, however, the Service's antipathy to the act was limited to National Office managers whose opposition was based upon loyalty to the Service or concern about their careers.

The tax protesters convinced rank-and-file employees that the Information Act was an evil to be resisted because it interfered directly with the work they were doing and threatened the physical safety of themselves and their families. Many of these employees were members of a generation which believed that unfair or evil laws should be neither enforced nor obeyed. Consequently, they frequently did whatever they could to avoid full compliance with the law.

Leaving taxpayer correspondence unanswered or destroying correspondence was completely outside the Service's traditions, yet the protester movement introduced these types of behavior through the simple device of overwhelming offices with frustrating requests. Local managers supported the behavior of their employees, partially because they shared the emotions on which they were based and partially because it was an easy way to maintain loyalty and commitment.

The records local offices sought to protect were frequently those which related to their employees or to tax cases. National Office managers had no serious concerns about the release of these types of records, being more interested in protecting records which related to the overall management of the Service. Thus there arose a conflict between National Office and local management in which each sought to protect its own interests. The Service's traditions of decentralization and the importance of managers reaching a consensus on actions to be taken made it impossible for the National Office to control processing in the field.

The proper administration of the Information Act requires a considerable degree of self-discipline and a willingness to sacrifice the immediate interests of the agency for the greater good of fair and conscientious administration of the law. Some offices had capable and dedicated disclosure officers who were able to achieve the proper administration of their programs despite the pressures created by the protest movement. In other offices, however, those pressures were too great, or the disclosure officers were too weak to permit the proper processing of Information requests without regard to the intentions of their originators.

Unfortunately, bad habits tolerated because their only victims seemed to be protesters who deserved no better treatment sometimes spread to other taxpayers, and the level of service to the general public declined. The tax-protester movement was designed to spread a doctrine of vigilantism. In the long run, it was difficult to tell whether the greater injustices resulted from lawlessness by their vigilantes or ours.

There was, however, one set of circumstances which seemed to justify any failure by Service personnel in processing Information Act requests which originated from protesters. From time to time, the Service received bomb threats. Sometimes there were Information requests for copies of our procedures for responding to bomb threats. One such request specifically wanted to know where we would search for bombs, how many trained persons would be involved in the search, and how long a thorough search of the facility would take. And sometimes there were real bombs.

Some of our most active requesters had already been convicted and incarcerated for homicide but continued to write from their prison cells to further the cause: the secession of the Pacific Northwest from the United States and the establishment of a white supremist state.

It is difficult to honor the information requests of such people.

Chapter Six

Needles in a Haystack

Beyond the handicaps created by our own attitudes and the exigencies of day-to-day law enforcement, the greatest inhibitors of compliance with the Freedom of Information Act and the Privacy Act of 1974 result from organizational patterns, work habits, and records-maintenance practices inconsistent with the objectives of public access to government records. In the Internal Revenue Service, provisions for public access to records were merely grafted onto existing procedures, with little willingness to alter anything to accommodate the new statutes.

Public-access laws seem to assume that agencies do business in a manner which will permit them to easily provide whatever records are requested. The truth of the matter is just the opposite. The Service is organized to administer the tax laws, and it keeps its records to allow it to do that job in the most efficient manner. The record the public requests is often something no one in the Service would otherwise ever pull out from wherever it has mercifully been permitted to come to rest. Bureaucrats like to put things where they can simply lie undiscovered until they fade away, for yesterday's records often interfere with today's urgent tasks. Remember, the Service is task-oriented, and the tasks at hand deal with right now, not with whatever may once have been. To the typical Service executive, a knowledge of history is nothing more than an impediment to today's decision-making process.

To the Service the past is not prologue, nor is the past a part of the present, nor is the past even the past. The past is simply an embarrassment. We really wish you would not ask us about it. Anyway, the past is packed away, and we will never be able to find it because we have forgotten where we put it.

The Amazing Croasmun Memorandum

A few years ago we received several Information requests for a document the requesters referred to with a tone of familiarity as the Croasmun Memorandum. More specifically, the requested document was described as a memorandum dated Feburary 26, 1973, on "Tax Rebellion in California," addressed to "Participants in the Conference on Tax Rebellion Movement." The originator of the memorandum was Homer O. Croasmun, Regional Commissioner, Western Region.

The National Office of the Service does not normally maintain copies of records originating in our field offices. It was no surprise, therefore, that our search failed to locate such a record. I telephoned the regional disclosure officer in San Francisco where such a record should have been on file, if indeed a copy still existed since it was then already about ten years old. He too was unable to locate the record, and we advised the requesters accordingly, adding that records of that age might have been destroyed pursuant to existing records-control schedules. Records-control schedules provide the Service its authority to destroy records whose retention serves no further purpose. These schedules are worked out with the National Archives and Records Administration and are approved by resolution of Congress. They provide specific periods for hundreds of categories of records which may be permanently retained, transferred to the National Archives of the United States, retired to Federal Records Centers for storage, or destroyed after the periods specified.

Much to my surprise, one of the requesters sent me a copy of the Croasmun Memorandum, explaining that he had purchased the copy at a "meeting" and had made his Information Act request to obtain verification that it was genuine. He now asked for any records or controls which might mention the memorandum or otherwise provide evidence of its authenticity.

The memorandum was merely a transmittal of minutes of a meeting said to have been held on February 9, 1973. As such, it would have had a very short retention period, but one sentence stated, "These minutes enumerate action items for the Los Angeles and San Francisco District Directors and for Regional Office officials." That sentence changed the nature of the memorandum and would have resulted in a longer retention period. In fact, it began to look like a document which should have been submitted to the National Office for review and should have been reissued as part of our Internal Management Documents System. A case could have been made that the memorandum should have been made available for public inspection as an instruction to staff. Why, then, could neither the National Office nor the Western Regional Office locate a copy?

The attached minutes proved to be one of the most amazing documents that I have ever seen. It began with a list of 14 participants, many of whom I recognized as people who had actually served in the positions identified. In several places, names of taxpayers were illegible, having been either deleted or highlighted on the original (yellow highlighting results in blacking out the text on photocopies). The format of the memorandum and the attached minutes seemed quite similar to the Service's way of preparing such documents. And yet I had my doubts...

Some of the contents of the minutes seemed to be what tax protesters' dreams are made of — confessions of the Service's obsession with a kook movement made to look important and powerful. I had seen copies of *Internal Revenue Manual* instructions which were deftly doctored to insert protester messages within the text. I had seen Service notices altered to evidence facts quite opposite to the original content. And I had personally exposed as a forgery an alleged Service news release which had been carefully numbered in accordance with a numbering system not in use on the date the news release was supposed to have been issued. Tax protesters like to create their own documentation to support their personal interpretation of reality. Was the Croasmun Memorandum a hoax? Was all of it a carefully fabricated fake, or was it a genuine document altered a bit here and there to make the movement seem heroic? Or was it an entirely genuine bit of Service exotica, something we could not find because it was better lost?

Some of the more interesting items included in the meeting minutes:

- "We must ... concentrate on the leaders of the movement attacking IRS."
- "We ... have now seized the initiative by infiltration of their organization so we know in advance of their plans before they execute them."
- "We must continue to stay aggressive if we are to enforce the revenue laws and to protect the Service from attack by tax rebel militants."
- "We are not limiting ourselves to the sanctions in the Revenue Code, but are using all the available law enforcement machinery whether it be federal, state or local laws; for example, if a tax rebel leader is violating a state law by carrying a concealed weapon, we should use state enforcement to prosecute him; and, if there is a firearms violation, ATF agents should be alerted."
- "Since [blank] spoke on the radio in Cleveland, there has been a flood of General Motors employees submitting false forms W-4."
- "[blank] of Ventura County ... is now leading the Mariposa camp of militants organized by [blank]."
- "The sheriff of Mariposa County has been checking on the activities."
- "In the Los Angeles District, Taxpayers Anonymous in Orange County, led by [blank] and [blank] is the most militant; and that we should keep this in mind in deciding our targets."
- "Often the state can move quickly to close up a tax rebel's business or revoke his license; that we should see that the state uses its enforcement machinery on those cases which are not our targets."
- "Commented on the problem of federal judges appearing to be anti–IRS based on a belief that IRS is highhanded."
- "There was a general discussion of the importance on meeting with U.S. Attorneys and federal judges to acquaint them with the full picture of the tax rebellion movement."
- "Suggested the possibility of requesting religious leaders to warn their following against participation in the movement, pointing to the beneficial effects of Mormon Church President Lee's message."
- "Federal judges ... had not full background information on some of the defendants to whom they had given light sentences."

The minutes went on to identify 11 action items for district directors:

1. Maintain the initiative in the attack on the tax rebels.
2. Know their plans before they arrive at our door to execute them.
3. Identify the leaders of the movement and concentrate on them.
4. Have a plan of action in coordination with the region rather than hit and miss defensive reactions.

5. Continue and step up infiltration in-depth of the movement.

6. Use all available federal, state, and local laws.

7. Use civil penalties on Porth-type cases.

8. Wage a campaign to educate U.S. attorneys and federal judges with the importance of prison sentences on cases.

9. District directors to continue to follow up cases of admitted or known false W-4's or W-4E's to advise employers of responsibilities in such cases and follow up to see that proper 1040's are filed at the filing season.

10. Use state taxing agencies willing to cooperate on enforcement of laws on tax rebels.

11. Los Angeles and San Francisco project supervisors to hold periodic planning meetings on common targets.

These items were followed by four action items for the region:

1. Use tax Executive Institute liaison to inform tax consultants and their client-employers of their duties on suspected false-exemption cases.

2. Consider requesting legislation or an IRS published ruling to require employers to file with service centers a copy of amended W-4 or W-4E forms.

3. Use Circular E, the *Employer's Tax Guide on Withholding*, to inform employers of responsibilities on suspected false-exemption cases.

4. Use trade journals to reach employers for same purpose.

The more I read the Croasmun Memorandum, the more I doubted its authenticity. No single statement in the minutes seemed inappropriate. There was really nothing that would embarrass the Service. A lot of what was said even seemed to be quite contrary to what one would imagine protesters would want spread about. If it was fake, if it was disinformation, it was damned well done, for its purpose was totally obscure.

I showed the memorandum to several experienced special agents in National Office. No one recognized it. It might or it might not be genuine. Either way, it was considered amusing.

I sent a copy to Western Region after explaining to the regional disclosure officer that we now had a request for any records which might authenticiate the Croasmun Memorandum as a genuine Service document. I made no mention of my belief that it was a protester product.

About two weeks later, the regional disclosure officer called to brief me on his findings. He had circulated the document, asking for information. No one had any record that would prove that the memorandum was genuine. Even the travel vouchers which would have proved that some meeting had taken place on the date shown had long since been destroyed.

Every office has at least one old-timer who remembers everything that ever happened and can expound at length on the most trivial details of the most trivial events. Every office has at least one nitpicker who will tell you exactly where something was put and then complain that it probably is not there anymore because some people cannot be trusted to leave anything alone. Every office has at least one packrat who makes a copy of everything because you never know when you might need it. The Western Region disclosure officer questioned all the old-timers and all the nitpickers and all the packrats. No one had ever seen the Croasmun Memorandum before; no one had any recollection of the events which might have surrounded its creation.

The general belief was that the Croasmun Memorandum was a clever forgery. And a special agent in Western Region came up with a rationale for its creation. If the Croasmun Memorandum was genuine and all the actions discussed had been taken in 1973 and the tax protest movement was still growing ten years later, it would prove that the Service's best efforts against the movement were ineffective.

We advised the requester that we could locate no records which would provide any indication concerning the authenticity of the submitted document. And we gave the matter no further thought for a few years.

Time passed, we experienced one or two reorganizations, a new regional disclosure officer was appointed, other personnel were replaced, I had occasion to inquire as to the types of Information Act requests being received in the Western Region. From the description of one item that was currently popular, it was immediately apparent to me that protesters were once again making requests for the Croasmun Memorandum. I expressed my familiarity with the document and asked how the Western Region was handling such requests. "Why, we're giving the document out," the new employee told me.

"Wherever did you find the damned thing?" I asked. I was shocked to hear the answer. "It was no trouble at all," the new employee explained. "Just about everyone had a copy!"

I asked if these copies came from old-timers. Were they found in old files, were they associated with other 12- or 15-year-old records?

"No," I was told, "for some reason someone sent a lot of copies around just a couple of years go. We don't know why. But a lot of the things in that memorandum seem just as valid today as they were years ago, so a lot of people kept them. There's nothing exempt in it, so we just decided to give it out."

It was readily apparent what had happened. The copies being released were not descended from the original Croasmun memorandum if there ever was one. They were generated from the copy a protester had sent to me, which I had sent to the Western Region, which the regional disclosure officer had circulated for authentication, authentication no one was able to give. It may never have been our record before, but it was our record now, and it was being released as genuine. The tax protesters had succeeded in using the Information Act to insinuate a record into our files and had gotten us to distribute it for them as a genuine document!

Record-Retention Practices

There can be no doubt that the outcome of the Croasmun Memorandum incident resulted from the Service's record-retention practices, which while designed to be practical for tax administration purposes, are virtually worthless for maintaining records of any historical integrity.

The Service does not have central files. The Service does not have indices of existing records. The Service does not have a catalog of the types of records maintained. The Service does not have a list of the locations at which records are being maintained.

Instructions for maintaining records are spread throughout the *Internal Revenue Manual* and generally pertain only to the specific types of records maintained by a specific function. Those sections of the manual which deal with the general rules for effective records maintenance consist primarily of good intentions and other pap, with the result that for many categories of records, managers will do whatever seems practical for their own immediate purposes.

Service records can be considered to fall into six broad categories: tax returns, documents which establish or alter tax liabilities, case records, correspondence, internal memoranda, and subject-matter files. Each is handled differently, and the treatment of each varies from an attempt to be perfect to something approaching the chaotic.

The processing of tax returns constitutes the major activity to which the Service devotes itself, and it is what the Service does best. From the moment that returns arrive in a service center, they are under precise controls and follow extremely exacting processing guidelines. Empty envelopes are even passed before light bulbs to make certain that nothing has been overlooked in the extraction process. Every return is immediately assigned a document locator number which will ultimately be the key to identifying it on a master file and permit its retrieval whenever needed. There have been cases, notably those uncovered by investigations following upon an unsuccessful processing season in 1985, of disgruntled or maladjusted employees destroying returns, but such incidents are extremely rare. In theory, tax returns can never be lost. A return can be misplaced within a file, or it can be charged out and never returned to the proper place, but by then all the information on that return has been recorded. Ultimately, returns are destroyed in accordance with applicable records-control schedules. The record of a return's receipt, however, made at the very outset of processing, is never destroyed. When no longer of any immediate practical interest, such records are transferred to retention registers for permanent storage. The only exceptions to the permanence of these tape files result from the fact that the earliest registers established did not use state-of-the-art techniques, and some of them have consequently deteriorated beyond any possibility of restoration. More recent data files are virtually indestructible. In fact, there need be no fear of fires, earthquakes, or other disasters, for duplicates of the major tape files are maintained at alternate locations.

In theory, the Service expects to resume operations within a few days of a nuclear holocaust, somehow believing that enough of its records, its staff, and the taxpaying public will survive to permit an active tax administration program.

Documents other than returns which establish or alter tax liabilities are subject to almost the same level of care. Basically, such records constitute the input documents to the master files. They too receive document locator numbers and are supposed to be readily retrievable as long as they are scheduled to exist. Many such documents, however, warrant only limited retention periods. And the trend is to replace the use of paper documents for input to master files with electronic transfers of information. Thus, while the records will be maintained for as long as necessary, there may never have been any paper for filing purposes.

Unfortunately, this theoretical striving for perfection in the retention and retrieval of tax returns and related documents does not produce the desired result. In 1989, a Service study revealed that about 2 million tax returns and related documents are known to be lost every year; the actual total that are lost may greatly exceed that number. The study showed that Service personnel annually send to the files for about 35 million documents in the course of performing their duties. Six million, or approximately 17 percent, of these requests are not successful in retrieving the record within a reasonable time and are resubmitted for another search. After these follow-up efforts have been completed, there remain 2 million documents, or about 6 percent of the total originally requested, which cannot be found. Since the Service receives more than 100 million returns annually, it may be assumed to be misplacing about 6 million of them beyond retrieval with reasonable search efforts.

Some Service employees have admitted that they prefer to make requests to state tax authorities with whom taxpayers have filed copies of their federal returns, as the states are able to provide more reliable service. It is not at all unusual for revenue agents to ask taxpayers under examination to bring their copies of returns, since the Service cannot find the originals, and then to suspect fraud if the taxpayer has also lost the return!

Further indication of the condition of returns files can be found in the program for providing taxpayers with copies of their own returns upon payment of a fee. About 800,000 taxpayers pay such fees annually; 21 percent of these get their money back because the Service cannot locate the returns within 90 days.

Other categories of records are not subject to the same level of good intentions. Case files, for instance, may virtually always be found as long as the case is open and the master file reflects assignment information. Once the case is closed, practices differ. In the Collection Division, closed cases for Taxpayer Delinquent Accounts (the records which reflect enforced collection efforts) are dropped into storage boxes. These boxes are not searchable except by determining the date the case was closed and then rummaging through the appropriate box on the assumption that older cases will be at the bottom of the box and more recent ones closer to the top. The Collection Division simply feels that there is not enough reason to retrieve such cases to warrant the effort of filing them alphabetically or numerically. Moreover, since case files usually consist of folders containing whatever documentation has been developed, there is no way to know whether they are complete.

Correspondence is controlled in the recipient offices. There is no way of knowing which office that might be unless there is knowledge of how the correspondence was addressed or an educated guess can be made based upon the subject matter of the correspondence. Every function maintains its own files. Even if it were known that a piece of correpsondence was handled in the

National Office, there would be hundreds of places where such correspondence could be filed. Even if it were known that within National Office the correspondence was assigned to Examination or Collection or any other function, there would still be dozens of locations where the item might be.

Internal memoranda are maintained by the issuing office, but there are no controls such as those for correspondence. In order to locate internal memoranda, it is necessary to know who produced it and when.

Finally, there are subject-matter files. Each office keeps its own. Their value and continuity vary widely between offices. Chief Counsel functions, Technical, Planning Division, Research Division, and a few others keep excellent subject-matter files. The enforcement functions — Examination, Collection, and Criminal Investigation — although excellent on case files, are usually quite poor on maintaining subject-matter files.

We have had occasions when high-ranking officials have made public statements such as "We have records which show that...." or "We have evidence that...." Then we received requests from the news media to see the records or get copies of the evidence. Unfortunately, we could find no file which would establish which records were being referred to or where they might be located. We could locate records which would have served the purpose of defending the statements which had been made, but we could not establish that these were the records to which the officials had been referring or even that these officials had ever seen these records. In fact, for most decisions made by the Service, it is virtually impossible to determine what background matter was seen or used by the deciding official. Even if we can locate an appropriate subject matter file, we have no way of knowing who has seen it or what was in it at any particular time or what has been subsequently added or removed.

Decisions on policy and practices of the Service are usually made at fairly high levels — commissioner, deputy commissioner, associate commissioner, or assistant commissioner. However, such officials' offices usually do not maintain files other than those few which relate to the official's immediate activities. The methodology for decision making usually consists of signing a document which has been prepared by a lower echelon. It is the lower echelon which maintains the relevant files.

But when we look at how these subordinate offices at the division or branch level maintain their files, we find some very strange situations. The *Internal Revenue Manual*, at IRM 1(15)53.3(2), identifies those records which warrant permanent preservation:

> Records identified for permanent preservation are produced in preparing and issuing policy, procedural, organizational, and reportorial documents and in providing executive direction to the Service's activities. These are records containing evidence of the organization and functions of the Service. They document the rationale of the policies of the Service and of decisions with respect to organizational and procedural matters. The records show how the Internal Revenue Service mission is directed and how its activities involve relationships with other governmental entities including foreign governments. Such

records are of archival value because they contain information useful for research in the administrative history of the Service and the Department; and they are of value to IRS because they contain information needed in dealing with organizational, procedural and policy matters.

One could easily assume that the Croasmun Memorandum, if it were genuine, would have met that standard for permanent retention. Of course, it might have been issued at too low a level. But when we ask the Commissioner's office for records of historical value responsive to Information requests, we are referred back to the functional offices which maintain the records!

When we refer to Records Control Schedule 102 for Examination Division—National Office, we find no mention of any records warranting permanent retention. The most relevant entries read:

> Examination Division subject file. Contains correspondence, reports, and other documents which have usefulness for reference purposes, and related control cards. This file contains narrative and statistical reports of the Division; reports and memoranda, and other papers on the organization and activities of the Division, etc. Destroy after 25 years.

> Monthly, Quarterly, Annual, and Other Periodic Management Information Reports. Includes computer generated reports produced from the Master File and other Management Information Systems of the Service to measure field accomplishments in returns and staff time, additional taxes and penalties proposed, and effected and related material.... Destroy after 5 years.

When we refer to Records Control Schedule 109 for Collection—National Office, we find yet another concept of what constitutes permanent retention:

> Administrative Management and Organization Records
> (1) Records, whether studies, analyses, or correspondence, which established the policies, practices, and programs for the management of the Collection Division. Included are organizational changes, functional realignments and responsibilities, long and short range planning documents.... Destroy after 10 years.
> (2) Record copies which document the history of the Collection Division. Correspondence and case files of this type documentation may contain analyses, coordinations, approvals and disapprovals, recommendations, plans and any background materials which contribute to an understanding of or provide an explanation of complete documents.... Destroy after 10 years....
> General Administrative and Housekeeping Correspondence.
> Routine correspondence, transmittals, teletypes, and requisitions that relate to administrative, housekeeping, and facilitative roles of the organization and not procedural in nature. Destroy after 2 years.

Thus it would seem that records which warrant permanent retention for historical purposes may be retained permanently or for 25 years, 10 years, 5 years, or 2 years.

Beyond the confusion about which records should be retained, how long they are to be retained, and who should retain them, another major problem results from the Service's fascination with the process of reorganization. Some function or another has been reorganized almost every year since the "great" reorganization of 1953. Major reorganizations took place in 1978, 1982, and 1986. Frequently, the dust from these reorganizations does not settle for two or three years, by which time the next reorganization is in progress. These reorganizations may benefit the management of future programs, but they destroy continuity and help records lose themselves. In fact, many managers consider reorganizations good times to purge their files of records whose retention may not be advantageous. We have repeatedly been told when searching for records, "We don't know who has them," "Is no longer our responsibility," or "Must have fallen into a crack."

Information Act requests for current case files seldom present any search problems. Requests for background files, materials in subject-matter files, documents of historical interest, invariably involve serious search problems. Moreover, the records released in response to such requests seldom represent a significant proportion of the records which could ultimately be uncovered with a conscientious effort by anyone with a probing mentality. Requesters in need of such materials should critically examine the records provided in search of internal clues for other files, other locations to be searched, and related subject matters to be requested. The employees who perform records searches in response to Information Act requests will not do the necessary spade work. They will perform a minimal search, respond on the basis of whatever is readily available, and hope that the requester will be sufficiently satisfied not to come back for more.

Any requester who has a serious interest in studying the operations of the Service and needs documents of historical value should hurry. The needles in the haystack are not only difficult to find; they are rapidly disappearing.

There is, however, some hope that historical material may yet be salvaged. In 1989, the celebration of the Service's 125th anniversary was capped by the appointment of the agency's first historian. Ostensibly, the agency's reason for hiring a historian was to avoid repeating blunders and to force management to face the many unfortunate incidents which they might prefer to forget. Unfortunately, the historian is an employee of the assistant commissioner for Human Resources Management and Support and is unlikely to have much influence with the less enlightened staffs in the enforcement areas, who often believe that history can best be managed by the prudent loss, shredding, or misplacement of records.

The historians's first task is to rescue abandoned records. She has stated, "I'm finding nooks and crannies all over the organization where there's a pile of records." Her second task is to set up a reference service providing "a centralized location where people within and from outside the organization can call if they need historical information." Eventually, additional historians, archivists, and clerical support are planned to staff the intended research center. The historian also plans to create a depositary of oral history of the agency by interviewing the participants in significant events.

How long the office of the historian will last is anyone's guess. She has stated, "The responsibility is not to protect and defend an organization." That sort of objectiveness has proved to be the undoing of many well-intentioned persons struggling to overcome the narrow self-interest of a bureaucracy. In the meantime, anyone having a need for historical records might do well to discuss the matter with the Service historian. Information Act requests for historical records should include a specific statement that the Office of the Historian should be included in the search.

Do not be surprised if any significant public use of the Office of the Historian causes the agency to reevaluate its need for such a position. When dancing the Service fandango, we always take one short step forward followed by two rapid steps backward.

Chapter 7

Philip and Susan Long

Of all the factors which came to influence how the Internal Revenue Service administers the Freedom of Information Act, none had greater effect than the activities of two taxpayers from Washington State, Philip and Susan Long. Much like characters in a Frank Capra movie, the Longs assigned themselves the role of the common man defending American values of fair play against the duplicity of the heartless bureaucrats of the Service.

To the bureaucrats who dealt with them, however, the Longs appeared to be tricksters who tried to beat the tax system by harassing the Service with unnecessary and unreasonable requests for information.

Doubtlessly both assessments were valid. Both the Longs and the Service acted in completely unreasonable ways and for more than ten years carried on what can only be described as an Information Act vendetta which cost the American taxpayers millions of dollars and precluded other taxpayers from receiving information services to which they were entitled.

The Service bears the responsibility for starting the contest. The abuses the Service committed created the Longs as an administrative bete noir. But there is a limit to getting even, and the Longs could have stopped once they achieved justice. Instead, they went on to seek retribution.

To understand the nature of the struggle and how it affected the administration of the Information Act, we have to go back to the very beginning and see how the Service implemented the act.

Implementation

The immediate response of the Service to the Information Act, which became effective July 4, 1967, was to issue instructions for implementation in the form of a *Manual* supplement. These instructions made it perfectly evident that the Service had an adequate understanding of the act's requirements, had no doubts about how the provisions were to be interpreted, was committed to properly administering the act, and was actually willing to go beyond the barest necessities to accommodate the public.

Each assistant commissioner was assigned responsibility for publishing all the materials produced by his function which were legally required to be published. Among the items assigned for publication were "statements of general policy."

Public reading rooms were to be established in the National Office and in each of the seven regional offices. The establishment of reading rooms went beyond the requirements of the act, which merely stated that certain items were to be available for public inspection and copying but made no mention of reading rooms. The reading rooms were to be under the administration of Public Affairs, an arrangement which further attested to the intention of achieving genuinely open government.

Each assistant commissioner was to be responsible for placing in the reading rooms all those materials required to be available for public inspection. Among the items to be placed in the public reading rooms were "those Internal Revenue Manual materials, and IRS training texts and materials, which are furnished to the reading rooms by the National Office as being open for public inspection and copying." The materials in the reading rooms were to be kept up to date. The instructions recognized that some items might require editing "to the extent necessary to exclude exempt material."

Requests for copies of materials on deposit in the reading rooms were to be honored by any office of the Service receiving the request to the extent that the materials were readily available at that location. Requests for records not placed in the reading room or for which no specific disclosure instructions had been issued were to be forwarded to the Collection Division's Disclosure and Liaison Branch for response. Responses were to be made with the concurrence of other interested functions. The tone of the instruction definitely implied that at least some such requests would be granted.

Had this initial implementing instruction been followed with a reasonable degree of commitment and integrity, there would never have been a struggle with Mr. and Mrs. Long or any of the other early requesters. Millions of dollars in unnecessary administrative expenses, numerous court cases, and years of wasted efforts could have been avoided. Unfortunately, the implementing instruction was not followed for very long.

Regression

I was assigned to the Disclosure and Liaison Branch about four years after the Information Act went into effect. One of my first duties was to familiarize myself with the administration of the act, at that time still regarded as a new statute not yet fully effective. My first act was to review the accumulated files of specific requests for records not yet placed in the reading room. These files were not extensive, as there had been well under 200 requests during the past four years.

After reviewing these files and the related statutes, regulations, and implementing instructions, I was puzzled by the fact that many of these requests appeared to have been processed in accordance with prior law rather than the statute in effect. Few records had been releasd. Those that were released seemed to have been responsive to the status or circumstances of the requester rather than the characteristics of the records sought. When I questioned more experienced technicians about this, I was handed another instruction for processing these requests which I had not previously seen.

The instruction was not part of the *Internal Revenue Manual*. It was simply a photocopy of about 30 typewritten pages. It was neither dated or signed, nor did it bear any other indicator that it was an official issuance. This instruction listed almost every existing variety of record and explained which exemptions permitted withholding the record from the public. It was explained that all I had to do when receiving a request was to find the requested records in this instruction and then copy the rationale for denying the request in my response. It made the job very easy. There was no need to retrieve any records, no need to analyze any records, no need to apply the law, and no need to release any records!

What was even more puzzling was that this tool for administering a law which called for open government and publicity for administrative instructions seemed to be designed as a secret instruction. No one seemed to recognize any paradox in this arrangement, nor was there anything in this instruction that in any way recognized the possibility that some records might become available to the general public.

My next action was to visit the public reading room. The room number was known to me, as it was listed in the regulations. I found that there was no sign that identified the location as the reading room. There was an outer room containing a few desks. Beyond this, there was an inner room whose walls were lined with filing cabinets. The cabinets, however, were the kind that closed, so it was impossible to see if there was anything in them.

A moment after I entered the room, I was followed in by a rather disagreeable woman who shouted that I had no business being there and that I should leave immediately. I asked whether this was not the public reading room which anyone could use. I was told that it was the reading room, but that it could not be used by anyone without permission from the "front office." The woman explained that she could not allow anyone into the room because the materials had to be maintained in good order for the public.

I then identified myself as a representative of the Disclosure and Liaison Branch who had been charged with responsibility for overseeing the administration of the Information Act. I was told that that made no difference. Whether I was there as a member of the public or as an employee, I still had to leave, and I could not see any records.

I reported this incident to my branch chief, who called public affairs and made arrangements for me to make another visit to the reading room. When I arrived, a very pleasant young lady made profuse apologies and explained that the older woman was a problem employee who had been assigned to the reading room to keep her out of public sight since no one ever went there!

A variety of documents were brought out of the cabinets and displayed on the desks for my review. Everything that I was shown was either specifically published for distribution to the public or related to public affairs such as news releases. There were no *Internal Revenue Manual* issuances, no policy statements, and no training documents. This was certainly not the reading-room collection envisioned by the implementing instruction. It made no contribution toward complying with the Information Act. I began making inquiries.

The first step backward from the implementation plan had come in August 1967, just a month after the effective date of the act. The intention had been to publish Internal Revenue Service Policy Statements in the *Federal Register*. However, on the basis of discussion with the Director of the Office of the Federal Register, it was concluded that the majority of the policy statements did not require publication in the *Federal Register*. Making them available through the reading room would be adequate to satisfy the law. The policy statements were printed as a handbook which was part of the *Internal Revenue Manual*. As such, it was decided, they would be included in the reading room as publicly available portions of the manual.

Thereafter, the reading room seemed to function as long as the Commissioner who originally authorized it, Sheldon S. Cohen, remained in office. As soon as Randolph Thrower became Commissioner, the assistant commissioners launched a campaign which ultimately resulted in the removal of the *Internal Revenue Manual* and the training documents from the reading room.

The training documents went first. It was pointed out that the law required "instructions to staff" to be available for public inspection. Technically, the training documents were instructional material, not "instructions to staff." That is, training documents told how to do something; they did not direct that it be done. Consequently, the training documents were removed.

The next step backward involved the *Internal Revenue Manual*. It was argued that practically no member of the public had actually visited the reading rooms, and since automatically placing manual materials in the room involved considerable expense, it would be more practical to devise some other means of access. I do not know how extensive the actual reading-room traffic had been, but I do know that there had been no attempt to make use of the facilities easy or convenient. And I was aware that at least one potential user (myself) had been thrown out.

I spoke to several of the technicians who had been involved in making the manual materials available to the reading room. Based upon their recollections, I estimated that the time devoted to this operation probably did not exceed a quarter staff year annually. It was therefore very unlikely that the efficient use of resources was the true motivation for removing the manual materials from the reading rooms. Nevertheless, Commissioner Thrower, whether he understood the implications or not, was prevailed upon to authorize the removal of the manual from the reading room.

The removal of the manual had very serious consequences. As part of the manual, the policy statements were also removed. The rationale for not publishing the statements had been that they would be in the reading room, but now they would no longer be there. These steps did not violate the law since there was no requirement to have a reading room in the first place.

The requirements of the law could still be met by making manual materials, training documents, and policy statements available to specific requesters. But my review of the responses to specific requesters showed that these items were not being released on request. The attitude was that the materials which had been removed from the reading room were not required to be there, and anything not required to be in the reading room need not be released.

I asked an experienced manager who had been involved in this process how the Service hoped to get away with withholding policy statements. "It's easy," he replied, puffing studiously on his pipe. "The law requires that we publish statements of general policy, and the Director of the Office of the Federal Register told us that our policy statements are not statements of general policy, and they are not statements of policy; they are policy statements. If the Congress wanted us to give out our policy statements, they should have said so!"

An Audit in Seattle

In 1969, as the Service's implementation of open government was collapsing in Washington, D.C., an audit was progressing in Washington State. The 1966, 1967, and 1968 personal income tax returns of Philip and Susan Long were being examined in the Seattle District. The returns of two small corporations which represented the family's real estate business were also examined.

As far as income and business activities were concerned, the Longs were in every way average taxpayers. In fact, the way the Service measures things, they would have been considered small-income taxpayers. Initially, the audit was uneventful. The necessary records were brought in, adequate cooperation was shown, and there was an expectation that the result would be some minor adjustment or perhaps even a "no change" closing.

The result was far different. The examiner proposed a tax of $38,144 added to the $21,412 tax already paid for those years. The Longs would have been more highly taxed than any other Americans; in fact, they would have been close to being in a nonexistent 100 percent tax category.

It is easy to imagine that the Longs must have been shocked, annoyed, and frightened by the proposed assessment. They not unnaturally asked how such a thing was possible, but they received no explanation of how the assessment had been arrived at. Instead, they were threatened with a jeopardy assessment, a device designed for use in enforcing immediate collection against gamblers, drug dealers, and defalcating businessmen expected to flee the country with their ill-gotten gains.

There were in those days no taxpayer-service personnel, ombudsmen, or disclosure officers to help taxpayers experiencing such difficulties. The route prescribed by the system for the Longs' situation was an informal conference with the revenue agent's supervisor, a more formal district conference, an appeal to the Appellate Division, and a complaint before the Tax Court or the payment of a portion of the tax and a complaint in a District Court. These remedies were not inadequate, but neither did they offer immediate satisfaction. The Longs had their own ways of doing things.

The Longs entered into the prescribed procedure for resolving the issue. But at a January 5, 1971, meeting with an appellate officer, they delivered an

Information Act request. The request sought all the investigative files on Mr. Long and his corporations, the *Closing Agreement Handbook* (a portion of the *Internal Revenue Manual* instructing appellate officers on compromising claims), and "code books." The law did not then require the release of investigative files, and no one ever knew what was meant by "code books." At least a part of the request could have been resolved locally, and the rest of it might have been clarified by discussion. The *Closing Agreement Handbook* had been in the reading room and could have been released. But this request was viewed not as a citizen's right but as an unfriendly act. Somehow, battle lines had become drawn, and instead of an administrative problem to be resolved, the Longs and the Service had become implacable foes, each considering the other totally unreasonable.

The Longs Do Battle

The Longs began publishing advertisements in the *Washington Post*, which they titled "Life Under the IRS." Ultimately, there were to be 11 such articles, each of which detailed in the smallest possible typeface some aspect of their struggle. Many of the ads seemed to be facetious. One implied that the Chief Counsel's staff of attorneys were blundering incompetents in a parody of "The Charge of the Light Brigade." Someone in the Service might have been annoyed, someone might have been embarrassed, but most of us were, I think, amused. Whatever the Longs intended to accomplish with these ads, the only apparent result was that they made it almost impossible for anyone in the Service to associate himself with their cause without losing the respect of his peers.

In 1970, the Longs made Freedom of Information requests for Pub 481, "Description of Principal Federal Tax Returns, Related Forms and Publications," and Pub 676, "Catalog of Forms, Form Letters, and Notices." The use of the term *Pub* (Publication) in these titles meant that they had been printed with the intention that they should be of use to the public. Both items were in the reading rooms, and consequently they were quickly provided. Soon thereafter, the Longs returned these books to the Service with a request that each of the blank forms marked with a blue check should be sent to them. Almost every item in both books was checked! There was no easy way to put together a collection of vast numbers of blank forms in those days, and servicing this request was a difficult and time-consuming task. After a few months' work, 1,577 blank forms listed in Pub 481 and 1,191 blank forms listed in Pub 676 were mailed in what was doubtlessly the first significant grant of records ever made by the Service.

The next move by the Longs was a visit to Washington, D.C., where they presented their problems to various congressmen and sought to meet with Service officials. By now, the Longs had filed a complaint concerning their tax case with the Tax Court. Service officials were naturally, and quite properly, unwilling to meet with them on matters already in litigation. They also asked to meet officials to discuss what they were now calling their investigation of the Service.

The chief of the Disclosure and Liaison Branch, Mr. Donald Virdin, was willing to meet with them and prepared for the meeting by putting together a stack at least 18 inches high containing various documents which explained how the Service operates.

Mr. Virdin, Mrs. Long, a stenographer, and I were present at this meeting. Mrs. Long began by complaining that responses providing the 2,768 blank forms were inadequate, took too long, and represented poor service. She then explained her objective of learning precisely how the Service operates and of obtaining statistics which could be used in studying and evaluating those operations. Mr. Virdin offered a pile of documents which he had accumulated as something to begin with. Mrs. Long refused to accept them, explaining that she did not want anything we were willing to give to her but wanted only those things we were not willing to give to her. Mrs. Long then explained that what she wanted was a series of meetings with top officials for each of several functions so that she could interrogate them on the types of records that existed and which she might request.

In the next few days Mr. Virdin made arrangements for a preliminary meeting between himself and National Office managers who might be able to suggest an approach for helping Mrs. Long. Almost 50 managers, mostly division directors and branch chiefs, accepted Mr. Virdin's invitation. Mr. Virdin, who was eager to comply with the law and to be of help to taxpayers, began by explaining the requirements for making information available. He presented the Longs' request in a positive way and then asked for suggestions on how to be helpful. Instead of suggestions, he received questions, which I have paraphrased to the best of my recollection:

- "Weren't these the people who put those silly ads in the *Washington Post*?"
- "Weren't these the people who were being so much trouble to the Seattle District?"
- "Weren't these the people who were up on the Hill bothering congressmen a few days ago?"
- "Didn't they ask you for thousands of blank forms? How could blank forms be of any help to a taxpayer disputing a proposed assessment?"
- "Didn't Mrs. Long complain about the forms you gave her? What makes you think that anything else that you give her will satisfy her?"
- "Didn't you offer her a lot of information, and didn't she refuse it just because she didn't want anything that you were willing to give to her?"
- "How can we justify taking time that belongs to all the taxpayers and wasting it on people who don't appreciate the need to work within established procedures?"
- "Why didn't they get an attorney or an accountant to help with their tax problems instead of flying to Washington looking for special treatment?"
- "What could we possibly know, what could we possibly have, what could we possibly say that would help them?"
- "Aren't they just trying to harass the Service, to blackmail us into letting them off without paying their tax?"

• "Aren't we already in litigation with the Longs? Why can't they work out their problem like everybody else? What's so special about them? Why not wait until the Tax Court rules, either they owe it or they don't?"

There were no answers to these questions. As the meeting began to break up, it was obvious that a consensus had been reached. Without voting, without anyone announcing a position, it was obvious that the management of the Service, meeting in a rare assembly, had decided upon the position to take. The Service was going to stonewall!

The Longs had lost their opportunity to win the Service's cooperation. They now began to make what appeared to be random requests for any record they were able to identify. The Service generally denied their requests for manual material, training documents, and statistics but did make some records available. Whenever a record was released, it was quickly followed by more requests asking for every form, every report, every record of any description which had been mentioned in the original record. The Longs, having been denied the meetings at which they were going to question managers on what records were available, were undertaking a search to identify what they were searching for.

Oddly, many of the items now being requested were the same documents Mr. Virdin had offered to Mrs. Long and she had declined. But the opportunity for easy access had passed, and documents once freely offered were now being denied.

One of the formerly available items was Doc 5988, "6 to 1 Yield Cost Study Report." This report, designed much like a comic book, offered simple-language explanations of how any funds spent for enforcement purposes would be repaid through additional assessments resulting from more audits. Frankly, it was propaganda prepared for distribution to congressmen and their staffs in support of budget requests. Hundreds of copies had been distributed on the Hill, and many of these had been passed on by staffers to any interested constituent who might want one. There was absolutely nothing confidential in this booklet, but now that the Longs wanted it, it had to be protected. The explanation for this sudden realization was that the statistics relied upon to calculate the 6-to-1 yield estimate could be misused for other purposes. The informal rationale offered by jaded National Office analysts was that if the booklet fell into the hands of anyone less gullible than a congressman, they might recompute the figures and realize that the 6-to-1 ratio had been backed into to justify someone's ballpark guess and had no real scientific basis. Not being a trained statistician, I am unable to offer any comment upon the validity of the 6-to-1 figure. However, in retrospect, I do find one thing odd. Almost 20 years later, despite changes in the level of audits performed, tremendous growth in the economy, drastic revisions to the tax law, computerization of many operations, and every other variety of change, we still see 6 to 1 mentioned as the anticipated return from expenditures for additional staffing. I guess when you have a really good figure, it lasts almost forever.

The meeting Mr. Virdin had called not only cost the Longs any chance of finding cooperation but also cost Mr. Virdin and the disclosure function the trust and respect of other Service managers. Shortly after this meeting, a reorganization was announced. Disclosure was split off from the Disclosure and Liaison Branch under the Collection Division and was established as the Disclosure Staff working directly for the Assistant Commissioner (Compliance). This change appeared on the surface to reflect the growing importance of Disclosure by moving it from within a division to a staff function above the division level. There were rumors, however, that the Collection Division was believed to be too soft on Freedom of Information matters and was not trusted to make an adequate defense of any Audit or Intelligence records requested. Therefore, Disclosure was put where the assistant commissioner could keep an eye on it and make sure that no Audit or Intelligence records were released.

A few weeks after Disclosure was transferred, Mr. Virdin was called to the office of the assistant commissioner on an urgent matter. When he arrived, he was told that the assistant commissioner had just received an important phone call and Mr. Virdin would have to wait. After waiting for some time, he was told that he could return to his office and he would be called when he was needed. No sooner had he arrived at his office than he was told to return, but when he got back to the assistant commissioner's office, another phone call had been received. For almost two weeks, Mr. Virdin was played like a yo-yo, repeatedly called to the assistant commissioner's office but never learning what the urgent matter was. He submitted his retirement papers, which were immediately accepted, and the urgent matter resolved itself without further difficulty.

Mr. Virdin was replaced by a longtime Audit Division (now Examination Division) manager who recognized the importance of defending the Service's records and knew better than to offer assistance to a disgruntled taxpayer trying to investigate the Service.

The Longs Litigate

On June 29, 1971, Mr. Long filed suit against the Service to compel production of all files relating to the business activities of himself and his corporations, the *Closing Agreement Handbook*, and certain "code books." On November 23, 1971, the U.S. District Court at Seattle ruled on that litigation.

The request for the investigatory files was dismissed as "much too vague." In regard to the other matters, the court quoted Mr. Long as saying, "The main reason I am here is I was audited nearly two years ago." It was therefore apparent that Mr. Long wanted the materials requested solely for use in current proceedings before the Tax Court. The District Court decided that despite the fact that the materials requested might be available through the Freedom of Information Act, a person already litigating in the Tax Court should seek the records through that channel. The District Court was simply unwilling to step on the toes of the Tax Court!

This result came very close to completely justifying the positions taken by the National Office managers at Mr. Virdin's meeting. The struggle was now centered in the Tax Court where it seemed to belong. It was generally believed that we would have no further Freedom of Information problems with the Longs. Unfortunately, there was no letup in the flow of requests.

In anticipation of requests for the same records being made through the Tax Court, I now visited the court's docket room where any member of the public was free to examine the files on matters before the court. The Longs' file contained copies of their tax returns and the proposed assessments. I was stunned by what I found.

The assessment against Mr. Long's corporations, which accounted for most of the tax involved, was based upon an obscure provision of the Internal Revenue Code designed to discourage wealthy investors from accumulating funds in "personal holding corporations." It was extremely unlikely that Congress ever intended the provision to be applied to small businessmen, and even if that was the intention, it seemed unlikely that it was being properly applied in this instance. Frankly, I believed the proposed assessment was unfair and unreasonable and that there was little likelihood that the Service would win the case. In fact, I wondered how such an assessment could have been proposed and how it could have survived all the reviews necessary to get into court. Generally, the Service wants to win its cases and will not litigate unless it believes that the case is a sure winner. This case looked like a sure loser. I could only surmise that the case had progressed much like the emperor's new clothes, which everyone could see did not exist but no one dared challenge.

What was even more shocking was that the provision the assessment relied upon was not designed to collect a tax but was intended to promote the payment of dividends to shareholders in order to generate taxable income. Mr. Long could have avoided the proposed tax at any time simply by paying himself and any other shareholders dividends and then filing an amended return. Despite their public protestations, the Longs were never really at risk for paying the proposed tax if they did not want to be. The balance of the tax claimed represented an unreasonable nitpicking which would have fallen apart once the main claim was disposed of.

It also became evident from the file that there were good reasons for not having pursued the request for records through the Tax Court. Nothing that the Longs had asked for, nothing which had been given to them, and nothing which had been denied to them was in any way relevant to their case. It seemed quite doubtful that record requests were actually being made to support the Tax Court case, but the case might have been manufactured to lend credence to the pursuit of the records.

The Longs now filed various legal actions to further their Freedom of Information campaign. On August 9, 1972, the U.S. District Court again issued a ruling concerning the *Closing Agreement Handbook* and a management information report, Doc 5342, "Source of Returns — Income Taxes." The Service argued that the *Closing Agreement Handbook* should be withheld because it is not an administrative staff manual which affects the public and therefore is not required to be released. In other words, we were claiming that this portion of the *Internal Revenue Manual* was not a manual!

The court ruled that the handbook was indeed a manual which affects members of the public and must be released. The opinion stated: "Although

the manual may not have been heretofore disclosed in its entirety in any proceeding, the government concedes that various portions thereof have been produced voluntarily or pursuant to court order in various legal actions." The
court then cited about a dozen instances in which portions of the manual were
released.

Fortunately, the court did not mention or was unaware that the original
instruction implementing the Information Act admitted that the *Internal
Revenue Manual* was an administrative staff manual, that the entire manual
had at one time been distributed to a major university, and that portions of the
Closing Agreement Handbook had at one time been in the reading room.

Document 5342, which detailed statistics pertaining to the sources of
returns for examination and the results of the examinations of income tax
returns, was also ordered released. Fortunately, the court did not mention or
did not know that at the very time these arguments were being heard, Document 5342 was among the *Quarterly Statistical Reports* on display in the
Department of the Treasury library. The Service frequently calls the same item
by different names, with the result that requesters sometimes demand records
they already have!

Thus, the Longs' first great victory, which they claimed had cost them over
$10,000 in expenses, was to obtain access to records which had once lain un-
noticed on reading-room or library shelves. I have never encountered any indication that the Longs have ever been able to make any use of these materials
or that they were found to contain anything that was in any way controversial,
worth pursuing, or worth defending.

The FOIA Policy Statement

The loss of records in litigation now prompted action at the Commissioner's level to promote a change of attitudes in the Service. There had seemed
to be an intention to release records on appeal (discussed in Chapter 2), but
somehow the recommendations of the managerial establishment were allowed
to prevail over the views of the Commissioner's assistant, which may also have
been the preferences of the Commissioner.

Commissioner Walters now created a task force, including representatives
from each function and headed by a representative from Planning and Research.
The purpose of the task force was to create a policy statement which would
overcome the bureaucratic resistance to releasing records and bring the Service
back to full compliance with the act.

The task force had no enthusiasm for the task, and most members re-
sented being involved in an activity they feared would earn them the enmity of
their division director or assistant commissioner. The statement which was ultimately drafted was almost entirely the work of the Planning and Research
member. Once the statement was drafted, the representatives were asked to
vote on it.

Some representatives asked whether they were permitted to vote against
the proposed statement and were simply told that the statement reflected the

Commissioner's preferences but their votes were desired anyway. Everyone thereupon returned to their offices to seek guidance from their supervisors. At the next meeting, the task force unanimously endorsed the proposed policy statement. We then signed a letter asking the Commissioner to issue the policy statement as drafted. On March 2, 1973, Commissioner Walters approved Policy Statement P-1-192:

> Freedom of Information Requests
>
> The Internal Revenue Service will grant a request under the Freedom of Information Act (5 U.S.C. 552) for a record which we are not prohibited from disclosing by law or regulations unless; (a) the record is exempt from required disclosure under the Freedom of Information Act; and (b) public knowledge of the information contained in such record would significantly impede or nullify IRS actions in carrying out a responsibility or function, or would constitute an unwarranted invasion of personal privacy.
>
> The administrative cost and impact on operations involved in furnishing the requested record(s) shall not be a material factor in deciding to deny a request unless such cost or impact would be so substantial as to seriously impair IRS operations.

The issuance of this policy statement, had it been adhered to, would not only have placed the Service in full compliance with the Information Act but would have given the public access rights well beyond the requirements of the law. The policy was a commitment to waive exemptions which did not have to be applied. No other agency in the government had espoused such a liberal principle.

The policy statement had been approved by Commissioner Walters on March 2, 1973. Manual issuances normally took about two months to be printed and circulated to the recipient offices. Unfortunately, Commissioner Walters's final day in office was April 30, 1973. Thus, all managers receiving the policy statement were immediately aware that it represented the preferences of a commissioner who was leaving. The immediate question upon everyone's mind was whether the next Commissioner would feel committed to the same policy. There followed an interregnum until May 25, 1973, when Commissioner Donald C. Alexander took office. No one was about to risk his career in observance of a policy which might momentarily be rescinded.

A few months passed until the opportunity arose for obtaining the new Commissioner's views on Information Act matters. The occasion was a meeting during which our experiences with the Longs and a few other requesters were being discussed. The policy statement was called to Mr. Alexander's attention and his opinion asked.

Donald Alexander was known to pride himself on his knowledge of good grammar and proper usage. He chose to consider the statement in grammatical terms and asked what the expression "significantly impede or nullify IRS actions" meant. No one volunteered an explanation. Someone then commented that we did not know what the statement was intended to mean. Mr. Alexander then ridiculed the statement as redundant and meaningless. He never said anything about whether the policy was valid. He had spoken only in terms of its grammatical construction. It was apparent, however, that no one need concern himself about the policy statement as long as Donald Alexander was Commissioner, and no one ever did. The policy statement has been ignored ever since.

Arbitrary and Capricious

The demolition of the policy statement and the tour of the reading room resulting in the removal of statistical reports (described in Chapter 2) were followed by an expression of concern about the Taxpayer Compliance Measurement Program (TCMP). Commissioner Alexander sent instructions to Disclosure that any Information Act request for TCMP information was to be referred to his office and was not under any circumstances to be answered by Disclosure or Planning and Research, which was responsible for the program. This instruction was then inserted into the *Internal Revenue Manual*.

There was at the time only one request for TCMP information, and that had been submitted by Mrs. Long. I forwarded the request to the Commissioner's office as instructed, expecting that it would come back with some instruction for denial. But weeks went by, and nothing came back.

I called the Commissioner's office to inquire what had happened to the request. A secretary checked on the matter and advised me that I should never again make an inquiry about the status of anything sent to the Commissioner, that the matter was being attended to, and that I should close out any controls that I was keeping and consider the request as transferred and disposed of. I did just that.

The Longs filed suit to obtain the TCMP data, beginning a series of court actions that were to span the next 12 years. Ultimately the Service was able to defend most of the TCMP data, but large portions not identifiable to any taxpayer were ordered released. And with the release order came a finding that the withholding of some of the data raised a question of whether the Service had acted "arbitrarily and capriciously." It was the responsibility of the Merit Pay Protection Board to determine if sanctions such as a suspension or removal from office would be appropriate.

I received a request from the Merit Pay Protection Board to testify on the matter. An investigator for the board came to my office. Our Chief Counsel's office assigned an attorney to advise me. At the outset of the interview, the attorney asked if there was any possibility of charges being brought against me in the matter. We were assured that there was not. I was told that the only reason for speaking to me was that no one else had any knowledge of the incident and the most directly involved persons had all long ago left government service.

In response to the investigator's questions, I related the story of how the TCMP request had been transferred to the Commissioner's office. I was shocked to learn that the Commissioner had never responded to the initial request and that that failure to respond formed a portion of the basis for finding the Service arbitrary and capricious.

Several months later, I received a formal letter from the board in which my responses were misstated, my attorney was quoted as a witness, and I was identified as the primary target of the investigation. Fortunately, the report concluded that too long a time had elapsed to be able to determine precisely what had happened and the investigation was to be discontinued without action.

Thus, although I never possessed the records, had no way to obtain the records, had no authority to release the records, was acting under the Commissioner's orders, and was in effect told by the Commissioner's secretary to mind my own business, I became the first person in the Service to be accused and cleared of being arbitrary and capricious in the withholding of records in violation of the Freedom of Information Act.

The Effect of the Longs

The Longs won their tax case in 1977. Their tax returns were found acceptable as originally filed. This did not diminish the flow of Information Act requests. The Longs' campaign continued for almost two decades from the time they filed their first request. It continues to this day.

At least 200 Information Act requests were filed. In addition, there were probably between 200 and 300 follow-up letters, clarifications, and appeals filed. There were 33 requests filed on a single day! But these counts relate only to pieces of correspondence, not to the items contained in requests. Some of Mrs. Long's requests covered as many as 65 major distinct documents. The denial of requests resulted in at least 13 lawsuits. The granting of requests resulted in the provision of many millions of pages of documents and in the later stages, numerous computerized tape files.

At one time, the Service maintained a storage room full of documents awaiting Mrs. Long's inspection. We toyed with the idea of locking her in the room and not letting her out until she had read all the records she had asked for.

For several years in the 1970s the resources allotted to servicing Mrs. Long's requests exceeded the total effort expended upon all other requesters combined. There were literally millions of dollars spent to confront or to accommodate what can justifiably be described as a single individual's ego trip.

None of the records involved, released or withheld, had any affect upon the Longs' tax case. The investigation embarked upon by these taxpayers produced no charges, no recommendations, and no increase in the public knowledge of how the Service operates.

In 1981, years after his involvement, Commissioner Alexander said of the Longs, "Dealing with them face-to-face gave me the impression that a snake must have face-to-face with a mongoose. . . . I was the target of something, and I knew it wasn't good."

The Longs, on the other hand, told an interviewer in 1981 that documents received in response to their Information Act requests enabled them to conclude that

The Revenue Service's explanation of tax law in its manual to auditors sometimes differs from the actual law. For instance, collection officers are instructed to tell taxpayers that full payment for delinquent accounts is required, when, in fact, partial payment is legal.

A taxpayer's chances of being audited vary by income level, where he lives and his source of income. In some states such as New York, Delaware and Nevada, a taxpayer's chances of being audited are several times greater than elsewhere.

The lower a taxpayer's reported income, the greater the chances of being audited. Persons earning under $10,000 are audited more than those earning between $10,000 and $50,000. And the I.R.S. spends more time auditing the returns of small corporations than large ones.

The more money at stake in a audit, the higher the chances of negotiating a favorable settlement with the I.R.S. The agency is more willing to compromise on larger alleged liabilities, settling for a smaller percentage, than on smaller liabilities.

Professional income tax preparers frequently make mistakes. So does the I.R.S. when it gave advice to taxpayers. The documents showed the I.R.S. as error-prone as tax return preparers. If a taxpayer relies on incorrect advice from the I.R.S., that is no defense in an audit.

About 8 percent of people audited under the Taxpayer Compliance Measurement Program are actually due a refund. Of those who do not file, more are owed money than owe the Government unpaid taxes.

The I.R.S. is more likely to detect a civil violation than criminal fraud. It also finds it difficult to effectively deal with the "underground economy," people who fail to report income.

If you find that these "conclusions" are not very impressive for the effort and expense that went into obtaining the records upon which they were based, it might be because others have been expressing the same opinions for years, basing their views on readily available public documents, including many statements issued by the Service.

In many ways, the excesses of the Longs' campaign might be considered responsible for having provoked irrational responses by IRS management to their requests. On the other hand, the Longs may justifiably claim that the excesses of the Service provoked their actions.

While engaged in this struggle, Mrs. Long pursued and received a doctoral degree, and currently teaches at a large university. She continues to make Information Act requests but primarily seeks statistical information for use in research that is only tangentially related to the Service. I am told that she has earned the respect of the professional community in her field. Two things are certain. Mrs. Long has matured, and she is not the enemy of the Service.

To this very day, however, disclosure personnel working on Mrs. Long's occasional requests find it almost impossible to obtain the cooperation of operational personnel in obtaining, copying, and shipping records. Some of the individuals who resent Mrs. Long's requests could not have been beyond grade school when the great struggle was taking place. If Mrs. Long has matured, in many ways the Service has not.

From time to time, someone would caution me that releasing a record might create another Mrs. Long. I would reply that not releasing a record might create another Mrs. Long. No one, it seems, has as good an understanding of what happened as those who were not involved.

The great fear of the Service is that its limited resources might be seriously diminished, thereby threatening its ability to accomplish its mission. What would have happened if there had been 2 Mrs. Longs, or 12 or 142? What would the costs have been then, and how could we have coped with them?

The truth is that these are not logically valid questions. The fact that there was only one such omnivorous requester creates the illusion that there might be more and that such increase would multiply costs.

The real cost of a records-access program does not depend upon the number of requesters but upon the number of records and the policies and practices by which they are to be released. If an agency can afford to create and maintain records, it can afford to make them public.

Chapter Eight

Project Haven

The early 1970s were a time of scandals for the Internal Revenue Service. The Watergate era gave us the "friends' list" and the "enemies' list." The Vietnam War gave us the Special Services Staff. We created the Intelligence Gathering and Retrieval System, Project Haven, and Operation Leprechaun.

Each of these affairs was to have an affect upon Service attitudes toward the Freedom of Information Act, for when you do not know what is coming next, you hestitate to release any information for fear that it might reveal yet another skeleton in the agency's closet. The affair which had the greatest affect on disclosure practices was Project Haven.

In Criminal Investigation parlance, a "project" is a broad investigation directed toward an area, an industry, a practice, or a group of persons which has not yet focused upon specific taxpayers. Ultimately a successful project will give rise to individual case files, but until then, it resembles a net which has been cast but has not yet dragged in its catch.

Project Haven involved the investigation of illegal tax havens operating outside the United States, especially in the Caribbean area. The scams consisted of complex real-estate deals, transfers of funds between hidden foreign bank accounts, and sophisticated record-keeping devices designed to disguise the true nature of transactions and avoid their tax consequences.

Many of the taxpayers involved were influential or well-known people, including sports and entertainment notables. But it was questionable whether these taxpayers understood the illegal nature of the tax activities their advisers had gotten them into. Without fraudulent intent, there would be no criminal case.

A number of extremely sophisticated tax attorneys were involved in setting up various portions of these deals, and some would be charged with conspiracy to defraud the government. But the question was to what extent did any individual intend to take part in an illegal act which was sufficiently a part of the series of manipulations through the use of corporate entites, corporate stock, domestic and foreign trusts, partnerships, backdated records and receipts, transfers of ownerships, phony commodities deals and franchises, to meet the definition of *criminal conspiracy*?

The real problem for the Service was how to gather evidence for such a complicated case, most of which took place outside the United States. The solution to this problem was to lead to charges of illegal government activities. Ultimately, however, the Supreme Court was to decide that some of the activities in this strange investigation which were initially characterized as wrong were actually legally permissible.

The most interesting and best known of the events in the investigation involved the use of informants. Our interest here, however, is not to dredge up the sordid (or fascinating) details of Project Haven, which any interested person may research in contemporary reports, but to understand the effect these events had upon the disclosure program.

An individual was hired by a special agent to act as an informant to secure information concerning the involvement of a Bahamian bank in the creation of offshore tax havens. The informant somehow gained the confidence of the managing director of the bank and learned that the banker was to deliver a list of names of bank clients to a law firm in Chicago but would be stopping in Miami.

In Miami, the informant had apparently subcontracted his duties to a young woman who had existed on the fringes of law enforcement activities by making herself useful to a variety of agencies. The informant arranged a meeting between the banker and the young woman in Miami. The banker had no idea that his benefactor was an Internal Revenue informant or that his date was an Internal Revenue subinformant.

The young woman got the banker to take her out to dinner and to leave his briefcase containing the list of names on a bed in her apartment. Sometime during the evening's activities, special agents removed the briefcase from the apartment, forced its lock, photographed the list, and returned the briefcase to its place on the bed in time for the unsuspecting banker to carry it to Chicago.

Needing further information, the enterprising young woman visited the bank's premises in the Bahamas. While the unaware banker was looking elsewhere, the talented lady filched a Rolodex file from the banker's desk and returned it to the United States where it came into the possession of the Service.

This entire effort, which provided the leads and taxpayer identities necessary to proceed with the Project Haven investigation, could only take place with the connivance of high Bahamian government officials. This complicity was allegedly purchased by first obtaining politically and commercially valuable information from criminal elements and then trading it to the Bahamians in return for their cooperation with the Service.

The special agents involved were quite proud of themselves. The successful conclusion of the investigation was quite an accomplishment. Commissioner Alexander, however, was not pleased. The Commissioner's posture was that he was upset with the use of illegal techniques by the Criminal Investigation Division (although the courts later found that the principal actions involving the compromised briefcase were not illegal). Special agents, meanwhile, had become disenchanted with the Commissioner's leadership and were whispering that the investigation was being torpedoed to protect friends in Chicago who were involved in the tax-evasion scheme.

By the time Project Haven intruded itself upon the disclosure scene, there were considerable ill feelings within the Internal Revenue Service. Mistrust, rumor, and accusations were rife. No one knew exactly what was happening. It was becoming difficult to distinguish right from wrong.

Congress Investigates

In 1975 Project Haven came under investigation by a subcommittee of the Committee on Government Operations of the House of Representatives, chaired by Congressman Benjamin S. Rosenthal. It was only after the initiation of this investigation that Disclosure became involved.

Commissioner Alexander sent to the Rosenthal subcommittee a copy of an internal memorandum which served as a sort of status report on the project. This memorandum prominently mentioned a Chicago attorney who was a prime target of the investigation (but who was never convicted of any crime).

Soon newspaper accounts appeared which contained very extensive and exact quotations from the memorandum. There obviously had been a leak, but the source was not known. The timing made it appear that the memorandum had been given out by congressional staffers, but it could just as well have originated in the Department of Justice or in the Service itself.

Immediately after these newspaper articles appeared, we received an Information Act request from the Chicago attorney asking for a copy of the document upon which the story was based. The technician who worked this case immediately recognized the source. The transmittal which sent the memorandum to Congressman Rosenthal had been prepared in Disclosure, so the technician was able to obtain a copy of the memorandum without seeking input from anyone else. Without discussing the matter with anyone or briefing any manager, the technician released the memorandum to the requester. He reasoned, not without logic, that if Congress could have it and if the press could get it, then the individual under investigation was certainly entitled to receive a copy. Nor could he see any way that a release would interfere with the investigation when it would merely confirm what was already in the newspapers.

Commissioner Alexander was reported to be furious upon learning of this release. Apparently he had not been upset by the leak to the press but was angry only about the release to the attorney. One factor which may have upset him was that the director of disclosure at this time was a former special agent whose sympathies obviously lay with the Criminal Investigation Division. This director, however, knew nothing about the release.

An Internal Audit

Commissioner Alexander suggested that Inspection should investigate the release to determine if the technician had committed a crime! As chief of the Freedom of Information function, I was given the opportunity to look into the matter and make recommendations on the advisability of such an investigation.

I found that the technician had simply done what he thought was right, without giving any consideration to the sensitive nature of the situation. Anyone else would have recognized the danger of offending the Commissioner and would either have waffled or gotten enough other people on board with the proposed reply to dissipate any adverse reaction. This individual's attitude had been simply that what is right is right and there was nothing else to consider.

I recommended against an investigation by Inspection on the grounds that such an investigation would have a chilling effect on the Freedom of Information process and could endanger our relations with the House Committee on Government Operations, which was a strong supporter of the Information Act and had in the past criticized IRS noncompliance.

I also pointed out that if Inspection were to investigate the release, they would also have to investigate the release to the Rosenthal subcommittee by Commissioner Alexander. This committee had no special powers to receive information from the Service, and if it were determined that the release by the disclosure technician was illegal, it would follow that the Commissioner's release was also illegal.

There was no investigation by Inspection. But the Assistant Commissioner (Inspection) also had under his direction the Internal Audit Division, which investigated inefficiency and procedural improprieties. A few months later an Internal Audit team called at my office and announced that they had been requested to investigate the Freedom of Information function. Although the Information activity had been a separate unit for less than a year and had only about six employees, four or five auditors were to spend the next three or four months going over our activities with a fine-tooth comb.

Such an audit of a National Office function was previously unheard-of. Moreover, the extent of the effort was completely disproportionate to the size of our operation. There was simply no managerial or economic justification for such an audit. It was, in my opinion, a vindictive act intended to inhibit Freedom of Information technicians in the performance of their duties.

Each and every Information case open or closed in the past year was carried away and photocopied for reasons completely incomprehensible to me. At the conclusion of this audit, we were given an inane list of recommendations, consisting primarily of findings concerning the timely acknowledgement of cases and how often we were to count a $25 change-making fund maintained for the convenience of users of a coin-operated photocopier in the reading room.

A year later, a new set of Internal Audit investigators came by and repeated the entire effort. This time we were told that investigating our operation was good experience! The results of several months' review of our records showed that the proceeds of our coin-operated photocopier were off about a dollar a month. Usually we had more money than the records showed we were supposed to have. It was not a very impressive result for an audit, but it did get the message across that an excessively generous response to a Freedom of Information request would be punished.

These events further detracted from the willingness of National Office managers to take risks in favor of compliance with the law, especially if the requested records might contain some indication of a possible agency impropriety. Thereafter, every manager knew that when it came to Information Act requests, you not only had to worry about doing the wrong thing, but you had to be very careful when tempted to do the right thing!

The major prosecutions resulting from Project Haven were lost, and the operation was abandoned despite ten years' effort. Several careers were lost along with the project. Some said that the unfortunate end of the project was inherent in the many illegal acts involved in the investigation. Others said that the fault lay in the fact that the major targets in the probe were not guilty of any crime other than having constructed a brilliant and completely legal tax-avoidance scheme. Some blamed Commissioner Alexander for having intentionally sabotaged the investigation. A few blamed the Information Act in the belief that our release of the already public memorandum triggered the debacle.

Before the saga of Project Haven was over, one unfortunate taxpayer was to take his case before the Supreme Court and learn to his dismay that the constitutional protection against the use of illegally procured evidence was effective only for persons who had a property right to the seized material or a legitimate expectation against such seizure. In other words, if the government improperly took something from me, it could not be used against me, but it might very well be used against you.

In another peculiar outgrowth of Project Haven, a *New York Times* reporter was accused of illegally divulging the contents of a sealed grand jury report concerning the investigation. Although the Information operation was not involved in this incident, this too was laid at our doorstep.

The Project Haven experience convinced many managers that disclosure personnel attempting to comply with the Information Act were disloyal pariahs working against the rest of the agency and deserved neither cooperation, trust, nor respect.

Chapter Nine

An Independent FOIA Operation

The original Freedom of Information Act permitted agencies to withhold investigatory files in their entirety, regardless of circumstances. Moreover, the act was silent on the question of whether any nonexempt material had to be identified and released from a record otherwise exempt. The Internal Revenue Service interpreted this absence of direction to mean that the presence of the slightest bit of exempt material was sufficient to warrant withholding a volume of material otherwise releasable.

In 1974 a major amendment of the Information Act altered these assumptions. Thereafter, investigatory records compiled for law enforcement purposes were exempt only to the extent that production would interfere with enforcement proceedings, deprive a person of a right to a fair trial, constitute an unwarranted invasion of personal privacy, disclose the identity of a confidential source of information, disclose investigative techniques and procedures, or endanger the life or physical safety of law enforcement personnel. Furthermore, any reasonably "segregable" portion of a record had to be released after the exempt portions were deleted.

These requirements brought complete consternation to the Compliance Divisions of the Service. The big automatic denials were no longer possible; after appropriate editing, almost every record might produce some releasable material. A few of us, however, realized that even these amendments to the law would not achieve much in bringing the Service into full compliance and giving the public its due. What was needed was an independent Freedom of Information operation!

The original instruction, under which Information Act requests were still being processed, stated that a proposed response required the concurrence of the division director whose records were involved before being submitted to the Assistant Commissioner (Compliance) for signature. This mean that no Audit Division record could be released until the director of the Audit Division agreed to the release. No Criminal Investigation Division record could be released without that division's director agreeing. And the Assistant Commissioner (Compliance), the boss of the Audit, Collection, and Criminal Investigation division directors, had the final say! Under those circumstances, the professional opinion of disclosure specialists was meaningless. We also knew from experience that the law enforcement mentality rampant in these divisions was capable of every conceivable fantasy in a determined defense of the most innocuous records.

We saw the drafting of new regulations needed to implement the 1974 amendments as the great opportunity to grab power by putting disclosure determinations where they belonged, into an independent Freedom of Information operation. We prepared the proposed regulations to read, "The Director of the Disclosure Operations Division or his delegate shall have authority to make initial determinations with respect to all requests for records of the Internal Revenue Service."

Not only would the authority be where we wanted it, but it would run directly from the Commissioner via the regulations to Disclosure. No intermediary, neither deputy commissioner nor assistant commissioner, would be able to interfere. No "owner" of records would have the final say. Determinations could be made solely upon the requirements of law and the exercise of reason. The realities of career survival, however, would still necessitate that such authority be exercised through persuasion or with the protection of the Commissioner. And therein lay the major problem. We already knew that the current Commissioner, Donald Alexander, had no sympathy for open government!

Much to our surprise, the new regulation was signed without anyone's having noticed this change. A few months later, someone did notice! A Planning and Research representative explained to me that Commissioner Alexander was not satisfied with the new regulation and wanted a policy statement issued to provide that no records were to be released without the concurrence of the originating function. Thus, the Service would once more take a giant step backward; each division director would again decide on the release of his own records!

I objected. Regulations had legal precedence over policy statements and it would be highly improper to restrict the authority granted by regulation through the use of a lesser issuance. I was soon advised that I was entirely correct; a policy statement would be improper. The vehicle to be used would be the *Internal Revenue Manual*, and I was to write the new provision!

Thus, although the regulations placed the authority to decide upon Information releases with Disclosure, the legally inferior *Internal Revenue Manual* required that prior to release, concurrence would have to be obtained from the director of the function whose records were involved.

In the event of a dispute between Disclosure and the functional directors, the issue was to be raised to their common supervisory authority for resolution. If the dispute was between Disclosure and Audit, Collection and Criminal Investigation, that common supervisory authority was none other than the Assistant Commissioner (Compliance)!

The public, by reading the regulations, was led to believe that disclosure determinations were being made on a professional basis by specialists trained in that activity. Few people read the manual, and none seemed to realize that the proposals of these independent specialists were always subject to being overruled by managers who lived in fear of their ox being gored. The Information Act required each agency to submit an annual report, including copies of its rules and instructions, to the Speaker of the House and the President of the Senate. The required report was duly submitted, but no one ever noticed the discrepancy between regulations and manual instructions.

It was to be more than ten years before we could set matters right and revise the manual to match the regulations. It now provides that recommendations of the function having primary interest or issuing authority for the records under consideration will be sought, but that "recommendations are not binding upon the official who has the authority to make FOIA determinations and who must release or withhold records in accordance with his/her interpretation of the law." Although the authority is now in place, no director of Disclosure has used it.

In 1976 the Internal Revenue Code was amended to revise drastically the disclosure rules for tax returns and return information. As a result, Disclosure gained a field component, consisting of disclosure officers in every district and regional office. Disclosure was placed in Taxpayer Service, then Support and Services, disassociating it from the overbearing influence of the compliance functions. The result was a golden age of disclosure in which the public received the best possible services, provided of course that they were not requesting sensitive documents not previously released and still under the control of any of the functions which continued to struggle against the Information Act.

No major category of records was ever initially released on a voluntary basis. Everything had to be dragged out of the Service through litigation. Whenever anyone requested a new category of records, a meeting would be held to decide what to do. Frequently, I or another disclosure representative would point out that the requested records did not appear to be exempt from disclosure and that we believed that they should be released. Next, an attorney from Chief Counsel's Disclosure Litigation Division would provide qualified support for the proposed release by explaining that no relevant exemption was readily apparent, that there was no precedent for withholding the records, that it would be difficult to make a viable argument against disclosing the records, or that they could hold out little hope for a successful defense. Often, a Public Affairs representative would be present and would explain that a quick release would probably draw little attention to the records and be unlikely to cause any problem, whereas litigation which resulted in their loss would create considerable notoriety and make it difficult to explain the Service's rationale in refusing immediate release. After receiving all this good advice, the official who had the power to withhold the record but no responsibility for disclosure matters would decide that the request should be denied.

Such decisions were not foolish. It was realized that few requesters would bother to file suit. Even if suit was filed, the requester might not see the case to completion. The likelihood was that any tax matter that prompted the request for records might be resolved before the FOIA suit was heard. It was even possible that the Service might win the case, for there have been instances in which the courts supported arguments which we did not believe. And two other considerations always lurked in the background.

First, no one had ever been subjected to sanctions for the arbitrary and capricious withholding of records. The likelihood was that any adverse results of denying access would not take place until the official had moved on to another assignment, so it was always safer to withhold records than to release them.

Second, there was an assumption that had worked its way into the folklore of the agency that if we voluntarily released records, we would have no recourse to alter that practice in the future. But if we fought tooth and nail against giving anything away, an understanding Congress might come to the rescue with remedial legislation to protect what we had lost in the courts.

Despite these problems and the reversals which occurred from time to time as newly assigned officials decided to wage new battles to defend records which had long before been released, the Service seemed to have made considerable progress, and most requesters were receiving reasonably prompt and fair consideration.

Many of the fears which prevented compliance with the Information Act were slowly being overcome. The influence of the Scientologists and the tax protesters, the odyssey of the Longs, and the many emotional restraints against releasing information were fading into the past. There was hope that with continued progress, dedicated disclosure personnel would someday bring the Internal Revenue Service into full compliance with the law.

Unfortunately, the Internal Revenue Service does not seem able to make much progress before it begins backsliding. In 1986, a new reorganization of the Service was decided upon. The office of Assistant Commissioner (Support and Services) was abolished. The disclosure function was transferred to the Assistant Commissioner (Examination), ostensibly for budgetary purposes. It was soon apparent that disclosure had been fed to the lions. Examination immediately set out to take control of the disclosure function with a view of making disclosure decisions not in accordance with the law or with the long-run benefit of the Service in mind but solely in accordance with the immediate interests of the examination program. The Internal Revenue Service was to return to the dark ages of pursuing irrational disclosure policies, and any who raised objections were about to be shunted aside.

Now that we have reached an understanding of the factors which influence the Service in fashioning its disclosure policies and practices and realize that those policies and practices are not getting better but worse, let us look at what the Freedom of Information Act actually requires.

Chapter Ten

The Freedom of Information Act

Applicability

Unlike the Internal Revenue Code, which is designed primarily to govern the operations of a single agency in great detail, the Freedom of Information Act is applicable to every government agency. *Agency* is defined to mean any executive department, military department, government corporation, government-controlled corporation, other establishment in the executive branch of the government (including the executive office of the President), or any independent regulatory agency. The Internal Revenue Service, as a component bureau of the Department of the Treasury, is a part of an executive department and is subject to the act.

The Publishing Requirement

There are three major requirements which every agency must obey — publishing, public-inspection, and specific requests. The first of these, the publishing requirement, is known as the "(a)(1)" requirement, referring to the section in which it appears.

The publishing requirement states that every agency will publish in the *Federal Register* five categories of information. This requirement is important because the act provides that unless a person has actual and timely notice of the terms of a matter required to be published in the *Federal Register* and not published, that person cannot be required in any manner to resort to, or be adversely affected by, that matter. In other words, if something should have been published but was not, and it has not been called to your attention in an acceptable manner, it cannot be used against you. Agencies are naturally very careful that they meet the publishing requirement.

The five categories of information which must be published in the *Federal Register* are

1. Descriptions of the agency's central and field organization and the established places at which, the employees from whom, and the methods whereby the public may obtain information, make submittals or requests, or obtain decisions.
2. Statements of the general course and method by which its functions are

93

channeled and determined, including the nature and requirements of all formal and informal procedures available.

3. Rules of procedure, descriptions of forms available or the places at which forms may be obtained, and instructions as to the scope and contents of all papers, reports, or examinations.

4. Substantive rules of general applicability adopted as authorized by law, and statements of general policy or interpretations of general applicabaility formulated and adopted by the agency.

5. Each amendment, revision, or repeal of the foregoing.

Obviously, these five categories constitute nothing more than the minimal information necessary to enable an individual to do business with the agency and to confrom to the agency's requirements. Since the primary purpose of the Internal Revenue Service is to get you to pay your taxes, the Service is going to make very certain that you know how, when, and where to do it. In all the years in which I was involved with the administration of the Information Act, no person ever made any serious allegation that the Service had failed to publish any information subject to the (a)(1) requirement.

Some of the information responsive to the publishing requirement will be found in the *Internal Revenue Bulletin* rather than the *Federal Register*. Publication in the *Internal Revenue Bulletin* provides "actual and timely notice" to persons needing the information and therefore meets the publishing requirement.

The act also provides that a matter reasonably available to the class of persons affected thereby is deemed published in the *Federal Register* when incorporated by reference with the approval of the director of the *Federal Register*. This provision simply provides a vehicle to permit extensive material to be mentioned in the *Federal Register* without all of it being reprinted in detail as long as the material itself is available through some other method to anyone needing it. The Service has not used this method of publishing because it was not considered a practical method for meeting the Service's information objectives.

The most important thing to remember about the publishing requirement is that (a)(1) material, information that has been properly published in accordance with this requirement, need not be made available to requesters under the specific-request requirement.

The Public-Inspection Requirement

The second requirement of the act, the public-inspection requirement, is known as the "(a)(2)" requirement. Three categories of records must be made available for public inspection and copying. The Service created its Freedom of Information reading rooms as a practical response to the public-inspection requirement, although the act does not specifically require reading rooms.

The three categories of records to be made available for public inspection are

1. Final opinions, including concurring and dissenting opinions, as well as orders, made in the adjudication of cases. This "final opinion" requirement is easily disposed of since the Service does not make final opinions or orders in the adjudication of cases. The Service does not adjudicate cases. Consequently, no records subject to this category exist.

2. Those statements of policy and interpretations which have been adopted by the agency and are not published in the *Federal Register*. It was this "statement of policy" requirement which caused the Service extreme internal turmoil, as already described. Ultimately, however, the Service's policy statements became public as part of the *Internal Revenue Manual* and are in the reading rooms. There are unlikely to be any further problems involving the availability of policy statements.

3. Administrative staff manuals and instructions to staff that affect a member of the public, unless the materials are promptly published and offered for sale.

The last is the provision the Service resisted by withholding the *Internal Revenue Manual* from the public for many years. The terms *administrative staff manuals* and *instructions to staff*, have not been subject to any final and exhaustive definition. There are many documents beyond the *Internal Revenue Manual* which may be subject to these requirements, some of which have never been considered for Freedom of Information purposes. Nor have there been exhaustive discussions on the meaning of "that affect a member of the public." One can reasonably expect that the public-inspection requirement, insofar as instructions to staff are concerned, whether manuals or not, will be subject to continuous growth and development for years to come. Many records currently being withheld from the public or currently beyond the scope of public interest may ultimately be released pursuant to this provision.

The act goes on to provide that a final order, opinion, statement of policy, interpretation, staff manual, or instruction that affects a member of the public may be relied on, used, or cited as precedent by an agency only if it has been indexed and made available for public inspection or published, or the party involved has been given actual and timely notice of such material. The Service never cites as precedent or relies on internal instructions in dealing with a member of the public in observation of this provision and in accordance with its assumptions about what constitutes proper administrative behavior. Such assumptions are far older than the Information Act and are well known and accepted by Service personnel.

Occasionally an employee will justify his actions by referring a taxpayer to a provision of the *Internal Revenue Manual* or some other internal instruction. Sometimes an employee will cite a document to a taxpayer and refuse to show it or explain it, telling the taxpayer that he must make an Information Act request to obtain a copy or that a copy will not be available under any circumstances. Every time such an event was brought to my attention, I found that the employee was acting in complete ignorance of the Service's procedures, as to the availability of the document and as to the proper source to be cited as a precedent. The correct citations always proved to be a statute, a regulation,

a published revenue ruling, or some other publicly available document which
was merely being parroted by the internal instruction.

If you find yourself in a confrontation with a Service employee who appears to be citing or relying upon an internal instruction, you may be able to
resolve the problem simply by asking his or her supervisor to assist you by identifying the statute, regulation, or ruling which is the ultimate source. The Service is extremely careful in basing its actions on well-established precedents
which can be upheld in litigation.

The prohibition against relying on or citing as precedent instructions
which have not become public also extends to instructions which have been
"used." I have been wondering for 15 years just what *used* means in this context. While every expert I have ever discussed this with has had some opinion
to add, I have never met anyone who was able to adequately define *used* in this
context. This is, consequently, another unresolved area. It may well be that a
creative definition of *used* may someday break loose additional documents
which are now considered exempt from the act.

The importance of the (a)(2) section lies not only in its success in making
the materials it covers available for public inspection but in its use as a tool to
pry loose information being withheld under the exemptions to specific access
to records. None of the exemptions to the Information Act are valid if the
records to which they are applied are found to be (a)(2) materials.

Secret Law

A major underlying purpose for the creation of the publishing and public-
inspection provisions of the Information Act is to prevent the development or
the continued existence of *secret law*, although that term is not mentioned in
the act. Since agencies cannot create law, secret or otherwise, there cannot really
be a *secret* law. The term, however, is extended to mean any procedure, instruction, assumption, operating technique, or other activity which tends to have an
adverse affect upon members of the public, interferes with the way they do
business with the agency, frustrates their use of existing procedures, or is otherwise harmful and whose existence, terms, and effects are known to the agency
but not to the public.

Agencies are aware of the need to avoid the creation of secret law, but it
is a difficult concept to understand, and even the best-intentioned bureaucrat
may be unaware of its existence. Secret law is a philosophic concept, and there
is little guidance to help agencies recognize it when it occurs. Secret laws, like
mushrooms, grow in dark places.

Let us attempt to invent an example of secret law. Assume that a processing unit in an agency finds it difficult to work with applications written in pencil. The manager, faced with performance standards and a program completion date, instructs his employees to place any applications written in pencil on
the bottom of the pile to be worked when time permits. This program distrib-
utes some benefit on a first-come, first-served basis, the later applicants being

less likely to be successful. Some applicants, who submit their applications written in pencil, never seem to do as well in obtaining benefits as do their neighbors. They know that they need to improve their applications and try to do so. They even send them in earlier, but they never guess that the fatal flaw lies in their use of pencils. Try as they may, they never succeed in obtaining what would otherwise be theirs. As innocent as the agency's reasonable efforts to process their workload may have been, this agency would have had a rule which effectively eliminates penciled applications from consideration. But because the effect is unintentionally buried in internal procedures, it may never become known to the public, some of whom will be destined to suffer forever the disadvantages which result. This set of circumstances would constitute secret law.

Agencies are no more able to recognize and remedy secret law than a batter is able to diagnose the causes of his hitting slump. That is what coaches are for. That is what the publishing and public-inspection provisions of the Information Act are for. When interested members of the public make a critical analysis of the procedures which affect them, they are likely to recognize the secret law (which would no longer be secret), and they may then conform their own behavior or take action to promote other remedies, including the revision of the agency's procedures.

Does the Service have secret laws? It almost certainly does, for the nature of secret law is that in the absence of full and conscientious disclosure, it seems to crop up here and there, now and then, in one connection or another. Consider that quota system which the Service is so willing to admit existed a few generations ago, but whose continued existence is so often denied. Either it exists, and its provisions contain extensive incidents of secret law, or it is an illusion. But if it is an illusion, that illusion must be based upon instructions which themselves harbor secret law. When over a period in excess of 60 years the Service, its employees, the National Treasury Employees Union, the taxpayers, the general public, and congressional investigators are unable to resolve what exists and what does not, then the Service must have a long way to go to reach the objectives of open government, and there must be a good deal of secret law which needs to be uncovered along the way.

In 1989 a situation came to public attention which dramatically demonstrated how easily secret law can operate. A small group of employees at the Memphis Service Center realized that procedures under which they were processing information concerning taxes withheld had the effect of stealing money from certain taxpayers. They raised the matter to their supervisor's attention but were told to do nothing about the problem because it was the taxpayer's responsibility to ask for a refund if one was due. The employees felt strongly about what they perceived as an injustice, so they became whistleblowers and exposed the matter to Senator Albert Gore, Jr., Democrat, Tennessee.

Senator Gore made the necessary inquiries and found that taxpayers were indeed being cheated, and to make matters worse, most of these taxpayers were the proverbial little old ladies who so often become the targets of swindlers. The Service was receiving information returns which stated the amount of tax withheld and matched these with tax returns on file. The primary purpose was to uncover returns which claimed more withholding credit than was justified. Sometimes, however, it was discovered that the taxpayer had more tax withheld than was being reported on his return and was entitled to a refund.

If the excess withholding appeared on a Form W-2 reporting wage and salary information, the Service quite properly made the adjustment which gave the taxpayer the refund to which he or she was entitled. But if the excess withholding appeared on a Form 1099 reporting interest, dividends, pensions and other nonsalary payments, nothing was done, in effect cheating the taxpayer out of money which should have been refunded. Withholding which appeared on the Form 1099 and was not reported on the tax return usually represented the tax which had been paid on lump-sum distributions from pension plans. Any taxpayer who did not take credit for the tax withheld would have to pay that tax *again* when filing his return.

Employees apparently had been complaining about this unfair practice for several years, but supervisors refused to act upon the complaints. Was anyone really trying to cheat the old folks who were unaware that they were entitled to a refund? Of course not. There simply was no procedure which demanded that the right thing be done, and the supervisors were apparently unwilling to disrupt processing routines to create a procedure which would accommodate these occasional exceptions. Thus, the processing philosophy became "Let them find their own mistakes" — in violation of the Service's announced policy "that taxpayers pay only the tax due — no more, no less."

Unfortunately, these elderly and generally law-abiding taxpayers could not find their own mistakes because they did not know they existed. Nor could any tax adviser, accountant, or attorney alert them to the potential for a refund, for none of these had any way of knowing that such a practice existed. The Service not only had a do-nothing practice, but it kept both the practice and the policy hidden, so that the public could not know that they existed, could not help themselves, could not obtain advice, could not do anything to promote change, and could not object. And that is the evil of secret law.

The Specific-Request Requirement

The specific-request requirement, also known as the "(a)(3)" requirement is the heart of the Freedom of Information Act. It is the provision which differed most from prior law and created the radical access to records which so many government officials found so offensive.

The specific-request requirement states simply that any record which has not already become public as a result of the publishing or the public-inspection requirement is to be released in response to any request made by any person which reasonably describes such records and is made in accordance with published rules stating the time, place, fees, and procedures to be followed.

Absolutely any person may make that request, regardless of that person's circumstances. Scholars or students, involved taxpayers or curious bystanders, concerned members of the public or frivolous amateurs, law-abiding citizens or convicted felons, American citizens or foreign nationals — the law made no distinction between persons, and every request was to be given the same consideration.

The desired records did not have to be accurately identified, only reasonably described. It was recognized that the general public could not be expected to have a detailed knowledge of an agency's records. The standard, therefore, became that if an experienced employee of the agency who was generally knowledgeable about the categories of records which appeared to be involved in the request could recognize what was wanted, the request was to be considered adequate.

Exceptional searches for records which *might* exist were not required. There was no need to search through files attempting to analyze each document, in effect comparing the content of the document to the description in the request in an attempt to establish whether this one or that one might be responsive. But if the agency could recognize what was wanted and locate it in accordance with its normal records-retrieval procedures or some other reasonable and appropriate effort, it was to be done.

The requester is under no obligation to explain why the records are wanted or what the requester intends to do with them. In fact, a request is completely valid in the absence of any purpose whatsoever.

There are definitions and exemptions which limit the records which will be released in response to a request. These will be discussed in the next chapter.

Agency Regulations

Agencies are required to issue regulations which state the time, place, fees, and procedures to be followed in making a request and processing such a request. The act includes extensive provisions concerning the establishment and computation of fees for search, duplication, and review of records. These fee provisions are discussed in detail in Chapter 14.

Unlike most agencies, the Service has several sets of regulations governing its Information Act processing. The first set is known as the departmental regulations because they were promulgated by the Department of the Treasury and govern all the Treasury's component bureaus. These regulations appear at 31 CFR (Code of Federal Regulations, vol. 31) Part 1. These regulations are further broken down to accommodate the needs of the various bureaus; Appendix B to 31 CFR Part 1 relates specifically to the Internal Revenue Service.

In addition, the Service maintains Information Act regulations at 26 CFR 601.701 and 26 CFR 601.702.

In the event of any disagreement in content, the departmental regulations take precedence.

Timeliness of Response

The act requires that an agency determine within 10 days (not including Saturdays, Sundays and legal public holidays) after receiving a request whether to comply. It must then immediately notify the requester of the determination and the reasons for making it. In reality, few agencies can meet such a stringent requirement on any but the simplest of requests. The 10-day requirement appears to exist not because compliance is realistically envisioned but because it serves to define the exhaustion of administrative remedies and permits the serious and eager requester to move on to quickly litigate the withholding of the records.

The act recognizes the difficulties inherent in meeting the timeliness requirement by permitting the agency an extension up to 10 working days to the extent necessary to cope with the need to search for and collect records from field offices or other locations that are separate from the office processing the request; the need to search for, collect, and examine voluminous records; or the need to consult with another agency having an interest in the records or to consult with various components within the same agency.

Even after the extension has been used and the requester has filed suit, the court may permit an agency additional time if the agency can show exceptional circumstances. Some agencies have been permitted a year or more to finish processing some unusual requests.

The issue of what constitutes timeliness in processing an Information Act request is extremely complicated. The timeliness requirements exist not only to ensure that an agency be reasonably prompt and that adequate resources are allocated to processing requests but to make certain that agencies do not stonewall requesters by delaying responses so that delay effectively becomes denial of access.

The requester must have an adequate understanding of the timeliness requirements and the actions which may be taken when they elapse. He must also have a realistic appreciation of what an agency can be expected to do and what it would be unable to do to know whether his request is being properly processed and whether further action on his part is appropriate. The timeliness of processing requests is discussed in detail in Chapters 16 and 18.

Appeal and Complaint

Whenever an agency withholds records, either by denial of a request or by failure to make a timely response, the requester may appeal the withholding to the head of the agency. For the first few years after passage of the act, the Service interpreted "head of the agency," to mean that the appeal was to made to the Commissioner of Internal Revenue. The authority to respond to appeals was later delegated to various assistant commissioners, but as the volume of appeals grew, even this level of response was considered too high for what was viewed as a technical rather than a policy decision. The responsibility for appeals is currently with the director of the Disclosure Litigation Division in the Office of Chief Counsel.

If a requester has not had a timely response to an initial request, she may elect not to appeal within the agency and go directly into litigation. If the request is appealed, the requester may file suit on the basis either that the appeal has been denied or that the records continue to be withheld because the agency has failed to make a timely response to the appeal.

Complaint may be made to the U.S. District Court in the district where the complainant resides or has his principal place of business, in the district where the agency records are situated, or in the District of Columbia. The court may examine the records, appoint a master to make the examination for the court, or may evaluate the records on the basis of agency affidavits describing their content and significance.

The burden is on the agency to demonstrate that the records may legally be withheld. The requester need make no argument. In its simplest form, a complaint need merely state what was asked for and that it was not made available. The court's determination is *de novo*, that is, based upon the court's evaluation of the records without regard to the actions taken by the agency in denying access. The court may order the records released to the requester and may enjoin the agency from future withholding of the records.

Whenever the complainant substantially prevails, that is, receives a significant portion of the records withheld, the court may assess against the United States reasonable attorney fees and other litigation costs reasonably incurred. In the event that the court orders the records released and the agency continues to withhold them, the court may punish the responsible government employee for contempt of court.

Whenever the court has ordered records released as having been improperly withheld and has assessed costs against the United States, the court may further find that the circumstances surrounding the withholding raise questions whether agency personnel acted arbitrarily or capriciously with respect to the withholding. If an employee is then determined to have acted arbitrarily and capriciously, that employee may be punished. No employee of the Service has ever been determined to have acted arbitrarily and capriciously. The act does not specify what an appropriate punishment might be, but based upon the legislative history, it is commonly believed that a six-month suspension with loss of pay and privileges would be likely.

Miscellaneous Provisions

The act provides that agencies having more than one member will maintain and make available for public inspection a record of the final vote of each member in every agency proceeding. This provision is intended to relate to agencies governed by a board with several members rather than headed by a single individual. The Service is not such an agency since the Commissioner is the unitary decision-making authority. There are therefore no Service records to which this provision pertains.

The act states that it gives no authority to withhold information from Congress. The intent of this provision is to preclude any agency from attempting to rely on the act to justify withholding information properly sought by Congress or any of its properly empowered committees or subcommittees pursuant to the body of law and precedents which govern the relationship between the Congress and the executive branch of the government. The provision does not pertain to Freedom of Information requests made by an indivdiual congressman acting as a citizen. A congressman making a request is entitled to the same response made to any other requester in the same matter.

Finally, the act requires that the Attorney General submit an annual report to the Congress listing the number of Information Act requests processed, the disposition of the cases, and the costs, fees, and penalties involved. The report is also to include a description of actions taken by the Department of Justice to encourage agencies to comply with the act. This report is a compendium of reports submitted by the various agencies, each of which reports upon its own activities. The report on the Service is incorporated into a unified report for the Department of the Treasury. Any researcher interested in the performance of the Service alone may request a copy of the IRS input to the departmental report from the Service's Freedom of Information Reading Room.

Exemptions

The Information Act often gives readers the impression that it provides them a legal basis for access to *any* information they want. There are, however, exemptions which provide that many types of records may be withheld from the public. Even as the act is drawn in broad strokes which encourage the impression of unlimited access, the exemptions appear to be so extensive that they easily encourage agency officials to believe that virtually every record may be withheld. The exemptions will be discussed in detail in the next chapter.

Chapter Eleven

The Exemptions to the Information Act

The illusion that the Freedom of Information Act provides access to every government record is swiftly shattered in practice by the exercise of the exemptions which permit withholding records. These exemptions are provided in sections (b) and (c) of the act. There are, however, limits to the act's reach which come into play long before the use of exemptions need be considered.

Agency Records

The word *information* in the title Freedom of Information Act is a misnomer which confuses many requesters. The act is not designed to access information; it is designed to access *records*.

No agency is required to answer questions, to explain anything, to collect information, or to create records which do not have a prior existence. You may request access to an existing record. If the agency does not currently possess such a record, it need not give the matter further consideration.

Even if a record is released, there is no guarantee that the record is current, accurate, truthful, or representative of the general thrust of information in the area to which it pertains. The agency is under no obligation to explain, validate, or qualify the contents of records released. There is no exemption which would permit withholding incorrect or irrelevant data and no requirement that the recipient be alerted to any record's imperfections.

The Internal Revenue Service, especially in National Office, will sometimes volunteer comments on the validity or significance of a record. Experience, however, has shown that requesters generally do not welcome such explanations and either ignore or dispute them in the belief that they represent further attempts at obfuscation. The willingness to offer explanation is further limited by the practical realization that explaining a record may lead the agency into creating new information, a trap which experienced disclosure personnel will assiduously avoid.

The requester must therefore realize that what she is permitted to seek is merely an existing record, which may mislead as easily as it may inform. Accessing government records introduces a new form of *caveat emptor* ("let the buyer beware"). If you are engaged in a dispute with the Service, you should be aware that it is your responsibility to analyze and evaluate any records received. What you receive may be evidence to its existence, but it may prove nothing beyond that.

What constitutes a *record* for Freedom of Information purposes? A record is a physical object created and maintained for the purpose of recalling some information contained therein. A record may take any form which technology permits, including written records, printed records, photocopies, photographs, motion-picture film, videotapes, blueprints, drawings, sound recordings, microfilm, microfiche, microdots, wires, tapes, disks, chips, or anything else which may be developed, providing its purpose is to extend the existence of information for future use.

The technology involved may create new problems in how to transfer the data to the requester, such as whether information on a computer tape could or should be transferred to a disk for the convenience of the requester. These, however, are logistical or technical problems which can be solved without recourse to legal issues if the requester and the responding agency are willing to work them out. However, we have had problems with some officials who indulged their desires to withhold information, refusing to accommodate requesters by altering the mode in which data is encoded on tapes, saying in effect, "If they can't use it the way we give it to them, that's their tough luck. We've done all the law requires."

Regardless of the willingness to cooperate, there are legitimate questions concerning the availability of data maintained electronically which remain to be answered. For instance, an agency may have data on tape which cannot be accessed with existing programs. Is the agency required to create a new program to service a request for access? Does creating a program to access currently irretrievable information constitute a record access and copying problem or does it involve the creation of new information? Thus far, the Internal Revenue Service has been willing to make minor modifications to a program as may be routinely attempted by an on-site programmer to facilitate day-to-day operations, but it has been unwilling to engage in more extensive programming efforts for Freedom of Information purposes.

The problem goes beyond the technical difficulties involved in electronic data processing. Physical objects not intended to maintain information are generally not considered records, even though they may be retained as evidence. The shirt worn by a shooting victim, the weapon used in the shooting, the bullets extracted from the body, or the body itself are not records and are not subject to access under the Information Act. But if photographs or laboratory reports concerning such objects exist, they would have to be considered pursuant to a request.

Do not expect to receive examples of the little red and blue threads embedded in dollar bills, the paper on which currency is printed, or a little pot of green ink. Such objects do not constitute records.

The Service once received a request for a copy of the printed insert contained in the Service's pocket commission, which, like a badge, is used to identify revenue agents, special agents, and revenue officers. Release of such a copy would have enabled the recipient to create his own identification and thereby impersonate a government officer. We refused to grant the request on the basis that the insert was an object which was intended to serve a purpose other than recording information and was not subject to the Information Act. Just in case that argument proved inadequate, we added that there is a statutory prohibition against copying official identification.

Now that we realize that not all information constitutes records, that not all physical objects are records, and that many things which might appear to be records are not, we consider the more difficult question of whether *all* records are subject to the Information Act. They are not. The access provisions of the act apply only to agency records. Most agencies possess many records which are not agency records.

Books, magazines, other printed materials, films, and recordings protected by a copyright are not agency records. They cannot be accessed under the Information Act.

Instructional materials, special procedures, computer programs, and other items may be borrowed, rented, or purchased from private businesses and would therefore not be agency records. An agency would not be permitted to purchase something from a private vendor and then make hundreds of copies for distribution under the Information Act, thereby destroying the owner's property value.

Sometimes government employees may create a computer program on their own time but use it in their official assignment. They may permit their co-workers to use it, or they may permit the agency general use. The program would nevertheless remain their private property and not be an agency record.

In some cases, the question of what constitutes an agency record can become very complex. For instance, an extensive and complicated computer program may have been created by the agency and be an agency record, but it may contain segments provided by employees acting on their own and may contain other segments or specific encoding devices provided by commercial vendors. Presumably, only those portions of the program which actually constitute an agency record would be releasable. Precisely how one can release portions of a program and what a recipient could do with them is another question.

Government employees may sometimes maintain personal calendars, diaries, notes, or memoranda which may not be agency records although they may have the appearance of dealing with government business, providing such records are intended for their own use and are not shared with other employees. For instance, we once received a request for the calendars maintained by regional commissioners. Our initial reaction was that such calendars might be personal to the officials maintaining them, and not subject to the act. That impression would have been correct if the facts had supported the concept that they were maintained for the personal use of the individuals who created them. However, we soon found that the calendars were actually maintained by the officials' secretaries, that persons acting on the officials' behalf in their absence referred to the calendars and made additional entries, and that in most cases the calendars were available for the inspection of subordinates wishing to schedule appointments with the officials. In other words, these were not personal calendars, but represented calendars of the *position* rather than the incumbent. The calendars were released, except for a few minor deletions of entries scheduling lunches, dental appointments, and afternoons on leave to play golf.

Generally, the personal notes made at meetings, reminders of things to be done, and those jottings most people make when trying to decide whether to create a more developed project worth turning in remain personal to the creator to the extent that they are not intended and not shared with anyone else in the agency.

There are, however, some circumstances which require great care and sensitivity when evaluating such personal notes. Both the Internal Revenue Code and the Privacy Act of 1974 include provisions which restrict the availability of information protected by those acts to employees who have a need for such information in the performance of their duties. During the time I was responsible for administering the Information Act, I would not permit any employee to attempt to defend as his personal records any document which contained a taxpayer's return information protected by the Internal Revenue Code or any other person's information protected by the Privacy Act. I reasoned that it was inherently inconsistent to claim an employee's personal right to information which he could possess only to the extent that it was necessary to perform his official duties.

I do not know if that policy will be continued or even if the paradox of claiming that someone else's information could be personal to an employee would be recognized. There is a problem in this position. If notes which are personal to the employee are not to be shared with the agency, how does the agency gain access to them to evaluate whether they are agency records? Someday some employee will be asked for his personal notes in response to a Freedom of Information request and will refuse to permit anyone to see them. That situation has never occurred, and the problem has never been faced.

These few examples should make it readily apparent that before any consideration can be given to whether any of the exemptions to the Information Act apply, it must first be established that the information requested actually consists of agency records available for evaluation. But before we look at those exemptions, we must first understand the concept of segregability.

Reasonably Segregable Portions

The act provides, "Any reasonably segregable portion of a record shall be provided to any person requesting such record after deletion of the portions which are exempt." Prior to the addition of this provision in 1974, it was possible to withhold an entire document on the basis of its containing a single item of exempt material. For instance, the Service attempted to withhold the huge *Internal Revenue Manual* on the basis of legitimately exempt portions which appeared throughout its many volumes. When ultimately edited for release, it was found that not more than 1 percent was actually to be withheld.

Without the concept of segregability, the Information Act was simply not functional since the act's disclosure requirements could be defeated by the presence of minimal exempt material which might not even have been relevant to the main thrust of the document. I was aware of several instances in the early 1970s when Service documents were salted with a few exempt statements only to justify withholding otherwise accessible information. Such salting was not only violative of the spirit of the act but was also contrary to the intent of the Internal Revenue Code, for taxpayers' identities and return information were sometimes included in documents which could just as well have been prepared in general terms.

After 1974, this scam could no longer be practiced, for the segregability concept meant that a document had to be reviewed so that only material actually exempt would be withheld. The balance of the material would have to be released if it contained any meaningful information. Just what constitutes a balance of meaningful information is difficult to say. Generally, documents would be released after deletions were made even if virtually nothing remained visible since it is easier to demonstrate that there is no meaningful remnant by release than to argue that a withheld portion was not meaningful. After all, if it is not meaningful, why bother to withhold it?

There are no firm rules governing the size of units being withheld as exempt. Certainly an entire document cannot be withheld because a portion is exempt. Nor has the Service ever claimed that an entire page may be withheld because of an exempt portion. Beyond that, sound judgment must be exercised in deciding whether to withhold by paragraph, by sentence, or by specific entry within a sentence. Sometimes deletions may consist of a single name. It may generally be assumed that the smaller the deletion, the more likely it is to be justified. Large blocks of deletions are likely to be based on more general rationales and may well represent excessive or poorly justified withholding.

The various exemptions discussed hereafter are to be understood to operate within the concept of segregability. That is, except when explained otherwise, an exemption is only valid to the extent that is necessary to achieve the governmental purpose for which that exemption was created. Anything beyond that is excessive and therefore illegal.

National Security

The first of the nine exemptions provided in section (b) of the act is intended to protect information which has been classified for reasons of national security.

> (b) This section does not apply to matters that are—
> (1)(A) specifically authorized under criteria established by an Executive order to be kept secret in the interest of national defense or foreign policy and
> (B) are in fact properly classified pursuant to such Executive order.

The factors to remember in understanding this exemption are that the material must have been classified pursuant to an executive order, it must relate to national defense or foreign policy, and the classification must have been proper. The current executive order is E.O. 12,356, dated August 1, 1982. The prior order was E.O. 12,065.

The Service seldom relies upon this exemption because it does not possess much properly classified information. The Service is not generally involved with national defense or foreign policy. When it does have such classified records, they would frequently also be return information of some taxpayer and be protected under 26 U.S.C. 6103. The Service would usually prefer to cite the exemption protecting return information without mentioning that it was also classified, thereby avoiding any hint of the nature of the withheld record. During 1986, exemption (b)(1) was cited only five times and therefore represents only 0.25 percent of the records denied by section (b) exemptions.

The courts will generally not attempt to question the expertise of an agency classifying records and will neither review nor reverse such agency actions. They will not try to substitute their judgment of what would adversely affect the national security for the judgment of the agency which specializes in such matters. But the courts will order the release of records which have not been properly classified and which therefore do not deserve protection under the executive order.

It would seem sensible to begin questioning the propriety of any (b)(1) withholding when appealing the initial denial which cited the exemption. There are several ways the Service might be making improper use of the (b)(1) exemption. The classifications available under the executive order are *Confidential, Secret* and *Top Secret*. The terms *Official Use Only, Limited Official Use Only, Restricted Information*, and variations thereof are not national-security classifications and are not protected by the executive order. Instructions limiting possession to the addressee only are not national-security classifications. And the very provocative designation *Eyes Only* is not a national-security classification. Trained disclosure officers know that they cannot cite (b)(1) to protect such materials, although they may be protectable under some other exemption based upon their content rather than their classification. Occasionally, Freedom of Information requests are worked by persons who are not fully trained. My experience in training new disclosure personnel has been that most Service employees have extensive misconceptions about the classification process and would be prone to accepting a variety of irrelevant terms as evidence of a national-security classification.

There are two types of classified documents which the service might possess; those received from other agencies and those classified by the Service itself. Each presents some opportunity for impropriety.

Few agencies who disseminate classified material will notify the recipients when such material is declassified. In those instances when the Service is advised of the declassification of documents, it may not be able to associate the new notice with the original record. I once received a package containing about 100 notices stating that documents had been declassified or downgraded from a higher classification to a lower. I was unable to find any evidence that we had ever received the original documents and consequently asked the agency not to send any more such notices.

On one occasion I received documents from another agency stamped *Confidential*. The records, however, contained only information which seemed similar to what was already in our tax-case files. I called the agency to ask how we should treat this information and was told that these records were developed from information which we had originally sent to them and they were returning the favor by showing us the extent to which they developed additional information about the taxpayers. None of the information involved national security. They were aware that the information we had provided was protected under the Internal Revenue Code, and they wanted to mark it to ensure that their employees properly protected it. Thus, they used the only rubber stamp available. The information was confidential under the Internal Revenue Code, but it was not *Confidential* under the executive order.

The Service still has many older records which were classified by other agencies using standards that are not consistent with the recent executive orders. I have seen dozens of older records classified *Secret* which have absolutely nothing to do with national defense or foreign policy. They may have been properly classified in accordance with some prior set of standards, but they would not warrant protection today.

In recognition of these problems, the regulations require that requests for records which were classified by another agency must be referred to that agency for advice prior to being withheld. In the absence of a timely response to such a request for advice, the Service will make its own determination on the releasability of the records. The *Internal Revenue Manual* requires that field offices requiring such advice from another agency are to transfer their case to National Office, which will contact the other agency and make the final response to the requester. Consequently, it does not seem possible that a field office will cite (b)(1) in denying a record to a requester; such denials should come from National Office. From time to time, however, we have found field offices citing (b)(1) without the National Office having any knowledge of the matter. Naturally, such instances could be indicative of a potential for error.

Information which originates in the Internal Revenue Service and is classified pursuant to the executive order is far more rare. In fact, I have never seen a record properly classified by the Service for national-security purposes. The only person in the Service who is authorized to make such classification determination is the Commissioner. He cannot delegate this authority to any other person. Another official may make the classification determination only if he or she is acting as commissioner in the absence of the Commissioner. The authority cannot be exercised by deputy commissioners, assistants to the commissioner, assistant commissioners, or any other person. No one in any field office has the authority to classify records.

Moreover, the Commissioner's authority is limited to the use of the classifications *Confidential* and *Secret*. Any item warranting a classification of *Top Secret* would have to be referred to the Department of the Treasury for approval.

The authority to declassify records rests with the classifying office, the Commissioner. Therefore, no field disclosure officer and no National Office

disclosure officer can make a decision concerning the releasibility of information classified in the Service and rely upon exemption (b)(1) without seeking a
final determination from the Commissioner. Presumably, such a request would
have to travel through the established channels and would either originate or
come through my office. Yet I have never seen such a request. It may be that
they occur only when I am on leave, but I have never been briefed by my people
on having had such a unique matter in my absence.

I have seen a few documents which might easily be mistaken for classified
national-security records. The procedure for seeking approval of a proposed
classification provides that the originator will mark the document with the proposed classification, which will serve as a tentative classification until approved
by the Commissioner. Such a tentative classification has no legal validity and
cannot protect a document, other than to preclude a careless release while the
need for classification is being pursued. Tentative classified documents are then
raised through channels to the Commissioner. Any reviewer in the chain of
command, either in a district office, a regional office, or the National Office
may disapprove the proposed classification as being unwarranted and not
worth the Commissioner's attention. No one wants to waste the Commissioner's time with something he need not see. Such rejected documents are then
returned to the preparer. But there is nothing in the procedure that requires the
removal of the markings resulting from the tentative classification. A person
who is not knowledgable about the classification procedure could mistakenly
assume that such documents are classified.

Finally, we must mention that the act of classifying records necessitates
some program to declassify them. Some years ago I suggested that we attempt
to survey the extent to which classified documents exist in the Service and
undertake considering their declassification. The proposal was not accepted because such documents were considered so rare as not to warrant such a program.

The fact remains, however, that in 1986, the (b)(1) exemption was cited five
times as the basis for withholding records, and I do not know how it was done
or why.

The chief instrument for the National Office's control of how exemptions
are used by the field is the ability of the requester to appeal any withholding
of records. Such appeals are processed by Chief Counsel's Disclosure Litigation Division. If the field or the National Office is denying access to records improperly, the Disclosure Litigation Division would alert my office to those circumstances, and we would then take any action necessary to prevent a recur-
rence. The Disclosure Litigation Division has never advised me of any pattern
of abuse concerning the (b)(1) exemption.

Although the (b)(1) exemption was used five times on initial denials in
1986, the Disclosure Litigation Division did not use it a single time to deny
records on appeal. That could mean that all five instances were reversed on appeal and the records released, which is extremely unlikely. It could mean that
the requester went into litigation before receiving an appeal response, which is
even more unlikely. It could mean that the records were withheld on appeal,
but the use of the (b)(1) exemption was abandoned in favor of relying on some

other exemption, which is quite possible but not very likely. Or it could mean, and it is extremely likely to mean, that the requesters were so awed by the use of the national-security exemption that they did not appeal the denials.

A person who has been denied access to documents on the basis that they are exempt for national-security reasons under (b)(1) should file an appeal. That appeal should focus on the possibility that the original classification and the continued classification of the records were improper.

Classified records are subject to the segregability requirements. Ask if any segregable portions can be released. Ask that the margins of the record, including the markings showing the level of classification, the date classified, and the identity of the classifying official, be released so that you may see whether the original classification was proper. Ask for copies of the history sheet or copies of memoranda referring records to their originating agency for advice. Ask for copies of the history sheet or copies of memoranda establishing whether the documents were evaluated for declassification and whether that evaluation was performed by a person authorized to declassify the records.

And finally ask whether the records are considered to be properly classified and warrant continuing classification. The Information Act does not require an agency to respond to such a question, but the Disclosure Litigation Division tends to write responses in order to create a favorable record in the event of litigation. You should be doing the same thing. Your appeal should raise questions that force the agency to give you every consideration to which you are entitled. And if the records are not released, your appeal and the agency response should give the court something to think about.

Internal Personnel Rules and Practices

The (b)(2) exemption provides that "This section does not apply to matters that are—related solely to the internal personal rules and practices of an agency." During 1986, this exemption was relied upon 629 times and therefore appeared in 32 percent of the denials issued by the Internal Revenue Service. It is seldom cited as the sole exemption relied upon and owes its frequency of use to being applicable to some aspects of investigatory records primarily denied pursuant to other exemptions.

In order to understand the (b)(2) exemption, we must first realize that it covers two very different types of records. It is in fact two exemptions rather than one. This dichotomy results from differences in the House and Senate reports explaining Congress' intentions in including the exemption in the original Freedom of Information Act.

The Senate report stated:

> Exemption No. 2 relates only to the internal personnel rules and practices of an agency. Examples of these may be rules as to personnel's use of parking facilities or regulation of lunch hours, statements of policy as to sick leave and the like.

The House report, however, stated that exemption (b)(2) was intended to cover

> operating rules, guidelines, and manuals of procedure for Government investigators or examiners ... but ... not ... all matters of internal management such as employee relations and working conditions and routine administrative procedures which are withheld under present law.

These two interpretations are not only different but would appear to be almost mutually exclusive.

The Senate thought that it was exempting rather innocuous housekeeping matters which would be of little interest to the general public but made no mention of the extremely important manuals of procedure described in the House report. The House concentrated upon exempting investigators' guidelines, thereby making a major contribution to the efficient performance of law enforcement agencies, while specifically excluding from exemption the internal-management matters the Senate was exempting.

This conflict in intent does not appear to have been error or accident but seems to reflect a difference in basic philosophy between the House and the Senate. Oddly enough, the House version reflects a sympathy for law enforcement agencies more usually associated with attitudes seen in the Senate, whereas the Senate version is similar to the liberal disclosure attitudes more often displayed by the House.

The Senate interpretation seems to continue the assumptions of prior law by permitting agencies to determine what constitutes the legitimate interests of the general public and thereby gives them extensive control over the release of their housekeeping records. The House, however, specifically states that the exemption does not cover the routine administrative matters "which are withheld under present law."

The two interpretations would appear to be basically irreconcilable. Agencies seem to rely upon whichever best supports withholding the records at issue, and the courts seem willing to uphold both positions.

The Internal Revenue Service has from the very first taken the attitude that it does not really need to protect the innocuous documents to which the Senate interpretation would seem to apply. In fact, during the early years, most of the records released by the Service could have been protected by the Senate (b)(2) interpretation had the Service chosen to do so. The Service generally seemed to feel that releasing information concerning unimportant personnel matters would create an image of cooperation which would facilitate withholding the important matters which were protected by the House version.

The (b)(2) exemption as interpreted by the Senate report is unique among exemptions because it permits withholding records whose release would cause no harm to any legitimate government function. The exemption serves only to protect agencies from wasting their resources on processing the release of records not considered to be of general public interest.

The Service's Policy Statement P-1-192 does not permit withholding exempt records unless the harm which could be anticipated to result from their release would be so substantial as seriously to impair Service operations. Thus, the Service has given away authority which the Senate said it might retain. Consequently, few of the Service's denials under (b)(2) pertain to the internal personnel rules and practices of the agency but instead deal with records which meet the much more significant House interpretation.

If you are denied access under exemption (b)(2) to records which you believe pertain to internal personnel rules and practices of the agency, you should appeal such a denial, calling attention to Policy Statement P-1-192 as a basis for not applying the exemption in the absence of any significant interference of the Service's operations.

There are circumstances in which the Service will apply (b)(2) on the basis of the Senate interpretation and contend that such use is consistent with the requirements of the policy statement. In such cases, the records would pertain to internal personnel rules and practices, and they would not be of legitimate interest to the general public, but they would not be inconsequential. On the contrary, the Service might consider them to be of the greatest and most urgent consequence and believe that their release would be extremely disruptive to the management of the Service.

One such case involved a document which reprinted the Service's contract with the National Treasury Employees' Union, to which were added the management interpretations of what the contract provisions meant. The document was intended for use by managers only, so that they might guide themselves in the proper observation of the contract provisions in dealing with their employees. The object was to promote a uniform compliance in accordance with management's understanding of what had been agreed to. The document was not to be shared with the employees.

The union requested a copy of the document. I reviewed the document and concluded that the contract meant exactly what it said it did. The management interpretations did not seem to me to alter the clear meaning of the contract provisions. I recommended that the document be released. Labor-relations experts differed with that opinion. They pointed out that there were nuances which would be highly meaningful to a person having a specialized knowledge of such matters. The release of the document could have adverse consequences upon future negotiatons. Even if the interpretations were identical to the contract provisions, that too would be information whose release could upset delicate negotiations. The document was withheld, and the denial has been upheld as a proper use of exemption (b)(2).

Although the withholding was a proper use of the exemption and completely legal, I still wonder if it represented a rational and constructive act. It would seem that the purpose of a labor contract is to reach an agreement on the basis of mutual understanding. If one party is to keep its interpretation of the agreement secret, it would seem to preclude any mutual understanding and defeat the purpose of having a contract. Moreover, how can an agency effectively manage its employees if neither the employees nor their representatives are to know what management expects of them? These, of course, are not Freedom of Information questions.

The far more common usage of the (b)(2) exemption is in connection with the House interpretation of operating rules, guidelines, and manuals of procedure for government investigators or examiners. This interpretation is highly relevant to the Service's extensive use of tolerances, case-selection criteria, standards for enforcement, and confidential law enforcement techniques. To understand this application of exemption (b)(2), we must reread the portion of the chapter on the Information Act which pertains to (a)(2) material so that we can appreciate the difference between records exempt under (b)(2) and those which must be made public as administrative staff manuals and instructions to staff that affect a member of the public. This application of exemption (b)(2) will be discussed in detail in Chapter 21.

Exempt by Statute

The third exemption, (b)(3), provides for the withholding of records made secret by the operation of some other statute. The original form of this exemption permitted any withholding statute to operate without further conditions. In 1976 the (b)(3) exemption was amended because Congress was concerned that in its original broad form, the exemption might have permitted agencies to avoid compliance with the Information Act on the basis of statutes not intended to have that effect. The current exemption:

> This section does not apply to matters that are — specifically exempted from disclosure by statute (other than section 552b of this title), provided that such statute (A) requires that the matters be withheld from the public in such a manner as to leave no discretion on the issue, or (B) establishes particular criteria for withholding or refers to particular types of matters to be withheld.

The parenthetical reference to 5 U.S.C. 552b has no relevance to our discussion since that reference is to the government in the Sunshine Act, which does not apply to the Internal Revenue Service.

The (b)(3) exemption is the most important and the most frequently used of all the exemptions available to the Service. In 1986 the Service cited (b)(3) 1,623 times. That means that 81 percent of all responses denying records on the basis of an exemption included a reference to (b)(3), creating the illusion that almost all records withheld by the Service were withheld because other laws required that result.

Virtually all citations to (b)(3) were based upon the confidentiality provisions of the Internal Revenue Code, 26 U.S.C. 6103. These are the provisions of the Code which require that tax returns and return information may be released only as specifically provided by the Code.

There are two major ways section 6103 may apply to a Freedom of Information request. First, it may be used to deny information to a third party, that is, anyone other than the taxpayer or some party otherwise authorized by the Code. This is the sort of denial which would result if someone else were to ask for information concerning you. The second type of denial results when the taxpayer, his representative, or some other legally authorized party seeks information the Service believes would interfere with tax administration if it were released. This is the sort of denial which would result if you requested access to some portion of an investigatory file concerning yourself.

The (b)(3) exemption, as amended in 1976, must meet either of two component tests. The first is that the statute must require that the matters be withheld from the public in such a manner as to leave no discretion on the issue. When tax returns and return information are withheld from a third party, this test is obviously and easily met. The second is that the statute must establish criteria for withholding or must refer to particular types of matters to be withheld. Withholding return information from a taxpayer because the release may interfere with tax administration may not always appear to readily meet the first test, but it definitely meets the second test.

Some courts have held that Code section 6103 is a valid (b)(3) statute because it meets the first test. Other courts have held that it meets the second test. Still other courts have developed a third theory, which holds that section 6103 need not be evaluated as a (b)(3) exemption because it was enacted to serve as the sole standard governing the disclosure or nondisclosure of returns and return information, and therefore displaces the Information Act.

In some cases, there might be a slight difference in the types and extent of information a court may permit to be withheld, depending upon which of the three theories it espouses. As a practical matter, the Service routinely wins litigation based upon section 6103. The overall assumption is that if the information is covered by section 6103, it may generally be withheld as long as the Service applies the standard of interference with tax administration in good faith.

Occasionally the Service will base (b)(3) exemptions on other statutes. Code section 7213 is sometimes cited, but this merely prescribes the penalty for an official who violates section 6103 by an unauthorized disclosure. Other times Code 7431 is cited, but this section merely provides civil damages for the unauthorized disclosure of returns and return information. These sections augment the 6103 prohibitions and should not be viewed separately.

Rules and regulations generally cannot trigger the (b)(3) exemption. Some rules, however, have been amended by or otherwise acted upon by Congress, so that they are considered statutes. For instance, in 1986 the Service cited Rule 6(e) of the Federal Rules of Criminal Procedure on five occasions. This rule governs disclosure of matters occurring before a federal grand jury and has the effect of law.

Two statutes which appear to tempt some officials but which do not meet the requirements of (b)(3) are the Privacy Act of 1974, 5 U.S.C. 552a, and the Trade Secrets Act, 18 U.S.C. 1905. No matter how often I stressed in training programs that these statutes cannot be relied upon for (b)(3) exemptions, some disclosure officer seemed to insist upon including one or the other in a (b)(3) denial. If you receive a response which cites one of these, you can conclude that the disclosure officer was not fully trained or was operating in some sort of a trance, but you will get little satisfaction beyond that. Invariably the records to which such statutes are applied will upon proper examination prove to be exempt on the basis of section 6103.

Any other statute cited in a denial by the Service should be looked upon with considerable skepticism. It is impossible to state a general exclusion of other statutes as a basis for (b)(3), but my experience has been that a large proportion of such innovative citations are based upon wishful thinking.

Since few requesters are so naive as to waste their time asking for someone else's tax information, the most frequent use of section 6103 involves the denial of information to a taxpayer seeking access to his own investigatory file. Such a denial will invariably involve the careful editing of the requested document since the segregability principle will apply to the determination of precisely which information would result in interference with tax administration.

Interference with tax administration may mean that the release would interfere with the collection or assessment of taxes, penalties, or interest from that taxpayer in that case or in some other case. It may also mean that the interference would affect some other taxpayer's case, which may or may not be related to the requester's tax affairs. In its broadest sense, the interference may be generalized to affect the overall process of tax administration, without regard to any particular taxpayer.

Some information must be withheld and therefore can involve no analysis. It need merely be present to trigger its immediate deletion regardless of circumstances. Such information consists primarily of discriminant-function scores and related matters whose release would nullify the effectiveness of the Service's process for selecting cases for examination. Since there is no discretion in the matter, there is nothing to be gained by appealing a denial of discriminant-function scores.

Other information in a case file must be carefully analyzed before a decision to release or withhold can be made. Such analysis involves the use of good judgment since it must consider what the nature of the interference is expected to be. Is it general, or is it specific to the case at hand? Either way, what is the adverse consequence which may be expected upon its release?

If the consequence envisioned is specific to the case at hand, how will the passage of time, the progress of the investigation, the collection of the tax, the completion of the litigation, or the expiration of the statutory period for taking action affect the result? Few adverse consequences specific to a case will continue forever, and information sensitive when it is current may well become innocuous upon the occurrence of some event. There are few categories of information, other than those associated with the discriminant function, which will lead to the same decision in every case since the circumstances which govern are always changing.

Enforcement personnel will frequently ask for broad definitions of information which can always be withheld or for a list of forms which are always confidential. Such definitions and such lists cannot exist, for they would defeat the application of sound judgment which is inherent in the protection of only that information whose release would interfere with tax administration.

Law enforcement officers frequently lack the good judgment necessary to evaluate their own case files. There is a natural tendency to overvalue the significance of projects to which one has been personally devoted and to imagine risks which do not exist. When the case under discussion is not simply a case, but "my big case," the natural effect of emotion is to encourage the defense of materials which do not deserve to be withheld.

Disclosure officers have to argue and compromise in an effort to pry loose such information. The level of release of such records will often be a function of the disclosure officer's dialectic skills and determinations, as opposed to the revenge agent's or special agent's obstinacy.

Unfortunately, in many district offices, disclosure offices lack the status necessary to overcome revenue agents' and special agents' proclivity toward the defense of their records. With the return of the disclosure function to the authority of the Examination Division, management can be expected to lean toward withholding rather than disclosing questionable portions of investigatory files.

My experience in reviewing hundreds of Freedom of Information case files over a period of years is that a very conscientious effort is made not to make more deletions than are necessary. Nevertheless, unjustified deletions are not uncommon, and in some offices they have been rampant. The more sensitive a case is, the greater notoriety attached to it, and the more management has been involved in directing the progress of the investigation, the more likely the deletions are excessive. Moreover, whenever the relationship between taxpayer and enforcement personnel has become degraded to a point of personal animosity and an open exchange of information would be appropriate to clear the air, the opposite result is likely to occur, and deletions will be based upon emotions rather than logic.

If you are a taxpayer who has been denied some portion of your return information on the grounds that the release would interfere with tax administration, appeal that denial. Additional information is generally released as a result of such appeals, and that additional information can sometimes be significant.

In order to determine objectively whether the Service is doing a reasonably acceptable job in determining what portion of taxpayers' investigative files may be released, some researcher must someday do a scientifically constructed test. One way would be to select a suitable sample of requesters who have had information denied to them and wait until the underlying tax case is devoid of any prospect for further activity. Then, when all the taxes have been disposed of and all prospects for litigation have been exhausted, request (with the taxpayer's authorization) the portions of the records which were denied. Since it would no longer be possible for any disclosure to have adverse consequence specific to that case, the most common rationale for anticipating interference with tax administration would no longer exist. The section 6103 prohibition against disclosure would no longer apply, and the (b)(3) exemption would no longer be available. The formerly withheld information would be released and could then be analyzed to determine if it had been properly withheld. Such an analysis could be invaluable in promoting improved compliance with the Information Act. The taxpayers, on seeing what information had been withheld when their cases were live, could ask themselves what might they have done differently had they known what was denied to them. How might that have altered the outcome of their cases and changed their lives?

Trade Secrets

The fourth exemption, (b)(4), is designed to protect commercial information. It functions to protect both the businesspeople who submit such information and the government's interest in having continued access without the flow of data being diminished by fear of leaks to competitors. The exemption reads: "This section does not apply to matters that are—trade secrets and commercial or financial information obtained from a person and privileged or confidential."

To begin with, it must be clearly understood that the vast volume of business information which the Service receives in the form of tax returns and return information is fully protected by section 6103. Such information will always be withheld from third-party requesters under exemption (b)(3). The Service will never cite exemption (b)(4) in connection with returns or return information since it is obviously advantageous to use the more powerful and less troublesome (b)(3) exemption.

Consequently, the Service uses the (b)(4) exemption to protect business information which comes to it through channels that cannot be construed as directly involved in tax administration. In 1986 the (b)(4) exemption was cited 19 times, which represented only 6 percent of all denials. Almost all the (b)(4) denials dealt with information contained in contracts for the purchase of goods and services necessary to the functioning of the Service. Most of these contracts related to the purchase or installation and maintenance of computers and related equipment. (The treatment of requests for contracts is covered in a separate chapter.)

A close look at the exemption reveals that it serves to protect two categories of information. The first covers trade secrets. True knowledge of what constitutes a trade secret would require an extensive understanding of each industry to which the requested information relates. In all probability such knowledge would have to extend to engineering principles as they might apply to methods of production or to the customs of commerce as they might affect a particular business. Naturally, there would be few people in the Service with adequate knowledge to determine what might constitute a trade secret since this is a very specialized field.

Fortunately, the courts have chosen to apply very broad standards to the term *trade secret* for exemption (b)(4) purposes. One court has defined a *trade secret* as "a secret, commercially valuable plan, formula, process or device that is used for the making, preparing, compounding, or processing of trade commodities and that can be said to be the end product of either innovation or substantial effort." If that is not sufficiently helpful, another court expressed the opinion that a trade secret is any information which would provide a competitive advantage. In actual practice, disclosure officers confronting information that might be a trade secret will telephone the person who submitted the information and ask whether that information is something commonly known in the industry and would be openly discussed with business associates, customers, and competitors. If the response is "No, that's a secret," we would generally be willing to protect the information, at least on the initial request.

The second category of the (b)(4) exemption has three components. It relates to information which is commercial or financial, obtained from a person, and privileged or confidential. These terms are given their ordinary meanings, and the category does not make any demands which are difficult to meet. "Commercial or financial" means simply that the information must relate to or be generated by a business. "Obtained from a person" merely means that some entity must have submitted it to the government, and it was not generated by the government itself. "Privileged or confidential" can mean that the government obtained the information by a promise of confidentiality or that the submitter had an expectation that the information would be held in confidence. Generally speaking, if the submitter does not want the information released, a basis for withholding it under exemption (b)(4) can be found.

One court ruled that information could be considered confidential if either one of two results could be anticipated from its release: The release would impair the government's ability to obtain necessary information in the future, or the release would cause substantial harm to the competitive position of the person from whom the information was obtained.

The Service has had few requests which involved the intricacies of the (b)(4) exemption to any great extent. One case, however, provides an interesting example of the complexities which might be involved and the unexpected twists which occur in working such a case. Some years ago, an individual wrote to the General Services Administration and asked for a copy of any documentation which formed the basis for deciding the level of reimbursement for government employees who used their own automobiles while traveling on official business. He wanted to know how it was decided that operating an automobile was worth so many cents per mile. The General Services Administration responded that the figure was based upon information provided by the Internal Revenue Service, and the request was soon in our hands.

No sooner did we receive the request than we realized that we already had requests for the computations which resulted in permitting a taxpayer to claim a mileage allowance for using a privately owned automobile for business purposes or in the pursuit of some charitable activity. We soon realized that requests for documentation of all these allowances were seeking the same thing. We made inquiries of the Assistant Commissioner (Technical) and found that all these allowances were based upon an average operational cost for the use of automobiles and that the average was based upon information appearing in a document called the *Runzheimer Report*.

The *Runzheimer Report* was a detailed study of the operational costs for every conceivable type of automobile. The information was compiled by a private firm which was in the business of selling its services as consultants to other businesspeople who needed to know the most efficient way to operate their fleets of vehicles. The report seemed to be part of a package of services which were being sold, which had value, and whose value might be destroyed if the report was released in response to an Information Act request. It seemed that this was definitely commercial information, it was confidential (at least until purchased), and its release would appear to damage the submitter's competitive position.

I soon learned that the report had been given to the Service free of charge. In fact, the firm which produced it made a free copy available every year. I expected that such a gift would have involved either a promise of confidentiality or at least an expectation of confidentiality. It was quite likely that if a copy of the report was released, our annual gift would no longer be forthcoming. Representatives of Technical advised me that it would be virtually impossible for the Service to produce such a report on its own unless we would be willing to go to very great expense.

The tests for applying the (b)(4) exemption all seemed to be in place. But upon further consideration, other complications were beginning to arise. If the deduction a taxpayer could take for the use of her automobile was based upon a computation which depended upon figures in a report which was secret, were not the American people being taxed on the basis of information of which they had no knowledge and which they could neither verify nor challenge? The hazy specter of secret law seemed to loom over the *Runzheimer Report*.

I discussed this aspect with the responsible specialists in Technical and in the Examination Division. They advised that the taxpayer would have no complaint since he was not required to use the established deduction but could claim his actual costs. Consequently, he was not being taxed on the basis of a secret report unless he elected to use the deduction provided and thereby save himself the trouble and expense of establishing his own cost computations.

Now I was really concerned. This response raised new questions. An individual who claimed actual expenses instead of accepting the deduction allowed would be asked to prove those expenses in an examination. I had once done precisely that in an examination of my own tax return, and I knew that it was a difficult and expensive task. Thus, there was considerable motivation to use the allowed deduction rather than the actual expense. But there was no need for an auditor to demand that taxpayers prove their actual expenses. I had the *Runzheimer Report* before me, and it listed the operational costs by year and make of car. The Service was asking taxpayers to prove something it had the capacity to know by reference to a report already in its possession. If the *Runzheimer Report* could be relied upon for an average allowable figure, then certainly the detailed input to such an average was equally reliable.

The significance of this lay in the fact that the use of an average meant that drivers of automobiles inexpensive to operate were permitted an allowance which exceeded their actual expenses, while drivers who had, but could not prove, greater expenses were permitted an allowance less than they deserved. Moreover, the driver who profited from the situation need prove nothing, whereas the driver who was disadvantaged could face a trying examination of his return. That seemed inequitable. And the knowledge that the Service had in its hands information which it demanded taxpayers prove but would refuse to release to those same taxpayers seemed to be even more inequitable.

As a sort of last straw, it occurred to me that the small cars enjoying this tax advantage were probably made in Japan, whereas the larger, more expensive automobiles denied an equitable deduction were made in the United States. In effect, in a small way at least, the secretive policy of the Service seemed to favor foreign industry at the expense of American manufacturers.

Secret law is a nebulous concept. But it seemed to me that although withholding the *Runzheimer Report* met the standards for exemption (b)(4), it might violate the open-government and fair-play concepts upon which the Information Act is based. I felt that the Service had an obligation to release the report, not because there was anything improper about the report but because its use facilitated practices by the Service the public had right to know about. Rather than exercise an exemption whose use was discretionary, the Service should be considering how it could make an appropriate release.

This in turn raised the problem of whether the Trade Secrets Act, 18 U.S.C. 1905, was applicable to the *Runzheimer Report*. This act does not give rise to a (b)(3) exemption, but it does contain criminal penalties for the unauthorized release of commercial information. Any analysis of whether information is to be withheld on the basis of the (b)(4) exemption must include consideration of the applicability of 18 U.S.C. 1905. A failure to exercise the (b)(4) exemption to withhold information covered by 18 U.S.C. 1905 would be a serious abuse of agency discretion and could lead to criminal penalties for the responsible individual. The statute reads:

> Whoever, being an officer or employee of the United States or any department or agency thereof, publishes, divulges, discloses, or makes known in any manner or to any extent not authorized by law any information coming to him in the course of his employment or official duties or by reason of any examination or investigation made by, or return, report or record made to or filed with, such department or agency or officer or employee thereof, which information concerns or relates to the trade secrets, processes, operations, style of work, or apparatus, or to the identity, confidential statistical data, amount or source of income, profits, losses, or expenditures of any person, firm, partnership, corporation, or association; or permits any income return or copy thereof of any book containing any abstract or particulars thereof to be seen or examined by any person except as provided by law; shall be fined not more than $1,000, or imprisoned not more than one year, or both; and shall be removed from office or employment.

This statute is the basis of "reverse" Information Act suits in which the submitter of the confidential information can petition the courts to order an agency not to release the information. In order to file such a suit, the submitter must know that a Freedom of Information request is pending and must have reason to suspect that the agency is about to release such information. The suit must be filed before the agency actually makes the release. Fair play, but no statutory requirement, dictates that the agency advise the submitter of its intentions to release her information in time to permit her attorneys to act.

The next step in working the case was to call the Runzheimer firm and ask for their input. I spoke to the manager responsible for the report. Much to my surprise, he stated that the firm did not have an expectation of secrecy when they gave the Service the report and had no objection to our releasing it. The report was only a small part of the product they were selling, and its release was unlikely to result in any harm to the company. He said that any of their customers might pass a copy of the report around and they could not control that. Nor did they worry about it. And he promised that they would keep sending us the report every year, regardless of what we did.

All of the (b)(4) elements evaporated as a result of this telephone conversation. But I found it difficult to accept that this was not a (b)(4) document and could be released. So I asked this gentleman if he could have an officer or owner of the business call me. I wanted to talk to someone who could legally bind the company.

The next day another individual called and again assured me that the firm did not wish to be involved in a defense of the report. I explained the basis for the (b)(4) exemption and was again told that the firm did not consider the document confidential. Finally the caller, who assured me that he could bind the firm, explained that I simply did not understand their business and that any minimal harm which might result from the release of the report could be more than offset by an increase in business resulting from the release.

I was now prepared to release the report, but I still needed the concurrence of the Assistant Commissioner (Technical). However, with the submitter supporting the release, that concurrence was inevitable. There was no basis for withholding the information without the (b)(4) exemption.

The next day, I met with representatives from Technical and Examination. The moral dilemma of not releasing a report which pertained to a subject which seemed to cry out for publicity was lost upon these gentlemen. The entire conversation revolved not around the exemption but the fact that if the *Runzheimer Report* was released, it might initiate a sequence of events which could drastically increase the cost of processing tax returns. There was no interest in the equitable treatment of the taxpayer. The sole concern was the convenient and efficient administration of the Service. This was not unusual since it was customary that the major if not the only factor given serious consideration in making a Freedom of Information determination was traditionally the unimpeded continued ability of the Service to function in an efficient and orderly manner.

When I reported that there was no support for the (b)(4) exemption on the basis of my two telephone conversations, I was told that either I had failed to explain what was involved or I had failed to understand what I had been told. At any rate, the Service's contact man with the firm would take up the discussions hereafter as he had an established rapport with the company and could better explain the problem.

A day or two later, the manager responsible for producing the report called and apologized for having misled me. It seemed that he had thought that we were speaking about some other report. The *Runzheimer Report* was a different matter altogether. The company had given the release of the report careful consideration and wished to do whatever was necessary to help support a denial pursuant to the (b)(4) exemption to protect its valuable commercial property.

The requests for the *Runzheimer Report* were denied. Litigation resulted, and ultimately the denial was upheld as being a proper application of the (b)(4) exemption. Regardless of the outcome of this litigation or any appeal that might have resulted therefrom, a method was found permanently to protect detailed automobile cost data from any Freedom of Information onslaught. In 1982 the Service contracted with Runzheimer International to provide figures for the average cost of operating an automobile. The contract was to run for five years and was renewed in 1988. Under the terms of the contract, the Service no longer received detailed figures for every automobile but only the average figure it announces to the public. You cannot ask the Service to give you what it has not got. Thus, while the question of whether using an average figure for automobile expenses has not been resolved, it is no longer an Information Act problem.

The Deliberative Process

The fifth exemption is intended to protect government employees from operating in a fishbowl subject to exposure likely to inhibit their frank expression of advice and opinions necessary to the effective formulation of agency policy. The (b)(5) exemption was cited in 516 denials, or 26 percent of all denials issued in 1986. The bulk of this use did not occur on documents which were solely dependent upon the (b)(5) exemption but supplemented other exemptions such as those for return information or investigatory files. The simple reason for this is that many investigatory files will include notations which interpret events, suggest future actions, speculate upon the significance of information, sketch the anticipated progress of the investigation, or construct a theory of the case. Such case entries could probably be withheld even if the (b)(5) exemption were not available, and the practice in the field as to how many exemptions are to be cited when more than one is applicable seems to vary depending upon the preferences of the individual disclosure officer.

The more interesting and purer use of the (b)(5) exemption involves the denial of the less frequently requested "thought documents" and legal files of the National Office. The (b)(5) exemption reads: "This section does not apply to matters which are—inter-agency or intra-agency memorandums or letters which would not be available to a party other than an agency in litigation with the agency."

You may find that phrase to be an appalling abuse of the English language. In 15 years of intimate involvement with the Information Act, I have never met anyone who claimed to be able to translate those words into any clearly meaningful sentence. Suffice it to say that the intent of the exemption is to protect those documents which would normally be privileged in the "discovery" phase of civil litigation. It may not always protect everything which would be unavailable in discovery, and it may sometimes protect something more than would be unavailable in discovery, but it is intended to equate more or less with civil discovery principles. There is considerable confusion in the Service as to what can be protected under this exemption. Managers will frequently insist that disclosure officers protect the most inappropriate documents, presumably in the mistaken belief that an incomprehensible exemption constitutes a comprehensive exemption.

The threshold test for applying (b)(5) is that the document must be an interagency or an intraagency memorandum. That is, it cannot constitute correspondence with a party outside government. It must have been generated within an agency with the intent that it remain therein or that it travel to another agency within government. However, within the context of this exemption, *agency* has a meaning somewhat more like "extended agency." For instance, the document may have been created by a consultant at the behest of the agency. That consultant may be performing with or without a contract, and he may be paid or unpaid. The document may have been created by or have been exhibited to a specialist outside the agency, or it may come from a state agency, a court, or some other person or organization which, within this context, was functioning as if it were a part of the agency and were taking part in the internal thought processes of the agency.

On the other hand, requests or proposals from persons outside the agency, gratuitous input from lobbyists, comments in response to the rule-making process, and similar documents do not share in the use of the exemption.

The document may be transmitted outside the agency to seek advice, comments, or additional viewpoints to assist the agency in its functions. It may not be intentionally released in a recipient's interest and then denied to others. A sort of fairness doctrine precludes withholding a document from the public after an intentional release to any person who is not taking part in the thought processes of the agency.

The basic rule is that when persons outside the agency create or receive the document, they must be doing so as a part of the agency function and therefore be considered an extension of the agency.

The second threshold is that the document must fall into one of three categories, in order of simplicity, attorney work product, attorney-client privilege, and deliberative process.

Attorney work product refers to all those documents created by an attorney or those persons who assist an attorney in contemplation of litigation. The intent is to preserve the integrity of the legal process by not permitting an adversary to extract documentation created for use in litigation. The anticipated litigation need not be on the immediate horizon, nor need a specific litigant be known, so long as the motivation for creation of the document is its use in litigation for which there is some reasonable expectation. It must be remembered that the document must be created as the result of the attorney's efforts. The exemption does not extend to an item of evidence by virtue of its accumulation but only to work product.

Attorney work product may sometimes be shared with persons outside the Service without losing the exemption, as when it is disclosed to a litigant in an attempt at settlement.

In the Service, attorney work product usually involves Chief Counsel records. Not all in the Chief Counsel organization function as attorneys, and some components, such as Technical and Appellate, do not litigate and therefore would rarely create attorney work product in anticipation of litigation. Some functions outside of Chief Counsel may also employ attorneys and engage in litigation, such as the Office of the Director of Practice.

The second category consists of records created pursuant to the attorney-client privilege. Such records need not relate to litigation. They consist of advice and opinions given by an attorney to her client. The client in the Service would be any of the operating functions receiving legal advice from an attorney. The purpose of this aspect of the exemption is to protect the legal process by maintaining the free flow of communication between attorney and client.

The confidentiality of advice from counsel is frequently compromised in the Service because National Office managers like to share good legal opinions with the field. They will transmit the legal advice in a manner which virtually ensures that the advice becomes an instruction to staff. A legal opinion may be transformed into secret law because the field acts upon such opinions as if they were instructions from the transmitting authority. In some cases, having been denied access to a Chief Counsel opinion dealing with an Examination, Collection, or Criminal Investigation matter, a request for any documents transmitting the opinion to the field may result in the release of the document or in laying the groundwork for successful litigation.

The third category, intended to protect the deliberative process, is the most difficult to understand and lends itself to the greatest potential for abuse. This category is available to protect documents regardless of the profession of the originator. The purpose is to encourage open, frank discussion in matters of policy between subordinates and superiors, to protect against the premature disclosure of proposed policies, and to protect against the confusion which might result from the disclosure of a rationale which may have been included in a proposal but which was not relevant to the adopted policy.

Such documents must be deliberative; they must express opinions or make suggestions on legal or policy matters. Technical opinions are generally not protected by this exemption. The Service has attempted to protect appraisals of real estate seized by revenue officers. Such opinions of value are not deliberative because they do not pertain to legal or policy matters and because the expression of an estimate of value represents the professional judgment upon which appraisers rest their reputation.

There is no risk of embarrassment and no risk of a loss of candor from the release of an engineer's estimate of the wiring necessary to support operation of a piece of equipment, an architect's estimate of the materials necessary to construct a building, or a programmer's estimate of the computer time necessary to run a program. These are not policy matters but merely technical opinions inherent in carrying out certain professional duties. Similarly, an opinion as to the revenue which will result from a certain program is not deliberative if it is based upon calculation, but might be deliberative if it is based upon speculation as to the behavioral response of the public to a proposed course of action.

Factual information which may be included in a deliberative document cannot be defended unless it is inextricably intertwined with the deliberative material. It is not easy to determine precisely what "inextricably intertwined" means; at least it is not easy to find examples which can be attributed to that state with any degree of confidence. Certainly statistical tables which frequently accompany or supplement a deliberative document would not be inextricable but would be clearly segregable and therefore releasable. Opening passages which recite the background to a problem or describe current procedures are not inextricable. Descriptions of a task force's assignment, the range of their responsibilities, the limits to their authority, the composition of their membership, the period of their tenure, are all items which may upon careful examination be found to contain factual information which is not inextricable. Bits and pieces of factual information contained within the deliberative text may be inextricably intertwined, but there is no easy yardstick for determining that, other than to make the attempt to separate the material and then evaluate the result. Most disclosure personnel will not make a serious attempt to identify any but the most obvious compilations of factual material for release.

It is occasionally suggested that the preparer's choice of which factual information is to be included in his document is itself a part of the deliberative process, and therefore factual information may be protected on the basis of its selection. The courts have rejected this argument, and factual information cannot be protected on the basis of selection. Nevertheless, this argument for withholding factual information periodically reappears at the suggestion of persons unaware of its history of rejection.

It is sometimes claimed that a draft is inherently a deliberative document. That claim has also been rejected. However, a draft may be a deliberative document if it is prepared as a proposal that the person having signature authority accept the *policy* enunciated in the draft. An early copy of routine correspondence which differs from the acceptable version only in matters of taste, composition, and grammar does not rise to the standards of (b)(5). Nevertheless, some disclosure personnel seem routinely to withhold all drafts as if they were deliberative of policy matters. Sometimes a draft will contain factual matter. It too is releasable unless inextricably intertwined with deliberative matter.

The identity of the preparer or of the members of the task force may sometimes be protected, especially if the proposal is seen as so unacceptable or inadequate as to be embarrassing. In other situations, however, the roster of persons serving on a task force may be so illustrious that their opinions virtually constitute a recitation of agency policy. Sometimes the status of the team members is so great that one may assume with confidence that their proposals are guaranteed of immediate and unquestioned implementation. In such cases, the identity of the team members would be public information, and the document itself may not warrant the (b)(5) protection because it is really not deliberative.

The document must be predecisional; it must constitute input to a determination not yet made. Explanations of why we did something are not subject to the exemption; explanations of why we should or should not do something would be exempt. Reconstructions of why a program failed would not be exempt; proposals for remedying a program's defects would be exempt.

Care must be taken that the proposal has not been converted into an action document, thereby losing the exemption. The Service once had a request for a document which was clearly a (b)(5) predecisional deliberative document. At least the copy we first saw met the requirements for the exemption. Before we made a determination to withhold the document, we learned of the existence of another copy. On this copy, the responsible executive had written, "This proposal looks good to me. Let's go with it." The document was no longer pre-decisional, no longer deliberative, no longer exempt; it was now an instruction to staff.

There are a great variety of ways an exempt document can become nonexempt. It need not be endorsed by an executive, but it can be circulated, filed, or reproduced in such a manner that it becomes clear to employees that the intent is that the proposal be carried out.

On the other hand, a proposal does not lose its exemption simply because some or even all of its points have been adopted, provided that implementation is made by some other document rather than by circulation of the proposal itself. The public need never know whether the final policy accepted all of a proposal, some of it, or none of it.

Care must be taken that proposals are not translated into instructions in such a way that there is no publicly available implementing document, for doing so risks the creation of secret law.

The level of authority of the originator of a proposal is an important factor to be considered. So too is the relationship between the originator and the recipient of the memorandum. If I send a suggestion to the Commissioner, it is far more likely to be exempt than if the Commissioner sends a suggestion to me, for the Commissioner is at liberty to ignore my suggestion. A proposal from a superior to a subordinate may well constitute an instruction to staff, and when it is mistaken for a mere proposal, it may be secret law.

It should be readily apparent that making a determination as to what constitutes a valid application of the (b)(5) exemption involves a consideration of the circumstances under which a document was generated, its content, and its subsequent use. This is not an easy determination to make, and there is a considerable potential for error. In the Service, memoranda are easily distinguishable from correspondence because they are typed on paper headed by half-inch-high blue letters: "Memorandum." There have been dozens of occasions on which top managers have held up a document and told me, "Look, this is exempt. It's a memorandum!" Upon closer inspection, they have almost always been found wrong.

Remember that to warrant a (b)(5) exemption, a document must first be an internal memorandum. It must consist of attorney work product, attorney-client privilege, or deliberative process. From time to time, some court will reach into the depths of historical precedent and common law to extract some other basis for applying the (b)(5) exemption to a unique situation, but the three categories mentioned will account for almost every document legitimately withheld.

If the only material denied to you pursuant to (b)(5) consists of those bits and pieces of rumination strewn about in an investigatory file, you may obtain some upon appeal, but most will continue to be withheld regardless of the strict applicability of (b)(5) because such items are likely to be protected by other, more appropriate exemptions.

   If the material you have been denied consists of attorney work product, there is little likelihood that you will obtain anything more on appeal, for this is a firmly established application of the exemption. Moreover, the application of the exemption to attorney work product has probably been made upon the recommendations of the same attorneys who will consider your appeal. And finally you must realize that all the world's attorneys, whether yours or ours, are firmly dedicated to the principle that whatever they produce in their professional capacity should not be exposed to those of us who are not attorneys.

   If the material you have been denied is subject to the attorney-client privilege, there is at least some possibility that the privilege has been negated by the abusive use of the document by the client, such as transforming the advice document into an instruction to staff or sharing it with other persons who stand outside the privilege. Such possibilities are worth exploring, and such denials are worth appealing.

   If the material you have been denied consists of deliberative-process material, there is a great likelihood that at least some of it may have been wrongly withheld. I would be tempted to appeal all such denials. In framing such an appeal, be certain to make mention of Policy Statement P-1-192. As we have mentioned before, that policy statement says that the Service will grant requests for records without using an available exemption unless public knowledge of the information would significantly impede or nullify IRS actions in carrying out a responsibility or function. It was the intention of that policy statement that most applications of the (b)(5) exemption for deliberative-process documents be waived since no significant harm would result from the release of such documents.

   The framers of that policy statement, and I was at every session at which it was discussed, believed that there was no harm in the public's learning that the Service considered a wide variety of proposals in formulating its policies; that those proposals included the good, the bad, the indifferent, and the irrelevant; and that management picked through proposals, choosing those it considered best. We saw no problem in letting the public know that before a decision was implemented, there were a variety of alternatives, each of which had its ardent proponents. We did not want to be seen as an unthinking monolith but as an organization capable of exploring alternatives and making rational decisions.

   Unfortunately, many managers do not share those beliefs. The Service does not generally involve the preparer of a deliberative document in its evaluation in response to a Freedom of Information request; the decision is made by the recipient of a proposal, not by its creator. I have, however, spoken to the people who submitted such documents on several occasions in the course of trying to learn the significance of the programs involved. I have never met anyone who was seriously concerned about having his proposals made public. I believe that the anticipated embarrassment which might result from the release of a rejected proposal and the "fishbowl" effect leading to the discouragement of future suggestions is a myth.

   Every submitter of a deliberative product that I have discussed this matter with was proud of his efforts, convinced of the value of his work (even when it proved to be wrong), confident of his continued involvement and value to the Service, and frequently eager to see his proposals released to the public. In fact, I suspect that some of the creators of deliberative-process documents had triggered the request for access to those documents by giving the requesters hints about the existence of their work.

I am convinced that if the people whose efforts are supposedly protected by this exemption were given the authority to make the disclosure determination concerning their own work, very few deliberative documents would ever be withheld from the public.

The decisions to withhold are made by the managers to whom the suggestions were made. Very few managers in the Service are motivated to act in the interests of their subordinates; decisions are usually made in the interests of the managers and in the furtherance of their careers. Deliberative-process documents are withheld because managers do not want the public to know that they had good proposals in hand and failed to act upon them, that the policies adopted are contrary to the advice upon which they were based, that actual practices run counter to the intentions of their creators, or that achievements fail to match their objectives.

There exists in the Service a constant struggle between the technical specialists who fully understand their subjects based upon experience and study and the managers who evaluate them. The philosophy that a manager need know only how to manage and need have no technical expertise produces a situation in which technical specialists who know everything about their subject produce totally correct proposals which flow up a management ladder on which every reviewer knows a little less than the reviewer before him but feels compelled to make revisions based upon his ignorance, until ultimately a product which is totally wrong is presented for final approval by an executive who knows absolutely nothing about the subject. The withholding of deliberative-process documents from the public serves to help perpetuate this system.

There are times when the application of the (b)(5) exemption is completely ludicrous. In 1987 a representative of the Collection Division showed me a report which had been prepared by a consultant. The report consisted of analyses, evaluations, opinions, comparisons, and proposals for further action. It was definitely a deliberative-process document, with the exception of small amounts of factual material. My initial reaction was that the report could definitely be withheld pursuant to exemption (b)(5).

The Collection Division representative replied that they did not want to withhold the report. The report had been prepared by a consultant who was paid to study an area of concern to the Collection Division. The report was submitted a year or two before. The consultant who had prepared the report was now making an informal request to use portions of it in a scholarly paper he planned to publish. There was no Information Act request. There was only a "friendly" inquiry. The consultant, as a scholar, had a need to publish, and some of this material could be useful to him. He had asked permission to use the material and had stressed that he would not press the matter if permission was not granted. He obviously retained hopes of further consultant assignments in the future.

The Collection Division did not want to withhold the report. They believed that the opinions expressed were favorable to the Service and that the proposals made were receiving attention. They believed that release of the document would contribute to a public understanding of how the Service operates and a greater appreciation for the problems the Service faces. All the Collection Division wanted to know was whether there were any disclosure rules which might preclude them from releasing the report.

I suspected that the Collection Division might have suggested that the consultant make the request, for they seemed eager to release the document. I gave the report a closer look and told the inquirer that according to the *Internal Revenue Manual* the director of the Collection Division had the authority to release that document, there were no disclosure rules which would preclude his doing so, but it should be realized that if they permitted the consultant to use the report for his purposes, it would lose its (b)(5) protection, and they would have to provide it to any Freedom of Information requester.

The consultant, of course, already knew the content of the document. But he had that knowledge, and may even have retained a copy, as a person taking part in the internal deliberative processes of the agency. If he was permitted to use that information for his own purposes, it would become available to the general public. The Collection Division representative said that they would be pleased to give this report to anyone who might want it and thanked me for my assistance.

The following day, he returned and said that the advice was just what they wanted, but his director would like to have it in writing. I was then a section chief, and section chiefs do not write to directors, so I had to prepare a memorandum for my director's signature so that the amenities of writing from director to director could be maintained. Unfortunately, my director did not trust my judgment in this matter and referred the memorandum to the Office of Chief Counsel for a legal opinion.

The attorney assigned to the matter obtained a copy of the original contract and found that it specified that the report was to be the property of the Service and that the consultant was to have no rights to the report or the information contained therein. Based upon this information, the memorandum to the Collection Division was rewritten to state that the consultant was not to be given permission to use the report because the contract provided against such use and that such denial was necessary to maintain the validity of the (b)(5) exemption so that the report could be withheld from other requesters. This, of course, was the same information which I had already provided to the Collection Division, but now it was inverted to preclude the release of the report, whereas I had been trying to accommodate the Collection Division's desire to release the report.

The Collection Division was confused and disappointed. The consultant was disappointed. I was amused.

Sometimes a dog does not know why it bites, and sometimes the Internal Revenue Service does not know why it withholds information from the public. Perhaps it is just the nature of the beast.

Invasion of Personal Privacy

The (b)(6) exemption to the act is designed to protect individuals from an unwarranted invasion of their personal privacy. The exemption reads: "This section does not apply to matters that are—personnel and medical files and similar files the disclosure of which would constitute a clearly unwarranted invasion of personal privacy."

The Service already uses the (b)(3) exemption based upon 26 U.S.C. 6103 to protect returns and return information. Consequently, the (b)(6) exemption is unnecessary to protect any information the Service may have concerning taxpayers. If it is necessary to protect personal information concerning a third party within a taxpayer's investigatory file, or which may be in an investigatory file which is not return information, a broader exemption is provided by (b)(7) than (b)(6). As a result, the (b)(6) exemption is not necessary for use with the vast bulk of the Service's records. During 1986, (b)(6) was cited 178 times, or about 9 percent of denials. Most of these uses related to records concerning the Service's employees. These uses are discussed in Chapter 33 on accessing information about Service employees.

The (b)(6) exemption applies only to information concerning individual persons, that is, real people and not artificial "persons." Corporations and other organziations or associations cannot have any privacy, thereby making it impossible to invade their privacy. The exemption states that it protects information in personnel, medical and similar files. This originally caused some controversy as to what was meant by "similar files." The Service has always taken the attitude that the intention of the exemption was to protect the type of information which might be found in personnel and medical files, regardless of where it would actually be located. Other agencies made similar interpretations, and this position was ultimately accepted by the courts. The meaning of "similar files" is irrelevant, so long as the nature of the information is such that its release would constitute an unwarranted invasion of privacy.

The continuing frontier of how to apply the (b)(6) exemption is just what is "personal" information and what is an "unwarranted" invasion of privacy. The definitions of these terms will vary widely with the circumstances involved, the status of the persons involved, the type of information being considered, and the relationship of the information to public duties of the person involved.

An invasion of privacy is deemed "unwarranted" if the adverse consequence to the individual exceeds the public interest in securing the information. Thus, if the public interest in release exceeds the reasons for withholding, the (b)(6) exemption would not be available. This requires a balancing test attempting to compare the public interest with the personal interest in the record. The public-interest part of the equation must, however, be truly representative of the public interest; a requester's personal interest in obtaining the information does not count. Nor does a private litigant's need for the information or a business' commercial interest in the information count. Frequently, the true public interest may lie in withholding the record, so that the public interest and the privacy interest coincide.

In applying this balancing test there are no absolute boundaries beyond which release or withholding cannot be considered. An extremely limited privacy interest would prevail over the absence of any bona fide public interest. A modest public interest might prevail over a limited privacy interest. And the most heartrending privacy interest imaginable might not suffice to prevent disclosure if the public interest in the information was considered overwhelming.

Such balancing requires good judgment, an understanding of the consequences involved, and a dedication to fairness, which is difficult for bureaucracies to maintain. Since the primary use of the (b)(6) exemption is in connection with information concerning the Service's employees, there is a natural and unavoidable bias in the performance of balancing tests.

My experience is that the Service will consider almost anything about a person to be personal information and almost any disclosure to be unwarranted. There have been instances in which managers wished to withhold information about their employees' training, awards, and professional qualifications at the same time that the employees had their office walls decorated with certificates attesting to these very accomplishments.

The Service will generally not apply a balancing test unless the requester states a public interest and requests such a test. Moreover, the Service will limit its test to those considerations the requester has raised, while feeling free to introduce every contrary consideration that it can think of. If you are seriously pursuing access to information likely to be withheld pursuant to (b)(6) either on initial request or on appeal after the exemption has been cited, consider it your responsibility to muster the most convincing public-interest argument you can. If you cannot make a respectable public-interest argument, you might wish to reconsider whether you really should be making the request.

The Service's proclivity to cloak its employees with anonymity and strongly defend them against even the most minute invasion of privacy is not without justification. The Privacy Act of 1974 established severe restrictions upon the release of information covered by that act, which is discussed in the next chapter. The Privacy Act does not protect personal information from access under the Freedom of Information Act, but it does create an inference that any exemption available to protect privacy should be exercised. And it gives some examples of what Congress considers a valid rationale for releasing such records. An agency which failed to strictly observe privacy considerations, consistent with Privacy Act objectives, even for its own employees, could be accused of an abuse of agency discretion.

Even if an agency has managed to make a universally acceptable determination on what constitutes an unwarranted invasion of privacy, there remain some very difficult decisions on how to apply that decision to a particular record. The segregability rule applies to (b)(6) material. That means that consideration must be given to which of the two major factors involved in personal information shall be withheld, the identity of the individual or the text describing the personal details concerning that individual.

If the request has been framed so that it must relate to a specific person or a small universe of persons, no exempt information can be released. But if the request is broadly drawn, it will usually be possible to release the personal information while deleting the identity of the individual. Some of the information might, however, hint at the identity, and this too would have to be withheld. An effective decision would have to take into account prior or even anticipated releases. An agency cannot today release a record from which identities have been deleted and information retained, and tomorrow release the same record with identities retained and information withheld.

To further complicate matters, some information in a record might not be exempt. The nonexempt material might permit inferences as to the nature of the exempt material. If nonexempt information is included in a document, it is unlikely that the identity could be withheld. That document would have to be processed by withholding the exempt information.

If a record included information on a series of persons, it would be necessary to consider whether those persons are related or unrelated by their placement in the series. All the determination made about the individual entries would have to be reevaluated, based upon what could be inferred from the series. It may be impossible to find a consistent approach for all the entries.

In some cases, information which could be released after the deletion of identifying details must be withheld because its nature is so traumatic that an individual recognizing allusions in the public press to his personal affairs would be deeply injured, although he alone would recognize the information as relating to him.

To a considerable extent, the disclosure officer's interpretation of the circumstances will govern the approach toward release on both the initial response and any response on appeal. Once a record has been released by deleting identities or by deleting information, that approach will be continued thereafter. Having made a wrong choice is not remediable. If you are seeking information of a personal nature, it is in your interest to decide whether you would prefer an identity-oriented or an information-oriented response. You should construct your request and your appeal in accordance with your needs. Explain what you need and why you need it; then expand upon the public interest involved. If the disclosure officer guesses wrong, the response may be opposite to your needs, even though you might have gotten something closer to your needs in response to a better-phrased request.

Law Enforcement Records

The seventh exemption is intended to protect records compiled for law enforcement purposes. The original (b)(7) exemption, as it existed from 1967 through 1974, was designed to protect investigatory files, and it protected them in their entirety. The investigation necessary to trigger the (b)(7) exemption could have pertained to criminal or civil law enforcement purposes. Consequently, the Internal Revenue Service used exemption (b)(7) to protect investigatory files maintained by the Collection Division (pertaining to the collecting of delinquent taxes and the securing of delinquent returns), the Examination

Division (pertaining to the audit of tax returns and the proposed assessment of taxes, penalties, and interest), the Appellate Division (pertaining to the appeal of additional assessments), the Criminal Investigation Division (pertaining to the investigation of tax fraud and other crimes under the Service's jurisdiction), and the Inspection Service (pertaining to investigations of wrongdoing by our employees and certain offenses by the public, such as attempted bribery).

Since the original exemption protected the entire contents of the investigatory file, these records were always denied in their entirety. In fact, the files were not retrieved for inspection prior to denial, since the actual content, substance, condition, and currency of the records were irrelevant to the decision to withhold the file.

In 1974, Congress amended the Freedom of Information Act and drastically altered the (b)(7) exemption to put an end to the practice of denying entire investigatory files without consideration of their content. Thereafter, the (b)(7) exemption applied to investigatory records compiled for law enforcement purposes, but only to the extent that their release would result in six specified forms of harm. If no harm resulted from the release of the record, the exemption would not be applicable.

The 1974 amendment also introduced the concept of releasing segregable portions of records, that is, those items within an exempt record which were not themselves exempt. Although records pertaining to the same types of Service activities continued to be eligible for exemption, they would thereafter have to be carefully examined to determine the extent to which an exemption applied. The result was that virtually every investigatory file contained extensive portions which could be released to the requester who was the subject of the file. But virtually every file relating to an open investigation also contained portions which were exempt and had to be withheld. An investigatory file which could be released without deletions or which could be withheld in its entirety would have been a great rarity.

In 1976, the amendment of section 6103 of the Internal Revenue Code created the requirement that return information, which included taxpayers' investigatory files, would be releasable to a requesting taxpayer, unless its release would seriously impair tax administration. Thus, there were now two standards for withholding records from a requester, the six enumerated forms of harm which exempted a record from the Freedom of Information Act, and the impairment of tax administration which resulted in a section 6103 prohibition against release, which in turn warranted application of the (b)(3) statutory requirement exemption of the Freedom of Information Act.

In order to be able to function, the Service had to make some assumptions which would permit a reasonable consistency between these standards. It was therefore assumed that Congress was familiar with both the Freedom of Information Act and the disclosure section of the Internal Revenue Code, and intended that they operate together in a rational and effective manner. Consequently, it had also to be assumed that the existence of any one of the six harms envisioned by the Freedom of Information Act which the Service felt compelled to assert would also constitute a serious impairment of tax administration.

If this assumption were correct, the Service would never have had to cite the (b)(7) exemption after 1976, for every item we determined to be subject to that exemption would also have been subject to the far stronger and far more convincing (b)(3) exemption. But we were not sure that our assumptions were correct. And we did not know if we could convince the courts that this was the way to approach taxpayers' investigatory files, for it could be seen as tantamount to the claim that section 6103 was the exclusive consideration for determining the availability of such records, which had not yet won acceptance by any court. Therefore, we generally cited both the applicable (b)(7) exemptions and the section 6103–based (b)(3) exemption. This dual use of exemptions became the custom and was continued even in jurisdictions where the courts would probably have been satisfied with the (b)(3) exemption alone.

For instance, in 1986, the Service used exemption (b)(7) 1,087 times, accounting for 54 percent of all denials. We also cited exemption (b)(3) 1,623 times, accounting for 81 percent of all denials. Had there been no other exemptions used, this would have totaled 135 percent of all denials. Obviously, except for a few requests which might have involved multiple records, these exemptions are being used in tandem to exempt portions of the same investigatory file, and generally were cited to cover the same items of information. In that manner, a court could choose any theory of prevalence between the Freedom of Information Act and the Internal Revenue Code the court found preferable; we would still have had one valid exemption to rely on. It would, of course, have made little practical difference whether our deletions were accepted as valid under (b)(3) or (b)(7).

The potential defect to this defense is that there might be some information in a taxpayer's investigatory file whose release would trigger one of the six harms but whose release might not be viewed as seriously impairing tax administration. If a court found such a situation to exist, the Internal Revenue Service could be barred from relying on a valid Freedom of Information Act exemption. The tax-administration-impairment standard is the only basis for withholding return information from the taxpayer the Internal Revenue Code provides. A requester might litigate for access under the Code and claim that Information Act exemptions are not relevant to return information. I am unaware of anyone ever reversing the "Internal Revenue Code is the sole avenue of access" argument in order to overcome an Information Act exemption, but the possibility would warrant always citing 6103 in addition to the Information Act when seeking access to return information.

In 1986, the Information Act was again amended. The amendment broadened portions of the (b)(7) amendment to permit easier withholding of some types of information, although the six harms were retained. The major change was that the words "investigatory file" were removed from the exemption and replaced with "records of information compiled for law enforcement purposes." This was a very important change, for the former threshold requirement for the (b)(7) exemption that the records be part of an investigative file no longer applied.

The (b)(7) exemption may now be used to protect law enforcement records which are not part of, or even related to, investigatory files. Moreover, information can now be protected even though it no longer resides in an investigatory file. Information compiled for law enforcement purposes may now reside in any file, or no file at all, and still warrant the use of the (b)(7) exemption.

As an example of the consequence of this amendment, let us consider the Criminal Investigation Division's accumulation of "program files." Program files differ from what the Criminal Investigation Division considers its case files in that they do not relate to a specific taxpayer but provide background information on some subject, industry, or particular type of offense. They serve as a sort of general informational resource for maintaining investigator awareness of potential problem areas which may suggest future targets for investigation. Since the files do not relate to a specific taxpayer, they could not be considered return information and could not be protected under section 6103 and exemption (b)(3). Since the files are created prior to an investigation being started or perhaps without an investigation ever taking place, they were not subject to the old (b)(7) exemption for investigatory files. Consequently some program files had to be released to requesters, although the release was anticipated to have resulted in harm to the Service's law enforcement activities because there was no relevant exemption. Large amounts of information on tax-protester groups became public through this circumstance. However, under the new (b)(7) exemption, these records could qualify for withholding because they were created for law enforcement purposes. Law enforcement manuals, although previously protected under other exemptions, can now be withheld under (b)(7), providing a stronger and more reliable defense for this type of material.

The final result of the new (b)(7) is that the exemption now covers considerable material which is not subject to section 6103 protection, so that in the future there will be fewer instances of the (b)(7) and (b)(3) exemptions being cited in tandem.

The current (b)(7) exemption reads:

> This section does not apply to matters that are—
> records or information compiled for law enforcement purposes, but only to the extent that the production of such law enforcement records or information
> (A) could reasonably be expected to interfere with enforcement proceedings,
> (B) would deprive a person of a right to a fair trial or an impartial adjudication,
> (C) could reasonably be expected to constitute an unwarranted invasion of personal privacy,
> (D) could reasonably be expected to disclose the identity of a confidential source, including a State, local or foreign agency or authority or any private institution which furnished information on a confidential basis, and, in the case of a record or information compiled by a criminal law enforcement authority in the course of a criminal investigation or by an agency conducting a lawful national security intelligence investigation, information furnished by a confidential source,

(E) would disclose techniques and procedures for law enforcement investigations or prosecutions if such disclosure could reasonably be expected to risk circumvention of the law, or

(F) could reasonably be expected to endanger the life or physical safety of any individual.

(b)(7)(A)

In order to understand the (b)(7) exemption, we must consider what its six component parts mean. What is meant by "could reasonably be expected to interfere with enforcement proceedings"? There are four components to the phrase: reasonableness, expectation, interference, and enforcement proceedings.

Prior to the 1986 amendment, it was necessary to demonstrate that harm would result from the release of information. This was too difficult a standard to meet, and courts were generally willing to accept something less than a demonstration that harm would in fact result. The new standard, a reasonable expectation, does not require establishing a likelihood of harm. It need only be shown that the anticipated harm could result and that the result is not so far fetched as to actually be unlikely. In actual experience, the tendency in the Service has been to base the anticipation of harm not on what is reasonable but upon any result which could be imagined.

There are occasions when enforcement personnel need to be creative and imaginative. Revenue Agents may have to construct "Blue Sky Assessments," computing a proposed tax without adequate information when taxpayers have provided no books. Revenue officers must sometimes compute penalties when employers have failed to pay over the taxes withheld from their workers and then experienced a spontaneous combustion of their records. Special agents must sometimes deal with taxpayers who keep two or three sets of books and a few scraps of paper tucked under the sweatband of their hat. These experiences have helped to foster a tradition of creativity and mental agility, which is sometimes applied in the justification for withholding records. Disclosure officers must constantly struggle against the tendency of Compliance personnel to withhold records in anticipation of adverse consequences that are totally divorced from reality.

At times, disclosure officers will be unable to prevail in the struggle to maintain a sense of reality, and denials will be based on unreasonable expectations. Hopefully, such denials will be reversed on appeal. Unfortunately, the attorneys who work appeals seldom have any experience in the enforcement field and will sometimes support the most outrageous flights of fancy.

There must be an expectation of an enforcement proceeding. That is, there must be an open case. If the investigation has been concluded so that it can be known that there will be no enforcement proceeding, there can be no valid (b)(7)(A) exemption. An investigation may be dormant and still have potential for a proceeding. The proceeding need not be imminent, but on the other hand, it would not suffice if it was something which merely hovered above a distant horizon.

A case may be closed but continue to have a potential to affect related cases, which would warrant continued exemption. For instance, a criminal scheme may not be apparent in a single tax year, but several prior years may have to be considered in order to warrant prosecution for the last year alone. Or the conclusion of a case against a single taxpayer may give rise to actions against other taxpayers involved in the same transaction.

In the Service, there are three levels of activities which may reduce the need to withhold records or lessen the likelihood of a proceeding, but only the final level actually eliminates the expectation of an enforcement proceeding.

At the first level, activity merely ceases. For instance, a revenue officer may report a delinquent tax as uncollectible. A revenue agent may close a case as a "no change" which does not warrant additional assessment. A special agent may close an investigation as having inadequate potential for criminal prosecution. These cases are administratively closed, and the Service may not want to withhold information from any of them. But they are not closed cases for purposes of applying the exemption, for each may be reopened in the event that new information becomes known, greater resources become available, or management review determines that the closing was inappropriate. The (b)(7)(A) exemption continues to be available if portions of such case files need to be withheld.

At a second level, the assigned action may have taken place, leading to the closing of the case. The delinquent tax has been collected or an additional assessment has been made. These cases are "closed" in accordance with Service parlance, but they are not closed for purposes of the exemption, since the possibility of a suit to set aside the assessment or to secure a refund is still possible.

Finally, at the third level, the true closing of a case takes place. The statute for assessment or collection has expired. Or the taxpayer has agreed to the assessment. Or the case has been litigated. It is only the final closing, which leaves the case devoid of any further potential for an enforcement proceeding, that removes the availability of the exemption.

But what is the result which is to be considered interference? Typical adverse results would be the release of information which discloses the scope and direction of the investigation, the premature release of evidence, and a release which makes it more difficult to obtain further data. In some cases, knowledge of imminent actions need be protected only long enough to permit the action to be successfully completed.

Finally, the enforcement proceeding involved may be the investigation itself since in the collection and assessment of taxes, the investigatory process and the resolution of the offense are inseparable. The revenue officer not only searches for concealed assets but seizes them. The revenue agent not only seeks to identify unwarranted deductions but disallows them. Except for criminal investigations, in which the Service initiates the prosecution of the taxpayer, tax litigation is usually initiated by the taxpayer in order to reverse the administration actions of the Service. Such litigation, for purposes of the (b)(7)(A) exemption, constitute enforcement proceedings.

(b)(7)(B)

The (b)(7)(B) exemption protects records whose release would "deprive a person of a right to a fair trial or an impartial adjudication." The intent is to avoid injuring the subject of the enforcement proceeding by the release of information which could cause prejudicial pretrial publicity. I am unaware that the Service has ever used this exemption. Since the Service deals almost exclusively with the release of information to the taxpayer himself rather than to unrelated third parties, there would appear to be little likelihood that it would ever be relevant.

One special agent did, however, suggest that we use the exemption to withhold all his criminal investigation files, since as far as he was concerned, the only fair trial was one which resulted in conviction.

(b)(7)(C)

This exemption is intended to protect the privacy of other persons who are mentioned in an investigatory file. It is somewhat similar to the (b)(6) exemption, except that instead of relating to a "clearly unwarranted" invasion of privacy, it merely relates to an "unwarranted" invasion of privacy. This constitutes a much lower standard for justifying the exemption. The intended purpose of a separate exemption for the protection of privacy in a law enforcement file is that the mere mention of a person in an investigatory file may cause a serious harm to that person's reputation. It is all too easy to assume that a person mentioned is engaged in some wrongdoing. As the Service's releases are primarily to the subject of the record rather than to the general public, concern about third parties' reputation is not a major factor. There are, however, other uses for the exemption.

The exemption also serves to protect the identity of witnesses, persons assisting with the inquiry, persons whose involvement has been ruled out, mere bystanders, law enforcement officers, and others who may be only casually involved with the events under investigation. As a practical matter, the majority of persons whose identity needs to be protected in an Internal Revenue Service file are the many clerical employees encountered when making inquiries at banks, business offices, and other locations. Frequently, such persons may have done nothing more than permit access to records to which the Service is legally entitled. They could, however, easily become the object of retribution by a vindictive taxpayer who may blame them for his troubles with the Service.

Revenue officers, revenue agents, and special agents always identify themselves to the taxpayer under investigation. Their identities and the identities of their supervisors are not protected. Investigatory records are full of the names of clerks who performed records searches, typists who prepared reports, secretaries who received messages, and other employees whose duties contributed something to the file but who could not be considered to have any real involvement in the development of the case. The Service is extremely sensitive to the need to protect the identities of such employees, especially from requesters who may be either known tax protesters or potentially dangerous or abusive persons.

The (b)(7)(C) exemption is not extinguished by the passage of time or the resolution of the underlying law enforcement action. For the most part, a recipient of records strewn with deletions on the basis of (b)(7)(C) would be well advised to disregard them as unrelated to his true interests. It would be appropriate to mention in any appeal that the release of such names need not be considered as they are outside the scope of the intended request. Such a statement can save a lot of time which would otherwise be wasted in reconsidering things that are neither wanted nor obtainable.

(b)(7)(D)

The (b)(7)(D) exemption is intended to protect the identity of confidential sources of information and in criminal investigations the information provided by confidential sources. Confidential sources may include the professional informants operated by the Criminal Investigation Division, the occasional informant seeking a reward for his submission of information, citizens providing unsolicited allegations of misconduct, persons responding to agency inquiries, commercial and financial institutions, state and local law enforcement officials, and virtually any other category person providing information and assistance in an investigation.

The protection of this exemption is not available to federal law enforcement officials. Its availability to complainants who wish the agency to redress wrongs against themselves is questionable. Its use to protect the identity of potential witnesses is a murky area. And it cannot be used to maintain the confidentiality of persons who might give evidence which would tend to exonerate the subject of the investigation.

The exemption is triggered whenever information is provided in response to an express pledge of confidentiality, a reasonable inference of confidentiality, an expectation of confidentiality, or a recognized policy of respecting confidentiality. The almost universal public belief that the Service respects the confidentiality of its sources is adequate to support the application of the exemption. However, this exemption is not available to protect the identity of a source who provides information under compulsory legal process, such as the service of a summons.

The nature and significance of the information provided and the nature of the investigation are irrelevant. The key to the exemption lies exclusively in the voluntary provision of information by a person who believes his identity will be protected. Although the law may not provide for such consideration, in practice the Service will take into account the character of the requesting taxpayer who seeks access to the records. Requests by drug dealers, members of organized crime, tax protesters, and potentially violent taxpayers will be very carefully edited in the belief that such requesters might prove a threat to any person identified in the file.

The fact that the requester already knows, or thinks he knows, the identity of a confidential source is irrelevant. It has been said that any taxpayer who has an informant need only assign one point each to his wife, his mistress, any rejected admirer, his secretary, and his bookkeeper. Add up the points. Whoever has the greatest total is the informant. Regardless of this or any other identifying device, the identity of a confidential source will not be released.

Information which may assist in guessing at the identity may also be withheld under this exemption. I have received calls from taxpayers who said that they know we will not identify an informant, but would I just tell whether it was a competitor or someone in the taxpayer's own office. The Internal Revenue Service does not give hints. In a criminal case, the information provided by the informant may also be withheld.

The (b)(7)(D) exemption is not extinguished by the passage of time or by the resolution of the underlying law enforcement action.

(b)(7)(E)

The (b)(7)(E) exemption was drastically modified in the 1986 amendment and now serves to protect law enforcement techniques, procedures, and guidelines. There are two parts to the exemption.

The first part protects law enforcement investigation and prosecution techniques and procedures. There is no need to show any harm which might result from the release of such records. Congress has already factored in the concept of harm in drawing the exemption. Thus all records which would disclose such techniques or procedures, whether they be recorded in an investigatory file and disclosed by inference or clearly stated in an established instruction, are exempt.

The techniques and procedures must, however, be unknown to the public in order to warrant protection. There have been instances in which the Service considered withholding investigatory techniques only to learn that the analyst who first included the technique in an instruction had obtained it from published materials he found in the public library. The question then becomes whether the fact that the Service uses a technique known to the public only in other circumstances can itself be withheld. The answer has not been established.

The second part of the exemption protects guidelines, but only to the extent that release could reasonably be expected to risk circumvention of the law. This provision is intended to prevent lawbreakers from tailoring their activities to escape detection and punishment by taking advantage of a knowledge of the agency's priorities for choosing which cases to pursue in order to use its limited resources most efficiently.

The Service is an agency which is forced to pick and choose among many competing challenges and thus has extensive guidelines governing almost all of its activities.

The (b)(7)(E) exemption is not extinguished by the passage of time or by the resolution of the underlying law enforcement activity. However, guidelines which are no longer in effect, and guidelines which frequently change may lend themselves to release without harm. Exemption (b)(7)(E) is discussed further in the chapter on law enforcement manuals.

(b)(7)(F)

The final portion of the (b)(7) exemption is intended to protect information whose release could reasonably be expected to endanger the life or physical safety of any individual. Prior to 1986, the exemption pertained only to the protection of law enforcement officers, although agencies used it to protect other persons as well. It may now be used to protect anyone.

The first impression is that this is another way to protect the identity of persons against an invasion of privacy, similar to (b)(6) and (b)(7)(D). It does serve that purpose. However, there is no duty to balance this exemption against any public interest accruing from release. In fact, a public interest in endangering anyone's life or physical safety is unthinkable. This exemption also covers federal law enforcement officers who are not covered by (b)(7)(D). Consequently, this is a stronger and more easily applied exemption than those which apply only to personal privacy.

The use of the exemption is not limited to personal information. The release of a law enforcement technique, a guard schedule, the nature of security precautions, and many other types of records could be protected if there existed a risk of endangering the life or physical safety of any person.

This exemption has a tremendous potential for being extended to many law enforcement documents which might not otherwise be so easily protected.

Financial Institutions

The (b)(8) exemption reads: "This section does not apply to matters that are—contained in or related to examination, operating, or condition reports prepared by, on behalf of, or for the use of an agency responsible for the regulation or supervision of financial institutions." This exemption was crafted to protect records which reflect upon the fiscal integrity of banks and to encourage candid communications between banks and bank examiners. It is an exemption which is rarely used by the Service, as few such records would be in the Service's possession and fewer still would come within the reach of Freedom of Information requests.

Even if the Service had such information, it would probably have originated in another agency and in the event of a request, be forwarded to that agency for resolution. The exemption was used twice in 1986, and that must be considered a sort of high-water mark, for it is seldom used.

Wells

The (b)(9) exemption reads: "This section does not apply to matters that are—geological and geophysical information and data, including maps, concerning wells." This exemption was not used in 1986.

If the data existed in the Service's possession, it would probably be return information withheld from third parties under exemption (b)(3) and from the subject taxpayer under some portion of exemption (b)(7).

It is conceivable that such data could be maintained by the Examination Division's engineers for use in establishing price or cost comparables and not be return information. There is little likelihood for the use of this exemption.

The (c)(1) Exclusion

The 1986 amendment provided three new methods for withholding information which were unknown to prior law. The first of these exclusions reads:

> Whenever a request is made which involves access to records described in subsection (b)(7)(A) and—
> (A) the investigation or proceeding involves a possible violation of criminal law; and
> (B) there is reason to believe that (i) the subject of the investigation or proceeding is not aware of its pendency, and (ii) disclosure of the existence of the records could reasonably be expected to interfere with enforcement proceedings, the agency may, during only such time as that circumstance continues, treat the records as not subject to the requirements of this section.

Criminal investigations by the Service normally commence with a special agent identifying himself and advising the subject of the existence and the nature of the investigation. Except in very rare instances of undercover investigations of organized crime activities, there is no likelihood of this exclusion being used.

Some disclosure officers have advised me that they do anticipate using the exclusion, although none was able to cite an actual case. I continue to be skeptical of the Service's need for this device.

You will, of course, never know if the exclusion is being used against you. If you are a major organized-crime figure, you need not use the Freedom of Information Act to determine if you are under investigation, nor need you be concerned about the use of the (c)(1) exclusion. You may safely assume that you are under investigation and it is simply a matter of time before we let you know about it.

The (c)(2) Exclusion

The (c)(2) exclusion reads: "Whenever informant records maintained by a criminal law enforcement agency under an informant's name or personal identifier are requested by a third party according to the informant's name or personal identifier, the agency may treat the records as not subject to the requirements of [the FOIA] unless the informant's status as an informant has been officially confirmed." The exclusion was intended to prevent a requester from identifying a suspected informant by making a request whose denial would supply the verification that the person about whom the inquiry was made was indeed an informant.

It has always been the Service's practice to respond to such requests by stating that informants' identities are confidential and the request is being denied without reference to our files to determine whether any records on the subject actually existed. Even the disclosure personnel making the response did not know whether the requester had hit upon a real informant. No one ever challenged this approach.

The new exclusion merely incorporates into the law the principle on which the Service was already operating.

The (c)(3) Exclusion

The third exclusion pertains only to records generated by the Federal Bureau of Investigation. It reads: "Whenever a request is made which involves access to records maintained by the Federal Bureau of Investigation pertaining to foreign intelligence or counter-intelligence, or international terrorism, and the existence of the records is classified information as provided in (Exemption 1), the Bureau may, as long as the existence of the records remains classified information, treat the records as not subject to the requirements of [the FOIA]." This exemption is obviously tailored for use by the Federal Bureau of Investigation and is unlikely to ever have any relevance to Service operations.

Conclusion

The reach of the exemptions and the exclusions may appear to be overwhelming. They may, indeed, justify the belief of many officials that virtually everything can be withheld. The truth, however, is that they really apply only to very specific and, generally, infrequent situations. In the vast majority of cases, most requested records may be released.

It is worth avoiding requests for materials which obviously will not be released. But the average requester should not be discouraged. Most of the records needed by taxpayers to understand their own tax affairs will be released upon request.

Chapter Twelve

The Privacy Act of 1974

The Privacy Act of 1974, usually referred to as the Privacy Act, attempts to regulate the entire process whereby government collects, maintains, uses, and disseminates information about individuals. The act includes records-access provisions and permits individuals to amend records concerning themselves under certain conditions.

The access provisions of the Privacy Act are seldom used, since the Freedom of Information Act appears to be a much simpler and much more direct vehicle. In a typical year, the Internal Revenue Service will receive about three dozen Privacy Act requests, which means that there is only one Privacy Act request for every 300 Information Act requests. There are probably not more than a dozen requests annually to amend records since the Internal Revenue Code contains a special provision designed to preclude such amendments in connection with tax matters.

Most of the Privacy Act cases worked by the Service have originated from its employees and, apparently, result from the Service's efforts to educate its people about the requirements of the act, which leads me to believe that there would be greater use of the act if the public had a greater understanding of its provisions. The act has certainly not captured the public's imagination. There is very great potential for those willing to search out novel applications of the act's many and varied provisions to successfully use the act to protect their privacy interests.

The act governs the records practices of all agencies in the executive branch of government. It is difficult, however, to relate its provisions to the actual activities of any particular agency. It certainly does not comfortably mesh with existing Service operations. Few people seem to understand its provisions, let alone how it may be applied to existing agency practices in any sensible manner.

The Act's Coverage

Congress, after lengthy hearings and moved by the spirit of Watergate, determined that legislation was necessary to protect the people's right to privacy. This protection was to be provided by an act which regulated the manner in which agencies maintained records about individuals.

The term *individual* was to mean a citizen of the United States or an alien lawfully admitted for permanent residence. The act served only to protect living persons, since the deceased are generally not considered to have any privacy rights. The Service decided at the outset that there was no need to observe distinctions concerning citizenship or residence. The Service would extend any rights available to an individual to every taxpayer who was a real person, as opposed to taxpayers who were artificial persons, such as corporations or partnerships. Thus, Privacy Act coverage was to equate with the Service's division of work between Individual Master File taxpayers and Business Master File taxpayers.

The Office of Management and Budget guidelines further defined *individual* so that most Privacy Act provisions did not apply to an individual acting in an entrepreneurial capacity. That is, an individual was covered as far as his personal activities were concerned but would not be covered to the extent that he presented himself to the public as a business entity. This concept meshed nicely with the Service's Individual Master File and Business Master File distinctions.

The term *record* meant any item, collection, or grouping of information about an individual, including but not limited to his education, financial transactions, medical history, and criminal or employment history. Obviously the type of information typically submitted on an individual tax return matched this definition of what constituted a record quite well. In order to avoid any unnecessary quibbling as to the kinds of information that created a record and to meet the "but not limited to" aspect of the definition, the Service proceeded on the concept that the act covered any information that told anything at all about an individual other than in an entrepreneurial capacity.

The act was applicable to a record without regard to the technology used to maintain the record. Consequently, every variety of record keeping, from the most old-fashioned set of index cards in a wooden box to state-of-the-art computer technology, is equally subject to the act.

Obviously, for a record to pertain to an individual, it must be identifiable to that individual. Thus, a record must also contain the individual's name, identifying number, symbol, or other identifying particular assigned to the individual such as a finger or voiceprint or a photograph. It made no difference what system of identification was used or whether the identifiers were scrambled or in some way disguised. If the system used permitted the agency to know to whom the record pertained, it met the requirements for coverage under the act.

One further characteristic was necessary to make a record subject to the act. The record had to be retrieved for the purpose of learning something about the individual, making a determination about him, or taking some action in regard to him. A record which is not in actual practice retrieved is not subject to the act. The Service assumed this to mean that the record was to be retrievable; that is, if it was part of a file designed to have the capacity to be retrieved, we assumed that it was retrieved and used. If the capacity for retrieval was absent, we assumed that it was in fact not retrieved.

This distinction is very important in determining which records are subject to the act, for a record may contain personal information about an individual, may contain a personal identifier, may have been used to make a determination about that individual, and may again be used for such purpose in the future, but if it cannot be retrieved by the individual's identity or some code representing identity, it is not subject to the Privacy Act. Correspondence which is filed by date of receipt is not subject to the act, assuming no cross-reference has been set up. Records which are filed by subject matter rather than by subject person are not subject to the act. Records which are randomly dropped into a receptacle are not subject to the act. Records ordered by priority or urgency are not subject to the act. Typically, spindle files, daily reading files, or accumulations of records of current interest do not have the capacity to be retrieved by individual identifiers and are not subject to the act.

These distinctions based upon method of access may break down into further complexities of coverage. For instance, if a file is organized by subject matter, such as automobile expenses, airline tickets, railway tickets, and travel vouchers, such a file would not be subject to the act. But if upon opening the drawer devoted to airline tickets we found the receipts were in alphabetical order by name of traveler, that would be a file subject to the act. On the other hand, if a new alphabetical file was begun each month, each quarter, or even each year, the current file would be subject to the act, while older files would lose that coverage. A record is not retrievable by individual identifier if it can be found only when the date of travel is known, as would be the case if locating the record requires knowledge of whether to look in the August file or the September file.

Sometimes records subject to the act may cease to be subject to the act due to a change in how they are treated. For instance, the Collection Division maintains its taxpayer delinquent accounts in a retrievable manner while they are open cases. They are subject to the act. Upon closing these accounts, they have little cause ever again to access the paper file. The cases are in many district offices dropped into a carton so that the most recently closed cases are closest to the top. If they ever wanted to access a case prior to its destruction in accordance with records disposition schedules, they would have to guess which carton it is in and how close to the top it might be. Then they would have to take up a handful and look through them until they find the one they want. The Collection Division feels that closed cases are sought so infrequently that this method is more cost-effective than expending clerical time to file all closed cases in an orderly fashion. These records cease to be subject to the act when they cease to be retrievable.

Thus, the Privacy Act covers records about identified individuals which are maintained in a fashion which permits them to be retrieved in order that they be used in some way which affects that individual. That does not cover everything which we know about you, but it does cover a great deal.

Statistical records are not subject to the act. Information which may otherwise appear to meet all the requirements of coverage by the act is exempt if it is maintained solely for statistical research or reporting purposes and is not used in whole or in part to make any determination about an identifiable individual. This provision can, however, be misleading. Information in the Service frequently flows from one function to another, so that what may appear to be maintained for statistical purposes may nevertheless end up in a file used to make a determination about an individual. Moreover, many case-selection and work-control techniques have the appearance of being statistical while nevertheless serving some nonexempt purpose. Consequently, care must be taken in considering all the ultimate uses of a record before it may be dismissed as being exclusively statistical.

Systems of Records

Before an agency may collect, maintain, use, or disseminate any information subject to the act, it must first establish appropriate administrative, technical, and physical safeguards to ensure the security and confidentiality of records and protect against any anticipated threats or hazards to their security or integrity which could result in substantial harm, embarrassment, inconvenience, or unfairness to any individual on whom information is maintained.

The agency must then establish rules of conduct for persons involved in the design, development, operation, or maintenance of systems intended to contain records. Employees must be instructed as to the requirements of the Privacy Act and the established rules of conduct. They must be alerted to the penalties which may result from noncompliance with such requirements.

Having established the rules and instructed the employees, the agency may then design and develop a system of records.

A *system of records* is defined as any group of records under the control of an agency from which information is retrieved by the name of the individual or by some identifying number, symbol, or other identifying particular assigned to the individual. In other words, the system of records is the file in which information is housed. However, the system need not have the physical characteristics of a file or exist in a single identifiable location. While it is easiest to think of a system of records as a file located in a cabinet or contained within a computer, the system may simply be a concept which encompasses a related group of records, regardless of their location. Since the Service is a highly decentralized organization using many different information technologies at many different locations with information flowing from one operation to another, it is important to understand that its systems of records are often conceptual. The records which comprise the system may never be physically associated.

Having established a system of records by creating the concept of what is to be encompassed and having made whatever provisions are necessary to permit the system to function, the agency must publish a notice of system of records. No information may be collected and no system may operate until the notice has been published. The purpose of such publication is to permit the public to understand what is intended and to raise any appropriate objections to the creation of the system. Such notices are reviewed by the Office of Management and Budget and are available to interested congressional committees prior to publication. Within the agency, awareness that any new system must pass the hurdle of publication serves as a restraint to ensure that only necessary and proper systems are proposed; outside the agency, publication serves as a protection that the agency will act responsibly and legally.

In addition to requiring publication of a notice whenever a new system is to be created, publication is required whenever an existing system is revised in such a manner as to serve a new function, cover a greater or different segment of the public, or risk some adverse effect upon the privacy of the individuals whose records are involved. Minor revisions to a system, as may be periodically necessary for housekeeping purposes without any envisioned effect upon the public, are routinely republished every few years.

Each notice, whether original or revised, must include nine types of information so that the public may know the nature of the system. First, the notice must state the name of the system and its location. The name is expected to be reasonably representative of the nature of the system, so that this fact alone will give the reader his first insight into the system's purpose and content. The name must also be meaningful to the agency employees who operate the system. Since all of the systems initially published related to long-established record-keeping activities, the Service balanced the need for descriptive names with the need for continuity. In most cases the Service used existing names whose meaning had to be expanded to cover the newly defined system rather than merely apply to a preexisting activity such as Individual Master File. In other cases, the Service invented names which are descriptive to the point of providing justification for themselves, such as the Defunct Special Service Staff File Being Retained Because of Congressional Directive.

The Service has long been a decentralized organization whose operations were based upon having one or more district offices in each state. Most systems directly affecting taxpayers were therefore described as being in the district offices. A few special-purpose systems were described as located in the National Office or at other places.

The second item of information to be published consisted of the categories of individuals on whom records are maintained in the system. These categories were intended to assist a person in determining whether there were likely to be records concerning him in the system and whether he need be concerned with the operation of the system. For the Service, these categories were directly related to the major tax-administration activities and included terms like Taxpayers Who File Federal Individual Income Tax Returns, Individuals Whose Returns or Claims Are Classified for Examination, or that ubiquitous term so beloved by the Service, Taxpayers. Surprisingly, a considerable number of systems of records relate only to the Service's employees and do not include any members of the general public.

The third type of information was to include the categories of records maintained in the system. The intention of this item was to give the public a further indication of what was contained in the system.

The fourth type of information was a listing of each routine use of the records in the system, including the categories of the user and the purpose of the use. This entry, however, does not tell the public how a record may be routinely used. It is misleading because the act provided a special definition of the term *routine use*. A routine use refers to a disclosure of a record for a purpose which is compatible with the purpose for which the information was collected. Thus, this entry identifies the situations in which a record may be regularly disclosed outside the agency and to whom it may be disclosed. The unfortunate part about this definition, in addition to the fact that it is misleading, is that no one seems to know precisely what is meant by a purpose which is compatible with the purpose for which the information was collected.

For instance, it can be argued that enforcing one law is certainly compatible with enforcing another law, so all law enforcement uses must be compatible. Collecting the revenue is certainly compatible with expending the revenue, so any information obtained might be released in support of any other program, so long as the routine use is properly published with the notice of systems of records. Fortunately, this problem of definitions is rendered moot by the fact that most of the information which the Service receives concerning taxpayers is return information protected by section 6103 of the Code and can therefore be disclosed only to recipients authorized by that section. Most of the Service's notices merely refer to the section 6103 restrictions as their routine uses.

The fifth type of information consists of the policies and practices of the agency regarding storage, retrievability, access controls, retention, and disposal of the records. For the most part, such policies and practices are complicated and extensive instructions published in the *Internal Revenue Manual*, and as a matter of convenience, the notices merely make references to the appropriate guidelines, generally IRM 1(15)59 and IRM 1(16)41.

The sixth type of information consists of the title and the business address of the agency official who is responsible for the system of records. Most Internal Revenue notices list two responsible officials. The first is the official who is responsible for the design of the system and for issuing the instruction under which it operates. This is generally a National Office official, such as the director of the Examination Division or the director of the Collection Division. These officials, while they control the system, have no access to its content. The second official identified is the official who has local control over the records actually maintained in the system. Generally this is the district director for the district which has jurisdiction over the subject taxpayer's records on the basis of area of residence. The purpose of these entries is to permit the inquiring individual to direct questions concerning the nature of the system to the National Office official and questions concerning his own records to the field official having possession and jurisdiction.

The seventh type of information consists of the agency procedures whereby an individual can be notified at his request if the system contains a record pertaining to him. The eighth type of information consists of the agency procedures whereby an individual may be notified at his request how he can gain access to any record pertaining to him contained in the system of records and how he can contest its contents. The act seems to envision a series of inquiries. First, is there anything concerning me? Then how may I ask for it? And finally, give it to me! The Internal Revenue Service rectifies this situation by merely directing the individual to ask for what he wants all at once. There are, however, exemptions whereby many systems may not be accessed, and these exemptions are identified in the notices. Most Service records are not considered subject to the provision for contesting the contents of records or amending them.

Finally, the notices must identify the categories of sources of records in the system. That is, they must state in general terms where the information they contain originated. Notices for systems consisting of investigatory materials compiled for law enforcement purposes are exempt from this requirement.

Information Gathering

Having determined that a record would be subject to the Privacy Act and having properly published a notice of systems of records without having encountered any opposition sufficient to deter it, an agency would now be free to begin gathering information.

If an individual is to be asked for information about himself for any purpose other than a criminal investigation, that person must first be provided with certain information to assist him in deciding whether he wishes to be responsive or prefers to refuse to answer. The information may be provided on the form requesting responses or it may be placed on a separate form which the individual may retain. You will doubtlessly recall having seen such a Privacy Act notice on your tax return or the instructions accompanying it.

The information to be supplied includes the authority, either granted by statute or by executive order of the President, which authorizes the solicitation of the information and whether response is mandatory or voluntary. The principal purpose or purposes for which the information is wanted must be stated. The routine uses of the information, meaning the disclosures which may be made outside the agency, are to be given. And the statement must explain the effects upon the individual of not providing any or all of the information requested.

If the individual is requested to reveal his social security number, he must also be informed whether response is mandatory or voluntary, by what statutory or other authority the number is solicited, and what uses will be made of it. This statement, usually included in the Privacy Act notice, generally explains that for tax purposes, the social security number serves as a tax identification number pursuant to 26 U.S.C. 6109 and is required on tax returns and other documents. There are no penalties or adverse consequences to an agency which fails to provide these required notices.

Restrictions

There are restrictions on what kinds of information may be collected and maintained. No agency may maintain a record describing how any individual exercises rights guaranteed by the First Amendment to the Constitution unless expressly authorized by statute or by the individual himself, or unless pertinent to and within the scope of an authorized law enforcement activity. The First Amendment reads, "Congress shall make no law respecting an establishment of religion, or prohibiting the free exercise thereof; or abridging the freedom of speech, or of the press; or the right of the people peaceably to assemble, and to petition the Government for redress of grievances."

Although the intent of a Privacy Act provision protecting First Amendment rights is both obvious and commendable, in actual practice it is virtually impossible to determine how the provision should be applied to the vast variety of records maintained by the Service. Few employees possess the sophisticated sensitivities necessary to observe adequately the requirements of the law, and enforcement personnel may be expected to blunder occasionally across the boundaries of impropriety.

Another provision which is difficult to interpret states that agencies may maintain only such information about an individual as is relevant and necessary to accomplish a purpose of the agency required to be accomplished by statute or executive order of the President. Both criminal and civil law enforcement records may be exempted from this provision, since it is impossible in an investigatory situation to know the ultimate significance of the information being gathered until the conclusion of the case. That same difficulty in judging the ultimate value of information extends to other types of files, although the exemption does not. There is little difficulty in recognizing relevance; the difficulty lies in judging necessity when knowledge of one fact may obviate the need for another.

Except for criminal law enforcement investigations, information is to be collected to the greatest extent possible from the subject individual whenever the information may result in adverse determinations about an individual's rights, benefits, and privileges under federal programs. All records, except criminal law enforcement records, which are used in making any determination about an individual are to be maintained with such accuracy, relevance, timeliness, and completeness as is reasonably necessary to assure fairness to the individual in the determination.

When viewed as a whole, the foregoing restrictions constitute a high standard of performance which can seldom be met. All supervisory personnel are responsible for the quality of work performed by their subordinates and should be making certain that these Privacy Act requirements are met whenever they are applicable. Most supervisors are far more comfortable confronting the need to maintain good production levels than they are in groping with the ethical standards of the Privacy Act.

Conditions of Disclosure

The Privacy Act restricts the disclosure of records, except as provided by 12 provisions of the act. When considering these provisions, it must be remembered that tax returns and return information can be disclosed only pursuant to the Internal Revenue Code; thus the Privacy Act provisions are primarily relevant only to records not subject to the far more restrictive requirements of 26 U.S.C. 6103. The following are the Privacy Act conditions of disclosure:

1. To those officers and employees of the agency which maintains the record who have a need for the record in the performance of their duties.
2. As required by the Freedom of Information Act.
3. For a routine use, that is, a disclosure of information for a purpose which is compatible with the purpose for which the information was collected and which was established by being published in the relevant notice of system of records.
4. To the Bureau of the Census pursuant to Title 13.
5. To a recipient who has provided the agency with advance adequate written assurance that the information is to be used solely for statistical research and the information is transferred in a form that is not identifiable to any individual.
6. To the National Archives and Records Administration as a record which has sufficient historical or other value to warrant its continued preservation by the government, or for evaluation by the archivist or his designee to determine if the record has such value.
7. To another agency or to an instrumentality of any governmental jurisdiction within or under the control of the United States for a civil or criminal law enforcement activity if the activity is authorized by law and if the head of the agency or instrumentality has made a written request to the agency which maintains the record specifying the particular portion desired and the law enforcement activity for which the record is sought. Shortly after the passage of the Privacy Act, representatives of most federal law enforcement agencies met and agreed to recognize and cooperate in granting each other's requests under this provision and to interpret head of the agency to mean any supervisor superior to the investigator desiring the record. Thus, this provision provides far less protection than its language would make apparent.
8. To a person pursuant to a showing of compelling circumstances affecting the health or safety of an individual if upon such disclosure notification is transmitted to the last known address of the individual.
9. To either house of Congress, or, to the extent of matter within its jurisdiction, any committee or subcommittee thereof, any joint committee of Congress or subcommittee of any such joint committee.
10. To the Comptroller General, or any of his authorized representatives, in the course of the performance of the duties of the General Accounting Office.
11. Pursuant to the order of a court of competent jurisdiction.
12. To a consumer reporting agency in accordance with section 3711(f) of Title 31, which pertains to the collection and compromise of claims of the government arising out of the activities of government agencies.

If a record is disclosed to any person other than an agency (that is outside the federal government) except when released pursuant to the Freedom of Information Act, the agency must make reasonable efforts to ensure that the released records are accurate, complete, timely, and relevant for agency purposes.

If a record is released under compulsory legal process, the agency must make reasonable efforts to serve notice on the individual when such process becomes a matter of public record, except when the record was part of a criminal law enforcement file. Fortunately, such events are quite infrequent, for the releasing agency has no readily available means of knowing when the process has become a matter of public record.

Accounting of Disclosures

Each agency which has made a disclosure outside the agency pursuant to any Privacy Act provision, other than a Freedom of Information Act release, must keep an accurate record showing the date, nature, and purpose of the disclosure, and the name and address of the person or the agency to whom the disclosure was made.

The Internal Revenue Code exempts some disclosures of returns and return information from the accounting requirement but creates a similar requirement for some records not subject to the Privacy Act.

The accounting of disclosure made pursuant to the Privacy Act must be retained for five years or for the life of the record, whichever is longer. Except for records which originate in civil or criminal investigatory files or records which are released for civil or criminal investigatory purposes, the agency must make information concerning accountings of disclosure available to the individual on request.

The purpose of the accounting provision was to document the extent that information flowed between agencies, to allow an individual to know which agencies have had access to his records, and to facilitate correcting shared records when that becomes necessary. There is, however, another reason for paying careful attention to the disclosure of your records. Each agency which has received your information is another source which you may pursue through the Freedom of Information Act for access to your own records. What may be denied to you by one agency may well be released to you by another.

Access to Records

Each agency which maintains a system of records is required to permit an individual, accompanied by a person of his own choosing if he so wishes, to inspect and obtain copies of any record in the system which pertains to him. This access provision appears at first glance to be very much like a Freedom of Information Act request. It is, however, an entirely different approach, which gives entirely different results. The Freedom of Information Act proceeds on the premise that the requester will seek specific records and will provide the agency with a reasonably accurate description of what is wanted. Thus, under the Information Act you would ask for A, B or C, and, if successful, receive just about what you asked for.

The Privacy Act access provisions envision a requester who is basically ignorant of what he is seeking. The prospective requester would review the notices of systems of records published in the *Federal Register*, paying special attention to the categories of individuals on whom records are maintained in the system and on the categories of records maintained in the system. Once he has located a system which is likely to include him as an individual on whom records are maintained and which relates to the type of records or the type of activity which is of concern to him, he would then request access to the system. That would be very much like asking for a bucket on the basis of a general description of its contents without knowing just what you are going to get.

Theoretically, the Privacy Act approach is the easier and likely to be the more popular for use by the average individual who lacks the knowledge upon which to base the more specific Freedom of Information request. In reality, just the opposite is true. Most requesters avoid the use of the Privacy Act. Those few who use it make serious errors, indicating that they either do not understand the scheme or have not adequately read the notices.

Privacy Act requesters will commonly seek access to systems which contain only records on Service employees when they are seeking information concerning their tax affairs. Taxpayers who have never been abroad will seek records from systems concerning International Operations. Taxpayers who have never been in litigation with the agency will seek records concerning court cases. Ordinary people have spent their time making Privacy Act requests to access systems which contain information on authors who have published materials concerning tax administration, files of newspaper clippings concerning employees and taxpayers whose tax affairs have been reported in the press, and biographies of IRS officials who are available to make speeches at public meetings! Making a successful Privacy Act access request requires a reasonable amount of research, a careful analysis of the published notices, and a degree of self-discipline.

The Privacy Act permits the head of an agency to exempt civil and criminal investigatory systems of records from the access provisions. The Service has used this provision to exempt every investigatory system of records which contains any return information protected by 26 U.S.C. 6103. The rationale behind the use of this exemption is very simple: 26 U.S.C. 6103(e)(7) permits disclosure of return information only "if the Secretary determines that such disclosure would not seriously impair Federal tax administration." Some disclosures (although not very many) would obviously impair tax administration. If the available exemptions for these systems had not been claimed, there would be no provision under the Privacy Act for withholding those records which could not be released. Thus, to make the Privacy Act access provisions consistent with the Internal Revenue Code restriction, all investigatory systems containing return information had to be exempted in their entirety. As a result, a Privacy Act request for access to any of the systems in which a taxpayer may reasonably be interested will be rejected out of hand, regardless of the nature of any records actually contained in the system. There will be no search made and no review of the records. There is no appeal from a denial of access to an exempt system.

This denial can easily be defeated. All the requester need do is to state in his request that it is also being made under the Freedom of Information Act. In effect, such a combined request has to be treated as if the Privacy Act reference to a system constitutes the description of the records and the Freedom of Information portion constitutes the actual demand. The result is that the records must be retrieved and reviewed. Any record from an exempt system which is not also exempt pursuant to the Information Act must then be released, including the segregable nonexempt portions of records.

There exists one further exemption to access under the Privacy Act, designed to offer some protection to records which are not part of investigatory systems. Any information compiled in reasonable anticipation of a civil action or proceeding may be withheld. This exemption applies to individual records and would apply only to something within a nonexempt system. It is basically consistent with the Information Act approach to withholding exempt records.

Amendment of Records

Once an individual has obtained access to a record, he may request that the record be amended. The agency must within 10 days correct any portion of a record which the individual believes is not accurate, relevant, timely, or complete, or the agency must inform the individual of its refusal to make the amendment, the reasons for such refusal, and the manner in which the refusal may be appealed.

Civil and criminal investigatory systems of records and portions of a few other systems are exempt from the amendment requirement. There are, however, systems which contain returns and return information which are not investigatory and might have been subject to the amendment requirement. Congress, however, was concerned that the Privacy Act amendment process might be abused to create an alternative method of affecting tax assessments without going through the established provisions for amending returns, making claims, appealing proposed assessments, or litigating tax issues in either Tax Court or District Court. The Internal Revenue Code was amended so that 26 U.S.C. 7852(e) provides that the amendment provisions of the Privacy Act shall not be applied, directly or indirectly, to the determination of the existence or possible existence of liability (or the amount thereof) of any person for any tax, penalty, interest, fine, forfeiture, or other imposition or offense to which the Internal Revenue Code applies.

The Service assumes that 26 U.S.C. 7852(e) precludes the amendment of any tax return or return information and automatically denies any such request. Appeals of such denials will not be considered. Congress may not have intended the exemption to be that broad, and there may be a small window of opportunity from which some requester may benefit, for there are items of return information which are not part of investigatory files and are not subject to any possibility of an amendment altering the tax consequences because the assessment has been agreed to or the courts have ruled upon the tax or the statute has tolled. No one has ever requested the amendment of such a record, so the question of whether it can be done has never been resolved. Few people have any interest in their tax records after all monetary matters are resolved, so such an amendment may never be requested.

In the event that a record which was subject to the amendment provision was not corrected, the individual may submit a statement of disagreement in which he can tell his version of the matters in dispute. The agency must associate the statement with the record.

If the record has been disclosed to another person or to another agency, that recipient must be offered or provided a copy of the corrected record or a copy of the statement of disagreement. The Service has little if any experience in making and sharing corrections since it seldom agrees to correct anything. However, in some circumstances, Privacy Act amendment requests will be processed within the existing channels for correcting records provided by the Internal Revenue Code. Such corrections are often easier to make than to attempt to construct a Privacy Act amendment of a record.

Civil Remedies

If the agency refuses to permit access to a system, refuses to make a correction to a record, or in any other way fails to comply with the Privacy Act, the individual may bring a civil action against the agency in a U.S. District Court. The court may order the correction of the defect and award reasonable attorney fees and other litigation costs to a complainant who has substantially prevailed.

An individual may also bring suit whenever an agency fails to maintain a record concerning him with such accuracy, relevance, timeliness, and completeness as is necessary to ensure fairness in any determination relating to the qualifications, character, rights, or opportunities of, or benefits to, the individual that may be made on the basis of such record, and consequently a determination is made which is adverse to the individual. If the agency's failure to comply with the Privacy Act or adequately to maintain the records can be shown to have been intentional or willful, the court may award actual damages to the injured individual. Such damages are not to be less than $1,000.

It is, of course, difficult to prove intent or willfulness, and it is difficult to establish actual damages, but these provisions have a tremendous unfulfilled potential for correcting the harm done in the course of excessive enforcement activity. Over the years one reads of case after case of unwarranted levies and seizures, and one cannot help but wonder if some of these unfair acts were not the result of adverse determinations resulting from inaccurate, irrelevant, untimely, or incomplete agency record-keeping practices in violation of the Privacy Act. I cannot help but feel that the Privacy Act is a far broader and far more powerful tool than either the public or the Service has yet realized.

Criminal Penalties

An officer or employee of an agency who willfully discloses information protected by the Privacy Act to a person or agency not entitled to receive it may be found guilty of a misdemeanor and fined not more than $5,000. A person who knowingly and willfully requests and obtains any record concerning an individual from an agency under false pretenses may be found guilty of a misdemeanor and fined not more than $5,000.

The possibility of someone falsely obtaining another person's records is a very real and a very serious problem introduced with the passage of the Freedom of Information Act and the Privacy Act. Prior to these acts, the Service rarely released any information to anyone. In other words, you did not get it, whether you were really you or not. This may have been unfair, but it maintained an adequate level of defense for individual privacy. Now, however, records must be released. Adequate precautions against an improper release do not sustain a perfect defense. An unprincipled requester cannot be deterred from obtaining another person's records. One of the unforeseen consequences of the Privacy Act may well be loss of any real protection against the invasion of privacy.

Any officer or employee who knowingly maintains a system of records without meeting the notice requirements of the Privacy Act may be found guilty of a misdemeanor and fined not more than $5,000. I believe that the maintenance of unpublished systems of records in the Service today is endemic. For years we struggled against the establishment of unpublished systems and were successful in preventing them because the logistics involved made it difficult to break the law without any indications becoming apparent to us. In the last few years, however, the ubiquitous spread of personal computers throughout the Service and the constant increase in storage capacity and speed in operation of these machines makes it possible for anyone, anywhere, at any time to create his own system of records without coming to the notice of anyone. I know that there were unauthorized systems of records in operation when I left the disclosure function, and I had initiated inquiries to locate and identify them so that a determination could be made on how to cope with the problem. After I left, however, this effort fell into the hands of persons who had little or no understanding of the problem and no commitment to resolving it. You may assume that the discovery of multiple unpublished and unauthorized locally established systems of records operating without the knowledge or approval of National Office will be the next scandal on the Service horizon.

Exemptions

Throughout this chapter we have mentioned various exemptions to provisions of the Privacy Act. These exemptions extend to the system of records, not to the individual record. The Service places extensive reliance upon these exemptions. In the event that the use of such exemptions seriously interferes with some purpose you are in pursuit of, keep in mind that Service's systems are generally conceptual rather than having any physical reality. In the beginning, a system of records was whatever I said it was; it contained whatever I considered reasonable for it to contain.

Take a closer look at the descriptions of the categories of records in a system. They are intentionally vague. No one knows how to find all the records in a system. No one can examine any group of records and accurately state which system they belong in. It is all an exercise in categorizing rather than a firmly established definition.

Most records move rapidly between systems as they are processed. Many records exist in multiple copies, each of which has become part of a different system. If you are stymied because of an exemption which extends to a particular system, challenge the propriety of that record being part of that system. And always remember that the availability and the treatment of return information, which covers most of the records most taxpayers are interested in, depends not upon the Privacy Act, but upon the Internal Revenue Code.

The Internal Revenue Code says simply that a taxpayer is entitled to access his return information as long as release will not seriously impair federal tax administration. That is really all that you need!

Chapter Thirteen

IRS Systems of Records

The Internal Revenue Service underwent a major reorganization in 1952. The changeover from manual processing of tax returns to automatic data processing took place in the early sixties. When the Privacy Act was passed in 1974, virtually all return-processing and record-maintenance programs which were to be considered systems of records had been functioning for a dozen years or more. But no index, no organized listing, and no set of definitions which could help determine what was to be considered a system of records existed.

The Privacy Act implementation team, of which I was the second in command and the primary strategist, put together all the existing guidelines for identifying potential systems of records, created a reporting form, and wrote to the field offices requesting their assistance. After studying their actual operations, the district offices, service centers, appellate offices, inspector's offices, regional offices, national computer center and data center submitted their completed reports, together with appropriate supporting documentation.

The implementation team reviewed the cartons of reports received and estimated that if each submission warranted recognition as a system of records, the Service could have about 2,500 systems. Inquiries with other agencies quickly revealed that such a total far exceeded what they were planning to report. The Service would have appeared to be the agency which constituted the most excessive user of personal information, a result that was politically unacceptable to management.

An agency could comply with the Privacy Act by designating all its records as a single system of records if it could adequately describe such a system, accept that it would be subject to a single set of rules and limited exemptions, and was willing to cope with access requests that could cover all the agency's records concerning a particular individual. An agency could comply equally well by describing a multitude of smaller systems, each differentiated from the others by some small but significant characteristic, providing that the agency was willing to create the detailed notices and be known as the most profligate personal record keeper.

The Privacy Act implementation team decided that the information received from the field should be massaged, combined, and redefined as necessary to come up with no more than 250 systems of records. Consequently, the number of systems initially reported, and their sizes and shapes, reflected this desire to stay within a safe limit rather than any objective reality of how many systems there really were. The team was successful. Since then, some of the original systems were combined or deleted in response to "drives" to reduce the amount of personal information retained by the government so that the current total appears to be about half what the Service started with, although there is no real difference in the amount of information being maintained.

At present the Service has 126 published notices of systems of records, identified as follows:

IRS 00.001 Correspondence Files and Correspondence Control Files
IRS 00.002 Correspondence Files/Inquiries About Enforcement Activities
IRS 10.001 Biographical Files, Public Affairs
IRS 10.004 Subject Files, Public Affairs
IRS 21.001 Tax Administration Advisors Resources File
IRS 22.003 Annual Listing of Undelivered Refund Checks
IRS 22.011 File Erroneous Refunds
IRS 22.026 Form 1042S Index By Name of Recipient
IRS 22.027 Foreign Information System (FIS)
IRS 22.032 Individual Microfilm Retention Register
IRS 22.034 Individual Returns Files, Adjustments and Miscellaneous
          Documents File
IRS 22.043 Potential Refund Litigation Case Files
IRS 22.044 P.O.W.–M.I.A. Reference File
IRS 22.054 Subsidiary Accounting Files
IRS 22.059 Unidentified Remittance File
IRS 22.060 Unit Ledger Cards
IRS 22.061 Wage & Information Returns Processing File
IRS 24.013 Combined Account Number File
IRS 24.029 Individual Account Number File
IRS 24.030 Individual Master File (IMF)
IRS 24.046 Business Master File (BMF)
IRS 24.070 Debtor Master File (DMF)
IRS 26.001 Acquired Property Record
IRS 26.006 Form 2209 Courtesy Investigations
IRS 26.008 IRS & Treasury Employee Delinquency
IRS 26.009 Lien Files (Open and Closed)
IRS 26.010 Lists of Prospective Bidders at IRS Sales of Seized Property
IRS 26.011 Litigation Case Files
IRS 26.012 Offer in Compromise (OIC) File
IRS 26.013 One Hundred Percent Penalty Cases
IRS 26.014 Record 21, Record of Seizure and Sale of Real Property
IRS 26.016 Returns Compliance Program (RCP)
IRS 26.019 TDA (Taxpayer Delinquent Accounts)
IRS 26.020 TDI (Taxpayer Delinquency Investigations)
IRS 26.021 Transferee Files
IRS 26.022 Delinquency Prevention Programs
IRS 30.003 Requests for Printed Tax Materials Including Lists
IRS 30.004 Security Violations
IRS 32.001 Travel Expense Record

IRS 32.003 Schedules of Collections and Schedules of Cancelled Checks
IRS 34.003 Assignment and Accountability of Personal Property Files
IRS 34.005 Parking Space Application & Assignment
IRS 34.007 Record of Government Books of Transportation Requests
IRS 34.009 Safety Program Files
IRS 34.012 Emergency Preparedness Cadre Assignments and Alerting Rosters Files
IRS 34.013 Identification Media Files for Employees and Others Issued IRS ID
IRS 34.014 Motor Vehicle Registration and Entry Pass Files
IRS 34.016 Security Clearance Files
IRS 34.018 Integrated Data Retrieval System (IDRS) Security Files
IRS 36.001 Appeals, Grievances, & Complaints Records
IRS 36.002 Employee Activity Records
IRS 36.003 General Personnel & Payroll Records
IRS 36.005 Medical Records
IRS 36.008 Recruiting, Examining & Placement Records
IRS 36.009 Retirement, Life Insurance, and Health Benefits Records
IRS 37.001 Abandoned Enrollment Applications
IRS 37.002 Files Containing Derogatory Information About Individuals Whose Applications for Enrollment to Practice Before the IRS Have Been Denied and Applicant Appeal Files
IRS 37.003 Closed Files Containing Derogatory Information About Individuals' Practice Before the Internal Revenue Service and Files of Attorneys and Certified Public Accountants Formerly Enrolled to Practice
IRS 37.004 Derogatory Information (No Action)
IRS 37.005 Present Suspensions and Disbarments Resulting From Administrative Proceedings
IRS 37.006 General Correspondence File
IRS 37.007 Inventory
IRS 37.008 Register of Docketed Cases & Applicant Appeals
IRS 37.009 Enrolled Agents and Resigned Enrolled Agents (Action Pursuant to 31 CFR, Section 10.55[b])
IRS 37.010 Roster of Former Enrollees
IRS 37.011 Present Suspensions From Practice Before the Internal Revenue Service
IRS 38.001 General Training Records
IRS 42.001 Examination Administrative File
IRS 42.008 Audit Information Management Systems (AIMS)
IRS 42.012 Combined Case Control Files
IRS 42.013 Project Files for the Uniform Application of Laws as a Result of Technical Determinations and Court Decisions
IRS 42.014 Internal Revenue Service Employees' Returns Control Files
IRS 42.016 Classification/Centralized Files and Scheduling Files
IRS 42.017 International Enforcement Program Files
IRS 42.021 Compliance Programs and Projects Files

IRS 42.027 Data on Foreign Corporations
IRS 42.029 Audit Underreporter Case Files
IRS 42.030 Discriminant Function File
IRS 44.001 Appeals Case Files
IRS 44.003 Appeals Case Data
IRS 44.004 Artist File
IRS 44.005 Expert Witness & Fee Appraiser Files
IRS 46.002 Case Management and Time Reporting Systems
IRS 46.003 Confidential Informants
IRS 46.004 Controlled Accounts—Open & Closed
IRS 46.005 Electronic Surveillance File
IRS 46.009 Centralized Evaluation & Processing of Information Items
IRS 46.011 Land Trust Files
IRS 46.015 Relocated Witnesses
IRS 46.016 Secret Service Details
IRS 46.022 Treasury Enforcement Communications System
IRS 48.001 Disclosure Records
IRS 48.008 Defunct Special Service Staff File Being Retained Because of
           Congressional Directive
IRS 49.001 Collateral and Information Requests
IRS 49.002 Competent Authority and Index Card-Microfilm Retrieval
           System
IRS 49.003 Financial Statements File
IRS 49.007 Overseas Compliance Projects System
IRS 49.008 Taxpayer Service Correspondence System
IRS 50.001 Employee Plans/Exempt Organizations Correspondence Con-
           trol Records (Form 5961)
IRS 50.003 Reports of Significant Matters in Technical
IRS 60.001 Assault & Threat Investigation Files
IRS 60.002 Bribery Investigation Files
IRS 60.003 Conduct Investigation Files
IRS 60.004 Disclosure Investigation Files
IRS 60.005 Enrollee Applicant Investigation Files
IRS 60.006 Enrollee Charge Investigation Files
IRS 60.007 Miscellaneous Information File
IRS 60.008 Security, Background, and Character Investigation Files
IRS 60.009 Special Inquiry Investigation Files
IRS 60.010 Tort Investigation Files
IRS 70.001 Individual Income Tax Returns, Statistics of Income
IRS 90.001 Chief Counsel Criminal Tax Case Files
IRS 90.002 Chief Counsel Disclosure Litigation Division Case Files
IRS 90.003 Chief Counsel General Administrative Systems
IRS 90.004 Chief Counsel General Legal Services Case Files
IRS 90.005 Chief Counsel General Litigation Case Files
IRS 90.006 Chief Counsel Interpretive Division and Employee Plans and
           Exempt Organizations Division and Associate Chief Counsel
           (Technical and International) Case Files

IRS 90.007 Chief Counsel Legislation and Regulations Division, Employee
Plans and Exempt Organizations Division, and Associate Chief
Counsel (Technical and International) Correspondence and
Private Bill Files
IRS 90.009 Chief Counsel Tax Litigation Case Files
IRS 90.010 Digest Room Files Containing Briefs, Legal Opinions and
Digests of Documents Generated Internally or by the Depart-
ment of Justice Relating to the Administration of the Revenue
Laws
IRS 90.011 Employee Recruiting Files Maintained by the Operations
Division
IRS 90.013 Legal Case Files of the Chief Counsel, Deputy Chief Counsels
(Policy and Programs) and (Management and Operations),
Associate Chief Counsels [(Litigation) and (Technical)]
IRS 90.014 Management Files Maintained by Operations Division and the
Deputy Chief Counsel (Management and Operations) other than
the Office of Personnel Management's Official Personnel Files
IRS 90.015 Reference Records of the Library in the Office of Chief
Counsel
IRS 90.016 Reports and Information Retrieval Activity Computer and
Microfilm Records
IRS 90.017 Correspondence Control and Records, Associate Chief Counsel
(Technical and International)

Should anyone wish to pursue a Privacy Act access request by naming one
of the systems rather than use the Freedom of Information Act by naming a
specific document wanted, they would first have to review the notices of systems of records as they appear in the *Federal Register*.

The most recent publication of the Internal Revenue Service notices was
at 53 FR 6378, March 1, 1988, where the full description of the Service's systems
runs to 180 pages of text. As the notices may be revised or added to, any serious
researcher must also refer to indices to locate the latest information. Persons
interested in earlier versions of the notices may research older *Federal Registers*
or may ask the Service to provide them with a copy of IRM 1272 Exhibit
(15)00-2, List of Systems of Records. This list identifies all systems of records,
past or present, and categorizes them as current, superseded, or obsolete. Current systems are those presently in existence. Superseded systems are those
which no longer exist as systems by virtue of having been combined with
another system but whose contents remain. Obsolete systems are those which
no longer exist because their records have been destroyed or they have been
determined not to be subject to the Privacy Act.

A requester should never assume that he may avoid necessary research
simply by requesting all records in all the published systems. Such a practice
is contrary to the intent of Privacy Act that the requester choose those systems
which pertain to him and will be strenuously resisted by the Service. Moreover,
Disclosure personnel are likely to assume that such a requester is a tax protester
or some sort of troublemaker totally undeserving of any cooperation.

The search to identify systems of records suitable to your needs is not as difficult as it would seem; it is not really necessary to review all 126 notices. Each system has an identifying number. The first two digits of that number represent the function which has responsibility for that system. The taxpayer who is seeking to unravel a problem with the Service need only know which function he is involved with and then review only that function's systems to make his choice. The systems are arranged in numerical order, so that related systems are published in sequence.

Series 00 General Items

There are only two systems in Series 00, both covering correspondence. The first is intended for nonexempt material, whereas the second covers correspondence related to exempt investigatory matters. These systems were intended to cover correspondence which is not specifically identified as part of some other system. Remember, the Service does not have centralized files or controls and these systems may be located anywhere. Only you know which office has been involved with your correspondence. Obviously, your own letters and the Service's responses are of little interest to you. These systems may also include documentation on how your communications were processed and could be useful in determining the extent of the effort made to resolve your problems.

Series 10 Public Affairs

There are two Public Affairs systems. They cover biographical data about IRS employees and news clippings concerning tax matters. They are generally not of interest to taxpayers.

Series 21 Tax Administration Advisors Resources File

The organization which maintains this system offers assistance to foreign tax administrations and state governments. The systems relate to Service employees and other officials and tax professionals. It is of no interest to taxpayers.

Series 22 Returns and Information Processing

There are 12 systems in this category. They relate to the processing of returns, payments, and information documents. Some of these systems may be helpful to taxpayers who have problems concerning lost documents, misapplied payments, erroneous data entries, undelivered refund checks, and similar bookkeeping matters.

Series 24 Computer Services

There are five systems in this series, all of which are related to the processing of returns and other tax documents in the service centers. Two of them can be very important to taxpayers.

System 24.030, Individual Master File, or IMF, is the major computerized system for processing and recording information on taxpayers. Think of the IMF as a giant string of social security numbers, one for each taxpayer in America, maintained in numerical order. Attached to each social security number is an entity section containing the taxpayer's name, address, and data concerning the Service's expectations of the type of return which should be filed. Each entity section is followed by tax modules, one for each tax period. Each of these modules contains postings for actions relevant to that account, such as return filed, refund mailed, tax paid, credit transferred, balance due, and interest or penalty computed, and literally hundreds of other possible transactions. The IMF is the heart of all tax processing; almost everything that the Service does flows in or out of the IMF.

The IMF is maintained in a series of codes that are compatible with data-processing requirements. In order to make the information of the IMF available to taxpayers in a comprehensible form, as required by the Privacy Act, the Service issues a Privacy Act transcript which restates the account in plain language. Anyone who has any serious problem with the Service should, at the very least, obtain a Privacy Act transcript in order to learn what entries are posted to his account.

A further value of the IMF is that entries generally are preceded by what is referred to as a Document Locator Number, or DLN. The DLN identifies the event or the document, which may be either another computer action or a paper document, which initiated the transaction posted to the account. The DLN maintains what is referred to as the audit trail, which permits you to track transactions to their origin. Once you have a DLN for a transaction which interests you, you have everything that you need to make a valid Freedom of Information request for that document.

The second system in this series which is of interest is 24.070, the Debtor Master File. This system relates to taxpayers who have delinquent obligations to a federal or state agency. It contains the amount owed and the agency to which owed. If you have a problem concerning money withheld from your refund check, this may be the place to look for information.

Series 26 Collection

The Collection Division has responsibility for the enforced collection of delinquent taxes and securing delinquent returns. There are 14 systems in this series, but most of them relate closely to Collection's main system, 26.019, TDA (Taxpayer Delinquent Accounts). A TDA is a statement issued to a revenue officer telling him how much money you owe and that it is time to go get it. Revenue officers have a variety of tools designed to assist them in their tasks and a great deal of imagination in how to apply them. Their efforts are sometimes painful to the taxpayer and sometimes embarrassing to the Service. I spent many years as a revenue officer, and the best advice I can give you is pay the man! When making a request for records from this system, remember that it will contain details of how the collection process operates, but it is not a good source for information on why you owe the tax or how it was computed.

Traditionally, such questions are not the concern of the Collection Division.

The second major system operated by the Collection Division is 26.020, TDI (Taxpayer Delinquency Investigations). A TDI is a notice to the revenue officer that the Individual Master File expects a tax return from you and has not yet received it. The revenue officer's function in this case is to locate you, determine whether a return is actually due, and secure it from you. The TDI file will relate the revenue officer's efforts to perform these duties, but it will generally not say anything about why a filed return may not have posted to the master file.

The source of a taxpayer's problem is unlikely to be found in the TDA or TDI files because if such information were known, those files would not remain open. Lost payments and lost returns can best be sought in Series 22 or Series 24 systems.

Series 30 Resources Management

This series has only two systems—30.003, Requests for Printed Tax Materials, and 30.004, Security Violations. The first system deals with persons who request printed materials and is basically a mailing list. The second system deals with Service employees and other persons having business on Service premises. These systems are of no interest to taxpayers.

Series 32 Financial Operations

This series has two systems which serve IRS employees who have travel expenses or other forms of reimbursements. These systems are of no interest to taxpayers.

Series 34 Facilities Management

This series has nine systems, all of which deal with Service employees and other persons closely related to the Service's housekeeping functions, safety, security, accident reports, and control of property. These systems are of no interest to taxpayers.

Series 36 Personnel

This series has six systems, all of which deal with Service employees in regard to various personnel matters. These systems are of no interest to taxpayers.

Series 37 Office of Director of Practice

This series has 11 systems. The director of Practice is responsible for maintaining the discipline of persons who practice before the Internal Revenue Service, including attorneys, certified public accountants, and enrolled agents. These systems are of no interest to other persons.

Series 38 General Training Records

This series contains a single system which deals with Service employees and other persons who have been involved in Service training programs. It is of no interest to taxpayers.

Series 42 Examination

The Examination Division has responsibility for auditing taxpayers' returns and proposing additional assessments, interest, and penalties. This series has 11 systems. With the exception of 42.014, which deals only with the returns of Service employees, all the systems in this series are potentially of interest to taxpayers under examination. Some of the system names assigned by the Examination Division are somewhat misleading since they seem to imply that they are merely control or scheduling devices when in fact they contain extensive taxpayer information.

I would suggest that a taxpayer having difficulty with the Examination Division request all the Series 42 systems except 42.014, possibly 42.017, International Enforcement Program Files, and 42.027, Data on Foreign Corporations.

Series 44 Appeals

The Appellate Division receives cases on appeal from the Examination Division. Two of the four systems in this series—44.001, Appeals Case Files, and 44.003, Appeals Case Data—would be of interest to taxpayers having cases in appeal status.

Series 46 Criminal Investigation

There are nine systems in the Criminal Investigation System. Systems 46.003, Confidential Informants; 46.011, Land Trust Files; 46.015, Relocated Witnesses; and 46.016, Secret Service Details, are specialized systems not of general interest to taxpayers. The other five systems would be of interest to any taxpayer under investigation by the division.

Series 48 Office of Disclosure

This series contains two systems. System 48.001, Disclosure Records, would be of interest to any taxpayer having concern about disclosure matters, including how his requests for records access have been processed. System 48.008, Defunct Special Services Staff File Being Retained Because of Congressional Directive, is not a Disclosure file at all. It is one of the most sensitive and most dangerous files maintained by the Service and would be of considerable interest to a narrow class of taxpayers. This file is discussed separately later in this chapter.

Series 49 International

This series includes five systems. The Assistant Commissioner (International) is responsible for tax administration involving U.S. taxpayers with interests outside the United States and foreign taxpayers with tax interests inside the United States. All of these systems would be of interest to those taxpayers who fall within those definitions and those who are aware that they have involvement with the Assistant Commissioner (International). None of these systems would be of any interest to the vast majority of taxpayers who are not involved with any international issues.

Series 50 Employee Plans & Exempt Organizations

This series consists of two systems which would be of moderate interest to the very small number of persons who have become involved with employee-plan or exempt-organization matters in an individual capacity. They are of no interest to the vast majority of taxpayers.

Series 60 Inspection

The Assistant Commissioner (Inspection) serves as the internal security officer of the Service. For the most part, his activities relate only to former, current, and prospective employees of the Service, other government employees, contractors, and tax practitioners, to whom 6 of the 10 systems in this series relate. Four systems, however, are likely to contain information on taxpayers: 60.001, Assault and Threat Investigation Files; 60.002, Bribery Investigation Files; 60.007, Miscellaneous Information File; and 60.009, Special Inquiry Investigation Files. System 60.001 is deceiving; although it would appear to relate to a small group of taxpayers, it has widespread ramifications for everyone. It is discussed in detail later in this chapter.

Series 70 Statistics of Income

This series includes only one system. Its overall thrust is statistical, and it is published only because the techniques and processes involved occasionally result in some records retaining an individual identity while in use. This system is of no interest to taxpayers.

Series 90 Office of Chief Counsel

This series contains 14 systems, all but 2 of which would be of interest to those taxpayers who are involved with Chief Counsel. Chief Counsel files deal extensively with matters already in litigation or with taxpayers who have sought legal opinions or otherwise approached Counsel. These systems are unlikely to be of interest to the general taxpayer who does not know himself to be involved with Counsel. Since many of the matters dealt with by Counsel would already involve a taxpayer's attorney, taxpayers are not advised to request access to these systems acting on their own behalf. Many of the matters involving Counsel originated in other functions. It is advisable that records be accessed before they are referred to Counsel since other functions are generally more cooperative and many items are released which would be denied by Counsel.

This analysis shows that of the 126 systems in use by the Internal Revenue Service, fewer than half are likely to be of any interest to any taxpayer. Those 60 or so systems which are of potential interest to the public are maintained by 10 different functions. It is very unlikely that any taxpayer would at any one time be involved with more than one of these functions. Thus, by first focusing in on the function of concern, the taxpayer need never review and choose from more than a dozen systems and frequently need only consider from 2 to 5 different systems. The Privacy Act access approach is therefore a lot simpler than it appears to be, although it cannot compare with the directness of a Freedom of Information Act request for those who know what to ask for. It should always be noted, however, that virtually all of the systems identified as being of interest to taxpayers are exempt from the access requirement and will be searched for records only if the request also cites the Freedom of Information Act.

The System That Never Was

The overriding interest of the Internal Revenue Service is to operate efficiently. The Service has only a minimal appreciation of privacy considerations and little concern for individual rights in general. Somehow, it assumes that all other considerations will resolve themselves in the face of efficient tax administration.

In 1977, three years after the passage of the Privacy Act of 1974, the Service proposed the implementation of a billion-dollar computer system designed to replace its aging and outdated equipment and serve as the major tool for tax administration for the next two or three decades. The new system would have been the largest data-processing project ever undertaken by the federal government and would have contained more information on individual citizens than had ever been possessed by any single federal agency. The basic concept involved the replacement and expansion of the existing systems of records into a centralized data bank which could be instantaneously accessed by some 48,300 employees throughout the country by use of 8,300 terminals.

The Service's plans, written budgetary submissions, and testimony before Congress were vague about the controls and protections to be built into the system. There is little wonder that they should be vague, for the concept of controls is inherently incompatible with the objective of efficient operation. Protections for the taxpayer mean restrictions upon the agency and its employees. Rules tend to prevent the agency from doing what it wants to do, which is simply to give the public the best possible service.

The Office of Technology Assessment studied the proposed system and reported that it could be seen as posing "a threat to the civil liberties, privacy and due process of taxpayers" and could ultimately result in "surveillance, harassment or political manipulation of files."

Public objections were raised by Representatives Charles A. Vanik, Democrat of Ohio; John E. Moss, Democrat of California; Charles Rose, Democrat of North Carolina; and Senators James Abourezk, Democrat of South Dakota; Birch Bayh, Democrat of Indiana; Charles M. Mathias, Jr., Republican of Maryland; Edmund S. Muskie, Democrat of Maine; Charles H. Percy, Republican of Illinois; and Abraham A. Ribicoff, Democrat of Connecticut.

As a result, the Service's massive leap toward efficiency came to a halt. The Service, however, continues to plan for the future with little awareness of the right to privacy, and individual officials continue to act with little respect for the rights of the public.

The Special Service Staff File

In 1970, I worked as a data-processing systems analyst in the National Office. One of my varied responsibilities was to secure printouts from the Individual Master File for taxpayers whose accounts seemed to indicate some error which might be representative of a systemic problem. These printouts were needed by data-procesing technicians for analysis to ensure that the system was functioning properly.

I would receive lists of social security numbers identifying each account to be transcribed, combine these requests into a single list, transmit the list to the National Computer Center where the Individual Master File was maintained, receive the transcripts, sort them out, and return them to the original requester. Although the requests contained only the taxpayers' social security numbers, the transcripts returned from the computer center included the taxpayers' names.

One office would routinely send a list of 15 or 20 social security numbers every few days. In the course of processing the transcripts, I noticed that many of the taxpayers' names seemed familiar to me. I soon realized that these were names about which I had recently read in the *Washington Post*. I began to be more careful about both my reading and my processing of the transcripts. I found that whenever a name appeared in the *Washington Post* in connection with civil rights or antiwar activities, there was a good likelihood that the name would show up on a transcript a week or two later. After a month or two, it was perfectly obvious to me that someone was performing a surveillance of political activists.

I advised my supervisor of the situation. After making some inquiries, he instructed me to continue providing the transcripts. I was to raise no further objections. The program I had noticed was perfectly proper. The Commissioner knew about it, the Congress knew about it, and the White House knew about it! Later, I visited the secret basement room used by the Special Service staff and observed several persons reading newspapers to identify potential subjects, cutting out articles, and placing them in file folders. These items served as the basis for obtaining transcripts of taxpayers' accounts and initiating tax audits and investigations.

The little that I could see of this operation convinced me that regardless of the level of approval, it seemed an immoral abuse of tax-administration authority for political purposes. But it never occurred to me that there was anything further that I could do about it, so I continued doing my job, serving as the conduit for information between the Individual Master File and the Special Service staff.

In 1972, a disgruntled former FBI agent blew the whistle on the Special Service staff. Once the operation became known to the public, the Commissioner, the Congress, and the White House forgot that they had known all about it.

By 1973, the Special Service staff had been disbanded and was under investigation by Congress. It was revealed that the organization began in response to expressions of concern by several congressional committees that some tax-exempt organizations might have been illegally funneling funds into political activities and that some individuals involved in such activities might not be filing returns or paying taxes.

During the three or four years in which Special Service operated, it accumulated records on about 10,000 individuals and organizations, and apparently attempted to prompt investigation of or enforcement action against some of these persons. There was little doubt that the intent of this operation was to create problems for persons who were politically involved. Based upon my own observations and conversations with persons who worked on the staff, this was an extraordinarily ineffective operation which achieved absolutely nothing. The Service is a very efficient organization, but I believe that in the case of the Special Service staff, devotion to efficiency rendered the organization's malevolent efforts useless because the staff's requests for investigations were not factored into the districts' program expectations and local management ignored requests for any activity that would burn up resources without contributing anything to meeting its production quotas.

In 1974, Commissioner Donald Alexander stated before a congressional subcommittee that he intended to take the records on the 10,000 victims of the Special Service staff out on the Mall and burn them in public sight, to be done with this unfortunate blemish on the Service's reputation. The response by Representative Bella Abzug to this eminently wise proposal was "Don't you dare!" It seemed that the subcommittee might someday want to take a further look at the file and did not want the records destroyed. Unfortunately, this well-intentioned remark by Ms. Abzug has contributed to the very problem which she would have wanted to prevent, for the file of the Special Service staff continue to exist to this very day and continue to constitute a threat to all those innocent taxpayers whose records are included therein.

The Special Service staff file was sealed and retained by the Collection Division as long as Ms. Abzug remained in Congress, in the belief that her statement constituted a continuing directive. Once Ms. Abzug left Congress, the Collection Division wrote to her successor on the subcommittee and asked if the file could now be destroyed. The response suggested that these records should first be examined by the archivist to determine if they were of historical significance. The records, however, constituted tax returns and return information which the archivist had no legal authority to examine. If it was assumed that congressional permission was necessary to destroy the file, that permission could not be obtained until the archivist examined the records, and it was illegal to let the archivist examine them, so it became inescapable that the files could never be destroyed.

At this point the Collection Division tired of holding the file. They became concerned that they could not resist the pressure from some enforcement personnel to access the file for information which might be useful in their investigations. The Collection Division therefore transferred the Special Service file to Disclosure, which at that time was believed to be relatively free from Compliance influence. By then, my career had advanced to where I had become chief of the Freedom of Information Branch in Disclosure, and I was given physical possession of the Special Service file, with instructions not to allow any person to access the file for alleged tax-administration purposes. The file was placed in a vault protected by additional locks, and a variety of access records were established to ensure that the Service did not abuse this file, which was held only so that Ms. Abzug or one of her successors might someday continue an investigation which was long ago completed.

As soon as I received the file, I raised objections to its continued maintenance. My concern was prompted by the knowledge that witch-hunts recur throughout history on a regular basis. Someday we may have another unpopular war which results in protests. It is only natural that governments seek to discourage protest. It would seem to me that under such circumstances it is not unlikely that someone will remember the existence of the Special Service file and reason that the same people who were considered activists then might be responsible for whatever protest movement might occur in the future. Thus, so long as the file continues to exist, there is a threat that persons once abused may once again come to the attention of a repressive program.

It was my belief that the continued maintenance of the Special Service file is clearly illegal. Notice 48.008 identifies the system as Defunct Special Service Staff File Being Retained Because of Congressional Directive. The notice further states, "This file is no longer being used by the Internal Revenue Service. The Special Service Staff was abolished August 13, 1973."

The Privacy Act states that each agency shall "maintain in its records only such information about an individual as is relevant and necessary to accomplish a purpose of the agency required to be accomplished by statute or by executive order of the President."

If the Special Service file has not been used by the Service for more than 15 years, how can the file be necessary to accomplish a purpose of the agency? Moreover, the original purposes of the staff were not required by statute or by executive order of the President. How, then, can the continued maintenance of this file be justified? The "Congressional Directive" mentioned in the notice was in reality nothing more than Ms. Abzug's statement that Commissioner Alexander should not burn the records. Could Ms. Abzug ever have imagined that her remarks would cause the Special Service file to live on in per-petuity?

I raised these arguments to the Office of Chief Counsel, but they were re-jected. My instructions were to keep the file under lock and key, and never let anyone use it for any purpose other than as necessary to respond to Freedom of Information Act requests, Privacy Act requests, related litigation, or that long-awaited resumption of a congressional investigation.

Unfortunately, that simple requirement proved to be beyond my capacity. Over the years, half a dozen requests were made by special agents to access the file. On each occasion, I explained the genesis of the file, how it came to be sealed, the commitment against its use, the rationale behind the Privacy Act notice, the effect of the Privacy Act prohibition against the use of unauthorized records. I added that to access the file would be illegal, would dishonor the In-ternal Revenue Service, would violate a Commissioner's commitment to the Congress, and would probably taint the investigation. On each occasion, the special agent backed off. All, that is, except one.

More than ten years after the Special Service file was sealed, I received a call from a special agent seeking access to the file in connection with an in-vestigation he was working. I repeated my usual arguments. The special agent then explained that his was a special situation. He was investigating Taxpayer X, whom I immediately recognized as a Special Service target. His current in-vestigation was inadequate to support prosecution, but there had been another investigation years before. It too was closed without a recommendation for prosecution. However, this earlier investigation involved certain persons who were willing to testify against the taxpayer or to serve as informants. These per-sons were identified in a memorandum which had allegedly been sent to the Special Service staff. The special agent had the old file available, but it did not name these persons. It mentioned the memorandum but did not contain a copy. If a copy of the memorandum had been maintained, the special agent would know the identity of these persons and would have enough evidence to obtain a conviction in the current case. All the special agent wanted was to retrieve a copy of a memorandum which was in the Special Service file but which had somehow not been retained in the Criminal Investigation file.

I told the special agent that no investigation was worth compromising the integrity of the Internal Revenue Service and I would not permit access to the Special Service file under any circumstances. The following day, the special agent's supervisor called and repeated the story. This time I questioned the relevance of a memorandum which was more than ten years old to a current investigation. The supervisor then claimed that the memorandum was much more recent than that and provided a date well after the Special Service staff had ceased to exist and its files had been sealed. I told him that it was absolutely impossible that such a memorandum could be in the file since nothing was ever added after the staff was abolished. The supervisor then claimed that they had not known that the staff was abolished and had continued to add documents to the file long after it was sealed.

In order to satisfy the supervisor, I offered to examine the file myself to verify that the memorandum was not there and inform him of that fact. If the impossible should happen and I located the memorandum somehow inserted into the file of a defunct unit, I stated that I was willing to refer the matter to the Office of the Chief Counsel for a legal opinion on whether such a memorandum was subject to the prohibition against access to the file. The supervisor replied that my examining the file would be inadequate, that only a special agent could examine the file, and that he would send his man down to the National Office armed with credentials and a summons and whatever else was necessary to gain access to the file.

I absolutely refused to permit anyone to enter the vault or to examine any portion of the file. The following day, the supervisor called again. He said he had discussed the matter with his district director, who was very eager to gain a conviction of Taxpayer X and that he did not think that Privacy Act considerations should stand in the way of effective law enforcement.

I again refused to permit access to the file. The supervisor thereupon stated that hereafter his director would deal with my director. I prepared a memorandum on the matter and briefed my director on the incident. My director supported my position and agreed that we could not permit access to the file.

Nothing further happened for several months, and this incident slipped from my mind. Then I had occasion to be away from the office for a week or two. When I returned, I asked the individual who acted in my place if anything unusual had happened in my absence. There was only one unusual incident. One day when my director was also absent from the office, there was a call from the individual who was sitting in for him stating that an assistant commissioner was curious what kind of records were in the Special Service file and wished to see a sample folder, which was then delivered to the front office.

I asked whether we had selected the sample. I was told the assistant commissioner had named a taxpayer whose folder he wanted to see as representative of the general content of the file, that of Taxpayer X. It was kept about an hour, certainly long enough to copy, and then returned. Less than a year later I read in the newspaper that Taxpayer X had been convicted of tax fraud.

I do not know that the Special Service file was breached. I do know, however, that if my name had appeared in the *Washington Post* between 1969 and 1973 and I had been in any way involved with antiwar or civil rights or some other political activity, I would make a Freedom of Information Act request to determine if there was any mention whatsoever of me in the Special Service file. If there was, I would make a Privacy Act request to have the record corrected by the total deletion of all information. If it was not done, I would consider the matter worth litigating. And if I had to go that far, I would feel that I might just as well ask the court to order the Service to destroy the other 9,999 records in the Special Service file.

The Potentially Dangerous Taxpayer

The Internal Revenue Service is intensely concerned with the problem of taxpayers who may violently attack Service personnel. In fact, one may say that the Service is obsessed with the problem. The Service has therefore established a Potentially Dangerous Taxpayer System. Unfortunately, the Potentially Dangerous Taxpayer System is potentially dangerous to the taxpayer. I believe that this system constitutes a serious threat to the civil liberties of all American taxpayers. This system is not a relic from the days of the Watergate scandals like the Special Service staff. This system is not an imaginative proposal which may never become operational. This system exists and operates today. Despite the protections of the Freedom of Information Act and the Privacy Act of 1974, no one seems to have noticed its existence. The Service has established the Potentially Dangerous Taxpayer System in a manner which renders it transparent, and its victims never know that they are victims.

If the notice for the Service's ubiquitous Individual Master File, 24.030 is examined, found buried in the description of Categories of Records in the System is the sentence "Recorded here are tax transactions such as tax amount, additions, abatements of tax payments, interest and like type transactions recorded relative to each tax module, power of attorney authorization transactions, and a code identifying taxpayers who threatened or assaulted IRS employees."

Despite the numbing effect of that sentence, keep in mind the last phrase "a code identifying taxpayers who threatened or assaulted IRS employees," and at the same time try to remember that the Individual Master File is the central system through which flows almost every operation involved in tax administration.

Now let us look at Inspection's notice for System 60.001, Assault and Threat Investigation Files. The entry for Categories of Individuals Covered by the System reads:

> Individuals attempting to interfere with the administration of Internal Revenue laws through threats, assaults or forcible interference of any officer or employee while discharging the official duties of his position, or individuals classified as potentially dangerous taxpayers, based on verifiable evidence or information that fit the following criteria: (1) taxpayers who physically assault an employee; (2) taxpayers who have on hand a deadly or dangerous weapon when meeting an employee and it is apparent their purpose is to intimidate the employee; (3) taxpayers who make specific threats to do bodily harm to an employee; (4) taxpayers who use animals to threaten or intimidate an employee; (5) taxpayers who have committed the acts set forth in any of the above criteria (1) through (4), but whose acts have been directed against employees of other governmental agencies at Federal, state, county, or local levels; and (6) taxpayers who are not classifiable as potentially dangerous through application of the above criteria (1) through (5), but who have demonstrated a clear propensity toward violence through acts of violent behavior to a serious and extreme degree within the five (5) year period immediately preceding the time of classification as potentially dangerous.

Notice how this description flows from persons who have actually done something to Internal Revenue Service employees to persons who have done something in regard to any other level of government to persons who have done anything at all in regard to any situation at all, until ultimately it includes persons who have "demonstrated a clear propensity" or who are simply "potentially dangerous."

This description, placed in a notice which is unlikely to be read by most taxpayers, would prompt some further inquiry. Since this is an Inspection system, we would expect to find instructions in Part IX of the *Internal Revenue Manual*, which pertains to Inspection. But Inspection went further than that. On June 5, 1985, they issued the instruction as Manual Supplement (10)G-34, cross-referenced to the Examination, Collection, Taxpayer Service, Employee Plans and Exempt Organizations, Appeals, and Criminal Investigation divisions, so that virtually every function having any face-to-face contact with a taxpayer is involved in the Potentially Dangerous Taxpayer System.

To make the universal application of this system even more apparent, the manual supplement explains that the Commissioner assigned responsibility for developing the system to Inspection as part of the IRS Strategic Plan, on May 9, 1984. The system therefore is not a fluke stemming from the frenzied excesses of overzealous employees; it is the considered, approved, and authorized approach to law enforcement adopted by the Commissioner of the Internal Revenue Service. Nor can it be argued that the system which was adopted went much beyond what was intended, for the implementing instruction, Manual Supplement (10)G-34, was issued over the signature of the Deputy Commissioner.

The Criminal Investigation Division and the Collection Division both provide extensive information in their manual instructions on how the system functions. With regard to who is a potentially dangerous taxpayer, Criminal Investigation tells us in IRM 9142.533 that

> in situations not involving an overt threat or assault but where an employee obtains information which indicates that a group or individual may pose a threat to the safety of IRS employees, the employee should report this information.... There must be documentation of the specific activities of the group or individual that indicate a propensity towards violence that leads to the conclusion that the group or individual poses a threat to the safety of IRS employees. Such terms as "known protester" or "known to be violent" without documentation will not be acceptable. If the information being reported are the names of members of a violence prone group, the basis for knowledge of the membership must be listed.

The Collection Division states in IRM 5145.51 that

> membership in an organized tax resister or protester group/movement which advocates violent resistance may be grounds for input of the potentially dangerous taxpayer code even though the taxpayer has not made a personal assault or threat of assault on a Collection employee. Care must be taken in identifying members of such groups, and the reasons for believing that a person is a violent tax protester or member of a violent tax protest organization should be thoroughly documented. Because of the possibility of misidentification through similarity of names, incorrect information, etc., thorough research must be performed in the identification process.

These instructions make it clear that the "potentially dangerous taxpayer" designation may be applied on the basis of group membership rather than individual behavior. More importantly, a strong linkage is made between the potentially dangerous taxpayer and the despised tax protesters who represent an organized threat to every Service employee.

In IRM 9142.52, the Criminal Investigation Division goes even further, stating, "In those instances where the circumstances of a particular situation represent a borderline case in the application of any of the criteria ... the determination should be made in favor of the PDT designation for the protection of Service employees."

It could easily be assumed that all of this is not too important if the sole result of being designated a PDT would be the taxpayer's inclusion in a system of records maintained by Inspection with which few taxpayers ever have any contact. But that is not the sole effect. IRM 9142.52(4) explains:

> Employees will be alerted to the fact that a taxpayer has been designated as potentially dangerous by an indicator which will be reflected on the following records and data bases:
>
> (a) National Computer Center (NCC) Transcripts (except Privacy Act Transcripts)
> (b) Microfilm Replacement System (MRS) Transcripts
> (c) Federal Tax Deposit (FTD) Alerts (Business Master File only)
> (d) Integrated Data Retrieval system (IDRS) Transcripts
> (e) Tax Module (TXMOD)
> (f) Entity Module (ENMOD)
> (g) Taxpayer Delinquent Account (TDA)
> (h) Taxpayer Delinquency Investigation (TDI)
> (i) Audit Information Management System (AIMS), including AIMS Weekly Updates, AIMS Charge-outs (Forms 5546), and AIMS Display (AMDIS)
> (j) Daily Transaction Register

These data bases represent virtually all the processing systems used by the major functions of the Internal Revenue Service, indicating that the potentially dangerous taxpayer designation, once established, permeates the Service's operations. The instruction goes on to say that the symbol "*PDT*" will be prominently displayed on these data bases and the documents which they produce. They might just as well paint *PDT* on your forehead in scarlet letters!

Chief Counsel's Disclosure Litigation Division has issued an opinion that the PDT designation is return information and may be made available to state taxing agencies so that they may benefit from this valuable information. Consequently, the PDT designation, once applied in the Internal Revenue Service, may be passed on to any recipient of return information, like some contagious disease.

Section 6 of Manual Supplement (10)G-34, ominously entitled "Internal Security Information Gathering Initiatives," makes clear that Inspection is not going to await complaints about taxpayer behavior passively. Each regional inspector is to designate an inspector as the Regional Employee Protection

Coordinator, who, among other duties, will establish liaison with other law enforcement agencies and coordinate information-gathering activities on violence-prone tax-protest groups. When the Service uses words like "information gathering initiatives" and "liaison with other law enforcement agencies," they can only be understood to mean the active pursuit of information on persons who have as yet had no contact with the Internal Revenue Service, let alone done anything illegal.

The Inspector's Section 6 duties include "Serving as a clearinghouse for all assault, threat, and violence prone tax protester information which did not result in the initiation of an actual assault/threat case. Relevant information will be forwarded to the Director, Internal Security Division, who will input the information to the Internal Security centralized data base." In other words, reports of incidents which are not determined to warrant any investigation will nevertheless be included in the system. Wouldn't want to overlook anything, correct?

Section 6 goes on to say, "Each Regional Inspector will assure through coordination with the Regional Commissioner, that an Employee Protection Committee is established and that the committee meets at least once each quarter. The committee will consist of the Regional Employee Protection Coordinator and, at a minimum, representatives from the Examination, Collection and Criminal Investigation Divisions. The committee will serve as a forum for the purpose of discussing information relevant to employee protection." It must be comforting for employees to know that an employee protection committee is functioning. To taxpayers having an historical perspective, the employee protection committees may be reminiscent of the public safety committees formed during the days of terror following the French Revolution. Hopefully, there will be no funds in the budget for the purchase of a guillotine!

Once a taxpayer has been designated as potentially dangerous, how long will such a designation last? The notice for System 60.001 states that events which transpired five years before classification may be taken into consideration in initially establishing the designation. The manual instructions state that once the designation is made, it is to be reviewed after five years. Presumably, it need not be removed at the first review. Some of the documents imprinted with the designation may have lives which far exceed its removal from the system itself. Consequently, we must consider this designation something which will last for five or ten or more years. Had a potentially dangerous taxpayer fulfilled his potential and actually attacked someone, he would probably be convicted, punished, released and rehabilitated long before the PDT designation is removed from his tax records.

The purpose of having such a system is to contribute to the protection of Service personnel. IRM 5145.51 explains that "the records of past threats and assaults show that most incidents occur without any prior warning. However, prior knowledge that a taxpayer has, in the past, threatened to assault or actually assaulted a Collection employee can be useful in preventing future incidents."

But how? The only suggestion the Collection Division makes is that revenue officers, who carry no weapons, may secure an armed escort when making visits to potentially dangerous taxpayers.

Special agents, who are armed, are told to coordinate potentially dangerous taxpayers' office visits with Internal Security personnel and to consider asking the PDT if he is armed or other safety-related questions.

Frankly, I doubt if there is anyone in the Service or any other law enforcement agency who is qualified to identify persons who are potentially dangerous. I object to the concept that persons who have been convicted of no crime, who are not even suspected of taking any overt action, can be fairly designated as potentially dangerous on the basis of some event or statement or association which may have had no lasting significance. I consider it ridiculous to assume that designating people as potentially dangerous can in any way contribute to a reduction in violence. I believe that such a designation creates the expectation of violence, which is likely to trigger a confrontation that may grow into a self-fulfilling prophecy. Law enforcement personnel cannot effectively carry out their duties, which require that they respect the rights of those they know to be guilty, if they begin with a belief that the taxpayer is potentially dangerous.

I believe that among the thousands of Service employees who encounter records prominently designated "*PDT*," there will be those who will treat these people differently, unfairly, or illegally. Human nature being what it is, the Potentially Dangerous Taxpayer System would seem far more likely to do evil than to accomplish any good.

The bottom line, however, is this. The system has been successfully disguised to withhold knowledge of its existence from the public or make it appear innocuous. The systems in which it resides are primarily exempt from Privacy Act access. The PDT indicator does not appear on Privacy Act transcripts. It can reasonably be assumed that Freedom of Information Act requests for records will not obtain the release of any information alerting any taxpayer to the existence of the PDT designation on his records. I have no way of knowing whether I have been designated a PDT; surely, you will never know whether you are on the list. Nor will you ever know what effect the designation will have on your relationship with the Service or with your state taxing agency.

There is no opportunity for you to confront your accuser because there is no accusation; there is merely a designation. You cannot protest, you cannot protect yourself, you cannot litigate the issue. You can only rely on the integrity of the Service and the goodwill of its employees.

I cannot even recommend that you dig for the information through Freedom of Information Act requests or that you seek to reverse a possible PDT designation through a Privacy Act request to amend records unless you are willing to litigate the issue without knowing whether it really is your personal problem.

If all of this gives you a sense of déjà vu, it is because Congress once determined that it was wrong for an agency to gather information about people, to make adverse determinations based upon that information, to record the information, and to share it with other agencies without the subjects of that information having any opportunity to know what was happening, to question the practice, and to challenge the results. Congress passed the Privacy Act of 1974 in order to prohibit such practices. But neither Congress nor the people have been sufficiently interested to make the act work. I find that very sad. And just a little frightening.

Chapter Fourteen

The Cost of Making a Request

The cost of making Freedom of Information Act and Privacy Act requests must be considered in three ways. First we consider the cost of the entire program to the Internal Revenue Service. Then we consider the portion of such cost borne by the requesters rather than the agency. Finally we consider what the cost of a typical individual request might be to that requester and how such cost is computed.

The Cost of the Program

There exists in the Internal Revenue Service a general assumption that the cost of performing FOIA services is onerous to the agency. Almost any FOIA activity will be resisted because it is believed that the Service cannot afford to perform it and that the cost involved will result in a major reduction in the agency's ability to administer the tax law and a loss of important services to the taxpayer.

Three factors seem to contribute to the existence of this almost universal assumption. The first is that no Congress has ever provided any funds for carrying out FOIA or Privacy Act operations; these items have never appeared upon any Service budget as separate and identifiable line items.

The second factor is that when fees for performing FOIA services are collected, they are deposited to the government's General Fund and are not reimbursable to the agency performing the work. Thus, insofar as the Service is concerned, all Freedom of Information Act and Privacy Act activities represent a total loss to the agency and a reduction in tax-administration capabilities, regardless of any payment the requester may make. This money is never credited back to the agency.

The third and major factor is that most Service managers think in terms of the 6:1 ratio between expending Examination funds and collecting tax dollars.

When these three factors are combined, they produce an argument that no money is provided with which to perform FOIA services and the fees collected cannot be used to offset the costs; therefore, FOIA operations are supported by withdrawing funds from other operations. The major available pool of money is that budgeted for the examination of tax returns. Every dollar spent on the FOIA program reduces the number of tax returns which may be examined and results in a loss of six dollars in tax. Consequently, the FOIA program is seen as an expensive operation which cannot be justified as providing the general public any worthwhile service but which detracts from the Service's limited ability to meet its legitimate objectives. Not unreasonably, the more dedicated a manager is to the public-service ethic, the more resentful he may become to responding to FOIA requests. The FOIA program is seen simply as wasteful and as interfering with the Service's single-minded dedication to increasing efficiency.

It is believed that since Congress engineered the circumstances in which FOIA operations are unfunded and unreimbursed, Congress could not seriously have intended that they would be performed. To Examination Division managers who live their lives in accordance with the demand that every dollar of resources be justified by appropriate accomplishments raising adequate additional revenue, these are very powerful and convincing arguments. And to the extent that quotas for production exist, time devoted to disclosure matters is not available for helping to fill return-examination programs and schedules.

In reality, statistics maintained over many years show that the Freedom of Information program and its costs are rather minimal. In 1986, the total participation time for technical and professional employees in servicing FOIA requests was 128,786 staff hours. Clerical and administrative support added 48,701 staff hours. These figures represent an average use of technical time which does not exceed a single staff year in each district office.

Based upon the average costs of the type of personnel involved, including factors for physical overhead and supplies, the total cost of the FOIA program for 1986 was $3,452,984. Even if we were to apply the highly questionable 6:1 ratio, the loss in anticipated income resulting from this program would not exceed $20 million. The statistics for 1986 are reasonably consistent with the Service's experience over the past decade.

The total cost of operating the Internal Revenue Service in 1986 was $3,841,983,050. The FOIA expenditure represented less than 0.1 percent of that total. To simplify things, I used to round the cost figures and tell people that the cost of the FOIA program was very close to zero percent of our budget.

Examinations of returns in 1986 resulted in assessing tax and penalties amounting to close to $20 billion. If we accepted that all FOIA efforts could have been applied to the examination of returns and would have produced an additional $20 million in revenue, that too would have represented only a 0.1 percent increase in the total revenue.

Despite these figures, the Freedom of Information program was viewed and continues to be viewed as an expensive and wasteful activity which should be curtailed in any way possible. No rational argument was ever able to overcome the emotional commitment to the doctrine that the Service could not afford the cost of the FOIA program, which was apparently based upon the subconscious determination that a program which is unwanted always costs too much and even the most minimal expense represented far more than it was worth.

There exist two further assumptions worthy of note. The first is a common belief among Service managers that the Freedom of Information Act has caused a hemorrhaging of operational information which has made it more difficult and more expensive to operate tax-administration programs. It is assumed that the act promotes interference by uncooperative taxpayers, that a knowledge of Service procedures makes them less effective, that the spread of information somehow contributes to taxpayer lawlessness, and that expensive programs are necessary to overcome these problems. Therefore, the actual cost of FOIA programs is just the tip of the iceberg, and in reality the FOIA causes an immense loss of effectiveness. These managers believe they can best serve the public when as much secrecy as possible is maintained and that the public must pay an awesome price in a loss of effective government in return for the information it receives. In espousing such beliefs, Service managers are no different than many other professionals, including doctors, lawyers, and educators, all of whom generally believe that they would not be able to serve the public as well as they do if the public understood how they practiced their professions.

The second assumption, held by many FOIA advocates but totally unaccepted within the Service, is that the release of information contributes to the effectiveness of government by eliminating undesirable practices and programs, promoting public understanding and involvement, and generating helpful comparisons, proposals, and initiatives. These advocates believe that the cost of administering the FOIA is a small price to pay for the tremendous benefits which will result and which will ultimately more than pay for the program.

Although I spent many years in an excellent position from which to see either of these results take place, I have seen no indication that they are anything more than theories unsupported by an actual experience. The functioning of the Service has not been hampered by the FOIA, and there is no secret cost lurking behind the minimal expense of administering the act. Nor could I identify any savings in agency operations which resulted from the application of the act.

In reality, the Service stands immutable before the Freedom of Information Act, having successfully withheld, delayed, or diminished the flow of information to guarantee that neither good, bad, nor indifferent results will ever occur.

The true cost of the FOIA program has been neither increased by the evil effects of releasing information nor diminished by the benefits of an informed public.

The Public's Share of the Cost

In 1986, the Service collected $154,646.47 in fees for releasing records pursuant to the Freedom of Information Act. Since the total cost of performing these services was $3,452,984, the government lost about $3,298,357 on the operation. In other words, reimbursement amounted to only $1 for every $22 spent.

Such figures are misleading, however. The public need only pay for the information which is released, whereas the costs of the program consist primarily of the efforts involved in withholding information which is requested. A more liberal release policy would drastically reduce the cost of the program while at the same time increasing the payments received from the public. The average request which resulted in the release of any substantial amount of records in 1986 cost the requester about $30.00.

Congress has long been concerned that the application of excessive fees might be discouraging the public from making requests for information. Neither the total amount collected nor the average cost per successful request would seem to support the assumption that the fees demanded by the Service were sufficient to discourage serious requesters. Consider that while the average request which obtained substantial records resulted in fees of about $30.00, the average additional tax and penalty assessed for each return examined by a Revenue Agent in 1986 was $14,051. Although these figures might not offer a genuinely statistically valid comparison, they would seem to be adequate to illustrate that most taxpayers seeking access to records concerning their tax affairs were getting enough for their money not to be seriously deterred by the fees involved.

For the most part, the Service assessed fees for FOIA cases fairly and reasonably. Unfortunately, there have been a few cases in field offices in which requests seem to have been intentionally interpreted to be more extensive than necessary to build up fees which the requester could not or would not pay. In one case, several district offices refused to process requests because there was an extensive bill outstanding against the requester in another district. The requester appealed to National Office, claiming that he could not possibly have a large balance outstanding for unpaid FOIA services. Upon inquiry with the original field office, we were told that they could no longer locate records which would document the compilation of the fees and they would prefer to drop the charge rather than attempt to recompute or justify it.

Requesters being confronted by unexpectedly large fees should telephone the disclosure officer to ask for an explanation of how the fees were arrived at, what could be done to reduce the costs involved, and how the request might be reformulated to minimize the costs, to both the government and the requester. The more the disclosure officer knows about what you really want and why you want it, the more likely he will be to be able to suggest ways to minimize your costs.

Computing a Requester's Fees

Requesters are generally responsible for payment of the fees resulting from their requests whenever such requests result in records being released. The fees are based upon the number of photocopies made and the length of time devoted to searching for the records.

The fee for photocopies is $.15 per page, assuming that pages are not more than $8\frac{1}{2}'' \times 14''$. The fees for larger copies are computed on a basis of $.15 for each 119 square inches or fraction thereof unless the copies are produced on equipment known to have an actual cost exceeding that rate. Copies of photographs, films, tapes, disks, and other materials are charged at the actual cost of reproduction.

Copying fees are charged at the same rates, whether the copies are made specifically in response to requests, drawn from existing stocks, or consist of surplus printed materials.

Copying fees may frequently be avoided by requesting to inspect the existing materials rather than obtain copies. Upon inspection, the requester may identify whatever portion of the materials he wishes copied on the basis of his interests. However, copying fees will be charged if it is necessary to produce copies to permit inspection, as when deletions of exempt portions preclude the inspection of originals, the storage media does not provide for visual inspection, or special equipment needed to permit inspection is not available at the site.

It is advisable that any proposed inspection be carefully discussed with the disclosure officer before being formally requested, as there may be unforeseen problems involved, the anticipated savings may not be realized, or special circumstances may exist. A variety of approaches to copying and inspection problems are possible. For instance, arrangements have been made to permit requesters to view training films at an IRS facility. Records have been shipped to local offices for inspection closer to the requester's home. At times requests for on-site inspection have resulted in copies being sent to the requester without charge because the inspection visit would have been inconvenient to the Service.

The manual provides that records may be released to a private contractor for copying, with the requester being charged only whatever fees are actually due to the contractor. Preferably, the requester would make his own arrangements with an establishment of his choice and make direct payment without the Service being involved beyond delivering the records to the contractor. Such arrangements could drastically reduce copying costs for extensive records or could provide for meeting the requester's special needs, such as having the records reproduced on microfilm, enlarged, reduced, or bound.

Shipping costs necessary to permit inspection or copying are billed at the actual cost involved.

Search fees were computed at a rate of $10 for each hour or fraction of an hour through the end of 1986. In 1987, the fee was raised to the current rate of $17 an hour. Search time includes planning and managing the search, preparing memorandums or making phone calls to the offices from which the records must be retrieved, preparing transmittal memorandums, reporting on the results of the search, and restoring documents to their proper place in the file.

The term *search* should be understood to mean records location, identification, retrieval, and filing costs. Some requesters have attempted to claim that there should be no search fees for retrieving records whose location is known, since search is necessary only when the records are misplaced. Such arguments have been firmly rejected.

Search costs are applicable to the efforts necessary to identify the records as subject to the request and may include the need to search for the requested information within a record. However, search does not include any time spent to determine if the records should be released or should be considered subject to the Freedom of Information Act.

Requesters may be charged when a search establishes that requested records do not exist or when the requesters have insisted upon a search against a disclosure officer's advice that such search would be fruitless. There is no charge for searches which fail to produce existing records, nor are there charges for inordinate search efforts resulting from misfiled records or otherwise attributable to causes which should not be considered the requester's responsibility.

In at least one instance known to me, unsympathetic field personnel intentionally conducted a wild-goose chase, looking for requested records in the most unlikely place before ultimately finding them to build up the requester's costs to a point where he could not afford to pay for the records.

Fees for the use of computers and related data-processing equipment are based upon actual costs to the Service, whether such operations may be characterized as searches, runs, matches, analyses, tape copying, or other terms.

Despite the extent and variety of activities which may be charged under the concept of records search, the fact remains that most Freedom of Information Act requests involve searches of not more than one or two hours. More extensive searches are usually the result of requests which include a large number of records which require individual searches.

The application of copying and search fees was drastically altered by the Freedom of Information Reform Act of 1986, which created several categories of requests, including Commercial Uses, Educational and Noncommercial Scientific Institutions, News Media, and all others. Each of these requests or requesters is now subject to special rules, some of which are designed to provide Freedom of Information Act services with reduced charges or no charges, while others are expected to carry the burden of full costs.

Commercial Uses

Whenever records are requested for a commercial use, the request is subject to the full charges for search and duplication. In addition, there is a charge for the review of the records to determine if they are required to be released. The review charge has been established at $21 per hour since it is assumed that review will require the services of higher-graded personnel than are needed for records search. Records requested for a commercial use will cost significantly more than records requested for some other purpose.

It is important to realize that this category applies to the purpose for the request and not the identity of the requester. The statute specifies a commercial *use*, not a commercial user. A business may be requesting records without intending to put them to a commercial use, that is, without expecting to employ them in a profit-making manner. This may prove to be a difficult determination, especially when the records are requested by an attorney acting on behalf of some other party. Consequently, it is necessary for the requester to state the nature of his request and in some cases elucidate the purpose for which the request is made.

The danger arises that in evaluating the intentions of the requester on the basis of identity, the nature of the records requested, the stated purpose, and whatever other insight the disclosure officer may bring to bear on the matter, disputes concerning fees may develop which could delay the response and thereby effectively withhold the records. Persons making requests which give the appearance of relating to commercial uses, such as those writing on business letterheads, who believe their requests should not be subject to the review charges are advised to present careful documentation of their intentions in order to justify another fee category.

The review charges are applicable only to the initial examination of a document to determine whether it must be disclosed or to withhold any portions exempt from disclosure. In other words, the requester must pay for the cost of the editing necessary to permit the release of the segregable portions of a document. Consistent editing of a complicated legal document can be a very time-consuming and expensive process. Requesters should not expect the review charges to come cheap. However, if the document has been previously released or the editing has been done for a prior requester, the charge cannot be applied to subsequent requesters.

The Service likes to charge the same fee to everyone making a request for the same service, out of a sense of fair play. For instance, when multiple requests for the same document were received, everyone was charged the search fee, despite the fact that only one search had been performed. Requesters concerned about substantial review costs may wish to inquire whether the document has previously been released and thereby avoid further review charges. In some cases, it may be prudent to delay making a request until someone else has obtained the document.

When reviewer costs have applied to the initial request for a document, they cannot again be applied at the appeal level. For instance, if you obtain a document from which a portion has been withheld at your expense and your appeal results in a further release necessitating a revised editing, you cannot be charged for the additional review. Nor can you be charged for any costs resulting from the resolution of issues of law or policy.

The Service frequently requires that proposed releases of documents be reviewed by various functions having tangential interests in the documents or by excessive layers of management prior to approval of a response. The review costs should only apply to the efforts of the persons who actually prepared the document for release and not to subsequent reviewers who are primarily engaged in establishing a management consensus in the proposed release by holding hands, stroking backs, and gilding lilies.

Institutional Requests

Requests which are not made for a commercial use and are made by educational or noncommercial scientific institutions whose purpose is scholarly or scientific research or are made by a representative of the news media are not subject to charges for search costs. Such requesters may be charged only for the reproduction of the records released; however, there is to be no charge for the first 100 pages released. The news media enjoy a further advantage. The Service has traditionally waived all fees for news media requests, which are considered to be in the public interest.

To be eligible for the statutorily established fee advantages, the request must establish that it is made by an eligible institution or by the news media.

Other Requests

"Other" requests include all those which are not made for a commercial use and which do not originate from the news media or from the institutional requesters described above. Most requests, including those from taxpayers seeking access to their own investigatory records, fall into the Other Request category.

These requests are subject to fees for search costs and copying costs, but those costs are limited to searches which exceed two hours and to reproduction which exceeds 100 pages. Every requester is therefore entitled to two hours of free search time and 100 pages of free copies.

The very interesting aspect of this provision is that in recent years the average charge to requesters successful in accessing Internal Revenue Service records has been about $30. Two hours of free search at a value of $10 each and 100 pages of copies at a value of $.15 each represent a total value of $35. Therefore, the majority of requests for records serviced by the Service under the 1986 revision to the statute will not result in any cost to the requester or will result in a very minimal charge.

Public-Interest Fee Waivers

The statute provides that documents are to be furnished without any charge or at a reduced charge if disclosure of the information is in the public interest because it is likely to contribute significantly to public understanding of the operations or activities of the government and is not primarily in the commercial interest of the requester. In addition to this general principle and the restrictions on fees contained in the statute, the Service has traditionally waived fees when it was considered in the public interest. Requesters must ask for and justify such fee waivers.

A determination to waive fees may be based on the characteristics of the information to be released and the characteristics of the requester.

Factors characteristic of information which could be released without charge include that the information has not been previously released or would not be readily available elsewhere; the information is of current significance; the information is of historical, scientific, or economic significance; the information is of interest to a broad segment of the population; the release of the information could contribute to a public understanding of the function of government or could assist in the accomplishment of the mission of the Service; or the release of the information could reduce government costs by obviating the need for other forms of distribution or reducing the volume of further FOIA requests for the same information.

Characteristics of the requester which could be relevant to a determination to waive fees include recognition as a scholar, researcher, or authority in a field related to the material requested; association with a university, laboratory, or research activity related to the information; membership in relevant professional associations; an established record of publication or dissertation on related subjects; reputation for impartiality appropriate to scholarly, scientific, or journalistic endeavors; capacity for publication, reprinting, or dissemination of the information; capacity for the preservation of the information as in a library, archive, museum, or other publicly accessible depository; and presenting a cogent proposal for utilizing the information in a manner primarily benefiting the general public.

Factors which would tend to indicate that a fee waiver would be inappropriate would include that the information is of limited interest to the public, the requester would be unlikely to disseminate the information because it would be personal to the requester, the information relates to the requester's own affairs, the information is wanted in connection with an administrative or judicial proceeding involving the requester, the information appears wanted for a personal purpose such as a hobby or genealogical research, the information is to be used in an entrepreneurial capacity or may be offered for resale, the request is one of many seeking similar information, or the request appears prompted by or the requester appears associated with movements inherently inconsistent with the public interest due to the advocation of discrimination, segregation, public disorder, or illegal activity.

Other Waivers

Disclosure officers may use their discretion in waiving fees under a variety of circumstances on the basis of equity and fair play. Records may also be released without charge by other employees acting in furtherance of assigned tax-administration duties.

Fees may be waived when the requester has demonstrated that the request primarily serves a humanitarian purpose intended to benefit a person other than the requester. Requests may be processed without charge for charitable organizations.

Fees may be waived for persons who can demonstrate that they are indigent. Incarceration, however, is not considered to constitute indigence, nor will fees be waived if the indigence appears self-induced for tax-avoidance purposes.

Almost any convincing argument may be raised in favor of waiving fees. The typical disclosure officer will not, however, seek out opportunities to waive fees if the requester does not raise the issue and present a good case in favor of the waiver.

Other Fee Structures

The Privacy Act does not make any provision for search or review fees. The only fee involved in servicing a Privacy Act access request is the copying fee, which is the same as the FOIA copying fee. Some requesters have attempted to avoid search fees by making Privacy Act rather than FOIA requests for records. However, since most Privacy Act records are in exempt systems and there are no provisions under that act for releasing segregable portions of records, these requests failed to obtain any records. When the requester asks that Information Act standards be applied to Privacy Act access requests, the FOIA fee schedule is applied, making the request subject to any search or review charges which may be applicable. Requests to amend records pursuant to the Privacy Act are not subject to any charges.

Copies of records may be certified as representing an accurate and complete version of the record as it appears in the Service's files. Certification of records is usually requested so that the records may be submitted to a court or to a foreign government for some official purpose. The cost for the certification service is $1.00 for each document certified.

Copies of tax returns are provided to the taxpayer at a standard fee of $4.25 per return, regardless of the size of the return or the effort necessary to secure the return.

Photocopies of exempt-organization returns and approved applications for exemption are made available at a standard charge of $1.00 for the first page and $.15 for each subsequent page of each return or application. Forms 990-PF (Return of Private Foundation) and 990-AR (Annual Report of Private Foundation) are also available as aperture cards. The cost of such cards is $1.00 for the first card and $.13 for each subsequent card for the same return. When the request is for a large number of cards not requiring individual searches, such as all the Forms 990-PF for a single year within one district or one state, the fee is reduced to $1.00 for the first card and $.13 for each subsequent card (instead of $1.00 for the first card of each return).

Copies of employee-plan documents are made available at a charge of $1.00 for the first page and $.15 for each additional page of each group of papers which represents a normally associated file.

Written determinations, including rulings, determination letters, and technical advice memoranda released pursuant to 26 U.S.C. 6110 are subject to special charges. Photocopies are available at $.15 per page. Requests for background files are subject to a search fee of $13.00 for each determination file requested and a deletion fee of $2.00 for each page which must be analyzed for potential deletions.

Manner of Payment

The Freedom of Information Reform Act of 1986 provides that no agency may require advance payment of any fee unless the requester has previously failed to pay fees in a timely fashion or the agency has determined that the fee will exceed $250.

In cases in which the standard for advance payment is met, the Internal Revenue Service will require payment before any services are performed. In all other cases in which fees have been determined to be due, the Service will complete the services necessary to process the request, advise the requester of the final fee, and hold the documents for release immediately upon receipt of payment. This method is designed to minimize the costs of billing, making collection, depositing payments, and keeping records.

For some years the Service mailed requested records with a bill for subsequent payment. It was discovered, however, that about 40 percent of all requesters never paid the bill. Consequently, there were extensive bookkeeping costs, collection expenses, and losses. Studies showed that many requesters anticipated that they would receive very useful documents and when confronted with records to which deletions had been made or which simply did not serve the purpose for which they were wanted, refused to pay the fees due.

The Information Act makes no guarantee that the records released will be useful, interesting, amusing, or otherwise satisfying to the requester. The fees charged are for the services performed and do not represent prices for the sale of the materials released. Records cannot be returned for a refund. Requesters should be aware that most government records are very dull and may be of little or no value to the recipient. Moreover, agencies have little choice as to what they release; if a requested file contains a sheet of paper with little or nothing on it, it will be dutifully copied and released.

Oddly enough, our studies showed that the most respectable requesters were the least likely to pay for their materials. Attorneys and accountants seldom paid for the records received. Tax protesters, on the other hand, almost always paid for what they requested, although a few attempted to use "money" they had issued but guaranteed was just as good as federal "greenies," which constituted a promise to make payment promptly upon demand, backed by nothing of value.

In view of the many difficulties involved in attempting to collect the fees for services rendered, the Service adopted a cash-and-carry approach under which the requested records are released as soon as the appropriate payment is received.

Planning Your Request

The statistics which represented the costs of accessing records through 1986 will doubtlessly become irrelevant in view of the revised fee structure established by the Freedom of Information Reform Act of 1986 and the implementing regulations of 1987.

Typical requester behavior may change. The laws of economics apply to records-access requests, as they do to other forms of human behavior, but it is difficult to foresee which of several conflicting factors will have the greater effect. The limits on fees for search hours and copying charges may discourage self-restraint and result in excessive requests. The 70 percent increase from $10 per hour to $17 per hour for searches going beyond the minimum may well have the opposite effect and reduce the size of requests. Certainly, commercial users will have to think twice before making requests when facing both a $17-per-hour search fee and a $21-per-hour review fee.

The behavior of Service personnel working requests may also change drastically. Under the old fee structure, I suspected that many disclosure officers were charging for a single-hour search rather than justifying a greater charge by making the effort necessary to document the time actually spent. The elimination of the charge for the first two hours of search, which is extremely offensive to many disclosure officers, may prompt them to realize that most searches take much longer. The chief result of providing most requesters with two free hours of search time may be that the average search necessary to process a request will increase from an hour or two to three or four hours, creating a new dynamic of human behavior: the extent of the search expands to reach the fee.

No one can predict the future demand for records, the cost to the Service in providing them, or the value to the public of obtaining them.

Except for the most intemperate requester, the cost of making an Information Act request will not be so great as to deter anyone who has a legitimate need for access to Internal Revenue Service records. In a sense, the controlling cost factor motivating requesters is not the search fee, the review fee, or the copying fee but the amount of tax involved in their dispute with the Service.

The costs involved can be great enough to warrant careful planning. Do not hesitate to ask your disclosure officer for assistance before you make your request. You might ask which user category he would think you fall into, what the costs of requests similar to yours have been, what alternatives are available to you to reduce those costs, whether the request you are about to make is likely to produce the information you seek, and whether he thinks that such information would be of benefit to solving your problem. Then ask him to suggest what he believes would be your best course of action. You do not have to take his advice, but you cannot lose anything by asking. And once he has offered an opinion as to the likely cost, no matter how informal, human nature would prevent him from subsequently computing costs much beyond his original estimate.

I am certain that the most successful requester will be the one who plans his request carefully, takes the established fees into account, exercises restraint in making his request regardless of the anticipated cost, seeks the assistance of the disclosure officer in formulating his request, and respects the public purse as if it were his own, which indeed it is.

Chapter Fifteen

Making Your Request

The opening pages of the first chapter stated that of 10,820 Freedom of Information Act requests made in 1986, 2,749 were so poorly constructed that they could be denied as imperfect without ever having to locate or evaluate a record for release. A further 1,224 requests asked for records which did not exist or which were so poorly described that the request failed to bring to mind the identity of any existing record. Another 640 requesters asked for records concerning themselves but failed to adequately establish their identity or in some cases even to include their name and address.

Thus, almost half of all the Freedom of Information requests made in 1986, a year which was very typical of the Service's experience for more than a decade, were so poorly constructed as to have served no purpose whatsoever. I suspect, however, that the remaining requests, those which received either a denial or the release of some records, frequently suffered unnecessary delays, excessive costs, and other problems as a result of being poorly prepared and improperly submitted.

The Freedom of Information Reform Act of 1986, which became effective in April 1987, and the subsequent regulations, which became effective in October 1987, have made the requirements governing the form of request more complex, with the result that an even greater portion of requests may be imperfect in the future.

The objective of this chapter is to identify the minimum requirements necessary for making a request which will be accepted and promptly processed at the least possible cost and with the greatest possible likelihood of receiving as many of the requested records as the law will allow. I believe that with a little attention to the information in this chapter, the number of imperfect requests could be reduced to zero.

The Ten Barriers

The Service's regulations for making Information Act requests describe the proper "form of request," which refers not to a printed form which must be filled out but to the requirements which must be met before a request can be accepted for processing. These requirements are designed to ensure that requests are adequate to be processed and that no requester can seek to litigate the Service's failure to be responsive to requests which may not have been

194

understood or recognized as subject to the Freedom of Information Act. In practice, however, these requirements serve as 10 barriers to making a request, which many persons find insurmountable:

1. The request must be made in writing.
2. The request must be signed by the person making it.
3. The request must state that it is being made pursuant to the Freedom of Information Act.
4. The request must be addressed to and mailed or hand-delivered to the office of the official having control of the records or to the director of the district in which the requester resides.
5. The request must reasonably describe the records requested.
6. If the records are confidential pursuant to section 6103 of the Internal Revenue Code or the Privacy Act of 1974, the request must establish the identity of the requester.
7. If the records are confidential as in item 6, the request must establish the requester's right to access the records.
8. The request must set forth the address to which the determination of availability of the records is to be directed.
9. The request must state whether the requester wishes to inspect the records or prefers to obtain copies without prior inspection.
10. The request must state the requester's agreement to pay any fees due, request a fee waiver, or limit the request to the services available without charge or some other limit.

These requirements may not seem overly formidable, but it must be remembered that the records most likely to be requested are those subject to protection under section 6103 of the Internal Revenue Code and the Privacy Act of 1974. Thus, many of the requirements listed above are subject to the complex conditions imposed by those acts to prevent such records from being disclosed to persons not legitimately entitled to access them. These provisions are necessary to protect our rights of privacy.

Many of the 10 requirements are subject to legal interpretations, precedents, practical considerations, and state laws of which the typical requester is likely to be totally unaware. The result is that the barriers can be truly insurmountable to thousands of requesters who have not been initiated to their mysteries.

The Statute of Reliance

Requests for access to records must state the statute upon which they rely, or they may be rejected or treated in some other manner which fails to provide the requester with all the benefits available under the Freedom of Information Act or the Privacy Act. This statement of reliance upon the statute of choice should be prominently displayed, either as a heading to the request or as the opening sentence, or it may go unnoticed.

It is extremely unwise to include a request for records access in a letter
which deals with other matters, especially those which concern your tax affairs.
Such mixed correspondence risks any of several common consequences. Disclosure offices work records-access requests, whereas tax matters are worked in
correspondence units which are under a different organization. One or more
parts of a mixed letter will necessarily have been sent to the wrong processing
unit. Whoever works that case will lack the expertise and the authority to deal
with some portions of it and will either ignore or mishandle what he is unfamiliar with. A 1988 study by the General Accounting Office showed that half
of all responses issued by Adjustments/Correspondence branches were incorrect, incomplete, unresponsive, or unclear. You do not want your records access request to fall into the hands of Adjustments/Correspondence branch tax
examiners.

Even if recognized as a disclosure matter and properly transferred, there
will be delays, and some portion of the letter may never be properly answered.
Finally, any responses which do result are likely to encounter difficulties in getting signed since different matters require different levels of authority for signature.

Mixed requests suffer from one further serious problem. Tax examiners
working adjustment cases which contain records-access requests may feel
threatened by the mention of the Freedom of Information Act or the Privacy
Act and consequently be less enthusiastic about providing the taxpayer with
adequate service. The disclosure officer may feel that the records-access request
is a secondary interest not deserving his best efforts. To obtain everyone's
cooperation and best efforts on your behalf, make certain that your access requests are distinct and unencumbered by any other matter.

Generally, requests for access should state that they are being made pursuant to the Freedom of Information Act. If you are seeking access to a system
of records and are not providing specific descriptions of the records you want,
you should also state that the request is being made pursuant to the Privacy Act
of 1974. Remember, however, that reliance upon the Privacy Act alone risks
denial on the basis that the system of records is exempt from access. To be truly
effective, a Privacy Act request must also cite the Freedom of Information Act
to reach the segregable portions of otherwise exempt records.

I recommend that if you are seeking access to your own return information, which includes Collection, Examination, Criminal Investigation, and
some Inspection files, you also state that the request is made pursuant to 26
U.S.C. 6103 and that you expect to receive all return information whose release
would not seriously impair federal tax administration, regardless of the applicability of any exemption from the disclosure requirements of the Freedom of
Information Act.

You may include a reference to Policy Statement P-1-192, reminding the
recipient that it is the policy of the Internal Revenue Service not to withhold
records unless they are both exempt and their release would nullify Service actions in carrying out a responsibility or function, or would constitute an unwarranted invasion of personal privacy. Exemptions which do not meet the requirements of the policy statement should be waived.

If the records you are requesting are likely to involve information whose release might constitute an unwarranted invasion of personal privacy, you should include a request that there be a balancing test to determine if the public interest outweighs the privacy considerations. You must provide the public-interest argument necessary to prevail in such a test. Remember, however, that if the records pertain to your own affairs, it is difficult to make a public-interest argument in favor of release.

Generally, the Freedom of Information Act, the Privacy Act of 1974, and 26 U.S.C. 6103 are the only statutes to be cited.

Under no circumstances should you invent oddball citations to such irrelevant documents as the Constitution, the Declaration of Independence, the Bill of Rights, the *Rights of Man*, the Code of Hammurabi, the Old Testament, the New Testament, English common law, the Magna Carta, or anything else which would identify you as a tax protester, a gadfly, or a fruitcake undeserving of any further consideration.

Do not include in your request any reminder that a response is required in 10 days. Disclosure officers are acutely aware of the need to meet this rather unreasonable and highly frustrating deadline, and any further mention of it is infuriating. Highlighting the 10-day response requirement could guarantee your response a permanent place at the bottom of the pile. On the other hand, if there is a genuine need to have a response within a certain time frame, because of a court date, an impending trip abroad, the need to submit materials to a prospective employer, the demands of your publisher, or some other reason, explain your circumstances in your request. Most disclosure officers will be considerate of the requester's needs and generally have some ability to arrange their work accordingly.

Do not threaten to appeal or litigate your request in the absence of a timely response. Such threats achieve nothing but may invite further delay. Some appeals and all litigation will lift the request out of the hands of the disclosure officer and to Chief Counsel's Disclosure Litigation Division. The prospect of such a fortuitous transfer might tempt a disclosure officer to slow down just enough not to have to face resolving a difficult case.

It is generally unwise to submit your request through a congressperson, send a copy of your request to a congressperson, or ask that a congressperson intercede on your behalf while your request is in process. The involvement of a member of Congress raises the signature level necessary on the response, thereby involving additional review and creating delay rather than inspiring the hoped-for prompt treatment. The disclosure officer, knowing that his work will be reviewed at a higher level, will pay more attention to unimportant details to protect his product from managerial nitpicking. And remember that in my experience, the higher the rank of the official approving the response, the less likely that any significant information will be released.

Reasonable Description

The records taxpayers request from the Internal Revenue Service, with few exceptions, fall into two very broad categories. The first consists of those records which are not particular to the requesting taxpayer and may be requested by anyone with the same likelihood of access or denial. The second consists of the requester's own records, usually return information which may be accessed only by the requester or someone who has derived his authority from the requester. The approach to reasonably describing the requested records will differ markedly between the two groups.

For the first group, the general records, there are several ways to face the problem of describing what you want. You may already know the formal title, the popular title, the identifying letters or numbers, or the readily recognizable description of the record's function or location, and therefore need only include in your request one or more of these identifiers. Or you may research the matter until you find adequate identifiers in this book or some other work of reference. Or you may make a series of requests, asking first for some of the descriptive documents identified in this book and then narrowing in on what you really want, using each document as a stepping-stone in your search.

The regulations state that a request for records must describe the records in sufficient detail to enable the Service employees who are familiar with the subject area of the request to locate the records without placing an unreasonable burden upon the Service. The requirement will generally be satisfied if the requester gives the name, subject matter, date, and location of the record. It is suggested that the requester also furnish any information which will more clearly identify the records. If the request seeks records pertaining to pending litigation, the request should indicate the title of the case, the court in which the case was filed, and the nature of the case.

Obviously, if the requester can provide the sort of reasonable description envisioned by the regulations, he would have to have extensive knowledge about the record and identify it in great detail. Most requesters, unable to be specific, will provide a general recitation of what the record is believed to do and will rely on function rather than description to identify the record. Unfortunately, if the attempted description is too vague, the disclosure officer will deny the request as imperfect. Such denials have been upheld by the courts.

If the description seems to strike a chord, the request will be processed. The difficulty with processing such requests is that the record search will come to resemble a childhood game demonstrating the effect of poor communication. The requester will have described a horse in such a manner that the disclosure officer recognizes it as a donkey. He approaches the usually knowledgeable subject-matter specialist with the description of the donkey, which the technician visualizes as being much like a giraffe. He sends a clerk to look for a giraffe, and the clerk concludes the search upon locating a camel. Naturally we refuse access to a camel, but the requester knows that there is no reasonable basis for denying him access to a horse. Ultimately, the matter may be litigated. If the Service wins its case, no one will ever learn that the document which we have successfully withheld from the requester was not what he wanted in the first place. If the requester wins, he will feel cheated because what he receives is not what he wanted.

No one knows how often the Service actually withholds records not responsive to the intent of the requester. I do know that it is very common for the recipient of records to be disappointed because the records received are irrelevant to his needs. Disclosure personnel and others working on requests will frequently disagree among themselves as to which of several alternatives best resemble the request. Some of us will opt for the simplest and most easily released document as being the most responsive because we think in terms of minimizing costs, avoiding conflict, living a long and happy life, and satisfying the requester as often as possible. Others, like salmon compelled to swim upstream, will insist that every request pertains to records which require extensive effort, conflict, and confrontation, and will in the end frustrate the requester's efforts. Thus, the reasonable description is not really very reasonable.

The regulations also provide that the requester shall be afforded an opportunity to confer with knowledgeable personnel to refine his request. I strongly urge that unless you are certain that you are asking for what you really want, telephone the disclosure officer in the district office servicing the area in which you reside before you make your request. Explain your needs. Find out if what you intend to ask for is appropriate. Obtain his suggestions on how to proceed. You will find that most disclosure officers are reasonable and helpful people, and you will demonstrate that you too are a reasonable person pursuing a rational cause of action which warrants his assistance. You can secure the disclosure officer's sympathy and cooperation while obtaining assistance in framing your request. You will make his job easier and increase the likelihood of securing the requested records or some reasonable alternative to meet your needs.

The request for your *personal* records should follow a somewhat different approach. Never, never, never ask for "all records" pertaining to yourself. The Internal Revenue Service does not maintain dossiers on taxpayers in which all their records would be associated in a single file. It would be virtually impossible for the Service to accumulate all records in response to a request. Such a request would be denied as imperfect. The courts have upheld such denials.

You may identify the Privacy Act system of records you wish to access and use that as the description of the records wanted pursuant to the Information Act. Such a request could result in obtaining many records you do not really want and might omit some which you would consider desirable.

The better alternative is to frame your request in the same terms in which the Service organizes its work. If your request is prompted by the examination of your return, efforts to collect a tax, or the pursuit of a criminal investigation, identify the function engaged in that activity and then cite the tax years involved and the type of tax or form number of the return involved.

A typical request would be for the Examination Division file on your 1987 income tax, or the Collection Division file on your second-quarter 1986 employment taxes, or the Criminal Investigation Division file on your failure to file 1986, 1987, and 1988 income taxes. Such requests are always adequate, easily understood, readily retrieved, and processed without error, confusion, or misunderstanding.

If you wish to clarify your request further, you may add that the file is currently in the possession of a particular revenue officer or revenue agent in a particular office. You may also reduce your request by eliminating some items such as copies of financial statements submitted by you or copies of checks obtained from your bank.

There is no requirement that any requester explain why he wants to access records. Frequently, however, a knowledge of the requester's objectives and circumstances will make it easier to determine which records he wants and will enable the disclosure officer to offer practical advice and assistance. Few requesters need or really want everything in their file, and it would be foolish to have to wait while a large file is being analyzed and copied when only a few items are needed.

The type of records you request will also determine the need to identify yourself and the location to which the request should be sent.

Identification

Requests must be made in writing, must be signed by the person making the request, and must state the address to which a response should be sent.

Obviously, a request shouted by a demonstrating tax protester or telephoned to the disclsoure officer can be ignored. Such items would not even count in the tally of imperfect requests.

The matters of signature and address become more meaningful when the records requested are protected by the Internal Revenue Code or the Privacy Act. Requests to access such records are legal documents which if falsified may have very serious consequences. Any person who knowingly and willfully requests or obtains any record concerning an individual which is protected by the Privacy Act may be fined as much as $5,000.

Disclosure officers have a responsibility to ensure that protected records are not accessed by persons other than the taxpayers to whom they pertain. The signature and the address shown on the request may be compared to those in the records requested to ensure that they are genuine.

Whenever records protected by the Internal Revenue Code or the Privacy Act are requested, the request must establish the identity and the right of the person making the request to access those records. The request must include the social security number of the requester-taxpayer.

If the request is delivered in person, it must be presented to an official such as a revenue officer or revenue agent who can attest to the taxpayer's identity on the basis of having dealt with him in the course of an investigation, or the requester must present a suitable form of identification containing a photograph such as a passport; a driver's license; a military, student, or employment identification card. The employee receiving the request is expected to examine the identification presented to verify that the requester is the taxpayer whose records are being accessed.

If the requester has no suitable identification bearing a photograph, two pieces of identification which show both the name and the signature must be presented.

If the request is sent by mail, it must include a clear photocopy of one piece of identification which shows both the name and the signature in addition to the name and the signature on the request.

Needless to say, the names, social security numbers, and signatures on the identification and the request must match. The name shown must be the same as the name of the taxpayer in the records being accessed unless evidence of a name change, marriage, or other acceptable reason for any difference is presented. Disclosure officers may compare any of the identifying materials to other records in the Service's possession and may demand additional proof to the extent necessary.

Disclosure officers are encouraged to be especially careful if the request for access alleges to be from a person whose tax matters may be of interest to the general public.

In lieu of the various forms of identification required, the requester may present a notarized statement swearing to or affirming his identity. Notarized statements are subject to state laws which vary by jurisdiction, but generally disclosure officers will insist that notarization appear on the document making the request and not on a separate piece of paper, which may have been prepared in connection with an entirely different matter. The notarized statement must conform to state law and include a raised seal when applicable. Only an original statement will be accepted; photocopies are not valid.

Occasionally, requesters will submit multiple requests to different offices, consisting of photocopies, or will submit sequential requests to the same office without including identification beyond the original request. Disclosure officers may accept such requests on the basis that they have previously received adequate identification, but they are not required to do so, and they may insist upon further identification whenever they believe that is necessary to protect taxpayers' records.

Taxpayers may designate other persons who may access their return information. However, such designations are not valid if they are made under duress. Taxpayers may also issue powers of attorney permitting access to their return information. Such powers must be received by the Internal Revenue Service within 60 days following the date on which the taxpayer signed and dated the authorization.

Designations and powers of attorney which merely authorize the holder to make Freedom of Information Act requests or Privacy Act requests are not valid to access return information. Such designations and powers must specify the type of tax return and the tax year for which they are valid. Persons other than the taxpayer who have a material interest recognized by 26 U.S.C. 6103 may access return information under the Freedom of Information Act and may issue powers of attorney authorizing the exercise of their rights.

In all these cases disclosure officers will expect the request to include adequate evidence to ensure that the taxpayer's return information is adequately protected. This may include proof of the taxpayer's identity and evidence supporting the claim of material interest for persons other than the taxpayer, documentation supporting the designation or power of attorney, and proof of identity of the recipient of the designation or the power of attorney.

Addressing the Request

The regulations require that Information Act requests be addressed to and mailed or hand-delivered to the address of the official who is responsible for the control of the records requested. At first glance it may appear to be unfair to require the requester not only to identify the records being requested but also to know who is responsible for control of those records. The system for addressing requests is, however, eminently fair and very practical.

The Service is decentralized to provide the taxpayer with the best possible service in an office reasonably close to his place of residence. The system for addressing access requests takes advantage of this decentralization. In addition, it is designed to deliver the request directly to the official who has the authority to make a determination on the records requested whenever possible. Properly addressing a request helps to identify the records wanted since most recipients of a request will make the natural assumption that the request is intended to access records in their possession.

Most Examination, Collection, and Criminal Investigation activities take place in district offices. Any request to access a taxpayer's return information, including the investigatory files of the foregoing functions, should be addressed to the district director serving the area in which you reside or, if the request pertains to the tax matters of your business, the district director serving the area in which your business is located.

If your interests relate to matters which have involved another district office because you have moved or for some other reason, you may address your request to the district known to be involved. In such case your return address will identify you as an out-of-district taxpayer, and the recipient may assume that you sent your request to the wrong office. To avoid any confusion, your request should explain why you sent it to that district.

The regulations also provide that a requester who is unsure where to send his request should mail it to the district director serving the area of his residence. If you choose this option, it would be helpful if you include a statement that you do not know the proper official to whom to make the request and you want it transferred to the proper office.

Disclosure officers will transfer requests between offices whenever it appears appropriate to do so, but it is sometimes difficult to know what the requester's intentions were. Anytime you intentionally send a request to an office not normally involved with the requested records, it would be helpful to explain what you are trying to accomplish. The recipient does not know whether you wanted an unlikely location searched for the records, have made a mistake, or are involved in some special circumstances. If you send multiple requests to different offices or send any office a carbon copy of a request showing multiple addressees, it would prevent unnecessary delay if you explained your intention and clearly stated to whom you have sent the same request, so that the recipient will know whether to transfer the request, work all or some of it, or reject it as imperfect. I have seen situations in which copies of an identical request were sent to several different offices, each of which transferred the request to one of the others and none of which made any substantive response.

If you do not know the location of your district office, you may find a listing appended to the Freedom of Information Act regulations and to the Privacy Act regulations. The simplest course, however, would be to refer to a local telephone directory's blue pages for Government Offices and look for United States Government — Internal Revenue Service — District Director. Call the number shown and ask to be connected with the disclosure officer. Every district has a disclosure officer, and he will be glad to advise you how to address your request or any other matter that will help you make a good, workable request.

Internal Revenue Service Centers, those cavernous data-processing facilities to which you mail your return, also have authority to process Information Act requests for their records. However, unless you have good reason to believe that they have records you wish to access, such as prior correspondence concerning a tax matter, service centers are probably not the right place to send an access request. Many records pass through the service centers for input to a master file and ultimate retirement to a federal records center, but these records generally continue to be under the jurisdiction of the district director, who would be responsible for any access requests concerning them.

Regional commissioners have authority to process Information Act requests, but regional offices are merely administrative centers responsible for the management of a group of district offices. They do not generally have records pertaining to taxpayers except as copies for review. Unless you know that you want access to regional-office records, such as those pertaining to their management functions, they are unlikely places to which to send your request.

The IRS Data Center, in Detroit, has authority to process requests for records, but the data center is unlikely to have records of interest to taxpayers.

The Director of Practice, Internal Revenue Service, 1111 Constitution Avenue NW, Washington, DC 20224, has authority to process requests for his records. The director of Practice does not maintain records on taxpayers, but has records concerning the enrollment of enrolled agents, and the discipline of attorneys, certified public accountants, and enrolled agents who practice before the Internal Revenue Service.

The Assistant Commissioner (Inspection), Internal Revenue Service, 1111 Constitution Avenue NW, Washington, DC 20224, has authority to process requests for Internal Audit Division and Internal Security Division records, whether those records are maintained in the National Office or in the various Inspection field offices.

The Assistant Commissioner (International), Internal Revenue Service, 950 L'Enfant Plaza, Washington, DC 20024, has authority to process requests involving foreign programs, tax treaties, assistance to state taxing authorities, and other matters under his jurisdiction.

The Director, Office of Disclosure, P.O. Box 388, Ben Franklin Station, Washington, DC 20044, has responsibility for processing all Freedom of Information Act requests for National Office records other than those of the director of Practice, the Assistant Commissioner (Inspection) and the Assistant Commissioner (International). The Director, Office of Disclosure, has overall responsibility for the Service's entire disclosure program and may therefore take jurisdiction over any disclosure matter arising anywhere in the Service. Any doubts about where to send a request or about how a request may be made which have not been resolved through contact with the disclosure officer in your district office may be referred to the Director, Office of Disclosure.

The National Office Freedom of Information Reading Room, a facility under the Director, Office of Disclosure, and sharing his mailing address, processes requests for reading-room shelf materials. The operation and content of the reading room is discussed in a separate chapter.

All Freedom of Information Act requests, except those addressed to the Director, Office of Disclosure, should be addressed to the attention of the disclosure officer. All requests, regardless of to whom addressed, should include the term *FOIA Request* as part of the address or prominently displayed elsewhere on the envelope.

Agreement to Pay

Every requester must attest under penalties of perjury his status within one of the available categories of users to determine the type and extent of fees to be charged. He must also state how the records are to be used within the context of the types of uses which affect the fees to be charged.

The available categories of users:

1. Commercial Use Requester. Any requester who seeks information for a use or purpose that furthers the commercial, trade or profit interests of the requester or the person on whose behalf the request is made.

2. Media Requester. Any person gathering news for an entity organized to broadcast or publish news to the public. Freelance journalists may be included to the extent that they demonstrate an expectation to publish through a qualifying news medium.

3. Educational Institution Requester. Any person who on behalf of a preschool, public or private elementary or secondary school, institution or undergraduate or graduate higher education, institution of professional or vocational education which operates a program of scholarly research, seeks records in furtherance of the institution's scholarly research and is not for commercial use.

4. Noncommercial Scientific Institution Requester. Any person on behalf of an institution that is not operated on a commercial basis, that is operated solely for the purposes of scientific research whose results are not intended to promote any particular product or industry.

5. Other Requester. Any requester who falls outside the above categories. Obviously, most requesters and all individuals making requests concerning their own tax affairs would fall into the "Other" category. They need not justify their intended use of the requested information beyond stating that it is not for a commercial purpose.

Having complied with the requirement to state her category and explain her proposed use, the requester may then request a waiver of all or a portion of the fees determined to be appropriate to her request and include her argument in favor of such a waiver or price reduction.

Every requester must then state that his request is to be limited to any services which are available free of charge or state his commitment to pay any fees determined to be due. Persons who have requested a fee waiver or a reduction in fees must state whether the request is to be withdrawn or the fees will be paid in the event that the waiver or reduction is denied. A requester may state a limit beyond which he would be unwilling to pay. Commonly, requesters have set this limit at $50.

The request must state whether the requester prefers to inspect the records prior to requesting any copies desired or prefers to secure copies without prior inspection. The choice would, of course, affect the estimated cost of servicing the request.

If the disclosure officer estimates that the stated limit would be exceeded or if no limit has been set and the expected cost will exceed $250, the requester will be afforded the opportunity to reformulate the request in a manner which would satisfy her needs without exceeding the fee limit. If the requester continues to desire services whose cost would exceed $250, the amount due would have to be paid before work on the request is commenced.

It is advisable that the requester include his telephone number and express a willingness to discuss any problems or interpretations which might arise. The requester may also ask that the disclosure officer call him to discuss the request before proceeding.

I strongly recommend that any request be carefully constructed and reviewed before submission so that the 10 barriers may be overcome and denial as imperfect be avoided.

Copies of Tax Returns

The Service processes some requests for access to documents in accordance with procedures established long before the Information Act went into effect. In these cases, neither the requester nor the Service need hold strictly to the FOIA rules. These procedures relate only to requests which are always granted and comply with the FOIA in that they are designed to provide the public with the quickest service at the least cost. The most important of these procedures concerns the provision of photocopies of taxpayers' own tax returns.

Copies of returns may be obtained by writing to the service center with which the return was filed. The request need only state the requester's name, address, social security number, and the tax year and type of return wanted. These requests are not serviced by disclosure personnel. They should not contain anything other than the bare request for the copy of the return.

The cost for each return provided, regardless of how many pages may be involved and what difficulties may be met in retrieving it from a records-storage facility, is $4.25.

There are several reasons why a person experiencing difficulties with the Internal Revenue Service might wish to obtain a copy of her return.

Taxpayers will sometimes prepare several versions of a return before deciding which to file. The copy filed may not be identical to the copy retained. Tax preparers will sometimes file a return which through error is not the same as the copy provided to the taxpayer. It is easy to omit a schedule or attach someone else's schedule. It is worthwhile under some circumstances to make certain that the document with which the Service is working is identical to the document the taxpayer intended to file.

In some cases, adjustments will be processed based upon processing errors. The General Accounting Office reported that the number of errors made in the coding, editing, and transcription of returns by service center personnel was significantly greater than the number of math errors made by taxpayers on their returns. Such errors would become apparent from inspection of the return on file.

Taxpayers against whom late-filing penalties are proposed could also benefit from inspecting a copy of their return. No late-filing penalty can be assessed unless the return has been stamped with a late-receipt date and an envelope showing a postmark later than the due date is attached. If these indicators are not present or some other marking on the return or the date in the document locator number stamped on the return is timely, no penalty can be assessed. I was once shown an envelope on which the stamp was canceled with a postmark past the due date, but the reverse of the envelope had a postmark ten days earlier, establishing that the return was mailed timely, but delayed in the mail; no penalty could be assessed.

If you are concerned about the likelihood of your return being selected for examination, there are a variety of markings on returns which might be of interest to you. For instance, a stamp reading "Accepted As Filed, Classification," would probably indicate that the return was identified as warranting examination on the basis of the DIF score but that a classifier decided against selecting it for assignment. If that makes you nervous, consider the message "Closed—Survey After Assignment," indicating that the return had gone beyond the classifier and been assigned for examination before being withdrawn. My favorite is "Survey Excess Inventory," indicating that the return of some extraordinarily lucky taxpayer has been selected, has passed the classifier, and has been assigned for examination before being withdrawn because there was too much work available. You may also find your return stamped with a small circle surrounding the letters *CI* and a single-digit number, indicating Criminal Investigation Division involvement. All of these markings indicate that the returns involved had been prepared in a manner that came close to warranting or actually warranted examination or criminal investigation but that the taxpayer had the good fortune to escape such disaster. Knowledge of these close calls might cause some to change their tax strategy. It might cause others to change their way of life.

There are other reasons for requesting a copy of your return. One such reason might interest long-shot players. After an examination has been completed, the Revenue Agent's Report is routinely associated with the return, and the two are filed together. The service center personnel who pull returns from the files, make photocopies, and fill requests for copies of returns are not trained in disclosure matters, are relatively low paid, are often temporary employees, and operate under work-planning controls which emphasize and reward the rapid repetition of simple actions. They are not paid to think. There have been instances in which taxpayers received copies of their returns from which the Revenue Agent's Report and other sensitive documents had not been removed. Thus, it is sometimes possible to obtain important documents without their having been reviewed by disclosure officers, without any deletions being made, without encountering the costs and delays usually attributable to Freedom of Information requests, and without the Service ever realizing what has been given to you.

Privacy Act Transcripts

The Privacy Act of 1974 provides that information from nonexempt systems of records must be available to requesters in a form comprehensible to them.

The Individual Master File, which records all transactions to a taxpayer's account, produces various printouts in coded form for Service use. In order to comply with the Privacy Act, the Internal Revenue Service created the Privacy Act Transcript, which contains all the entries on the Individual Master File (except the potentially dangerous taxpayer designation) arranged in a simple practical fashion and written in plain English. This transcript is a valuable tool for anyone encountering difficulties with the Internal Revenue Service, as it can serve as a sort of scorecard or road map recording actions taken on the taxpayer's account.

A Privacy Act Transcript of the Individual Master File may be obtained by requesting it from the district director. There is no cost.

Associated with the Privacy Act Transcript is the Privacy Act Accounting of Disclosures. Certain disclosures of records to other agencies must be recorded as Accountings of Disclosure. Persons who are interested in knowing of such disclosures may find this record valuable. In some cases it may be possible to obtain from other agencies information which was not available pursuant to requests to the Internal Revenue Service. Thus, knowledge of the disclosures made could provide leads for making further information requests.

Persons wishing to pursue this route (which is likely to be of value only to those who are experiencing serious problems, such as an investigation by the Criminal Investigation Division) should request a Privacy Act Transcript and specify that they also wish to obtain the Accounting of Disclosures portion.

IRM 1272(18)54 provides: "In order to prevent a requester from obtaining premature knowledge of the existence of an investigation and thereby defeating the law enforcement process, accountings of disclosure must be reviewed prior to release and those which are exempt should be withheld." Many of the items to be withheld as a result of that instruction are based upon very dubious assumptions. I do not believe that they would be sustained against a Freedom of Information action, but the Service would probably try to withhold anything which would be of any value to a requester.

If you believe that such information could be of serious value to you, make your request for the Privacy Act Transcript and the Privacy Act Accounting of Disclosures under the Freedom of Information Act and 26 U.S.C. 6103. Specify that you expect any deletions to be justified by FOIA exemptions and to meet the return-information standard that disclosure would seriously impair federal tax administration. Be certain that your request overcomes the 10 barriers, and be prepared to appeal any withholding.

FOIA Request Checklist

OPTIONAL	Call disclosure officer for advice	
REQUIRED	Cite Freedom of Information Act	*in text*
REQUIRED	Cite Freedom of Information Act	*on envelope*
OPTIONAL	Cite Privacy Act of 1974	*in text*
OPTIONAL	Cite 26 U.S.C. 6103	*in text*
OPTIONAL	Cite Policy Statement P-1-192	*in text*
OPTIONAL	Request public-interest balancing test	
REQUIRED	Make request in writing	
REQUIRED	Sign request; conform to name on return	
OPTIONAL	Explain any name change	
REQUIRED	Identify self if confidential information	
OPTIONAL	Notary statement in lieu of photocopy IDs	
REQUIRED	Social Security number if confidential information	
REQUIRED	Establish right to access if not taxpayer (TP)	
REQUIRED	TP Designation/Power of Attorney if not TP	
REQUIRED	Provide return address	
REQUIRED	Specify whether copies or inspection wanted	
OPTIONAL	Specify preferred location for inspection	
OPTIONAL	Request certification of released records	
OPTIONAL	Specify format for copying automated record	
OPTIONAL	Include arrangements for contractor to copy	
REQUIRED	Reasonably describe records requested	
REQUIRED	Identify case and court if current litigation	
OPTIONAL	State function, tax year, and type of return	
OPTIONAL	Suggest location or describe desired search	
OPTIONAL	Identify unwanted portions of records	
OPTIONAL	*Never* ask for "All My Records"	
OPTIONAL	Explain your needs and ask for suggestions	
OPTIONAL	Omit extraneous requests and comments	
OPTIONAL	Justify urgent or preferential treatment	
REQUIRED	State user category and explain intended use	
REQUIRED	Make commitment to pay or not pay excess	
OPTIONAL	Request fee waiver and provide justification	
OPTIONAL	State fee limitation	

OPTIONAL	Telephone number, request disclosure officer call
REQUIRED	Mail or deliver to authorized official
OPTIONAL	Request district director forward request
OPTIONAL	Advise of identical requests sent elsewhere
OPTIONAL	Request return of receipted copy of request
OPTIONAL	Express appreciation to disclosure officer

Chapter Sixteen

Processing Your Request

A knowledge of how your request will be processed will prove helpful in preparing your request, dealing with the disclosure officer, understanding what is transpiring while you await a response, and knowing when to appeal or file suit for nonresponse.

The processing of a request can be broken down into nine steps which are typical of what will take place in any office of the Internal Revenue Service: analysis of the request, acceptance of transfer, records search, acknowledgement, records review, making deletions, securing concurrence, demand for payment, and response.

Analysis of Request

Correspondence which purports to be a Freedom of Information Act request or which appears to be a Freedom of Information Act request is forwarded to a disclosure officer for analysis. Initially, the disclosure officer will cull for more appropriate handling any items which have been misdirected or which cite the act but actually request only services readily available under some other procedure, such as requests for copies of returns.

The disclosure officer will then reject certain types of letters (generally written by tax protesters) which give an appearance of being or which claim to be Information Act requests but do not conform to the intentions of the act and cannot be processed by locating, analyzing, or releasing existing records.

The most common of these types of correspondence are known as pseudo-requests. Some characteristics of pseudo-requests:

1. They tend to ask questions rather than request access to records.
2. The questions are frequently phrased in an accusatory or devious manner, so that they appear to be intended to serve as harassment rather than to seek clarification of any tax related subject.
3. The correspondence may consist of, or imitate, form letters and may be part of an organized campaign involving similar requests from different requesters.
4. The originators of the letters are generally adherents of groups opposed to taxation, and the letters often contain references to tax protests, constitutional

rights, or obscure matters concerning silver or gold coinage and monetary policy.

5. Any requests for records included in the correspondence are usually extremely extensive, poorly described, incorrectly addressed, or otherwise contrived to make it difficult to respond, the objective appearing to be to force a denial rather than to secure access to records.

Another category of strange correspondence which falls into the lap of the disclosure officer is referred to as K letters. The symbol *K* has no meaning, having been selected merely as an available letter for coding entries in the National Office's Freedom of Information and Privacy Section's correspondence-control system, but this correspondence has come to be known as "kook letters":

1. Correspondence received directly, or as a courtesy copy, or forwarded from other government offices, in which the writer attempts to revoke his social security number, birth certificate, marriage license, driver's license, fishing and hunting license, or other document issued by federal or local authorities. The assumption would appear to be that the writer has the right to do whatever he pleases without authorization from any government agency and therefore has no need of the document to be revoked.

2. Such correspondence may cite various arguments designed to attribute some basis in law for such action.

3. It may include references to biblical injunctions against being counted, bearing the sign of the beast or the number 666.

4. It may announce having experienced an act of manumission, enjoying a God-given right or being "free, white, and twenty-one."

5. It may somehow imply that all or some of the above exclude the writer from any legal requirement to file returns or pay taxes.

A third category of correspondence requests all the records or background information concerning certain "decisions" or "determinations" allegedly made by the Internal Revenue Service concerning the writer, such as:

1. "I am a person required to file a tax return."
2. "I didn't file a tax return."
3. "I am a person as defined by the Internal Revenue Code."
4. "My commercial activity or employment is taxable."
5. "Classifies my job description as a taxable activity for revenue purposes."
6. "I am an employee or an employer or an individual engaged in trade or business as a sole proprietor."
7. "I received diversification of corporate profits."
8. "I am a fiduciary of a trust or estate."
9. "I am required to possess a social security number absent any income from any source."
10. "A Substitute for Return has been or will be prepared for me."

In all these situations the disclosure officer must study the correspondence to decide whether it contains the elements necessary to a Freedom of Information Act request, warrants being rejected as imperfect, or deserves some other reply or no response. She must decide whether it should be retained on file and for how long. The correspondence may be transferred to interested compliance functions if it is believed to be useful in identifying previously unknown non-filers. Some of these letters may contain threats, which would identify the writer as a potentially dangerous taxpayer. On one occasion, such a letter was referred to the Secret Service, as it appeared to contain a threat against the life of the President.

Much of this correspondence is lengthy, poorly written, and almost irrational. It is difficult to ferret out the elements of a Freedom of Information Act request, if they exist. Disclosure officers may sometimes overlook a valid request hidden in what may appear to be the ravings of madmen.

Only the correspondence which is determined to constitute valid Freedom of Information Act requests or imperfect requests failing one or more of the 10 barriers will be counted in the FOIA statistics. The rest is considered detritus which does not warrant being counted as a disclosure work item. The *Internal Revenue Manual* states, "Pseudo-requests should not be permitted to drain disclosure resources needed to administer the FOIA and other programs. They should be responded to in a minimal fashion consistent with statutory requirements."

The "real" FOIA requests are then analyzed to determine if they pass the 10 barriers. Some disclosure officers will accept a request which does not meet all the criteria if the defect is not considered critical to working the request or will call the requester to obtain additional information or clarification rather than issue a denial.

Other disclosure officers will prefer, usually with the blessing of local management, to be "chicken" and reject every request not absolutely perfect in all respects, especially if they work in a district plagued by tax protesters. I once reviewed the work of a district office which had excellent production statistics and found that virtually no requester ever received any records. That, of course, is the easy way to obtain the maximum number of closings with the least effort. I stated in my report that an unsympathetic reviewer might easily conclude that the district was in total disregard of both the spirit and the letter of the Freedom of Information Act. Many of the denials issued by this district were based upon the 10 barriers or at least upon perverse interpretations of the 10 barriers.

In one unforgettable instance, the taxpayer had made an adequate request for records, but his letter did not include his social security number. He had, however, attached a copy of a notice received from an IRS Service Center, which included the number. The disclosure officer, who had rejected the request as imperfect, explained that she thought the rules required that the requester provide his social security number. When he merely encloses our notice showing the number, it is we, not he, who are supplying the number.

In another memorable case, the taxpayer had received a notice of proposed assessment of additional tax from a revenue agent, together with a self-add-ressed envelope, so that he might return a copy of the notice signed in agree-ment to the proposed assessment. The taxpayer returned the notice to the reve-nue agent with a letter which met all of the necessary elements of a request ex-cept that the only description of the records wanted was the statement "I cannot agree to anything until I see my file." The disclosure officer rejected the request because it did not reasonably describe the requested records. When I asked the disclosure officer if it did not seem obvious that the requester wished to see the file concerning the proposed assessment mentioned in the enclosed notice, she explained that she did not think she had to make such an assumption in the ab-sence of a clear request and that since taxpayers were often illogical, the re-quester could have meant anything.

The *Internal Revenue Manual* was promptly revised to make absolutely certain that such enclosures be considered when evaluating the adequacy of re-quests, but I suspect that anyone who doubted the logic of the taxpayer's re-quest and who had management's blessing for doing so could just as easily doubt the validity of the *Internal Revenue Manual*.

No one really knows how fair or effective disclosure officers are in making their initial analysis of the request. It is assumed that the readily available remedy for having a request denied as imperfect would be the prompt submis-sion of whatever additional information is necessary to perfect that request. I suspect that quite a few requesters never make that second try.

Analysis of the available statistics would seem to indicate that most im-perfect requests are never perfected. Most of the disclosure officers with whom I have discussed the matter agree with that analysis.

Once the request has been determined to be imperfect, the requester is ad-vised of the defects on Letter 1526. The description of the defect given on this form is quite succinct, and it may not always be clear to the requester what needs to be done to perfect his request, especially when there are multiple de-fects. The form does provide the name and phone number of the disclosure officer so he may be called for assistance.

Acceptance or Transfer

Valid requests will be taken into inventory if they appear to be intended for the office which received them. Controls are established so that the inven-tory may be measured, the status of requests tracked, timeliness estimated, and required statistical reports prepared.

Some valid requests cannot be taken into inventory because they appear to warrant transfer to other offices. In the absence of any clear guidance from the requester as to his intentions, the disclosure officer can only guess as to the proper treatment of requests which originate from out-of-district addresses, appear to seek records under another office's jurisdiction, or seem to be one of multiple copies of the same request.

The disclosure officer must perform research to determine where the re-quested records might be and where the request should go. Sometimes she may have to call or write the requester for clarification. At the very least, she must call her counterpart in another office to determine if transfer is appropriate and will be accepted. Sometimes the request has to be split and partial responses prepared by various offices.

These efforts cause unnecessary delays and may result in the wrong choices being made. Consequently, requesters should always make their intentions as clear as possible when dealing with distant districts or sending multiple copies of requests. They should avoid including requests for dissimilar or unrelated records in the same letter.

Sometimes requesters will ask several offices to supply the same record or to supply the local versions of closely related records. These requests appear to be attempts to shop around for the best treatment in the belief that one office may release a record which others would deny. Or there may be an attempt to compare the products of various offices in search of error and inconsistency. Disclosure officers are sufficiently sophisticated to recognize such strategies and coordinate responses with other interested offices. Many requesters have become furious when their carefully planned multiple requests resulted in the receipt of a single response speaking for all the recipient offices. Inconsistency is anathema to the bureaucracy, and every effort will be made to avoid its appearance.

Requesters who have a legitimate need to obtain similar records from various jurisdictions are advised to make their request to the National Office, which will perform the necessary coordination and make the quickest response.

Records Search

Once the request has found its way to the proper office, the records search may begin.

The Service does not have centralized files, nor do its local offices have such files. Nor are there catalogs listing the great variety of records which may exist and the locations in which they may be found. The greatest skill a successful disclosure officer may have is a knowledge of how the Service operates, how it is organized, what types of information may be contained in various records, who may maintain them, and where they may be located. The most successful disclosure officers are those who have long experience serving in the greatest possible variety of other jobs within the Service before specializing in disclosure matters. Unfortunately, persons with this breadth of experience are not readily available at the grades allotted to disclosure officers.

We once had an experienced Examination manager assigned as a team leader in the National Office. As soon as this individual arrived, production fell off sharply, typing backlogs increased, the timeliness of responses suffered, and other functions began to complain that their efforts were being wasted with unnecessary records-search requests. We found that although this individual had more than ten years experience in the Examination Division, he knew absolutely nothing about the rest of the Internal Revenue Service and had not the faintest idea what any other function did. As a result, perfectly clear requests for readily recognizable records were being misinterpreted and forwarded to the wrong functions. When he realized his shortcomings, he attempted to cover the waterfront by sending duplicate search requests to a large variety of functions in the hope that one of them might be the proper source.

Although this may have been an unusually flagrant example, it is not uncommon for new disclosure officers to lack the skills necessary to make a proper records search. A field disclosure officer once received a request for the background file which resulted in an assessment of additional tax. The records search was sent to the Collection Division, which replied that they did not have the requested record. This was not at all surprising since the Collection Division is not generally in the business of assessing additional tax, the primary function of the Examination Division. Nevertheless, the disclosure officer accepted the Collection Division response as the basis for informing the requester that the desired records did not exist. The requester, unable to imagine that no one had looked where the record was most likely to be, accepted the response without further inquiry or appeal.

In 1986, 1,224 requesters were told that the requested records did not exist or that their request would require the compilation or creation of a new record. Not one of them followed up with a new request to access the file which recorded the efforts made to service their prior request so that they might evaluate the adequacy of the records search performed. If you wanted to see the background file concerning the assessment of additional tax against you and were told that such record did not exist, you might find it worth your while to see just how effective an effort had been made on your behalf. And if you were being charged an inordinate search fee, as if someone had searched here, there, and everywhere for your records instead of focusing in on where they ought to be found, you might want to see that file also.

A FOIA request has to contain a reasonable description of records adequate to permit an agency employee familiar with the subject matter to recognize what is wanted, but the disclosure officer has to know how to get the record-search request to that employee. Those knowledgeable employees with whom the disclosure officer must deal are known as functional coordinators. Every function, that is, every separately organized activity in the Service which does not have its own disclosure officer, has a functional coordinator.

The functional coordinator is the person to whom the search memorandum will be sent. He is responsible for advising which records fall within the scope of the request, conducting the search (or passing the search on to some even more specialized person who has an even more detailed knowledge of some aspect of the function's records), analyzing the records, suggesting possible editing and preparing the function's recommendation upon the disclosure or withholding of the records. Some functional coordinators are former disclosure officers; some are future candidates for disclosure officer positions; most have had some formal disclosure training.

Obviously, the disclosure officer is almost totally dependent upon the goodwill, cooperation, and effectiveness of the functional coordinator. The functional coordinator, however, works for her managers, not for the disclosure activity, and her responses will reflect what her management wants said or done. Often, the disclosure officer may not know how appropriate or how complete the materials received are. She must somehow reconcile the materials received; the recommendation of the function; the requirements of the disclosure laws, regulations, precedents, and policies; and the desires of the requester. And she may, through accident or intent, be working with the wrong documents or with incomplete documents.

Acknowledgement

If a response is not imminent within 10 working days from the receipt of the request and there has been no other contact with the requester, the disclosure officer must choose between two forms of acknowledgement.

Generally, the simpler requests can be closed within or shortly after the 10-day response requirement, especially in the field offices, and therefore need not be acknowledged. In most cases, the need to acknowledge will arise after the records search has been initiated but before any records have been received from the function.

Form 5683 is available to acknowledge receipt of the request and to provide a response date. In practice, this form is seldom used because the disclosure officer cannot know the response date until the case has progressed to the point where she would consider response imminent. It would, of course, be foolish to acknowledge something promising a response date which is only a few days away.

The far more popular alternative is to use Letter 1522, which advises the requester of his appeal rights because the 10-day response requirement has not been met but which asks for a voluntary extension of 30 days unless exceptional circumstances require a greater period. The letter assures the requester that his request is being worked on and will be answered as soon as possible.

There are three things you should know about the voluntary extension letter.

The first is that the mere fact that you are receiving such a letter means that response is not imminent and the fact that the disclosure officer has declined to use the more specific Form 5683 means that he does not feel comfortable with promising a specific date of response.

The second is that since the disclosure officer has probably not received the records from the function, she has no idea when a response is likely and has no control over getting hold of those records. She may actually expect a considerable delay. In National Office, we routinely used the 30-day voluntary extension letter to requesters asking for Chief Counsel records, although we knew that such records were frequently not made available to us until a year or two after we asked for them.

The 30-day figure does not in any way relate to an actual expected response date to your request. It is a magic number suitable for use in every circumstance. I decided upon 30 days because most reasonable people would not hesitate to allow an agency an additional 30 days, whereas a more realistic request for a longer extension would probably provoke the average person to demand quicker service, thereby defeating the intent of obtaining a voluntary extension. There is no more than a 50 percent likelihood that the 30-day extension will be met. In fact, in National Office an FOIA case is not considered to be over-age and warrant supervisory intervention until it has been in inventory for 90 days.

The third thing you should know about the voluntary extension letter is that its intent is to prevent or delay the filing of a suit for nonresponse to the request. Consequently, the letter speaks of filing an appeal to the Commissioner as the alternative to allowing additional time. Actually, there is no requirement to appeal nonresponse; the failure to respond within 10 days permits you to file suit immediately. The hope is that if you are unwilling to let the Service procrastinate by granting the voluntary extension, you will let it procrastinate by filing an appeal.

Records Review

As soon as the disclosure officer receives the records, he is able to begin his review. Reviewing extensive or complex records for disclosure purposes is not an easy task.

To begin with, it is generally necessary to read the entire file to become familiar with the contents before even thinking of what should or should not be released. Often, it will be necessary to make notes on what the file contains, the sequence of events recorded in the file, the flow of documents in and out of the file, and the significance of each document and each event. It is impossible to make disclosure determinations without understanding both the nature of the file and the nature of the activity which prompted its creation.

The next step is to analyze the recommendations made by the function as to what they believe should be withheld. The disclosure officer should now have a good feeling for the direction this case will take. She will go through the file a second time, paying special attention to the need to answer several questions. She will want to know whether the undesirable consequences the function anticipated are likely to occur. She will question whether the items they wish withheld can be protected by available exemptions. She will want to know if the withholding of those items will necessitate withholding others for purposes of consistency. She will wish to identify other information she is legally required to protect but which the function did not include in its recommendations. And she will seek to identify information which clearly must be released.

In answering these concerns, she will begin to make notes identifying the items which she has tentatively decided to withhold. She will probably have to confer with the functional coordinator to resolve doubts about the meaning or significance of parts of the file. Ultimately, these notes will evolve into an index listing every item which is to be withheld.

The disclosure officer will search her knowledge of the law, the Service's disclosure policies and practices, the court precedents, and how Counsel has ruled on appeals involving similar questions. She will also have to seek to accommodate the preferences of the function to the extent that it is legal to do so. The result will be the creation of an extensive index identifying each item to be withheld and associating the appropriate available exemption with that item. The whole product must conform to a theory of how the law should be applied in connection with that particular case. She may have to refer back to the records repeatedly in order to ensure consistency. The entire purpose of reviewing records for disclosure demands the utmost consistency. You cannot withhold in one place what must be released elsewhere.

Some cases are so extensive that they require a team approach. In that case the disclosure officer must serve as the team leader, manager, or coach. But when several people work one case, that goal of absolute consistency becomes extremely difficult to achieve.

Making Deletions

Having decided upon the types of information which are to be withheld, the disclosure officer must identify the detailed entries to be deleted from their surrounding releasable information in accordance with the principle of segregability. This requires first identifying the entry and then making the physical deletion.

Identifying the entries to be deleted requires considerable judgment. We once performed a test in which each of seven or eight experienced disclosure technicians were asked to sanitize seven or eight identical pages of text. We found that no two of the technicians had made the same deletions. Nor could we find a single page of text which had been treated the same by more than two or three of the technicians. But none of the results could be shown to be wrong, careless, incomplete, or ineffective; they were just different. The larger and the more complicated a document, the greater the variety in editing styles which may be expected.

Case files which have been carefully sanitized by field disclosure officers will invariably yield further releases when reviewed by Disclosure Litigation Division attorneys on appeal. The prudent requester will not only appeal responses which have been sanitized but will also request similar documents from different sources or the same documents at various time intervals since each effort at sanitization will yield different results.

The average taxpayer requesting her own investigatory files knows so much more about her own affairs than did the creator of the file that she is likely to be able to fill in the gaps in sanitized records, and even knowledge of where the gaps appear is likely to be helpful. All the bits and pieces which might be obtained through a further request for similar records are likely to help in reconstructing the document.

Few disclosure officers are so careful in making deletions as to guard against allowing the form of the verb in the released portion of a sentence identify whether the deleted subject was plural or singular.

Measuring the length of a deleted typewritten word can reveal quite a lot. I have seen edited documents in which the deleted pronoun referring to an informant left a space large enough to have been *she* but a bit too wide to have been *he*. The numbers one, two, six and ten all leave the same space, but the spaces left by four, five and nine, or three, seven and eight, differ. The same may apply to place-names, dates, and every variety of detail which careless redactors thought they had protected.

I once reviewed a group of forms which had been sanitized to hide their origin by deleting the names of our regional offices and the signatures of the regional commissioners. The technician had very neatly removed all that he believed necessary but never considered that our seven regions have five different-length names and that any remaining doubt could be resolved by the fact that one regional commissioner signed his name with a huge first letter and one letter that had a tail dangling near the end of his name, a second wrote his name in tiny neat letters each of which was of precisely the same height, and the third signed by trailing her pen off the edge of the paper as if she had fallen asleep while writing her name. The technician was amazed that I was able to read the spaces just as easily as if the words were still there.

The shrewd redactor will block out handwritten information with uniform deletions large enough to protect everything that appears and some of the surrounding space. Key words in typewritten text should be deleted in a manner that takes away enough to disguise what was there before, even if an extra word or some unused space at the end of the line is also removed. Most disclosure officers do not bother.

Once the exact size and shape have been determined, a variety of techniques for making deletions are used in the Internal Revenue Service. These are razor cutting, yellow highlighting, red taping and white taping.

Razor cutting requires that the deletions actually be cut from a photocopy of the record using a razor or some sort of hobby knife. It is practical when a few small deletions are made from each page, but it is not at all practical when the deletions are large or extensive or many pages are involved. Either the cut pages or photocopies of the cut pages are released. The method is unpopular since keeping the cut copy creates messy files and giving them away seems to upset the requesters more than if they received photocopies. The biggest problem with this method is keeping track of the cutouts. These snippets of paper seem to store static electricity, with the result that they cling to the back of the sheet from which they have been cut. One of my technicians once tried to mail a requester a document which had all the deletions adhering to the back. All the recipient would have had to do is fit them into the correct holes.

Yellow highlighting requires a broad felt-tip pen which is drawn through the material being deleted. The photocopying process copies the yellow highlighting as a solid black mark which obscures the text beneath it while the original remains legible. The fallacy is that frequently the text is not really obscured and may still be read by anyone having better eyesight than the technician who made the deletions. Moreover, the use of such a pen frequently leaves the tops and bottoms of letters uncovered or fails to extend to the end of the word. I consider it a lazy man's tool which does not produce a quality product.

Red taping is the preferred method in the Internal Revenue Service. A very satisfactory red Freedom of Information editing tape was once marketed but is no longer manufactured as there was inadequate demand. Various types of red draftsman's tape serve almost as well. The tape is transparent on our file copy, but produces a sharp-edged deep black when photocopied. The problems with red taping are that not all photocopiers black out the image equally well and not all settings, work as well on those copiers which do black out the image. Actually, the newer and better machines tend to allow too much of the image to come through. It is difficult to keep clerks working on the older (but better for this purpose) copiers rather than on the newer and faster machines. It is obvious that all forms of copying for the purpose of making deletions produce results which have to be carefully reviewed before being released to the requester.

White taping consists of using typist's correction tape to block out the deletions before photocopying. This entirely opaque tape produces the most reliable deletions but is seldom used because it generates complaints from the requesters. Quite rightly, requesters claim that whiting out the material hides the extent of deletions since there are no obvious black marks to identify the gaps. We have been forced to provide new sets of copies to some requesters who complained of the white-out method because copies did not make the deletions readily apparent and actually misrepresented what was being released.

Some years ago, we received information from a requester who claimed that copies produced by both the yellow-highlighting and red-tape methods left an impression undetectable by the naked eye but which could be restored by burning a malodorous substance readily available at drugstores and subjecting the photocopies to its smoke. I don't know whether this individual was a practical joker trying to make a fool of me, but I burned a lot of sulfur in my office trying to verify the claim without ever being able to read any deletions. Some of my employees claimed that if the tax protesters had been able to smell my office, they would have considered it as evidence that I had raised the devil and bore the mark of the beast.

The alleged restoration of deletions was reported to the Department of the Treasury, which had laboratory tests made and reported that there was no known method which could successfully restore the image on copies which had been properly produced by the red tape method.

Despite this result, I am personally convinced that the edited records now being released by the Internal Revenue Service could someday be made fully legibile by the use of chemical, electronic, or computer enhancement techniques.

In the meantime, there is one thing which might prove helpful to requesters. The Service frequently cites a variety of exemptions in its denial letters but fails to indicate on the records themselves which exemption is applicable to each separate deletion made or to each page withheld. Knowing the applicable exemption could be helpful in trying to guess what was deleted. If the deletions are not properly linked to specific exemptions, ask the disclosure officer for another copy which includes this information or for an index which shows this. If he does not provide it, consider either filing an appeal for this information or making a separate request for each deleted item, so that the response will refer only to those exemptions actually applicable to the requested item.

Securing Concurrence

Once the disclosure officer has completed her work, she requires the concurrence of all other affected functions before anything can be released. She does not require concurrence to withhold information. Consequently, withholding information is an easier task than releasing it.

If the proposed response does not release any more information than was agreed to by the function in making its recommendations, no further concurrence is required. However, if there is any disagreement, nothing can be released until it is resolved. In this process of resolution, the function has the advantage because from its point of view, no response is just as good as the response it wants. The disclosure officer, however, is under pressure to dispose of the case. She can do this only when the function agrees. She must therefore sooner or later give in as much as necessary to obtain an agreement.

The disclosure officer may raise an unresolved matter to whatever level has authority over both disclosure and the function to force a decision. Unfortunately, field disclosure officers now work for the Examination Branch chief. If the records in question involve the Examination Division, which is the Service's major component, there is little likelihood that any disclosure argument will prevail over an Examination interest. Records may be found to involve other functions as well, and they too must concur before anything can be released.

As a result of these concurrence requirements, the response which ultimately is issued may not reflect the professional opinion of the disclosure officer who prepared the response. Do not assume that because the Service says information is exempt from release, it really is exempt or even that the Service believes it is exempt. It frequently is not exempt.

At the very moment that this is being written, the Examination-dominated Office of Disclosure is exploring ways to place the bulk of the Service's investigatory case files beyond the reach of the Freedom of Information Act.

Demand for Payment

When all questions of what should be contained in a response are resolved and all necessary concurrence is obtained, the disclosure officer will again consider the question of fees. If there are no fees due, or the fees are so minimal as not to warrant billing, the response will be issued.

If there are significant fees due, the disclosure officer will write to you advising that a response is ready and will be issued as soon as full payment of the remaining balance is made. This letter will imply that some information will be released to encourage you to pay the fee, but you might just as well be facing a complete denial.

If no payment is received, no further response will be made. The delinquent requester's name will be retained on a list of poor payers or nonpayers, and no future request will be worked until payment is received in advance. Payment for the prior request and interest thereon may also be required before a further request is worked. Having once been listed as a poor payer, prompt payment of future amounts will not necessarily result in a restoration of privileges. Poor payers may continue on the poor-payer list despite catching up with the arrears.

If the proper payment is received, the disclosure officer will make the final copies and issue the response. Response must be made within three days of receiving payment.

The Response

The response which constitutes a full grant, with no records denied and no deletions made, is a mere transmittal letter stating nothing more than that the requested records are enclosed or that arrangements for inspection have been made as requested.

Responses which include denials of some or all of the requested records, or which provide records to which deletions have been made, must identify and explain the exemptions upon which such denials are based. They must also identify the statutes upon which any mandatory denial rests.

Finally, the response must explain your right to appeal such denials. Unfortunately, in 1986, less than half of the requesters who received denials and were advised of how to make appeals bothered to do so.

The problem which results from so massive a failure to take advantage of appeal rights is that when the disclosure officer tries to get the function manager to agree with the proposed release of records, he may argue that undue withholding will result in an appeal which would not only mean more work but could embarrass the district director before the National Office and therefore detract from everyone's career prospects. The function manager may then smugly reply in full reliance upon the statistical evidence, "We needn't be concerned about that. They're unlikely to appeal. After all, they hardly ever do!"

Chapter Seventeen

Investigatory Files

The most important records which individual taxpayers may request from the Internal Revenue Service are the investigatory files maintained by the Collection, Examination, and Criminal Investigation divisions and the Assistant Commissioner (Inspection). The information in these files may flow from one of these functions to another as cases are transferred or referrals are made between them, and the same or similar information may also flow into the files of the Appellate Division and the various functions within the Office of the Chief Counsel. Because these files may often contain the same or similar information, we will consider the availability of their contents in terms of substance rather than the responsible office which creates or maintains them.

Generally, however, the Collection Division and the Examination Division are able and willing to release a far greater portion of their files than the Criminal Investigation Division. The Internal Security Division is often the least likely to make extensive releases. The Office of Chief Counsel will avoid the release of even seemingly innocuous information to maintain the integrity of the discovery process in litigation. Investigatory files should always be requested while still in the possession of the investigating division since they may become virtually unobtainable once referred to Chief Counsel.

It is worth knowing what kinds of information may generally be released and what kinds must be withheld or may be withheld. This knowledge will help you to decide whether to make a request, when to make a request, and what to ask for. It will also help you fill in the gaps when information has been deleted from records by providing you with an understanding of the missing pieces which may fit into the puzzle. Finally, understanding what should or should not have been withheld may help you to construct your appeal of any denial.

Before proceeding, let me remind you that (with the exception of some Inspection investigations) persons who are subject to enforcement activity leading to the creation of investigatory files are always informed of that fact by letter or in person. Do not attempt to stir the pot by asking for an investigatory file without knowing that you are in fact under investigation.

One of our best disclosure officers told me of an assertive taxpayer who requested any investigatory files being maintained on him. The disclosure officer performed the necessary research and found that his district had no record of any current activity by the Collection, Examination, or Criminal Investigation divisions. The requester immediately explained that he wanted to know if he was under investigation for tax fraud. The disclosure officer made specific inquiry of the Criminal Investigation Division, which reported that they had no record of the taxpayer. Unable to accept this, the taxpayer insisted that the disclosure officer look into the possibility that the Criminal Investigation Division was hiding something since it was inconceivable that they would not have a case on him. The disclosure officer took this suggestion of impropriety quite seriously. He obtained an Individual Master File transcript and studied it for any indication that the taxpayer might be under criminal investigation. There was none, but there were a series of curious entries which the disclosure officer called to the attention of the functional coordinator for the Criminal Investigation Division, who thought they might warrant a look at the taxpayer's recent returns. Shortly thereafter, a new response went to the taxpayer. This time it read, "At the time of your request, there had been no investigatory records concerning you; however...."

Easy Releases

If you nevertheless intend to request your file, you may expect that certain items will almost always be released to you. The Collection Division and the Examination Division would never have any reason to hide the existence of an investigation. They will always release records which initiated and control the investigation and such basic materials as normally form the skeletal file.

The Criminal Investigation Division may in theory have some rare circumstances in which an investigation in a very preliminary stage not yet subject to control might not be revealed to a requester. However, in 12 years of close involvement with disclosure matters, I have never encountered an example of such a situation. The Criminal Investigation Division has repeatedly advised me that as soon as an investigation is established by the posting of an appropriate transaction code on the Individual Master File, that information is releasable to the taxpayer. The Internal Security Division, on the other hand, may frequently have valid reason for withholding knowledge of their involvement, as when confronted with an attempt to bribe a Service employee.

Most investigatory files will include readily releasable materials such as file debris and innocuous folders and routine forms which would not indicate the direction or progress of the investigation. Transmittal forms, case transfers, requests for records, transcripts of taxpayer's accounts, correspondence between the Service and the taxpayer, copies of publicly filed documents such as notices of liens and levies, material originally submitted voluntarily by the taxpayer, items previously shown or discussed with the taxpayer, and information which Service employees would ordinarily release to the taxpayer in the course of dealing with his tax affairs are readily released. Information concerning the taxpayer's prior criminal record can be released after obtaining concurrence from the agency which provided the information.

News clippings found in the file are released, except in the rare instances in which the investigator may have highlighted sensitive items, the clippings have been selected in a manner which would reveal the direction of the investigation, or the clippings would identify other persons involved in related investigations.

Transcripts of verbatim statements or affidavits taken from and signed by the taxpayer or an authorized representative are released.

Copies of the taxpayer's returns are released if the condition in which they exist in the file is substantially the same as when filed. In some cases, copies of returns may have been marked to highlight items which are important in the development of the case and might be withheld if the release of those markings would have an adverse effect on the investigation at the time requested.

Any other items, including the history sheets which disclose the progress and the management of the case, may be released unless prohibited by statute, provided that the responsible investigator feels that the release will not have an adverse effect on the law enforcement process or create a serious impairment of federal tax administration.

Examples of interference with enforcement proceedings include anything which would alert the taxpayer to the nature and direction of the government's case, the type of evidence being relied upon, the identities of witnesses and informants, the specific transactions being investigated, and the scope and limits of the government's investigation. The importance and sensitivity of these types of interference diminish with the progress of the investigation and are generally extinguished with the closing of the case.

A great deal more information will become available after its usefulness dissipates. Generally, information which would reveal the investigator's intended actions will be withheld until those actions have been completed or have become inconsequential.

Memoranda of Interview

Although transcripts of verbatim statements or affidavits are released, memoranda of interview and the special agent's notes concerning them pose special problems. These memoranda are produced at a meeting of the special agent with the suspect under criminal investigation at which the taxpayer is afforded an opportunity to explain his actions and thereby avoid prosecution. They often contain attempts to justify or excuse behavior which may range from the fanciful to the most outrageously contrived fictions. The release of such memoranda must be considered on a case-by-case basis.

Obviously, the prospect of being provided a copy of a statement given to the special agent could serve as an inducement to obtaining the taxpayer's signature. Once signed, the statement would be released; special agents are naturally loath to release a copy of any statement which the taxpayer has refused to sign. The refusal to release the unsigned copy serves as an impetus to sign.

Memoranda of interview frequently become the subject of FOIA requests. Not unusually, the statement will have been made without the presence of an attorney, and once an attorney is obtained, her most immediate interest will be to learn precisely what her client has said. Special agents hate to give these statements away and lose the advantage they perceive they might have under such circumstances. There are, however, no readily available exemptions to protect these statements from release in most cases.

Disclosure officers wishing to support a denial must make a careful examination of the memorandum with the assistance of the special agent to determine whether its disclosure, or the disclosure of any portion, could reasonably be expected to interfere with enforcement proceedings. Line-by-line identification of contemplated interference, accompanied by specific justification for such anticipated interference, must be documented. Examples of entries which would support withholding would include admissions or confessions of the taxpayer or conflicting or contradicting statements the disclosure of which would permit the taxpayer or his counsel to develop explanations negating the impeachment value of such admissions, confessions, and statements.

The philosophy underlying the treatment of memoranda of interview is simply that the taxpayer has lied in her interview and that having lied, she will be incapable of maintaining a consistent defense in the absence of any documentation to assist her recollection of what she said. Sooner or later, she will trip herself up. To the special agent, this approach is eminently logical since the offense being investigated, tax fraud, is inherently based upon an extensive web of intricate prevarication. To a court hearing an FOIA case, the taxpayer is merely a requester seeking access to records. The entire element of fraudulent behavior, which is central to the special agent's view of the taxpayer, is absent from the FOIA case unless it can be clearly demonstrated from the memorandum of interview itself. If no admissions, confessions, contradicting or conflicting statements can be identified, defense of the document would have nothing to rely on except general conclusory statements that release would interfere with law enforcement. Affidavits based upon such conclusory statements have not been adequate to win these cases.

Typically, the general or introductory portions of statements, including the biographical portions, cannot be withheld under any circumstances. Records of taxpayers' own statements can seldom be defended.

The Service has lost several cases in which it tried to withhold memoranda of interview from FOIA requesters, but it has also won some. Moreover, even in those cases which were lost, judges elected to comment that there could be circumstances which would warrant withholding such records, thereby encouraging future denials. As a result, there has been some controversy between the Criminal Investigation Division and the Chief Counsel's Disclosure Litigation Division on the advisability of attempting to withhold memoranda of interview. Individual special agents seem unwilling to release the memoranda and tend to exaggerate the need to protect them. Disclosure officers tend to be unable to get special agents to be more realistic in evaluating the documents and restricting their defense to the more deserving cases. Disclosure Litigation attorneys are unappreciative of the special agents' concerns and are fearful of losing further litigation.

As a result of these circumstances and in view of the possible importance of these documents, it would seem prudent to appeal any denial of any portion of a memorandum of interview.

Third-Party Return Information

Investigatory files will sometimes include the return information of other taxpayers. Such information must be deleted in conformity with 26 U.S.C. 6103.

In the simplest situation, the files will include transcripts, printouts, or microfilm produced from the Individual Master File or some other automated file, which contain information on several totally unrelated taxpayers. The information will be in your file only because it happened to appear on the next line of the product; it is totally unrelated to your affairs. Such items are deleted without providing exemptions, denials, or appeal rights because they are not considered subject to your request for records. They do leave a gap when removed, and you may wonder what was in that blank space.

There may be references to other cases, basically unrelated to your interests, such as notations saying, "Review of books discontinued as supervisor directed I work on the Jones case" or "I will attempt to prepare the analysis using the methods employed in the Smith case." All such references to other taxpayers will be deleted, although enough information may remain to permit you to understand the situation.

There may, however, be entries which are related to your case and may be so entwined that some other taxpayer's return information has become your return information, as when the entries deal with a business associate some but not all of whose activities may involve you. In these cases there is a transactional relationship which will extend to some facts but not to others. The disclosure officer must sort out the entries in order to determine which must be released to you and which denied. Similar problems will arise when the file deals with the activities of spouses having filed joint returns for some years and not others. Determining what may be released becomes a difficult sorting process. As not everyone will perform such a sort with equally adequate logic and skill, denials involving mixed taxpayer return information are well worth appealing.

Third-Party Identities

The names of a great number of unrelated persons other than taxpayers may appear in a file. Some of these may be Service employees, some employees of other government agencies, some persons who cooperated or served as sources of information, and others nothing more than innocent bystanders.

The names of special agents, revenue agents, and revenue officers assigned to the case are always public, as these employees routinely identify themselves to the taxpayers whose cases they work. The names of persons who sign correspondence for the Service are released. The names of supervisors and managers having some involvement in the case are also released. Every case involves the services of large numbers of clerks, whose names may appear simply because they typed, photocopied, filed, or recorded something. Such names are usually deleted.

The names of persons in other agencies and in local government who may have made some contribution to the case are also deleted, as are the names of the many secretaries, receptionists, bank tellers, and others whom one encounters when making inquiries in the field.

The names of sources of information are deleted. These sources may be anyone from the doorman who said that you were not at home to your bookkeeper, accountant, secretary, partner, competitor, neighbor, sister, brother, wife, husband or girlfriend who may have volunteered to serve as informants, revealing all the details necessary to rid themselves of you for a long, long time. The Service may even withhold the name of a person of whom you have never heard who did nothing more than tell the investigator that he has never heard of you.

Any list of persons who have not yet been interviewed will certainly be withheld, as will the names of potential witnesses whose identities must be protected until released in the course of the judicial process.

Plans and Instructions

Case files may include remarks placed there by supervisors indicating their satisfaction or displeasure with the progress made thus far, evaluating the investigator's performance or proposing future courses of action. Such remarks are often deleted.

Investigators may place entries in the file outlining their intended course of action, explaining why some actions may not have been taken, or discussing their alternatives should some future circumstance warranty a variety of actions. Such ruminations are frequently deleted.

Some investigators pursuing a technical aspect of the case, such as preparing a report or performing a difficult analysis, may associate the manual instructions with the file as a convenient guide to assist them. If such instructions relate to future actions and may divulge the direction of the investigation, or if they constitute part of the *Law Enforcement Manual*, they would be withheld. On the other hand, instructions readily available to the public which relate to innocuous actions already performed may be released. Some disclosure officers may simply remove all such extraneous materials on the theory that they do not constitute records subject to the request.

Some file entries would be so detailed that they would tend to reveal law enforcement procedures exempt from release to the public. Entries may also tend to give away tolerances, case-selection procedures, and law enforcement criteria not available to the public. These too would be withheld.

Commercially Obtained Records

Investigatory files may sometimes contain records which need not be withheld but which a disclosure officer would hesitate to copy and release because they were obtained from a commercial source.

For instance, a taxpayer whose return was under examination was asked to provide copies of a great many checks issued in connection with his business. He failed to do so, in effect refusing to cooperate with the examination. In all probability, he failed to submit the checks because he would have had to obtain copies from his bank, which would have entailed a considerable fee. Ultimately, the revenue agent had to secure the checks from the bank by use of a summons, which necessitated the payment of a considerable fee by the Service.

The taxpayer then realized that he could obtain copies of his checks from the Service at a bargain price since the Freedom of Information copying fee was far less than the bank copying fee. The taxpayer even went so far as to ask that the checks be copied three or four on a single page. The additional labor to perform such copying wouldn't cost the requester anything, while the reduction in the number of pages would produce an additional saving.

Initially, the Service could see no way legally to avoid performing an expensive service at the bidding of a miserly taxpayer, even though it seemed totally irrelevant to the objectives of promoting access to government records. It then occurred to us that in addition to being a part of an investigatory file and the taxpayer's return information, the copies of the checks were commercially obtained records which were part of a service the bank provided its customers at a fee. For the government to release copies at a lesser fee would in effect deprive the bank of an economically valuable function. We decided not to perform such copying in the future, but it has never been determined whether the Service actually has a legal right to refuse to make such copies.

Similarly, investigatory files may sometimes contain copies of legal records, appraisals of real estate or works of art, studies of comparative pricing, reports on securities, and a variety of other products which have been purchased at a fee and which if released under the Freedom of Information Act might violate the commercial rights or economic interests of the original provider. Such records may be withheld, depending upon the individual circumstances or may merely be offered for inspection. A denial may even provide the name and address of the source from which copies may be purchased.

Transcripts of court records, although clearly public records, will generally be denied because they were obtained from court stenographers who based upon the rules of the court retain the sole right to distribute such copies for a fee.

Reports from credit bureaus and various commercial establishments may have to be denied because they remain the property of the organization which provided them and are merely lent to the recipient for limited uses. The requester's recourse in such cases is to the provider of the information.

DIF Scores

The letters *DIF* represent the term *discriminant function*, which is the statistical system used to select returns for examination. The Service considers this system to be its most important and most valuable law enforcement tool (although no one really knows whether it works). The Service is almost totally dependent upon its confidentiality as the key to maintaining and improving productivity, and 26 U.S.C. 6103(b)(2) exempts from disclosure the standards used or to be used for selecting returns for examination or data used or to be used for determining such standards. The exemption is intended to protect the data used to develop the current scoring formulas, the specific formulas, and the specific scores associated with any particular return. Not only are current and future formulas protected, but no information will be released about past formulas, nor will any information be released which would reveal whether there were past formulas no longer in use. The Service is extremely conscientious in protecting this material.

DIF scores, which appear in many Examination case files, were once made public in the belief that it was the formula which needed protection and not the individual scores which, without any definition, were merely meaningless numerals. Such releases, although they seem not to have caused any harm, were discontinued when 6103(b)(2) was enacted. Today, the Service protects anything remotely related to DIF. In fact, many disclosure officers will withhold any entry which appears to record a DIF score as 000 or 0000. Actually, these are space saving devices which appear on some automated output to indicate a position in which a DIF score would appear if one were generated. Do not bother to appeal the denial of anything remotely related to DIF (i.e., denied as protected by 26 U.S.C. 6103(b)(2)). You won't get it.

PDT Designation

Equally difficult to obtain, although not protected by law, is the PDT designation, potentially dangerous taxpayer. Apparently the theory is that if a potentially dangerous taxpayer knew that he was a potentially dangerous taxpayer, he might become even more dangerous. There is no way to know if you have been denied PDT information since you obviously would not be told that it was the designation which was deleted. However, if confronted with any document produced from the Individual Master File which shows a deletion of three or five spaces which might have contained the designation PDT or *PDT*, you might suspect that you have been designated as potentially dangerous.

Currency Transaction Reports

Currency Transaction Reports (CTRs, or Forms 4789), Reports of International Transportation of Currency or Monetary Instruments (CMIRs, or Forms 4790), and Reports of Foreign Bank and Financial Accounts (FBARs, or Forms 90-22.1) are reports made to the Secretary of the Treasury pursuant to the Financial Recordkeeping and Currency and Foreign Transaction Reporting Act of 1970, 31 U.S.C. 5311–5322. These forms are generically referred to as Title 31 reports.

The purpose of the Title 31 reports is to control the flow of large amounts of currency or financial paper to aid the struggle against drug dealers, organized-crime money-laundering operations, and other frauds or criminal operations.

Under some circumstances, the Service will process or have possession of these forms or information derived from them. They are not generally considered Internal Revenue Service records but are Department of Treasury records.

Title 31 reports and records of them, including the mere mention of their existence in a case file, are confidential. They are specifically exempted from access under the Freedom of Information Act by 31 U.S.C. 5319. When these items are deleted from a requested file, they will be denied, citing 5 U.S.C. 552(b)(3) based upon 26 U.S.C. 6103(e)(7) since any reference to 31 U.S.C. 5319 would call attention to the very documents whose confidentiality is being protected.

Knowledgeable disclosure officers will never permit the release of any information which even hints at the existence of these records in a file. Nor will they be released or acknowledged on appeal. Despite these efforts, the defense of Title 31 reports, especially the Currency Transaction Reports, may be quite soft.

In 1987, the director of the Office of Disclosure directed me to prepare procedures which would direct disclosure officers to release Currency Transaction Reports to taxpayers making Information Act requests, regardless of the status of any investigation. This would have reversed a long-standing prohibition against release, which was not only required by statute but was viewed by most Service personnel as virtually a sacred trust. I repeatedly explained to the director that such release would be a clear and direct violation of the law. I also pointed out that there would be little likelihood of prevailing upon Congress to change the law since my contacts in the Department of Treasury and the Criminal Investigation Division were aghast at the suggestion that such a valuable law enforcement tool should be shattered by making the forms subject to FOIA release.

The director was not in the least bit perturbed by these arguments and took the position that it was in the Examination Division's interest to release the information. He did not care about Criminal Investigation Division or Treasury programs. I repeatedly told him that it was nonsensical to write a manual procedure establishing the release of documents contrary to the specific requirements of the law. However, he seemed totally unable to understand or accept the requirement of the law. He directed me to prepare the manual instruction releasing the Currency Transaction Reports and to let him worry about getting it published.

Since the Service requires its employees to obey their superiors' orders, even when doing so would lead to violations of the law, I prepared a draft manual issuance and sent a copy to Chief Counsel's Disclosure Litigation Division with a note explaining that the instruction had been prepared because the director required me to do so. I hoped that alerting counsel to the potential for violation of th statute would result in their killing the document before issuance.

In preparing this manual instruction I had to work closely with some of the director's cronies in the Examination Division. I found that they were glee-ful at the prospect of releasing the CTRs since it would somehow enhance their civil programs. They were totally indifferent to the sacrifice of the criminal in-vestigations for which the reports had been designed. In the course of these dis-cussions, I was told that there were at least two types of documents currently being released to requesting taxpayers which recorded the existence of CTRs on those taxpayers. The Examination Division already had the potential to leak statutorily protected information to organized-crime taxpayers and according to what I was told, was already doing so.

I reported this to the director and suggested that rather than preparing manual instructions to release the CTRs, we should be looking into those poten-tial leaks and plugging them before there was a serious violation of the law. The director replied that looking into leaks was not part of my assignment and I should confine my activities in this matter to drafting the manual instruction as told. I suspect that those leaks have not been plugged, although I do not know precisely where they are. If you have recently deposited or transferred or dealt in large amounts of cash or securities, you might want to examine carefully any master-file printouts associated with your Examination Division case file.

Grand Jury Information

Grand juries are juries of inquiry summoned by a court. They meet in pri-vate session to receive complaints and accusations in criminal cases, hear the evidence, and return indictments when they are satisfied that a trial is war-ranted. Federal grand juries are subject to special secrecy requirements con-tained in Rule 6, Federal Rules of Criminal Procedure.

There are three sets of circumstances under which the Service becomes in-volved with grand jury activities. These circumstances may result in the Service possessing or appearing to possess grand jury information, either properly or through inadvertence. Such information may constitute Service records subject to access pursuant to the Freedom of Information Act, or it may constitute in-formation prohibited from release pursuant to Rule 6(e) and exempt pursuant to 5 U.S.C. 552(b)(3), or it may not be an agency record of the Internal Reve-nue Service and therefore not subject to Freedom of Information Act considera-tion.

Unfortunately, it is frequently virtually impossible to determine the proper disclosure status of grand jury information found in the Service's investigatory files or in the associated files of the investigatory functions.

The first circumstances encountered is the situation in which the Service makes information from its files available to the grand jury. Obviously, the in-formation released would have to constitute a copy of return information which exists prior to the release to the grand jury. Such release does not alter the disclosure status of the original material. But the transmittal which iden-tifies the material released is secret, as may be the very existence of the grand jury investigation. I have seen instances in which the same markings placed on the transmittal to identify it as containing grand jury information were then placed on the original document, mistakenly implying that it too was secret. The belief exists among some field personnel that the original information gains secrecy as a result of being divulged to the grand jury. Actually, such information in the Service's records should continue to be treated as it was before a copy was sent to the grand jury.

The second circumstance encountered is that in which information flows from the grand jury to the Internal Revenue Service under a Rule 6(e) order which may permit its use for tax-administration purposes. It continues to be grand jury information subject to secrecy and is usually properly marked to that effect. However, once the information is used for a tax-administration purpose, its disclosure status will depend on how it was used. It would be subject to the entire gamut of 26 U.S.C. 6103 requirements and may become subject to Information Act access unless otherwise exempt. But it is still marked as grand jury information, and anyone who does not think too deeply may treat it as secret forever.

Once grand jury information is used in a judicial or administrative hearing which places it on the public record, the Rule 6(e) secrecy provision is no longer applicable.

The third circumstance exists when Internal Revenue Service personnel are authorized to assist or are on loan to the Department of Justice in a grand jury investigation. In such situations, they are not acting as Service employees when working for the grand jury. Any records which they have access to or develop are not Internal Revenue Service records and should not become commingled with Service files. But they do become commingled. Employees working for the grand jury may retain their desks and their assignments in Service offices. Later, they may be unable to say which days were devoted to which agency, which actions were taken on whose behalf, or even which records were created or obtained for which employer. Nevertheless, grand jury records in the possession of IRS employees working for the grand jury are not agency records for FOIA purposes.

It may sometimes occur that personnel are on loan when the grand jury requests Service records. They ask for Service records, which they know exist, on behalf of the grand jury and then go back to their IRS office to prepare the transmittal submitting the records to the grand jury. Later, they recognize some grand jury records which the Service might find useful and initiate the action to obtain a Rule 6(e) order releasing them. After their loan to the Department of Justice is completed, they return to the Service and work the IRS cases which developed from the grand jury investigation.

Criminal Investigation Division files, despite every conscientious effort to preclude such confusion, may contain various types of grand jury information, including some which should never have been in the Service's possession. All these records will be carefully marked with legends intended to clarify the status of the information. Often these markings will have been erroneously applied. Moreover, even when a legend correctly states, "Caution, this document contains Grand Jury information," it may be difficult to determine whether all the information came from the grand jury or just some of it.

When an Information Act request for such records is received, which may be years later, it becomes almost impossible to reconstruct which IRS employees were working for the grand jury at what point, how the information came to be in our files, and whether it continues to be secret if indeed it ever was secret. There will, however, be a lot of legends on various documents cautioning people not to release secret grand jury information.

To make matters worse, I have frequently received bundles of documents from the Department of Justice asking us to give consideration to releasing or protecting what they described as our information which they found in their grand jury files. Most of the time, I had to return those bundles to the Department of Justice because I was unable to determine that they were actually Internal Revenue Service records. They appeared to me to be grand jury records.

Whenever we scheduled continuing professional education classes to keep experienced disclosure officers up to date on new developments, someone would ask that we include a session on grand jury records. Whenever we asked just what they wanted covered, we would be told that it might be a good idea to start at the beginning and try to make the whole thing as simple as possible. We always tried.

Statistical records do not reveal how many grand jury–related records were released or denied on FOIA or 26 U.S.C. 6103 grounds, or how many were treated as not being agency records. However, in 1986, Rule 6(e) was cited five times as a statutory prohibition against disclosure. I would think that any denial which appears to be related to a grand jury secrecy rationale would warrant careful consideration at the appeal level.

Other Agency Records

Investigatory files will sometimes contain records which were obtained from other federal agencies and require special handling when requested under FOIA.

Records in the possession of the Internal Revenue Service must be referred to the originating agency for direct response or for recommendations whenever the requested records are classified or bear any other designation restricting their release. Some records state that the originating agency retains ownership and the records should be returned when they have served their purpose or when they are requested. Other records will merely be inscribed with a prohibition against any further distribution. All these restrictions and any others encountered will be recognized by the Service as the equivalent of being classified.

Whenever such records are encountered in a requested file, the requester will be informed that coordination is taking place and the receiving office will transfer the records to National Office, which serves as the contact with all other federal agencies. Ultimately, the requester may receive a response from the originating office, from the National Office of the IRS, or even from the field office to which the original request was addressed, depending upon what appears to be the most practical approach in any situation.

If the other agency's record is not classified or restricted in any way, the Internal Revenue Service may make its own determination on whether to release. Some other agency records will be withheld for Service purposes; others will be released when that result appears obviously appropriate. In many cases, the proper disposition of the records will not be apparent, and it will be referred to the originating office for a determination.

Records obtained from state and local agencies will be treated in a similar fashion, except that the National Office will not serve as the contact point.

The frequency with which other agency records are encountered is probably far less than the average taxpayer would guess. In those few instances when it does occur, it appears to create some difficulties. All law enforcement agencies are extremely eager to maintain cordial relations with all other law enforcement agencies. As a result, coordination between agencies sometimes leads to a "we'll defend it if you want us to" attitude. The requester may find himself receiving a denial from whichever agency feels most confident that it has a good basis for defending the record.

Joint Committee on Taxation

Section 6103(f) of the Internal Revenue Code provides special rules by which committees of the Senate and the House of Representatives may access tax returns and the return information. Such access requests may be made by the chief of staff of the Joint Committee on Taxation.

These joint committee requests and documentation relating to them are sometimes found in investigatory files and require special disclosure consideration. The requests do not constitute agency records of the Internal Revenue Service and are not subject to the Freedom of Information Act.

If a request seeks access to a file found to contain a joint committee request but does not specifically ask for the joint committee document, that document and any material making reference to it will be removed from the file. No exemption will be cited and no mention will be made of the existence of any joint committee involvement.

If a request specifically seeks to obtain a copy of the joint committee request or any related documentation, the requester will be advised that the materials do not constitute agency records within the scope and reach of the Freedom of Information Act. No exemptions will be cited.

History sheets or other documents which record information concerning the joint committee request will be edited so as not to reveal anything about the content of the request. The records, presumably return information, released to the committee would continue to be available to the taxpayer, but they could not be released in a manner which would in effect alert the taxpayer to the parameters of the joint committee request.

Section 6405 of the Internal Revenue Code provides that the joint committee is given reports of any refund or credit in excess of $200,000. Such reports are agency records and are subject to Information Act considerations in accordance with their content. If the report was requested and its release contemplated, the matter would first have to be coordinated with the joint committee. Presumably, the Service would give careful consideration to any recommendations the joint committee might make concerning the release of such report.

Any follow-up request or other document generated by the joint committee resulting from a refund or credit report would not be an agency record and would not be available under the Freedom of Information Act.

Foreign Government Contacts

The Service occasionally receives information from foreign governments concerning taxpayers. Tax treaties provide that under some circumstances the Service may provide information and assistance to foreign governments. At times, there may be consultations or exchanges of information concerning persons of interest to several taxing jurisdictions, or questions may have to be resolved concerning the extent to which any taxpayer's affairs are subject to either government's jurisdiction.

Such events would give rise to records, either in separate files or within investigatory files, which may be extremely sensitive. Their release could adversely affect the relationship between governments.

Field disclosure officers may deny such records to requesters whenever adequate exemptions are available, but they have no authority to release records relating to contacts with foreign governments. Only the National Office may release such records and then only with the concurrence of various involved functions, the Assistant Commissioner (International), other agencies of the U.S. government, and the foreign government involved.

Taxpayers who have made specific requests for such records are advised that their requests have been transferred to the National Office for resolution. Taxpayers who have made general requests for an investigatory file (which happens to contain such records) will be informed only that some part of the requested records have been referred to National Office for response. They are not told the nature of the records referred.

Some foreign governments do not share our enthusiasm for releasing records to requesting taxpayers and will insist upon withholding the records. Since the Service is interested in maintaining the best relations with foreign governments and protecting our sources of information, any request to withhold information, no matter how innocuous it might seem, is likely to be complied with.

Responses denying access to records of contacts with foreign governments would be framed in terms of the disclosure's being prohibited by the Internal Revenue Code as seriously impairing federal tax administration. The rationale behind such denial would be that the release of (even quite harmless) data, if offensive to the foreign government involved, would cause the loss of the future cooperation of that government and of any other governments which might share similar concerns. This rationale is, of course, unlikely to appear in the response, which would try not to reveal the existence of foreign government contacts if not already known to the taxpayer.

Records concerning information received from Interpol, the International Police Organization, would be treated in a similar fashion.

Other Factors

There is, of course, no limit to the types of records which might be found in an investigatory file. Nor would there seem to be any limit to the considerations which might cause a disclosure officer to apply the available exemptions in more or less stringent fashion. Requesters should not be surprised to receive responses which release more or less information than anticipated since no two cases will involve the same circumstances.

There are, however, four factors which the *Internal Revenue Manual* states should be considered in determining the level of disclosure in a particular case:

1. The presentation by the taxpayer of falsified records or the possibility of the use of the records for impeachment purposes during the tax proceeding.

2. Involvement of organized-crime or narcotics figures.

3. A record of violence on the part of the taxpayer which indicates the possibility of threats toward Service employees or other persons, or prior record of crime involving assaults.

4. Attempts to bribe or attempts to threaten the investigating officials.

Although the statutory justification for this guideline is not readily apparent, it has appeared in the publicly available portion of the *Internal Revenue Manual* for more than ten years without adverse comment or challenge from any quarter.

Chapter Eighteen

Appeals and Litigation

To appeal the withholding of records to the head of the agency and to litigate the withholding in a federal court are the driving engines which obtain agency cooperation in making the Freedom of Information Act process work.

Unfortunately, in the experience of the Internal Revenue Service, these motivating forces are not used often enough to serve as convincing arguments to obtain adequate cooperation. Almost every manager faced with a records-access request acts on the assumption that there is little likelihood of an appeal or a suit. This assumption also governs the level of staffing available to process requests, the procedures established, and the practices tolerated. The assumption that requesters will fail to pursue their requests to ultimate resolution usually proves to be correct.

In 1986, the Internal Revenue Service denied access to records 1,996 times. There were, however, at least 1,000 cases in which a response claimed no record existed or could be located, or otherwise exercised a disposition which might have warranted an appeal. Even among those requests granted, there must have been hundreds of instances in which response was so long delayed as to warrant appeal or litigation.

Despite this extensive field of opportunity, the year's activities produced only 802 appeals. Of these, 496 were treated as nonappeals; that is, the ordinary process of initial response was continued in total disregard of the appeal. Thus, all this activity really produced only 198 firm responses to appeals, which included 21 full grants, 65 partial grants and 112 full denials.

During 1986 there were a total of 48 FOIA suits filed against the Service. Of these, 28 were taken on the basis of exhaustion of administrative remedies because the agency failed to respond within the applicable time limits.

Of the 10,820 FOIA requests received during 1986, only 7 percent were appealed, less than 2 percent received appeal responses, and less than 0.5 percent resulted in litigation. Such statistics would indicate that either requesters are quite satisfied with the way the Service administers its FOIA program or requesters are unaware of the availability of the right to appeal or litigate, or view those rights as too difficult or too remote.

My experience in discussions with requesters, including some attorneys for prestigious Washington law firms, was that they were not aware of their options, they were unable to distinguish between appeals and litigation, or they did not appreciate the ease with which either could be undertaken.

Appeal or Litigation

Appeal or litigation may be instituted whenever properly filing an initial request results in the withholding of records. This withholding may consist of the denial of access in a response to the initial request, or it may consist of a failure to make a timely response. Thus, it is not necessary to await a response before taking an appeal or filing a suit.

If the Service fails to make a response granting or denying access within 10 days (excluding Saturdays, Sundays, and legal public holidays) of receiving the request, the requester has the choice of appealing within the agency or immediately filing suit. Such actions may be delayed by the agency invoking an extension, which may not exceed an additional 10 working days. However, the Service never uses such an extension at the initial-request level, preferring to save it for use when an appeal has been filed. The acknowledgments and voluntary extension letters the Service issues have no power to delay appeal or litigation. Thus, upon nonresponse, administrative remedies are considered exhausted, and the requester has the choice to appeal or to rush into court.

If the Service has issued a determination, the requester is precluded from initiating an immediate suit and must take the appeal route if he wishes to proceed further. If a requester who could have filed suit because of nonresponse fails to do so until an initial determination is issued, he is forced to take an appeal in order to exhaust his administrative remedies.

Appeal must be taken within 35 days of the date of the response or the date of the transmittal letter providing the last of the records being released as a part of that response. Failure to meet this deadline could preclude any further action on that FOIA request, although in practice there have been several instances in which the Service accepted appeals which were filed several days after expiration of the appeal period.

If the agency denies the appeal or fails to respond to the appeal within 20 days (excluding Saturdays, Sundays, and legal public holidays), the requester may file suit. However, the Service may at the expiration of the 20 days invoke the 10-day extension which was not used for the initial response, thereby delaying suits slightly. In practice, both the appeal response and the requester's initiation of litigation occur long after this 10-day extension becomes irrelevant.

Appeals and suits are not necessarily limited to those instances in which a request has been denied or there has been nonresponse. Requesters have taken such actions in cases involving fee-computation disputes, failure to allow fee waivers, alleged inadequacy of search, objections to claims that records do not eixst, claims that wrong records were supplied, or even situations in which full grants were alleged not to have included all the records requested. There would appear to be no limit to the possibilities in which records may have been improperly withheld, although the agency may view itself as having complied with the request.

A decision to appeal or to file suit and when to do so will depend upon the requester's needs, the types of records involved, whether patience may be anticipated to result in a release or merely a long delayed denial, and the requester's perception as to whether his request is being worked and is progressing adequately, is legitimately awaiting its turn in line, or is being ignored or intentionally delayed.

Several factors must be considered in making such judgments. When records are subject to editing to release the segregable portions, it is to the requester's advantage to allow a second reviewer the opportunity to release a portion of what was withheld by the first reviewer. In that circumstance it may be worth some delay, to permit a complete initial response and an appeal response prior to litigation. If, however, there are indications that procrastination is being practiced, immediate appeal or litigation may be preferable. If the procrastination on initial request involves Chief Counsel records, there may be little sense in taking an appeal to Counsel, which would only make matters worse, since Counsel works its appeals no more rapidly than its initial requests. Finally, if the requester is demanding records unlikely to be released, it would obviously make good sense to rush into litigation as soon as possible.

On the other hand, in the Internal Revenue Service, field officials generally act within far shorter time frames than National Office officials, the administrative side of the house usually acts much faster than the attorneys in Chief Counsel's Disclosure Litigation Division, and the slowest of agency actions may proceed more rapidly than would litigation. A quick appeal or immediate litigation may not speed up the processing of a request but merely delay it further.

Before deciding on an appeal of nonresponse or a quick recourse to litigation, I recommend discussing your situation with the disclosure officer handling the case. If he has actually received the records, you can usually rely on his estimate of a completion date. If he has not received the records, he is as helpless as you are. He may actually welcome an appeal or a suit to resolve his dilemma in not being able to secure the records. Some assistance in planning strategy may be had by considering the time frames which may be expected in the processing of requests.

Processing Time Frames

Field offices are generally able to respond to about half of their requests within the statutory requirement of 10 business days. When a field office requests a 30-day voluntary extension, there is an excellent likelihood that the extended date will be met unless the requested records are very extensive or complicated. Most field offices do not have backlogs of requests causing delays unrelated to the case at hand. Exceptions to this rule may occur at times, especially in the Western Region where Los Angeles and Anchorage districts have a history of sudden receipts of large numbers of tax-protester requests, causing a virtual paralysis of the disclosure operation.

When nonresponse of field cases is appealed, the most likely result is that Chief Counsel's Disclosure Litigation Division will ask the field office to continue working the case, so that the appeal is closed as a nonappeal. The other possibility, most likely to happen only when Disclosure Litigation has some interest in the records and is afraid the field might release something, is that the case will be lifted into National Office for a formal appeal response. Thus an appeal risks taking the case from a more liberal to a less liberal processing environment. I would hesitate to appeal a request being worked in the field so long as there was an appearance of a likelihood of response within a reasonable time.

In the National Office, few requests other than the simplest can be completed within the 10-day requirement. Approximately half of all National Office requests will be completed before the 30-day voluntary extension expires. About 90 percent of all cases received will be closed within 60 days of receipt. A few more cases will be closed in the next 30 days. Any case not closed within 90 days of receipt is quite likely to continue to be open a year or even two years later.

These over-90-days cases almost all consist of requests for Chief Counsel records which the Office of Disclosure cannot process until the Disclosure Litigation Division makes the records available. Typically, this will not happen until any significance of those records has been rendered irrelevant by the passage of time. Most such requests originate from attorneys or other tax professionals, but they are generally neither appealed or litigated.

As the months went by and no records were received from Counsel, my technicians would call their counterparts in the Disclosure Litigation Division pleading for the release of records or for some explanation which would account for these outrageous delays. Invariably, they would be told that the records had been collected and reviewed by an attorney and a memorandum containing recommendations to us had been prepared. These items were claimed to be on a branch chief's desk awaiting review and approval, but that review and approval would never take place. Months later, the promised records would still be awaiting review or have been returned to the responsible attorney for a "second look."

Sometimes I would call the responsible Disclosure Litigation branch chief and demand that the records which had been awaiting review be released to us. Invariably, I would be told that something would be coming down to us in a day or two. But nothing ever came.

Many of these older requests are never answered. The Office of Disclosure will periodically write to the requester to ask if the records are still needed and point out that if the request is withdrawn, no fees will be charged for the services performed. If these letters do not result in the withdrawal of the requests, periodic telephone calls will be made. Ultimately, we would get lucky and learn that the requester no longer worked for the law firm from which the request had been made and no one else knew anything about the request. Other times, the requester no longer remembered making the request. Sometimes our letters would be returned as undeliverable, or we would learn that a telephone had been disconnected. Several times we learned that the requester had died while waiting for our response. All of these cases would ultimately be included in the "Closed Without Determination" category in our statistics. In 1986, we had 333 requests closed without determination.

Portrait of Procrastination

If any doubt exists that the Disclosure Litigation Division practices procrastination for the purpose of avoiding the release of sensitive Chief Counsel files, that doubt can be resolved by detailing the actions involved in a single request which lingered in inventory for more than two years without resulting in the release of any records.

On February 15, 1985, a well-known and highly respected organization specializing in tax matters made a Freedom of Information Act request, which read as follows:

> In reporting to shareholders on Forms 1099 for 1984, the American Telephone & Telegraph Co. (AT&T) has taken the position that a sum amounting to approximately 39¢ per share should be excluded from current income. The sum relates to transactions between AT&T and the Pactel Group during the AT&T divestiture. The IRS reportedly has taken the position that this sum should be included in dividend income by AT&T shareholders.
>
> We are currently working on a news story relating to this dispute between AT&T and the IRS. In connection with this story, we would like to obtain any documents in the Service's possession which outline the basis for the IRS' view that a sum amounting to 39¢ per share should be treated as dividend income by AT&T on Forms 1099. Our purpose is to present to the public the legal, or other justification, for the Service's position in this dispute. AT&T, of course, has already made public its reasons for disagreeing with the IRS' viewpoint.

Here was a perfected request from a responsible requester asking for records which were of legitimate current concern to the public. Presumably, such well-described records would easily be located and would be subject to some established disclosure principle which would result in their prompt release or denial, whichever was determined to be appropriate. It was, in fact, a request which any ordinary application of good judgment would have identified as warranting prompt if not preferential treatment.

The request was immediately forwarded to Disclosure Litigation Division. As usual, no records were forthcoming. Periodic follow-ups were made. The usual excuses were provided: the records had been reviewed, recommendations were being reviewed, the materials would soon be available. The requester received a request for a voluntary extension but chose neither to appeal nor to file suit.

More than a year after the request was made, the Office of Disclosure continued to be completely frustrated in its attempts to secure records from Counsel. On April 4, 1986, we wrote to the requester stating that several months had passed since we had last written concerning the request, that we were still not able to respond, that we were working on the request, and that if the records were no longer needed, the request could be withdrawn. The letter went on to advise that the delay could be considered a denial of the request and that an appeal could be filed. The statement that we were working on the request was something of a white lie, for we had no records on which to work, and as far as we could tell, Disclosure Litigation Division had done nothing for months. It was hoped, however, that this letter would either elicit a withdrawal of the request or provoke an appeal. Either one would have removed the item from our inventory.

Much to our consternation, the requester thanked us for our letter and stated that they would be grateful if we would continue to process the request. Unfortunately, such a polite and considerate response provided us no cudgel with which to beat Counsel into compliance with the law. We continued to press Disclosure Litigation for the records. In September 1986, a year and a half after the request, the attorney working the case told us that he could not give us a response because "there is considerable interest in this case at this time." We were told that the materials might already have been released to another media representative and that a denial was contemplated but it was feared that a suit might be filed.

In October we were told that the request seemed "dormant" but that further contact with the requester might prompt a suit. In February, exactly two years after the request was filed, we were told that there was no change in Counsel's position, that the case appeared to be dormant and that we should do nothing because the requester "had not pressed for the information."

Shortly thereafter, the director of the Office of Disclosure called the Disclosure Litigation branch chief concerning this case and was told, "No problem!" But that pleasant response did not mean that we could now obtain records, only that we could now talk to the requester.

On March 9, 1987, slightly over two years after the original request, I was able personally to explain to the requester that we were encountering some difficulties in processing the request. I was unable to give any hint what those difficulties might be since I had never seen the records and had no idea why they were not promptly released. The requester, however, was nice enough to agree that the issue seemed to be a dead horse and we could close the case.

The amazing part about Disclosure Litigation Division's procrastination efforts is that it is the director of the Disclosure Litigation Division who is delegated authority to serve as the appeals officer for the Service and is the agency's chief expert on the Freedom of Information Act, which is much like putting the fox in charge of the henhouse.

My strongest recommendation is that whenever a request is made for Chief Counsel records, do not bother with an appeal and certainly do not allow even a single day to pass beyond the statutory period for response. Always file an immediate suit on the very first day that you may do so. Nothing else will secure Counsel's attention and compliance with the law.

Filing an Appeal

Filing an administrative appeal is an extraordinarily simple procedure. There is no cost. No requester should ever hesitate to appeal in the belief that an appeal would require some significant effort.

The appeal must be made in writing and signed by the requester. It must be addressed and mailed to Freedom of Information Appeal, Commissioner of Internal Revenue, c/o Ben Franklin Station, P.O. Box 929, Washington, DC 20044. This address serves to maintain the fiction that the Commissioner is involved in considering appeals. Actually no Commissioner of Internal Revenue has seen any FOIA appeal in at least 10 years. The official actually handling appeals is the director, Disclosure Litigation Division, who, naturally is able to abuse this responsibility to provide extra protection for Chief Counsel records. Thus, an appeal of nonresponse to a request for Chief Counsel records is a request for prompt action directed to the very person responsible for the policy of procrastination.

The walk-in address for hand delivery of requests is more candid: Office of the Director, Disclosure Litigation Division, Chief Counsel, National Office of the Internal Revenue Service, 1111 Constitution Avenue, Washington, DC 20224.

The appeal must reasonably describe the records requested, set forth the address to which response may be sent, specify the date of the initial request, petition the Commissioner to grant the request for the records, and state any arguments in support thereof. Portions of these requirements can be met by attaching a copy of the initial request and a copy of any denial or other response received.

Requesters are not seriously expected to be able to state arguments in support of their appeals and may simply state the belief that the records withheld are not exempt. It will usually be worthwhile to stress in the appeal the need to adhere to the requirements of Policy Statement P-1-192 and request that any exemptions which need not be asserted be waived.

It would also be appropriate to request a balancing test for records which might be withheld on the basis of an unwarranted invasion of privacy but could better be released in recognition of the public interest. If the record being requested constitutes your return information, it would also be worthwhile to cite 26 U.S.C. 6103 and object to the use of any FOIA exemption to protect records whose release would not seriously impair federal tax administration.

Some sophisticated requesters present detailed arguments based upon legislative history and legal precedent to support the release of the requested records. Such arguments may be of some benefit in any future litigation, but I doubt that anyone working an appeal would pay attention to them.

Some requesters include their appeal in the initial request, asking that if no response is made by the tenth day or a response withholding any of the requested records is issued, the request should be immediately transferred to the Office of the Commissioner for consideration as an appeal. Such a request would appear to violate the regulations and is ignored by disclosure personnel working initial requests.

Litigation

The scheme for litigation presented by the Freedom of Information Act appears to be extremely simple. The litigant merely files a complaint; the court examines the documents and releases those found not to be exempt. This apparent simplicity has prompted some requesters to litigate on their own behalf, without an attorney, and some requesters have been successful, winning major precedent-setting cases by their own efforts.

Unfortunately, there have also been cases in which the Service was successful in the defense of cases which, in my opinion, had no merit. I believe that the litigating process in Information Act cases is far more complicated than it appears to be. Gadflies seeking the satisfaction of prevailing single-handedly against the establishment may wish to indulge themselves, but serious requesters are strongly urged to seek the best available legal services and to back those services up with the assistance of a consultant familiar with the creation, use, and maintenance of the agency records at issue.

The expense of an attorney need not fall entirely upon the requester. The act provides: "The court may assess against the United States reasonable attorney fees and other litigation costs reasonably incurred in any case under this section in which the complainant has substantially prevailed." Thus, the successful litigant has some hope of not having to bear the total costs of bringing the suit.

In order to be eligible for an award, the requester must substantially prevail; that is, the court must order the release of at least a portion of the records at issue. The released portion must be something more than a trivial mite, but it need not be all or nearly all of the records requested. In addition, the court must in its discretion find some public benefit in the request beyond the immediate personal needs of the requester. A commercial benefit to the requester reduces the likelihood of an award.

Most important, however, the agency's withholding must not have a reasonable basis in law. If the agency withheld the records to frustrate the requester, avoid embarrassment, or hide evidence of wrongdoing, there would obviously be no reasonable basis in law. If, however, the agency withheld records which might arguably have been exempt and the agency merely failed to have as good an understanding of the law as the court, an award would be unlikely. The existence of the Internal Revenue Code provisions prohibiting the release of return information which would seriously impair federal tax administration provides the Service with a good basis for arguing that even somewhat excessive efforts to protect such information would be consistent with the intent of the law.

The amount of an award would be based upon the quality and the extent of the work performed by the attorney and the prevailing local rates for attorneys providing services appropriate to the case. In one Internal Revenue case, a requested attorney fee was severely reduced by a judge who commented that a simple Freedom of Information case should not require the expenditure of efforts which would have been more appropriate to a complicated public-utility rate-making case.

Having balanced the anticipated costs, the likelihood of some reimbursement, the chances for a successful outcome, and the importance of the requested records, the litigant proceeds by filing a simple complaint with a Federal District Court.

The complaint may be filed in the district of the requester's residence, principal place of business, locality in which the records are known to exist, or the District of Columbia. The District of Columbia is usually favored by requesters because the District Court has more experience and expertise in FOIA matters than may be found in other areas. Within the Internal Revenue Service, however, there is a general apprehension, based upon some embarrassing defeats, about suits filed in the Ninth Circuit (covering Alaska, Arizona, California, Hawaii, Idaho, Montana, Nevada, Oregon, and Washington).

The complaint must demonstrate that the requester has exhausted administrative remedies by having made a proper request and received an initial and an appeal response, or by the expiration of the statutory time requirements for response. The proper agency must be named as a defendant, and the complaint must state the facts concerning the requested records and allege that the withholding was in violation of law. The complaint should ask for an order for the production of the records by the agency and may ask that the court expedite the suit, award attorney's fees and costs, find that the withholding of the records raises questions of arbitrary or capricious action warranting referral to the Merit Systems Protection Board, and request an injunction preventing the agency from improperly withholding the records in the future.

A copy of the complaint must be served upon the Internal Revenue Service by delivery to the Commissioner of Internal Revenue: Attention: CC: GLS, 1111 Constitution Avenue, Washington, DC 20224. The government must provide an answer or plead to the complaint within 30 days of service. This answer, however, generally does nothing more than state that the agency considers its actions to have been correct.

At this point the procedure becomes more complex, and questions of legal strategy requiring the assistance of a competent attorney arise. The requester may file a motion for summary judgment, or the government may file such a motion. There may then be a cross-motion for summary judgment, or the requester may file an opposition to the government's motion and seek discovery to contest the government's claims of exemptions.

Since the requester does not know the nature and contents of the records at issue, it is virtually impossible to propose much of an argument in favor of disclosure. To overcome this problem, the court may require the government to submit an index which describes each document or segregable portion withheld and offers detailed justifications for its exemption. However, the agency will construct the index not to reveal the very details it is attempting to withhold. Consequently, the index may add little to the requester's ability to argue in favor of release. Further motions may then become necessary to expand upon the government's generalized or ambiguous descriptions. The adequacy of the search for records may be questioned.

Ultimately, the court may inspect the records or may proceed on the basis of affidavits provided by the agency. The advantage to the requester would appear to lie with the court's making an examination of the records since the affidavits tend to support the agency's arguments in support of withholding. Disputes as to issues of fact may arise, requiring the presentation of testimony and the use of expert witnesses.

Once a decision has been rendered, either the requester or the government may pursue available appeals. The Service had been involved in Freedom of Information cases which lasted years, went from district courts to circuit courts and were remanded back again, and ended when heard by the Supreme Court.

The placement of the burden of proof upon the government, the general assumption of the releasability of records in the absence of a showing to the contrary, and the consideration the courts tend to give requesters litigating on their own behalf may enable some requesters to prevail without legal assistance.

The bottom line is a simple one. You will almost certainly do better with the assistance of an attorney. You may become lost in the maze of legal procedure if you proceed on your own behalf. But if you do nothing, you will get nothing. And if enough people do nothing, the Freedom of Information Act becomes totally ineffective.

Chapter Nineteen

Reading Rooms

The Freedom of Information Act provides that each agency make available for public inspection and copying final opinions made in the adjudication of cases, statements of policy and interpretation, and administrative staff manuals and instructions to staff that affect a member of the public. The act does not specify how these items are to be made available for public inspection and copying, and the Internal Revenue Service does not necessarily have, or admit to having, all the types of material covered.

The Service decided to comply with this inspection and copying requirement by establishing a National Office Freedom of Information Act Reading Room and seven regional reading rooms. Over the years, as the Service began to admit that materials were subject to this requirement, they were added to the reading room collection. In some cases materials were added because it was not considered worth arguing that they were not subject to the inspection requirement; in other cases materials were added because doing so seemed to offer some advantage to the Service. The reading room began to serve as an adjunct to the disclosure operation by providing a means for the inexpensive distribution of materials whose availability under the act was no longer at issue. There are currently about three dozen categories of records which have been designated as reading-room shelf materials.

The materials available from the reading room constitute a vast reservoir of information on how the Service operates. In addition, they serve two important functions in connection with your request for your own records. They provide the explanations and the background information which can make your personal records meaningful, and they can help you to identify other records which you may wish to request, either concerning your personal tax affairs or documenting how the Service operates.

There are two major advantages to requesting shelf materials directly from the reading room rather than through a field disclosure officer: The reading room fills most requests for copies within three or four days of receipt, and there is never a search fee for shelf materials.

The National Office FOIA Reading Room

Some materials are far too extensive to be useful, and reading-room personnel are often able to suggest ways to limit a request to a reasonable portion

or a small sample which would prove helpful without becoming burden-
some.

The reading room is located in room 1569 of the Internal Revenue Service's
National Office. Persons who use the Tenth Street and Pennsylvania Avenue
entrance may enter the reading room without having to pass the building guard
or identify themselves. An assistant is always present, but all materials are
located on open shelves and a self-service copying machine is provided.
Anyone who wishes to remain anonymous is able to enter the room, use all its
facilities, and copy any of its records without having to identify themselves.
The reading room is open from 9:00 A.M. to 4:00 P.M. and is accessible to handi-
capped persons.

The mailing address to request copies of shelf materials:

Freedom of Information Reading Room
OP:EX:D:F:RR
Internal Revenue Service
1111 Constitution Avenue, N.W.
Washington, DC 20224

Persons who wish assistance in framing their requests or have questions about reading room operations may call (202) 566-3770.

The Shelf Materials

The following documents are currently maintained on the National Office
reading-room shelves:

- *Actions on Decisions* (AODs). An Action on Decision is a document
which determines whether the Service will recommend appeal of an adverse
decision in Tax Court, District Court, or Claims Court. In a Tax Court case,
the AOD also determines whether the Commissioner will acquiesce or nonac-
quiesce in such issue. Nonacquiescence signifies that the Service will further
litigate the issue in cases where the facts and circumstances are substantially the
same as those in the case decided adversely. The acquiescence or nonacquiescence in a Tax Court case is published in the *Internal Revenue Bulletin*.

- *Actuarial Rulings.* Rulings issued by the Employee Plans Technical and
Actuarial Division containing actuarial computations based on specific facts
and circumstances.

- *Approved Master or Prototype Plans.* Retirement plans which have been
determined to comply with all existing code and regulatory provisions, and
which could serve as suitable models for the construction of other plans.

- *Art Advisory Panel and Art Print Panel Opinions.* Evaluations of
works of art for purposes of determining permissible values for estate tax and
contribution purposes.

- *Bulletin Index-Digest System.* A research tool designed to help find the
Service position on any tax issue contained in documents published in the *Internal Revenue Bulletin*.

- *Catalog of Federal Tax Forms, Form Letters and Notices (Publication 676).* A list of federal tax forms and letters and notices issued to taxpayers, including short explanations of their intended use. Permits finding the titles when only the form numbers are known.
- *Chief Counsel Orders and Notices.* Documents which establish the policies and practices of the Office of Chief Counsel, including the *Chief Counsel Manual.*
- *Comments Received in Response to a Notice of Proposed Rule Making.* The reading room maintains copies of comments considered to be of current interest. Older comments can be retrieved with advance notice. These expressions of the public's views on pending regulations are not only informative but can be used as a measure to determine how responsive the Service is in conforming the final rules to the popular will.
- *Commissioner's Advisory Group Meeting Minutes.* Minutes of the meetings of a group of attorneys, accountants, scholars, and businessmen which considers tax-administration matters in order to make policy recommendations to the Commissioner.
- *Commissioner's Annual Report.* A report which states the significant achievements of the Service during the year. Contains extensive statistical tables on returns processed, taxes collected, and other actions taken. Comparison of various issues permits the reader to recognize the Service's changing focus and trends. The reading-room collection is complete back to 1863 and constitutes a valuable historical collection.
- *Cumulative List of Organizations (Publication 78).* A list of organizations with current ruling or determination letters permitting contributions to be deductible. Extremely comprehensive, although not all-inclusive at any particular time. Provides names and locations of organizations and serves as a source for information upon which to base requests for access to exempt organization returns.
- *Cybernet.* Invoices for equipment and services processed by Contracts and Procurement. Serves as source for information on which to base requests for access to the related contracts.
- *Exempt Organizations Continuing Professional Education Technical Instruction Program.* Contains essays on exempt organizations technical topics. Recaps current technical developments.
- *General Counsel's Memorandums (GCMs).* Formal written legal opinions that are prepared in the Interpretive Division, Employee Plans and Exempt Organization Division, and General Litigation Division of the Office of Chief Counsel. A GCM contains the analysis and conclusion of the division preparing the opinion and is used as a research source by Counsel personnel but is not a statement of the policy or position of the Service. Positions contrary to an existing GCM may be taken only after consultation with the issuing division.
- *Historical Tables.* Fiscal-year budget messages and proposals for the various IRS functions.
- *Internal Revenue Bulletins.* The reading-room collection contains cumulative bulletins from 1919 to the present and weekly bulletins prior to the

inclusion in Cumulative Bulletins. The *Bulletin* constitutes the major IRS publication for acquainting the public with Revenue Rulings, Revenue Procedures,
Treasury Decisions, Delegation Orders, and various announcements concerning tax administration.

• *Internal Revenue Code.* Title 26 of the United States Code, the basic law
governing all Internal Revenue Service activities.

• *Internal Revenue Manual.* The massive loose-leaf service which constitutes the instructions to staff which direct Internal Revenue Service personnel
in the performance of their duties. See Chapter 20.

• *Internal Revenue Service Financial Plan.* The Service's budget and how
it affects the accomplishment of programs.

• *Internal Revenue Service Input to the Departmental Annual Report to
Congress on the Freedom of Information Act.* Statistical details on the performance of FOIA services. Includes the name and title of every official who
denied an initial request or an appeal for access to records.

• *Keyword in Context (KWIC) Index by Regions.* An index to regional,
district and service-center issuances which supplement the instructions to staff
contained in the *Internal Revenue Manual.* Helps to identify instances in which
local instructions may differ from the procedures established by the National
Office. See Chapter 20.

• *News Releases.* Public affairs issuances to the news media, intended to
announce items of topical interest and frequently the source of local news items.
Tells you what the Internal Revenue Service wants you to know about its
operations.

• *Privacy Act of 1974, Resource Material.* A compendium of the basic law
and regulations, Notices of Exempt Systems, and listings of Notices of Systems
of Records. A convenient reprinting of the major Privacy Act documents but
infrequently revised, so that much of the information is out of date.

• *Publications Catalog.* A listing of printed materials designated as Publications or Documents. An excellent source for identifying further materials
useful in researching the Service's operations and a good basis for making additional FOIA requests. See Chapter 24.

• *Regulations or Rules.* Title 26 of the Code of Federal Regulations,
containing the rules which govern administration of the Internal Revenue
Code.

• *Reports and Information Retrieval Activity (RIRA) Table 107 Pending
Cases.* Chief Counsel's list of pending tax cases identifies the issues currently
before the courts and may help you to locate other taxpayers litigating the
issues of concern to you. The issues are identified by the Uniform Issue List
number, and a request may be made for all pending cases under a given
number.

• *Statistics of Income.* Documents containing statistical information
compiled by the Internal Revenue Service, including the number of returns filed
and taxes paid by various income groups and occupational categories.

• *Strategic Plan.* Management's tool to guide the Service's future to improve effectiveness of tax administration. (Release was long resisted by the Service but basically says only that we will do better next year.)

- *Tax Court Briefs, Service Sheets, and Memorandums Sur Order.* Copies of government briefs and reply briefs filed in U.S. Tax Court cases, Service Sheets listing briefs transmitted daily, and memorandums "sur order" containing unpublished opinions of the Tax Court.
- *Tax News.* A newsletter prepared by Taxpayer Services discussing new procedures to assist taxpayers.
- *Tax Rates and Tables for Prior Years.* All the tables and rate schedules necessary to permit the delinquent taxpayer to catch up with prior-year self-employment tax, Federal Insurance Contributions Act (Social Security employment taxes), and Federal Unemployment Tax Act returns.
- *Technical Information Releases and Information News Releases* (1956 to present). Announcements of changes in IRS procedures and new items of interest.
- *Technical Memorandums (TMs).* Summaries and explanations of published IRS regulations, originally prepared to accompany the regulations through the review process. TMs state the issues involved, identify controversial legal or policy questions, discuss the reasons for the approach taken by the drafters, and provide other background information.
- *U.S. Tax Week.* A commercially prepared weekly report of significant federal tax developments. Although not issued by the Service, a set of reports is maintained for the convenience of reading-room users.
- *Uniform Issue List (Publication 1102).* List of index terms used by the Service for describing legal issues arising under the Internal Revenue Code and for locating materials which have been indexed according to the system. When used with the Code, the Uniform Issue List becomes the chief locator for accessing information such as pending tax cases.
- *Written Determinations.* Private letter rulings and Technical Advice Memorandums which were originally issued to specific taxpayers but which are available to the public in sanitized form pursuant to 26 U.S.C. 6110. See Chapter 25.

Special Order Materials

Although the primary function of the National Office reading room is to make shelf materials available to the public, the personnel assigned to the room also process written requests for several types of materials which must be retrieved from other locations.

- *Background Files Related to Written Determinations.* The files consist of the taxpayer's request for the written determination, any information submitted in support of the request, and any communications between the Service and the requesting taxpayer. See Chapter 25.
- *Employee Plans Materials.* Applications and supporting documents filed with respect to the qualification of a pension, profit-sharing, or stock bonus plan. See Chapter 29.
- *Exempt Organization Returns and Approved Applications for Exemption.* Returns in the 990 series filed by exempt organizations and the application

which recognized the exemption; available pursuant to 26 U.S.C. 6104. See Chapter 28.

* *Training Materials.* The student texts and instructor guides used in IRS training programs, to the extent that these have been determined to be available to the public. See Chapter 23.

The Impressive Collection

When the entire list of the contents of the reading room is considered, it constitutes an impressive collection which would easily convince the average person that the Service is making a considerable effort to comply with the Freedom of Information Act. That is precisely what it was intended to do.

I have frequently taken congressional staffers, visitors from other agencies, and representatives of the news media on tours of the reading room, calling their attention to the rows of shelf materials, their vast variety, and the ease with which any member of the public could access them. It was and it continues to be an impressive collection. What went unmentioned was the fact that the major items in the collection were not included voluntarily, in a spirit of cooperation with the legal disclosure requirements, but were added only after litigation forced their begrudging release to the public.

Users of the reading room should be aware that their access to shelf materials represents the successful litigating efforts of other members of the public who were willing to devote the time, effort, and wealth necessary to pry information from the Service's web of secrecy. They should also be aware that if these materials are not used frequently, they may, as has happened so often in the past, again disappear from public view.

The *Internal Revenue Manual* and the Chief Counsel Orders and Notices are in the reading room because the Service lost the case of *A. Kenneth Hawkes v. Internal Revenue Service* in 1974 (see Chapter 20). The Private Letter Rulings and the Technical Advice Memorandums are in the reading room because the Service lost the case of *Tax Analysts and Advocates and Thomas F. Field v. Internal Revenue Service et al.* in 1975 (see Chapter 25). The General Counsel's Memoranda, the Technical Memoranda, and the Actions on Decisions are in the reading room because the Service lost the case of *Taxation With Representation Fund v. Internal Revenue Service* in 1981.

The withholding and the subsequent defense in district and appeals courts of the General Counsel's Memoranda and the Actions on Decisions are especially enlightening as to the Service's attitudes toward the disclosure of records. With regard to the Actions on Decisions, the executive assistant to the director of the Tax Litigation Division, Office of Chief Counsel, testified that publication would not, in his personal opinion, cause any harm to the Service. Despite this absence of harm, the Service was seeking to continue to withhold Actions on Decisions!

With regard to General Counsel's Memorandums, the director of the Interpretative Division, Office of Chief Counsel, admitted in response to interrogatories that from 1926 until 1953, selected GCMs were published in the

Internal Revenue Bulletin. No clear reason appeared in the record as to why publication ceased. Despite this 27-year precedent of publication and despite the fact that no one in the Service could remember why they had become confidential, the Service was seeking to continue to withhold General Counsel Memorandums! Fortunately, the Service lost the case, the records became public, and no adverse consequence ensued.

Regional Reading Rooms

Seven regional reading rooms have been established. One reading room is located in each of the seven geographical regions into which the Internal Revenue Service is organized. These reading rooms have neither extensive collections nor the excellent facilities available in the National Office. Some of the regional reading rooms are nothing more than "reading areas," small spaces in larger general-purpose rooms which have been set aside for public use when needed.

The regional reading rooms are not required to maintain any items as shelf materials but need only have the capacity to retrieve and provide certain required items when requested. The items which must be available include the *Internal Revenue Manual,* the Chief Counsel's Directives System (*Chief Counsel Manual*), and any regional commissioner, district director, and service center issuances which supplement the *Internal Revenue Manual.* Other materials may be available but are not required.

The regional reading rooms are more extensive than the National Office in one respect: They maintain the complete regional commissioner, district director, and service center director issuances, whereas the National Office has only the KWIC Index identifying these issuances without having the materials themselves. Each region, of course, maintains only its own local issuances, and there is no reason to assume that any item issued in one office will have an equivalent issued by any other office.

It is advisable to telephone the regional disclosure officer before visiting any of these reading rooms, or you may find that they have a somewhat nebulous quality about them. In fact, you may not find them at all. The addresses of the regional reading rooms:

Central Region:
201 West Fourth Street, Covington, KY 41019.

Mid-Atlantic Region:
600 Arch Street, Philadelphia, PA 19105

Midwest Region:
230 Dearborn Street, Room 1980, Chicago, IL 60604

North Atlantic Region:
120 Church Street, 11th Floor, New York, NY 10007

Southeast Region:
275 Peachtree St., NE., Room 342, Atlanta, GA 30043

Southwest Region:
1100 Commerce St., Room 11B15, Dallas, TX 75242

Western Region:
450 Golden Gate Ave., Room 2307
San Francisco, CA 94102

Local Inspection

Internal Revenue Service managers prefer not to let the public know about or use local inspection procedures, but the regulations contain special provisions for persons who are unable or unwilling to visit an established reading room but nevertheless wish to inspect reading-room shelf materials. Such persons may request to inspect the materials at any office of the Service. That includes not only the various district headquarters located throughout the regions but also the tiniest neighborhood office.

To the extent that the reading-room shelf materials are readily available in the local office, they must be provided for inspection. Of course, many of the shelf materials maintained in the National Office could not possibly be located in local offices. But every office is certain to have a copy of those portions of the *Internal Revenue Manual* which govern the activities of employees in that office, together with any related local issuances. There may, of course, be other items available.

Initially, you would have to ask the disclosure officer in the district headquarters to make inspection arrangements for you, since the local employees are unlikely to know of this provision and equally unlikely to know that the *Internal Revenue Manual* constitutes reading-room shelf material available for public inspection. Once the necessary arrangements have been made, there is no reason why a person needing to research the manual should not walk into the local office and refer to the manual whenever she chooses.

Chapter Twenty

The *Internal Revenue Manual*

We have already discussed the Internal Revenue Service's inability to make a rational and realistic evaluation of its manual and the emotions and attitudes which contributed to attempting to keep the manual secret. Ultimately, the *Internal Revenue Manual* became available to the public as a result of litigation initiated by an Information Act requester named Kenneth A. Hawkes.

Mr. Hawkes was indicted for criminal tax fraud in June 1970. To prepare his defense, Hawkes requested access to various records, which included those portions of the *Internal Revenue Manual* which related to the examination of returns, the interrogation of taxpayers by agents, and other matters in the Examination Division and Criminal Investigation Division parts of the manual. These requests and the resulting appeal were denied in keeping with the Service commitment to the defense of the manual. Hawkes filed suit.

National Office managers in Examination and Criminal Investigation were elated at the prospect of this suit. As a defendant in a criminal case who was considered almost certain to be convicted, Hawkes was seen as an opponent who was unlikely to have the sympathy of the courts and would not have any public support or media interest. Moreover, the portions of the manual he sought included some of the most sensitive (and easiest to defend) items the Service had. Among the items he wanted were the case-selection criteria for examining the returns of closely held corporations which paid their executives excessive salaries, thereby disguising what in reality were returns on capital investment to the owner-employees. Certainly, no one had any sympathy for overpaid executives. The Service could not have picked a better case for defending the manual. In the words of one of the disclosure attorneys involved in the case, "Hawkes is a dead duck!"

To make matters even better for the Service, Hawkes' FOIA suit was assigned to the same judge who was presiding over his criminal case! There would be no need for the Service to harp upon its favorite theme: Freedom of Information Act requesters seeking access to the manual were criminals desperately trying to avoid retribution!

The Service moved to dismiss the case on the grounds that Hawkes could have requested the manual materials through criminal discovery processes and should therefore be barred from using the Freedom of Information Act. As a second line of defense, the Service argued that even if his suit were proper, the manual is exempt from the disclosure requirements of the Freedom of Information Act. The exemption cited was (b)(2), which is applicable to matters that are solely related to the internal personnel rules and practices of an agency. The District Court accepted these arguments, stating, "We conclude that the Government's motion to dismiss is well taken and that the action should be dismissed."

It appeared that the criminal-discovery argument was so persuasive that the court was willing to issue a decision which seemed to accept the (b)(2) exemption without giving it much thought, for the decision did not indicate which of the two arguments was "well taken." In the future, the Service could claim that a court had accepted its interpretation of the (b)(2) exemption, which was based solely upon comments in the House Report on the Freedom of Information Act and not upon the language of the act itself.

Elation turned to virtual delirium when on February 18, 1972, the District Court found Hawkes guilty of criminal tax fraud and sentenced him to prison. Hawkes was disposed of, and the manual was secure. Someone suggested that future requesters of the *Internal Revenue Manual* should be reminded of what had happened to Hawkes, the last person who had asked for it.

But Hawkes was not disposed of. Although his conviction destroyed any usefulness the manual may have had in his defense, it did not end his interest in obtaining it. He appealed the District Court decision to a higher court. On September 25, 1972, the Court of Appeals issued its decision. It analyzed the discovery argument and the (b)(2) argument separately.

Insofar as discovery was concerned, the court stated that access under the Freedom of Information Act is not limited to persons with a particular reason for seeking disclosure. Records are available to any person seeking them. The defendant's conviction in the criminal case did not diminish his right of access, but it did extinguish his right to discovery. The Court of Appeals was under an obligation to take into consideration any changes in fact or law which had occurred during the appeal period. Since the only change was that the discovery process was no longer available, but rights of access under the FOIA still existed, those rights would have to be recognized.

The Court of Appeals then considered arguments made by the Service that the manual was not (a)(2) material which had to be available for inspection and copying but was (b)(2) material exempt from disclosure under the act. The Service's argument against the (a)(2) requirement was based upon a statement in the House Report: "An agency may not be required to make available those portions of its staff manual and instructions which set forth criteria or guidelines for the staff in auditing or inspecting procedures, or in the selection or handling of cases, such as operational tactics, allowable tolerances, or criteria for defense, prosecution or settlement of cases."

The court, however, found that the House Report's comment violated the language of the act itself and was in conflict with the Senate interpretation. Under the circumstances in which the act was adopted, the House comment did not govern interpretation.

The question of availability of a manual was governed by the report of the Senate Committee on the Judiciary, which accompanied the bill on its passage: "The limitation of the staff manuals and instructions affecting the public which must be made available to the public to those which pertain to administrative matters rather than to law enforcement matters protects the confidential nature of instructions to personnel prosecuting violations of law in court, while permitting a public examination of the basis of administrative action." Thus, the distinction between what was available for inspection under (a)(2) and what was not available was between administrative and law enforcement matters. And it was not the intent to exclude from public access everything which might in some way relate to law enforcement matters but only information which if known to the public would significantly impede the enforcement process.

The decision went on to say that law enforcement is adversely affected only when information is made available which allows persons simultaneously to violate the law and to avoid detection. From an (a)(2) perspective, the distinction with regard to a specific manual passage could be resolved only by in-camera inspection of the material.

The (b)(2) argument against disclosure was similarly based upon differences between House and Senate reports. The House Report stated: "Matters relating solely to the internal personnel rules and practices of an agency: Operating rules, guidelines and manuals of procedure for Government investigators or examiners would be exempt from disclosure." The Senate Report stated: "Exemption No. 2 relates only to the internal personnel rules and practices of an agency. Examples of these may be rules as to personnel's use of parking facilities or regulation of lunch hours, statements of policy as to sick leave and the like."

Unfortunately for the Service, two prior decision by district courts concluded that the Senate version should be adopted. The Court of Appeals agreed because the Senate version was closer to the plain language of the act and because adoption of the House version would have created irreconcilable conflicts between (b)(2) and (a)(2).

The Court of Appeals ordered the case remanded to the District Court for reconsideration in light of its construction of the act and for in-camera inspection if necessary. The District Court would have to decide whether the manual passages being requested constituted law enforcement information whose release would significantly impede the enforcement process.

The euphoria in the Service soon disappeared. The emotional view which formerly supported the myth of some great evil taking place if even the tiniest portion of the manual was released was now replaced by an urgent need to identify the specific passages which warranted defense and which offered the best hope of victory. A closer inspection of the materials being withheld in their entirety revealed that there really was not as much that required protection as originally believed. The Service furnished Hawkes with substantial portions of the requested manual material rather than submit them to the District Court for review. Only the really hard-core passages were submitted for in-camera inspection.

The core was not hard enough. The District Court held that "the disclosure of none of these materials would have the sole effect of enabling law violators to escape detection."

The decision provided the Service with some consolation by expressing "some doubt" that instructions "having to do with the selection of returns for audit" should be disclosed but concluded that "even here in view of the complication of the directions and the checks and balances contained therein, we do not believe that knowledge of this would be of any substantial aid to a fraudulent taxpayer in avoiding detection." The District Court ordered all the requested manual instructions released but sealed the documents pending an appeal.

The Internal Revenue Service did appeal. But before appealing, it pared the materials at issue still further by releasing substantial portions of the records which had been before the District Court, so that the hard core to be considered on appeal was even harder than before. This time, the material being defended had been reduced to fewer than 70 paragraphs whose release was believed to threaten to substantially impede the Service's law enforcement program. The paragraphs still at issue constituted only a very small portion of what was originally denied to Hawkes. The Service argued that the District Court had improperly applied a "sole effect" standard instead of the "significantly impede" standard provided by the Court of Appeals and that the District Court had admitted that the "bureaucratic jargon" of the instructions made them "very difficult to understand."

The Court of Appeals found no distinction between the standards applied, saw no indication that the District Court had made an inadequate review, and concluded that no mistake had been made. The Court of Appeals reviewed each of the disputed paragraphs and found that the District Court's conclusion was not clearly erroneous as to even a single one.

The best that the Appeals Court's December 23, 1974, order could do was to express its recognition of the Service's "sincere belief that its enforcement activities will be inconvenienced by the District Court's disclosure order."

It promised not to be a very merry Christmas at the Service. In less than five years a convicted felon who had presented the Service with the perfect opportunity to defend the integrity of the *Internal Revenue Service Manual* in its entirety had wrested from the Service everything he had asked for. Despite its vigorous defense of a case which could not be lost, the Service was unable to protect even a single paragraph. But the bleakest December is soon followed by a happy New Year. It was not long before the architect of the total confidentiality of the manual announced that it was a good thing that Hawkes had not asked for anything really important. Now that we had a better grasp of the rules of the game, we could release the chaff and get down to the important business of protecting the real hard-core material that demanded an avid defense.

Shortly thereafter, the Commissioner directed that a thorough review be made to identify and extract from the *Internal Revenue Manual* those law enforcement instructions which met the standards developed in *Hawkes* and other relevant cases. The vast bulk of the manual became available to the public as the *Internal Revenue Manual,* which is described in this chapter. A very small amount of text was removed from the *Internal Revenue Manual* and inserted in a newly established *Law Enforcement Manual*, described in the next chapter. This distinction between publicly available *Internal Revenue Manual* and highly confidential *Law Enforcement Manual* remains to this day.

The Internal Management Document System

Properly speaking, what is under consideration here is not simply the *Internal Revenue Manual* but a larger umbrella of administrative instructions to staff known as the Internal Management Document System.

Understanding how the Internal Revenue Service functions, or at least how management intends it to function, requires a familiarity with this system. This is no easy task. Many Service employees, including quite a few managers, live through their entire careers without ever having more than a vague concept of how the instructions under which they operate are organized.

If you wish to know how your case is being processed, what to expect the Service to do next, where the Service has deviated from its own instructions, what internal conflicts exist within those instructions, where a Service employee has leeway to choose among several available courses of action, what the Service's true objectives are, or which materials might profitably be requested under the Freedom of Information Act, you must have access to the publicly available instructions in the Internal Management Document System. To have access, you must know how the system is organized, what to ask for, and how to use it.

Most employees have available for their use only those minimal portions of the Internal Management Document System which management believes are relevant to their immediate assignments. Since the *Internal Revenue Manual* alone exceeds 25,000 pages, you too will wish to focus on only those parts likely to affect your interests.

The Internal Management Document System consists of the following six categories of issuances:

1. The *Internal Revenue Manual*, or IRM.
2. Automatic Data Processing handbooks and ADP handbook supplements.
3. The *Law Enforcement Manual,* or LEM.
4. Memorandums and telegrams containing instructions or guidelines addressed to a group of officials.
5. Information Notices.
6. Local Issuances.

Basically, all of the Internal Management Document System except the *Law Enforcement Manual* is available to the public. Each of the other categories, however, may have specific issuances or portions of issuances which have been designated as LEM material and are protected accordingly.

ADP Handbooks and Handbook Supplements

The Automatic Data Processing handbooks and their supplements were established in 1961 as a special series of documents designed to cover the needs of personnel employed in the service centers where returns are processed. They are currently being converted into sections of the *Internal Revenue Manual*, primarily Parts II and III. Ultimately, the ADP handbooks will be discontinued as a result of this conversion, but presently extensive data-processing instructions continue to exist as ADP handbooks.

The ADP handbooks are available to the public and are on the shelves of the National Office Freedom of Information Reading Room. They are seldom requested, however.

The greater difficulty with the ADP handbooks is that they consist of such extremely technical jargon as to be virtually incomprehensible. Even persons who have extensive experience with service-center operations have difficulty reading the handbooks. The material is organized in a manner which reflects work flow and makes portions of instructions available to personnel involved with specific technical tasks, but they lack any sense of continuity and cannot be read as narrative. They seem to have a bits-and-pieces approach which requires the reader to know where to pick up next. They include the use of a great many processing codes which would be unfamiliar to the average taxpayer. Finally, since data processing involves a great many tolerances and criteria, substantial information has been removed from the handbooks and inserted in the *Law Enforcement Manual,* thereby leaving gaps which make the material all the more incomprehensible. Persons who do not have a strong technical interest, a background in data processing, and a real need to research some aspect of service-center processing are advised not to involve themselves with the ADP handbooks or to secure the assistance of a qualified person, such as a retired National Office ADP systems analyst.

Memorandums and Telegrams

Publishing and distributing Internal Management documents can take weeks or even months. Consequently, National Office must sometimes use memorandums or telegrams in order to make the initial distribution of instructions to staff in the field. Such documents, which contain instructions or guidelines and are addressed to more than one official, constitute administrative instructions to staff which must be available for inspection pursuant to section (a)(2).

The Service requires that such memorandums and telegrams be republished as instructions in the *Internal Revenue Manual* or some other suitable format within five days of issuance, but this requirement is virtually never met. In practice, three situations are likely to occur. The instruction is published long after it went into effect; the instruction is altered when published; or the instruction is viewed as temporary and is allowed to expire without ever being recognized in the manual. As a result, the actual instructions in effect may differ considerably from what appears to be required by the *Internal Revenue Manual.*

Persons who need to know precisely when a procedure began or who doubt that the Service actually followed the precise instructions in the manual may wish to ask for any memorandums or telegrams which may exist. The request should be sent to the National Office. It should identify a specific manual instruction and an appropriate time frame and ask for access to any memorandums and telegrams implementing, revising, or otherwise affecting the instruction during the period in question. The request should point out that the requested material would be (a)(2) material available for public inspection and should not be subject to any search fees.

Information Notices

Information Notices do not properly contain instructions to staff, but they do contain announcements and may call attention to policies or instructions which already exist in the Internal Management Document System. They will rarely be of interest to taxpayers but should be requested as part of a comprehensive search concerning some procedure which may be of great importance.

Information Notices are numbered by a calendar-year prefix and a serial-sequence suffix. Unless you are aware of the number of a particular Information Notice, ignore that numbering system in your request. Instead, refer to the manual section which you are researching and ask for all Information Notices within the years of your interest which reflected a distribution to that section or to a broader manual citation which would include that section. Requests are made to National Office and should cite (a)(2) to avoid search fees.

Local Issuances

Each regional commissioner, regional director of appeals, district director, and service center director is authorized to issue materials which supplement the National Office issuances as local circumstances require. These Local Issuances have effect only within the jurisdition of the issuing official. They should neither repeat nor conflict with National Offices issuances but should conform with, supplement or expand upon National Office positions.

In reality, the desired conformity is difficult to maintain, and Local Issuances may drastically differ from National Office instructions and may be quite contrary to what is in the manual. The Southeast Region was the experimental implementing area for many early data-processing efforts and still appears to believe that they should be a step ahead of the rest of the country. The Southwest Region prides itself upon its compliance initiatives and frequently shows considerable independence in its local issuancs. The Western Region sees itself as a breed apart, and its issuances tend to deviate extensively from National Office instructions.

Thorough research of the manual procedures relevant to your circumstances should include access to the Local Issuances for your area. Local Issuances are listed in the KWIK Index in the National Office reading room, but they are best obtained by a request to the appropriate regional reading room, which is required to have both the index and the materials themselves.

Regional commissioners, regional directors of appeals, district directors and service center directors issue (respectively) RC-Memorandums, RDA Memorandums, DIR-Memorandums, and SC-Memorandums. These memorandums contain instructions intended to complement the *Internal Revenue Manual* or the ADP handbooks. They are cross-referenced to manual or handbook sections and should be requested by reference to the IRM or ADP HB section of interest to you.

Regional commissioners, district directors, and service center directors issue RC-Circulars, DIR-Circulars, and SC-Circulars. These circulars are similar to Information Notices, except that they may be used to distribute temporary instructions affecting IRM or ADP HB procedures. They may be requested by reference to the IRM or ADP HB section to which they are distributed.

Regional commissioners, regional directors of appeals, district directors, and service center directors issue RC-Delegation Orders, RDA-Delegation Orders, DIR-Delegation Orders, and SC-Delegation Orders. Delegations Orders delegate authority from an official to his subordinate. They are usually issued to a position rather than to a person and are seldom of interest to taxpayers. Delegation Orders are sequentially numbered and are therefore not easily identified when the number is unknown. They may be requested by reference to the type of authority delegated, the official making the delegation, or the official receiving the delegation; or a requester may inspect all the Delegation Orders at a regional reading room.

Organization of the IRM

The *Internal Revenue Manual* consists of Manual Transmittals, basic text, Handbooks, and Manual Supplements.

The Manual Transmittals serve to issue any manual materials and to authenticate the materials transmitted as proper official issuances. Since the manual is a loose-leaf compendium consisting of about 25,000 pages, some portions of it are likely to change every day. Issuances frequently become obsolete. The Manual Transmittals are designed to keep track of all this material. Each transmittal relates to an identifiable segment of the manual and is numbered to show that manual segment plus a sequential number in a series beginning when that segment of the manual was established. Each part, chapter or handbook in the manual has its own series of Manual Transmittals. A statement of purpose further identifies what is being replaced. A statement of the nature of changes provides a short explanation of how the transmitted materials will alter the content of the manual. Filing instructions then state which pages are to be removed and which pages are to be inserted. The reverse of the Manual Transmittal lists the page numbers of all the pages which remain current at that time, together with the dates on which each page was first issued. Finally, the Manual Transmittal lists all the current Manual Supplements. Consequently, a complete set of Manual Transmittals will reflect the history of the related manual section from its establishment until its most recent change.

Handbooks are nothing more than segments of manual text which cover a closely related set of topics, are more extensive than other segments within the chapter, and (generally the most important factor) have a distribution pattern which differs from that of the surrounding text.

Manual Supplements consist of text which might have been inserted within a manual chapter or handbook were it not for special distribution or timeliness factors. Manual Supplements are used for trial instructions or temporary instructions or for materials whose distribution is limited to some managers rather than the wider audience addressed by the balance of the manual chapter. The most common reason for using Manual Supplements is that their instructions are addressed to personnel in various functions or who use various parts of the manual, and it is easier to create a cross-functional distribution of the Manual Supplement than to take the time to revise numerous segments of the manual. Whenever researching a manual instruction, it is important to ascertain whether that instruction is augmented by a Manual Supplement.

Numbering of the Manual

The manual numbering is similar to the Dewey Decimal System. Each segment has a number which tells where that segment belongs.

The manual is divided into 15 Parts, identified by Roman numerals. Each part is either of general applicability or is specific to a particular function of the Service. Thus Part IV contains all the material in the manual issued specifically to apply to the Examination Division. All text, Manual Transmittals, Manual Supplements, and Handbooks within Part IV will begin with an Arabic number 4; conversely, all manual material beginning with a 4 belongs to the Examination Division. Thus, by knowing that your return is under examination, you also know that the instruction of interest to you will be in Part IV and that all those instructions will begin with a 4.

Within each part, there are further breakdowns into chapters, sections, subsections, and smaller segments, each of which is represented by a further digit. But none of these numbers tell us anything about their contents.

Unless the specific segment of the manual which you wish to access is already known to you, three options are available in making a request. You may describe your area of interest to the best of your ability and hope that the National Office technicians who work your request will understand what you want, conscientiously research the matter, and provide you with the correct materials. You may request one or more of the handbooks or chapters mentioned below as being of particular interest. Or you may request the available indexes and tables of contents and perform your own research in anticipation of making your further request.

The entire manual is indexed in a document which you may request from the National Office reading room as the Internal Revenue Manual Numerical Index. This index, however, breaks materials down only as far as listing the titles of parts, chapters, handbooks, and other indexes. Actually, it is much more like a very general table of contents than an index.

Each part has an index of its own, generally arranged by key words in the titles of each segment within the part. There is no true index to the manual similar to what might be found in any scholarly book.

Each chapter and each handbook has a table of contents, and some handbooks have their own KWIC index.

A serious researcher might wish first to identify the part of the manual of concern to him and then use either the index to the manual or the index to a part to identify those chapters and handbooks within that part he wishes to access. Then he might telephone the National Office reading room to find the approximate cost, if any, to obtain those chapters and handbooks. If the cost goes beyond his willingness to invest, he might ask for the more important materials immediately and order the rest a month later, thereby being entitled to 100 free pages with each request.

I strongly recommend against attempting to identify segments of interest smaller than a chapter or handbook. Bits and pieces of the manual, taken out of context and without benefit of their surrounding material are likely to be extremely misleading and difficult to understand.

Parts of the Manual

Part 0

IRM Part 0 is of general applicability and deals with Personnel, and Training and Development. As the part deals entirely with the treatment of the Service's employees, it is of little interest to taxpayers. You might, however, wish to access IRM 0735.1, Handbook for the Rules of Conduct, which details the manner in which employees are expected to conduct themselves in dealing with the public and with their fellow employees in order to maintain the confidence and the esteem of the taxpaying public.

Part I

IRM Part I is also of general applicability and deals with Administration. Most of Part I relates only to internal matters of little interest to taxpayers, but there are several chapters and handbooks which might be of interest to the serious researcher:

• IRM 1100, Organization and Staffing, is useful in determining the duties of the various functions, the relationship between National Office and the field offices, and how the Service operates. The chapter includes a short history of the Service and describes the major reorganizations the Service has undergone.
• IRM 1218, Policies of the Internal Revenue Service Handbook, contains all those statements of policy which were once withheld from the public and provides excellent insight into the rationale behind many of the Service's operations.
• IRM 1230, Internal Management Document System Handbook, contains

all the information necessary to understand the preparation, issuance, and use of the manual and its related materials in far greater detail than this chapter, an excellent document for those who have a serious interest in the *Internal Revenue Manual.*

• IRM 1272, Disclosure of Official Information Handbook, is the bible of the disclosure function for those who need more information than they have found in this book. If you ask for IRM 1272, be certain also to request a set of all current Disclosure Information Digests, a set of newsletters which deal with disclosure matters and sometimes supplement IRM 1272.

• IRM 1279, Problem Resolution Handbook, details how the problem-resolution program is to operate, provides the criteria for including cases in the program, and tells you what you may expect the problem resolution officer to do for you.

• IRM 1(15)59, Records Control Schedules, identifies the types of records which the Service maintains and tells when they are to be retired to the Federal Records Centers and when they are to be disposed (i.e., destroyed), an invaluable reference for serious FOIA requesters. However, since there are very many different schedules, you may wish to limit your request to the functions and the location of special interest to you.

• IRM 1(16)00, Physical, Document, and Computer Systems Security, contains security standards, crisis-management and risk-analysis procedures, and instructions for safeguarding documents. Handbooks 1(16)31, Classified Defense Information Handbook, and 1(16)41, Physical Security Handbook, would be of special interests to persons pursuing requests for classified defense or foreign policy data or having a general interest in how sensitive documents are handled.

• IRM 1(19)00, Public Affairs, provides guidelines for Public Affairs activities, news coverage of tax prosecutions, and issuance of news releases.

Part II: Data Processing Services

Part II contains highly technical information relating to the management of the Service's data-processing operations. There is unlikely to be anything of interest or value to the typical taxpayer in this part. However, prospective vendors and contractors are likely to be very interested in subjects like IRM 2300, Management of Automatic Data Processing Resources; IRM 2340, User's Handbook for Automation; IRM 2500, ADP Software Standards and Guidelines; and information appearing throughout this part.

Part III: Revenue, Returns and Accounts Processing

Part III deals with the management of service centers and some aspects of data-processing operations. This part is generally of no interest to taxpayers.

Part IV: Examination

Part IV contains instructions for the Examination Division's office auditors and revenue agents. Many chapters and handbooks are of considerable interest to taxpayers whose returns are being examined. It is not practical for most taxpayers to request all of Part IV, as the index alone runs over 250 pages. Some of the more frequently requested chapters and handbooks include the following:

• IRM 4100, Classification, Screening and Identification for Examination of Tax Returns, Claims and Information Items, explains (to the extent that the Service is willing to release to the public) the procedures whereby the Examination Division selects its workload.

• IRM 41(12)0, Classification Handbook, contains more information for the use of classifiers in selecting returns for examination.

• IRM 4200, Income Tax Examinations, discusses various Examination procedures and programs, including Tax Protesters Program, Church Tax Inquiries and Examinations, and Tax Shelter Program.

• IRM 4231, Tax Audit Guidelines for Internal Revenue Examiners, provides examiners with auditing techniques for use in income tax cases. Includes sections on Planning the Examination, Audit Techniques, Small Businesses, Fraud and Tax Protesters.

• IRM 4232, Techniques Handbooks for Specialized Industries, provides assistance for the examination of industries having special characteristics or requiring information beyond general business principles. Each Handbook relates to a separate industry:

IRM 4232.1 Insurance
IRM 4232.2 Auto Dealers
IRM 4232.3 Textiles
IRM 4232.4 Timber
IRM 4232.5 Brokerage Firms
IRM 4232.6 Railroads
IRM 4232.7 Construction
IRM 4232.8 Oil and Gas
IRM 4232.9 Financial Institutions
IRM 4232.(10) Public Utilities
IRM 4232.(11) Mining
IRM 4232.(12) Barter Exchanges

• IRM 4233, Tax Audit Guidelines, Partnerships, Estates and Trusts, and Corporations, provides guidance for field examinations concerning the income tax matters of entities other than individual taxpayers.

• IRM 4234, Currency and Banking Reports Handbook, deals with the Bank Secrecy Act, reports on the transfer of cash and securities, and examination procedures for compliance with record-keeping and reporting requirements for casinos.

• IRM 4235, Techniques Handbook for In-Depth Examinations, provides suggestions for examinations which include special problems, fraud, or other criminal aspects. Segments deal with Strike Forces, Swiss Banks, Garbage Removal, Vending Machines, Labor Unions, Contractors, Trucking, Bars, After Hours Clubs, Pornography, Stocks, Stolen Securities, Loan Sharking,

Gambling, Credit Card Fraud, Extortion, Narcotics, Prostitution, Fencing and Arson.

• IRM 4236, Examinations Tax Shelters Handbook, assists examiners on Tax Shelter cases and includes segments on Motion Pictures, Real Estate, Farms, Coal, Commodity Options and Futures, Equipment Leasing, Research and Development, Energy, and Off-Shore Tax Havens.

• IRM 4300, Estate and Gift Tax Examinations.

• IRM 4350, Examination Technique Handbook for Estate Tax Examiners.

• IRM 4600, Employment Tax Procedures, deals with withholding of employment taxes on employees, Federal Insurance Contributions Act (Social Security Taxes), Federal Unemployment Tax Act, Railroad Retirement Tax Act, withholding on gambling winnings, tip income, fraud, and penalties.

• IRM 4700, Excise Tax Procedure, includes instructions on excise tax, wagering tax, and windfall profits tax examinations.

Part V: Collection Activity

Part V contains the instructions governing the enforced collection of delinquent taxes and the securing the delinquent returns by the Collection Division. Information of interest to taxpayers occurs throughout Part V. The most frequently requested and the most valuable chapters and handbooks:

• IRM 5100, General Procedural Guides, contains considerable internal administrative material which would be of little interest to taxpayers, but the chapter does cover interest and penalty provisions and has a significant segment on Potentially Dangerous Taxpayers and Illegal Tax Protesters.

• IRM 5200, Delinquent Return Procedures, covers efforts to locate stopfilers (persons who once filed returns but no longer do so) and nonfilers (persons who never filed returns). Since most persons who avoid filing returns wish to remain anonymous, they are unlikely to make FOIA requests which require their stating a current address. Nevertheless, the chapter may be of interest to those who have already been caught.

• IRM 5300, Balance Due Account Procedures, is the major instruction covering the enforced collection of delinquent taxes after assessment. It contains extremely valuable information on Jeopardy Assessments, Installment Agreements, Liens and Levies, and the designation of Uncollectible Accounts.

• IRM 5600, Collection Field Function Techniques and Other Assignments, tends to deal with the collection of business taxes and covers Trust Funds, One Hundred Percent Penalties, and Seizures and Sales of property and business premises.

• IRM 5700, Special Procedures, contains very valuable but somewhat technical material. The Special Procedures section performs services of a legal nature for Collection personnel. The chapter covers Federal Tax Liens, Seizures and Sales, Litigation, Bankruptcy, Offers-in-Compromise.

• IRM 57(16)0, Legal Reference Guide for Revenue Officers, is not instructional in the sense of providing a directive to act, but it provides supporting information concerning virtually all the procedures established in the rest of Part V. The Legal Reference Guide provides the fundamentals of legal knowledge needed by revenue officers in their daily activities, and they are advised to give it their "constant study." It is one of the most important segments of Part V and probably the best written portion of the entire *Internal Revenue Manual.*

Part VI: Taxpayer Service

Taxpayer Service personnel are the "happy little helpers" of the taxpayer. Consequently, their activities have seldom engendered requests for their manual instructions. Much of Part VI consists of administrative details of little interest to the public, and Taxpayer Service personnel rely extensively on other functions' instructions to unravel the problems which confront them. Those who are interested in how Taxpayer Service personnel approach their tasks, which taxpayer problems are considered "common situations," and how "where's my check" refund inquiries are handled should request IRM 6810, Taxpayer Service Handbook.

Part VII: Employee Plans and Exempt Organizations

Part VII, while of great value to the few persons needing information on the administration of the Employee Plans and Exempt Organizations programs, is of no interest to most taxpayers.

• IRM 7751, Exempt Organizations Handbook, covers various exempt organizations such as Religious, Charitable and Educational Organizations, Social and Recreation Clubs, Fraternal Beneficiary Societies, Veterans' Organizations, Political Organizations, etc., and has sections on Taxation of Unrelated Business Income and Cooperatives.
• IRM 7752, Private Foundations Handbook, deals with the restrictions, requirements, taxes, and penalties affecting Private Foundations, including self-dealing, failure to distribute income, excess business holdings, and investments which jeopardize charitable purposes.

Part VIII: Appeals

Part VIII is a relatively small handbook of fewer than 350 pages which is of interest only to those taxpayers involved in the appeals process. It is seldom requested. The most important segment is IRM 8(13)10, Closing Agreement Handbook, which derives additional historical interest from being the manual section which the Service fought tooth and nail against releasing to Mr. and Mrs. Long. Other portions of interest to taxpayers in special circumstances include:

IRM 8300, Tax Shelters
IRM 8900, Joint Committee Cases
IRM 8(12)00 & 8(13)00 Offers-in-Compromise
IRM 8(15)00 Cases Involving Criminal Prosecution
IRM 8(18)00 Bankruptcy & Receivership Cases
IRM 8(19)00 Transferee and Jeopardy Assessments
IRM 8(20)00 Windfall Profit Tax Cases

Part IX: Criminal Investigation

Persons wanting copies of the Criminal Investigation portion of the manual frequently have an urgent need for that document. There is important information throughout Part IX, and any segments which might be identified as of no interest are small enough not to bother eliminating. I recommend that if you need Part IX, get *all* of it. Make your request for Part IX, but be certain to specify that you also want IRM 9781, Handbook for Special Agents, which constitutes the greater and more important portion of the Criminal Investigation Division instructions.

Part X: Inspection

Inspection is divided into Internal Audit, responsible for auditing Service activities and making reports to management in order to improve operations, and Internal Security, responsible for protecting the integrity of the Service by investigating criminal misconduct and serious administrative misconduct by Service employees. The instructions for both operations are of interest to any serious student of the Service, but those for Internal Security may also be of interest to taxpayers under investigation for bribery attempts, certain refund swindles, and other crimes.

IRM (10)200, Internal Audit, and IRM (10)260, Internal Audit Handbook, cover the audit of Service operations. IRM (10)300, Internal Security, and IRM (10)311, Inspector's Handbook, cover the investigation of employee misconduct and certain criminal activities.

Part XI: Technical

Technical is responsible for the design of tax forms and public-use forms, the preparation of technical publications, and the issuance of Revenue Rulings. The material in Part XI is generally of no interest to taxpayers.

Part XII: Centralized Services

Centralized Servies provides mass-processing support of a technical and administrative nature to the operating programs of district offices. The material in Part XII is generally of no interest to taxpayers.

Part XIII

Whether due to superstitution or to some other consideration, the *Internal Revenue Manual*, like most hotels, which have no thirteenth floor, has no Part XIII.

Part XIV: International

The growing importance of multinational business has been recognized by the Internal Revenue Service by the creation of an Assistant Commissioner (International). Part XIV of the manual has been designated for the use of this expanding function. As this is written, however, no material has been distributed to Part XIV.

Chief Counsel's Directives Manual

The *Chief Counsel's Directives Manual* (CCDM) is not part of the *Internal Revenue Manual* but is described here because its organization, format, and use is very similar to those of the IRM. The CCDM is divided into 10 parts, identified as Parts (30) through (40), most of which are further divided into chapters. All but one of these parts are quite small; the largest part has no subordinate chapters. Consequently, the most practical unit for requesting portions of the CCDM is the Part. The CCDM has an index, and most chapters have tables of contents, so that persons who prefer this method may order only these items and then select individual segments for further requests.

The CCDM is on the shelf of the National Office reading room, and requests for copies should be sent there. The CCDM would usually be of interest only to those taxpayers who are involved with Chief Counsel through litigation or some other means. The most interesting portions of the CCDM are listed below.

• CCDM Part (31), Criminal Tax, includes prosecution considerations, referral of cases of prosecution, and referral for grand-jury investigation.

• CCDM Part (32), Disclosure Litigation, covers disclosure, testimony, the production of documents, disclosure litigation, the availability of records (pursuant to IRC 6103, 6104 and 6110), the Privacy Act of 1974, and the Freedom of Information Act.

• CCDM Part (34), General Litigation, includes bankruptcies, decedent's and incompetent's estates, erroneous refunds, actions to open safe deposit boxes, one hundred percent penalty cases, summons enforcement, wrongful levy, jeopardy assessments, reducing tax claims to judgement, foreclosure of tax lien, fraudulent conveyances, enforcing a levy, and offers in compromise.

• CCDM Part (35), Tax Litigation, is the largest and most frequently requested portion of the CCDM, providing procedural guidance for attorneys defending proposed assessments in Tax Court.

Effective Dates

Once you have received the instruction which appears to relate to your set of circumstances, you will want to ascertain that what you have secured was in effect on the dates when the actions of interest to you took place. The *Internal Revenue Manual* includes several devices to assist in making this determination.

If you have the latest Manual Transmittal, you will know that all the instructions transmitted were in effect on the date of that transmittal and continue to be in effect until a further transmittal is issued. The reverse side of the transmittal lists each page number which is part of the transmittal and shows the date on which that page originally went into effect. Nothing on that page could have changed between that effective date and the present. If the date of your action fell between the page date and the present, you know that your action was covered by that instruction.

If the date of your action preceded the page date, you should look at the instruction itself. Each segment of text which is headed by a title in bold print is called a TRIDOC, or a Technical Reference Information System Document. The TRIDOC is the smallest unit which may be revised. Directly above the bold-print title is the section number or subsection number which identifies the TRIDOC. To the right of this number is a date in parentheses. All the text which follows this group of number, date, and bold-print title until the next group of number, date, and title is encountered, constitutes a single TRIDOC. The date shown is the date upon which that TRIDOC was first transmitted in precisely the same form as it now appears. If your action took place after the TRIDOC date, you know that the governing instruction was exactly the same, even though the page may have been printed and transmitted a dozen times since then.

If your action took place prior to the TRIDOC date, you will need to research further. The National Office maintains a historical file which contains all prior versions of all *Internal Revenue Manual* issuances. You should now request a copy of the latest Manual Transmittal dated immediately prior to the date of your action but specify that you do not need all the material which was transmitted but want only the pages which reproduce the TRIDOC under the applicable section or subsection number.

In most cases, such a request would provide the instruction which you need. Sometimes, however, you will find that there has been a general renumbering of the text, and the number which you specified will relate to an entirely different subject. In that event, review the Manual Transmittal portion entitled "Nature of Changes" for hints. If this does not help, obtain the Manual Transmittal page for the TRIDOC date and review the Nature of Changes to determine where that instruction originated; it may have been brought in from an entirely different chapter, or it may have had no prior existence. Once involved in a renumbering situation, a series of requests may be necessary before the actual source is located. Unfortunately, National Office disclosure personnel have seldom been willing to provide much help in tracing old manual provisions to determine the instruction in effect on a particular date.

In addition, keep in mind that whatever the manual provision was on a given date, it may have been overridden by a memorandum or teletype to a group of field officials, or it may have been supplemented by a local issuance.

Internal Audit Reports, NORPS and RORPS

If you are convinced that your problem resulted from a failure of Service personnel to follow existing instructions, a defect in the instructions, a conflict between various instructions or some similar situation, you may wish to search for records confirming the existence of such situations or establishing that other taxpayers have encountered the same type of problem.

The Service maintains a wide variety of records which may provide you with precisely the information which you need. The Assistant Commissioner (Inspection) is responsible for evaluating the proper functioning of Service programs. In doing so, his teams of auditors prepare Internal Audit Reports which document their findings. These reports, which may be helpful to you, have been made available in response to Information Act requests after deleting recommendations and opinions and return information. The segregable, factual portions of the reports should be the only parts that you want. Your request should be addressed to the Assistant Commissioner (Inspection) and should state that you want any Internal Audit Reports which relate to the function (Collection, Examination, Criminal Investigation Division, etc.) and the particular operation described (or governed by the cited manual section). You might wish to limit your request to a time frame, perhaps a year before and two years after your experience. You should specify whether you intend your request to relate to events in a specific district office or the entire country.

If the materials received in response to your request are of interest, you may wish to make a further request for the background file of materials upon which the Internal Audit Report is based. The functions whose operations are criticized by Internal Audit Reports make management responses to the reports, which may offer additional facts and explanations or may make a commitment to remedy the defect. These may also be requested.

The National Office is responsible for evaluating how well a regional office manages the districts and the service centers subject to its authority. To carry out this responsibility, the National Office administers a National Office Review Program (NORP), usually on an 18-month cycle, which results in the issuance of a NORP Report. This program has a history of being emphasized, deemphasized, and reemphasized, so that NORP Reports are not necessarily produced every 18 months as scheduled. Moreover, the NORP process tends to be something of a hand-washing operation since National Office officials are loath to criticize their regional counterparts or even to say anything that might be interpreted as offensive. Consequently, the NORP Reports themselves are unlikely to contain anything worthwhile. The background files, however, are rich with observation of local procedural deficiencies since most National Office officials like to start the process with lots of ammunition for discussion purposes and then back away from actually reporting any adverse information. You may request the NORP Reports and their background files, limited to items of actual interest to you, from the National Office.

The Regional Office maintains a similar program for evaluating its districts and service centers called the Regional Office Report Program (RORP). Regional officials are not as sophisticated as National Office officials; consequently RORP Reports are generally more detailed and more useful than NORP Reports. RORP Reports and their background files may be requested, limited to items of actual interest to you, from the regional commissioner having jurisdiction over the district office which handled your tax case.

Most National Office and regional office functions have analysts or technicians assigned to exercise continuing oversight for specific manual sections. These technicians maintain background files documenting the needs for future revisions, problems under consideration, materials generated by the suggestion program, and other documentation relevant to their programs. Such technicians also make field visits to observe their procedures in practice. Each such visit must be recorded in a Trip Report. These background files and Trip Reports, although never before requested, would doubtlessly be available to the public after suitable deletions have been made. The requester seeking corroboration of the treatment which he received might well find these background files and Trip Reports a gold mine.

The directions a records-access campaign might take are limited only by the types of records which exist. The uses to which the records received might be put are limited only by the imagination and ingenuity of the requester. The most important uses will always be simply the right to be an active participant able to know and influence your own affairs.

Chapter Twenty-One

The *Law Enforcement Manual*

The final decision in *Hawkes* releasing all of the requested manual material and withholding nothing prompted an immediate project to divide the *Internal Revenue Manual* into an administrative staff manual available to the public, which was to retain the name *Internal Revenue Manual*, and a small hard core of properly protected material which was to become the *Law Enforcement Manual*.

Many of us were afraid that it was already too late to save the more important instructions. The Internal Revenue Service functioned more like a bank and a lot less like a police station. The harsh line drawn in *Hawkes* between protected law enforcement material and the "criteria or guidelines for the staff in auditing or inspecting procedures, or in the selection or handling of cases, such as operational tactics, allowable tolerances, or criteria for defense, prosecution or settlement of cases" envisioned in the House Report might already have rendered our efforts vain.

Chief Counsel's disclosure attorneys provided guidelines describing what could be withheld. Each function then had the analysts who were responsible for maintaining manual instruction review thier own segments and withdraw from the *Internal Revenue Manual* those items which were to be placed in the *Law Enforcement Manual*. Once approved, the *Law Enforcement Manual,* or LEM, would be printed and distributed. Immediately thereafter, the newly sanitized *Internal Revenue Manual* would be reprinted, distributed, and placed in the reading rooms for public access. It was a massive task, for the *Internal Revenue Manual* at that time contained approximately 36,000 pages of text.

My assignment was to receive the proposed LEM segments as they were drafted and review them to ensure that they came reasonably close to meeting Counsel's guidelines, that one function did not attempt to protect material which another function was releasing, that the final product would represent an integrated whole rather than a lot of disjointed bits and pieces, and that there were no unforeseen problems which might jeopardize the project.

Much to my amazement, the whole thing came together as if it had been planned in heaven. There were no disagreements between functions, no unreasonable attempts to protect more than could be justified, and no major problems of any kind. The dozens of technical specialists involved demonstrated that they really did understand the Freedom of Information Act and were willing to make the effort necessary to bring the Service into complete compliance. Several persons told me that they were relieved to be able to release the bulk of their instructions with management's blessing rather than have to continue the struggle to manufacture defenses for materials they considered innocuous. The final result released well over 90 percent of the manual, and the little which was being withheld had the look and feel of a document which justified defense.

The proposed LEM was passed on to Counsel, which promptly approved it and submitted it to Commissioner Alexander for signature prior to issuance. And there all progress came to a halt. The proposed LEM was returned to me. It was not to be issued as prepared. I soon learned that the Commissioner did not trust the efforts of the technicians and the disclosure experts who had produced the LEM and were believed to be "soft" on law enforcement. The Commissioner wanted the LEM to be produced by Chief Counsel personnel rather than functional technicians. Disclosure attorneys were not to be involved; the work was to be done by attorneys involved in the defense of tax cases. Rather than review the materials protected in the proposed LEM, they were to start from scratch and review the entire *Internal Revenue Manual* to identify everything which could possibly be defended. The function of Counsel in the project had been reversed from keeping unwarranted material out of the LEM to getting as much material as possible out of the IRM.

Counsel's task was virtually impossible. Not long after learning of these circumstances, I was approached by a Counsel employee who asked to borrow a copy of the original proposed LEM for "comparison" purposes. Several months later, Counsel completed the task, the Commissioner approved it, and the LEM was printed and distributed. It was no longer possible to compare the Counsel product with the original technician product, but it did not seem much different or noticeably more extensive. The difference was that we could no longer be certain that everything in the LEM represented the selection of the most knowledgeable technicians of what had to be protected to prevent interference with the law enforcement processes for which they were responsible.

The First LEM

This Counsel product, possibly largely plagiarized from the technician proposal, was the first LEM issued. It was to survive unchallenged and virtually unchanged for more than five years. The mere fact that the Service had produced an LEM seemed to overawe the public, so that it was seldom requested and never litigated. But what was in this LEM?

Only a very small proportion of the LEM would obviously meet the *Hawkes* standard that the law enforcement process is adversely affected only when information is made available which allows persons simultaneously to violate the law and to avoid detection. The preponderance of the LEM consisted of tolerances and criteria designed to permit the Service effectively to apply its limited resources. These materials were much more similar to those described in the House Report as warranting exemption but were released by the court in *Hawkes*.

Tolerances and criteria constitute those levels, often arbitrarily set, which differentiate between the circumstances which warrant taking action, and those which may be ignored either because they are minimal, reacting to them would seem unreasonable, or no organization can afford to do something about everything.

If you owed a creditor $1,000 and paid him only $999.99, you would not expect his computerized billing system to mail a demand for the remaining penny. It would be equally foolish if he billed you for a dime or even for a dollar. There must, of course, be a point at which a balance is large enough to warrant mailing a bill. If that point was $10.00 and every debtor knew that fact, might not a good many people simply reduce their payment by $9.99 and call the matter quits? How large would a balance have to be to warrant a second bill? How large a balance to warrant turning the matter over to a collection agency? How large a balance to justify employing an attorney to file suit? How would knowledge of such precise amounts affect the behavior of debtors? Presumably, the more they knew, the less they would pay.

The Service is faced with the same problems, except that the Service has literally thousands of different actions which can be triggered or delayed or avoided, depending upon the sum involved. The sum involved is not simply a question of money but may relate to how many returns, incidents, lines left blank, errors on a return, days late, almost anything. . . .

Release of any one of these tolerances might be entirely harmless. Release of all of them could significantly increase the cost of tax administration, could force the government to raise taxes to make up for lost revenues, or could make the Service far more severe in its treatment of taxpayers. Ultimately, knowledge of all the tolerances and criteria by the public could destroy our system of taxation. But could any of these consequences be demonstrated to a court, and would they qualify under the law enforcement standard?

The possibility existed that if the same court which ruled against the Service in *Hawkes* looked at the Service's LEM, it might decide that most or even all of it was not a LEM at all.

There were other problems with the LEM. The concept of withholding information from the public in order to avoid adverse consequences inherently requires that the information be secret to begin with. The tolerances and criteria in the LEM are needed by Service personnel performing a wide variety of duties. Although the LEM has a limited distribution within the Service, it cannot be restricted to any great extent without defeating its purpose as an operating instruction. Knowledge of the information in the LEM is widely available to the Service's 100,000 employees. Can anything which is known by 100,000 people be characterized as unavailable to the public?

Prior to the creation of the LEM, sensitive tolerances and criteria were hidden among the innocuous instructions in the manual, but with the issuance of the LEM, they were concentrated so that anyone could carry them out the door. Moreover, thousands of Service employees resign or retire every year. Many of them are attorneys and accountants or will become enrolled agents or return preparers. Can anyone be sure that knowledge of tolerances and criteria protected by the LEM are not readily known and taken advantage of by the tax-practitioner community?

Although it is commonly believed that public knowledge of tolerances and criteria would have serious adverse consequences for tax administration, no one actually knows that the assumption is valid. The Service has never performed any studies or any tests to determine whether the anticipated consequences would occur. It is not known what the true cost, if any, of releasing any tolerance might be. Nor have there been any studies to determine whether simple palliatives might not be adopted in order to ameliorate the consequences. The Service has never seriously explored whether there are alternatives which might permit it to operate without tolerances and criteria. For the most part, the attitude has been as long as we can withhold tolerances and criteria from the public, why should we bother to explore any alternatives?

Despite these misgivings, all of us who were involved in the creation of the LEM were convinced that it was a good LEM. We might not be able to successfully defend much of it; we might not be able to convince a court that our concerns for protecting tolerances and criteria were justified; but we had no doubt that the vast majority of the information placed into the LEM was legally exempt from disclosure. Our efforts to protect the information in the LEM were reasonable and entirely in the public interest.

The Purloined LEM

In 1980, the existence of Service tolerances and criteria attracted national prominence. An alleged portion of the *Law Enforcement Manual* was surreptitiously passed to an unauthorized person who publicized its contents.

The August 11, 1980, edition of the *National Law Journal* reported that the Criminal Investigation Division had directed it special agents not to recommend prosecution for tax fraud in cases which involved complex tax-evasion schemes which would be difficult to demonstrate or prove. They were to concentrate upon cases which were simple, readily understood, and easy to prove. But under no circumstances were they to recommend prosecution of any taxpayer unless the underpayment of tax averaged at least $2,500 per year for three consecutive years.

There had never before been any reliable indication of the level of noncompliance necessary to trigger prosecution, but it was commonly believed that a single instance involving $1,000 in tax would be adequate. The new guidelines were attributed to a July 15 classified directive from the director of the Criminal Tax Division and therefore appeared to be both genuine and authoritative. The guidelines were also quite shocking.

The guidelines, if genuine, would mean that any taxpayer could commit any size fraud without fear of prosecution, provided he filed an honest return once every three years. Or a less audacious taxpayer could consistently cheat for an unlimited number of years, provided the amount of tax never added up to $7,500 for three consecutive years. Tax experts pointed out that the guidelines would permit a married taxpayer earning $20,000 annually never to file a return without risking criminal prosecution, even if he were caught. Depending upon an individual's circumstances, there would be no end to the number of permutations which would permit escape from prosecution. Anyone who legitimately received a refund would have a license to do whatever she pleased for the next two years. Any new filer having had no income in the prior year would be exempt from filing until his third taxable year.

There would still be civil penalties, but there could be no criminal penalties.

Three conclusions suggested themselves from this situation: (1) The Service's tolerances and criteria are extremely important information which would be of urgent interest to large numbers of taxpayers. (2) Tolerances and criteria could have immense effects upon tax administration and could virtually eliminate provisions of tax law. (3) Some tolerances and criteria could be constructed in a very foolish and almost irresponsible manner.

The Service refused to confirm or deny that the published information, which was picked up by major news media throughout the country, was based upon any official document. A spokesman stated, "The jails are full of people who thought they knew what they could get away with." Unofficially, the word went out that any criteria which remotely resembled the published guidelines would immediately be changed and that the Service had a program designed to catch people who were motivated to cheat by this incident.

Freedom of Information requests for the guidelines or for any instructions which replaced them were denied. No one appealed. No one litigated. The LEM seemed safe as long as no one carried it out the door!

The Second LEM

About 1982 a strange set of events took place which so altered the LEM that it could thereafter be called the second LEM.

An investigator for the General Accounting Office had visited a service center to evaluate the returns-processing activity. As a result of this visit, a letter or report was produced in which the Service was advised to attempt to secure legislation which would permit it to withhold from the public definitions of its computer processing codes to assist in maintaining the integrity and security of its computerized files.

This suggestion, which was not an official finding of the General Accounting Office but seemed to be casually thrown in with unrelated matters, was brought to my attention by Data Processing personnel. It seemed a very strange suggestion, for two reasons. First, the subject of code books had been a part of the original Freedom of Information Act litigation brought by Philip and Susan Long; second, I had at one time personally espoused the protection of computer processing codes for security purposes.

When the first LEM was being constructed, it occurred to me that it might be worthwhile to try to protect such codes. My inquiries, however, led to two very firm conclusions. One was that there was no legal basis for such codes to be exempt. The second was that there was no rational basis for wanting to do such a thing. Conversations with data-processing specialists and security technicians showed that there was no way that having knowledge of our codes would enable a person to enter, alter, or destroy any of our computerized files. There was no telephonic or other off-premises access to our files. A person wanting to interfere with our files would have to physically enter a computer center and access a terminal to do so. Knowledge of the codes would be useless without breaking in. Breaking in would have provided access to the LEM as well as the terminal without using the Freedom of Information Act to pry codes loose.

Since there seemed to be no reason to protect the codes, I dropped the idea. All of our computer processing codes were in the public portion of the *Internal Revenue Manual* and had been on the reading room shelves for more than five years when the suggestion to obtain legislation to protect them was made. I suspected that the idea had been planted with the General Accounting Office investigator by some misguided Service-center employee who might have had a vague recollection of the litigation with the Longs. I did not expect the suggestion to be taken seriously, especially since it had been data-processing personnel who had ridiculed protecting the codes years before. I was wrong.

The suggestion to seek legislation to protect the computer codes hit the Service like an invitation for knights to go in search of the Holy Grail. Soon, Disclosure had a formal request from Data Processing asking for our support in the quest. We reasoned that withholding the codes was currently illegal and that the suggestion to seek legislation inherently recognized that illegality; consequently we could agree that legislation was needed to withhold the codes even if we could see no reason why anyone would want to withhold them. Thus far, Data Processing had provided no scenario which might make such withholding in any way useful. The supporting rationale was Data Processing's responsibility, not ours. We certainly did not want to appear to oppose someone else's grand quest. Moreover, we were still concerned that the many tolerances and criteria in the LEM might not be able to withstand a challenge. Anything that Congress might do to help protect any aspect of the Service's processing of returns could prove to be helpful. We concurred in the Data Processing request to seek legislation.

Chief Counsel's disclosure experts also concurred, apparently in the belief that Congress would not be responsive to the request anyhow. They were right. The request for legislation went to an appropriate subcommittee. The informal feedback from congressional staffers friendly to the Service was that it would not be acted upon because it was unconvincing and there was no sympathy in Congress for expanding FOIA exemptions.

Shortly thereafter, I was invited to a meeting to be chaired by Data Processing and attended by the deputy commissioner, the number-two man in the Service. The meeting was to discuss what to do next. Chief Counsel was also to send a representative. I met with the Counsel representative, and we agreed to maintain a joint position to argue that withholding the codes was illegal, Congress was unwilling to change the law, the codes had been in the reading room for more than five years without adverse consequence, no rationale for withholding the codes had ever been presented, there was no problem, no solution was required, and nothing could or should be done.

The Counsel representative and I arrived at the meeting a few minutes before the appointed time. Much to our surprise, we learned that the meeting had begun half an hour before, the subject had been thoroughly discussed, and a decision had been made without any input from Disclosure or from Chief Counsel. The computer codes and any related information would be moved into the LEM. The Counsel representative immediately stated that that would be illegal. The response from the deputy commissioner was a vague reference to some other action that was being taken to remedy that and a request that we do the best we could to support the Service's position. The deputy left us to work out the details with Data Processing.

All that we could learn about what had transpired at the meeting was that there was a belief that the proposal before Congress was not really dead, that the General Accounting Office was an arm of Congress, and that the initial suggestion resulted from strong support in the Congress. Other agencies were said to be going in the same direction, and it was a question of everyone doing his or her part until things came together. In the meantime, the Data Processing people would begin moving their codes into the LEM, I was to prepare a theoretical basis for the protection of the materials by revising instructions in the Disclosure of Official Information handbook, and Chief Counsel was to protect against any litigation which might result before things came together.

I reported the results of the meeting to my director, and the Counsel representative reported to his director. I do not know what the two directors might have said or known about the project, but a few days later I was asked to get moving on the new instructions as this thing was really important. I soon learned what the related items which required protection were. Data Processing wanted to protect the identity of the specific line items on returns which were to be transcribed. It was reasoned that if a person knew that a particular line item was not transcribed, he could readily conclude that the computer could not analyze that information and this would identify a place where he could cheat without getting caught. While this seems logical, I've never really found an example of a line item which was not transcribed but could affect the outcome of someone's tax liability. If such line items exist, one might ask why they are not transcribed or why we should ask taxpayers to provide the Service with information which is not used.

In addition, Data Processing wanted to protect any illustration of the appearance of data on display screens since people might somehow discover the meaning of codes, the items transcribed, or the analyses made from these illustrations.

To accommodate the new standards for the LEM, I revised the existing instructions to read as follows:

> (3) The classification of data processing materials serves four objectives:
>
> (a) To protect information from Law Enforcement Manuals of other functions such as Examination, Criminal Investigation, and Collection which may be reflected in data processing instructions.
>
> (b) To preclude taxpayers from altering their filing practices or avoiding the payment of taxes by protecting tolerances and criteria,

details of computer analysis and specific identity of items which may or may not be transcribed.

(c) To prevent invasions of individual privacy by protecting computer access codes and to reduce the harm of any inadvertent disclosures of records containing tax return information or other highly confidential personal information by protecting the definitions of data processing codes.

(d) To prevent interference in the computer processing for purposes of fraud or disruption by protecting data processing codes, routines and safety and security provisions.

These instructions were intended to provide a theoretical basis which would make the new deletions seem proper, necessary, and in the public interest. Two problems remained which had to be resolved to make the new scheme workable. The first was that the very codes which were being protected frequently appeared and were defined on correspondence directed to the taxpayer. The second was that the Privacy Act provided that records concerning individuals which were not exempt had to be made available in a form comprehensible to them; consequently, we had an obligation to define any codes appearing on any records released to the taxpayer. These problems were addressed in an instruction which read:

(4) In applying the foregoing objectives, the intent should be to deny public access to definitional materials and extensive listings of data processing codes, such as might prove useful to a person attempting to abuse such information. It is not intended that every mention of an otherwise innocuous code be deleted from every public document in which it might appear, since such occasional disclosure of limited information would not permit a reconstruction of the extensive nature necessary to threaten our computer processes. Moreover, individual requesters are generally entitled to receive records which pertain to them and to receive an adequate explanation of their content.

It should be readily apparent that the instructions identified as (3)(b), (c) and (d) were meant to justify the new LEM, whereas the instruction in (4) was designed to prevent the new LEM from destroying our existing Freedom of Information assumptions on individual taxpayer records or conflicting with the Privacy Act. Frankly, I considered these instructions to be a lot of double-talk meant to support a program with which I personally disagreed.

There were, at the time, many people who took an interest in the Service's programs, but no one took any notice of these public instructions. No congressional staffer apparently took any notice that the Service was unilaterally implementing a program for which it had sought legislation refused as unwarranted or undesirable.

In the next few months, thousands of pages of ADP handbook instructions were withdrawn from the reading room shelves. Nobody noticed. The LEM grew and grew and grew. At least no one could any longer carry it out the door. What had been a hard core of material genuinely believed to be exempt from public access had become trash. The vast majority of the contents of the

Law Enforcement Manual, including many thousands of pages, was not exempt from the Freedom of Information Act. And every Service official who was involved with the creation of the second LEM knew that it was illegal.

The Roberts *Case*

A taxpayer named Glen L. Roberts filed suit against the Internal Revenue Service demanding the release of the entire *Law Enforcement Manual.* On April 23, 1984, the District Court rendered its decision.

The decision describes the *Internal Revenue Manual* and the *Law Enforcement Manual* as consisting of a total of 42,000 pages. This is broken down as 24,000 pages in the publicly available *Internal Revenue Manual* and 18,000 pages in the protected *Law Enforcement Manual.* The 18,000-page LEM total was further broken down as 17,500 pages of Automatic Data Processing information and 500 pages of other information. The overwhelming size of the ADP matter makes it clear that this litigation involved the grotesque second LEM and not the highly selective hard-core first LEM. The figures stated for the size of the IRM and the LEM are probably incorrect. The error seems to result from the manner in which the ADP LEM is produced.

The non–ADP IRM and the LEM are written so that they may be read independently. The IRM text contains occasional references which state "See LEM," followed by a numeric citation. The LEM contains only minimal introductory material and the bare tolerances, criteria, or procedures described. A reader can follow the complete text in the IRM and choose whether to turn to the LEM in response to each reference. Since there is virtually no duplication between the IRM and the LEM, the pages in each would add up to the total number of pages in the combined manuals; i.e., the sum of the parts equals the whole.

The ADP handbooks and the ADP LEM use a different system. Service-center employees frequently have to follow handbook procedures step by step to perform their jobs. They cannot read along in one text and then stop and refer to another for a missing step. Consequently those ADP handbooks which have LEM material (not all handbooks have LEM material) are produced as a complete text. Each line or each illustration which is considered to be LEM material is identified by the character # placed to the right of the text. The ADP LEM produced for the use of Service employees therefore contains all the publicly available materials plus all the LEM material. In some cases an ADP LEM may contain a 100 pages of publicly available text and no more than a half-dozen lines of #-signed LEM material. After the ADP LEM is produced, all the #-signed lines and illustrations are covered by opaque tape, producing a camera copy which consists only of the public material.

A limited number of these sanitized public versions of the ADP handbooks are then printed for distribution to the reading rooms. Sometimes the public version will consist almost entirely of pages which have headings and page numbers but are otherwise completely blank. As a result, the total of all the public pages and all the LEM pages is much more than the total size of the ADP handbooks; i.e., the sum of the parts is greater than the whole.

Consequently, I agree with the figure of 24,000 pages of publicly available IRM, including ADP handbooks, and I agree with the figure of about 500 pages of non–ADP LEM, but I estimate that the ADP LEM which did not merely duplicate the publicly available material was no more than 10,000 to 12,000 pages. This difference in size was never noticed by the District Court because it never looked at a single page of the LEM; it merely relied entirely upon what the Service told it!

The Service responded to the suit by filing a motion for summary judgment supported by affidavits from ten Service officials. Seven of these officials — the Assistant Commissioner (Examination), the Assistant Commissioner (Criminal Investigation), the Assistant Commissioner (Collection), the Assistant Commissioner (Employee Plans and Exempt Organizations), the Assistant Commissioner (Planning, Finance and Research), the director of the Appeals Division, and the director of the Disclosure and Security Division — filed affidavits in defense of the less than 500 pages of non–ADP LEM. This material was virtually unchanged from the first LEM, and I have no doubt that all these officials could in good conscience defend material which was truly exempt.

Two officials, the Assistant Commissioner (Returns and Information Processing) and the Acting Assistant Commissioner (Computer Services), filed affidavits in defense of the 17,500 (10,000 to 12,000 by my estimate) pages of ADP handbook LEM. How they were able to give a convincing account of exempt materials, the vast majority of which had been recognized by all concerned to be nonexempt and were on the reading room shelves less than two years before, is beyond my comprehension.

The tenth affidavit was submitted by an attorney in the Disclosure Litigation Division of the Office of Chief Counsel who described the broad outline of the *Internal Revenue Manual* and the *Law Enforcement Manual*, and the process whereby law enforcement provisions were segregated from those provisions that could be disclosed to the public. You can be certain that he did not mention the meeting at which a Counsel representative and I argued that ADP codes are not exempt and were directed to cooperate in stuffing them into the second LEM.

This affidavit was prepared by an attorney because originally I had been requested to prepare it as chief of the Freedom of Information Branch and the most knowledgeable person in the Service on the creation of the LEM. However, I had declined to do so, pointing out that my filing an affidavit could result in my having to submit to questions from plaintiff's attorneys, and I might prove too knowledgeable.

The judge was obviously impressed by the size of the LEM and the affidavits submitted by the Service. He was not impressed by the plaintiff's response and in his opinion stated:

> Plaintiff, in his response to this motion, does not attempt to controvert any of the factual representations set forth in the government's affidavits. Rather, he argues that there continue to remain material questions of fact in this case, although he does not identify which facts remain in controversy. Further he has failed to produce any admissable

evidence, by way of affidavit or otherwise, in support of his contention. Consequently, he has failed to satisfy the requirement of Fed.R. Cicv.P. 56(c) that

> When a motion for summary judgment is made and supported as provided in this rule, an adverse party may not rest upon the mere allegations or denials of his pleading, but his response, by affidavits or as otherwise provided by this rule, must set forth specific facts showing there is a genuine issue for trial.

This would appear to be a rather harsh burden to place on an FOIA plaintiff. The plaintiff, obviously, has never seen any of the documents at issue. He can know nothing about them. That is the very basis for his suit — to obtain access and learn what they contain. How, then, is he to present evidence to controvert the affidavits? That is the very reason the act places the burden of proof on the government. But when the government's affidavits are accepted as a basis for issuing a summary judgment, the court is acting as if they constitute evidence from a disinterested party rather than the self-serving justifications of the defendant. What difference is there between the plaintiff merely repeating his request for access in his response and the government merely repeating its denial in the form of affidavits? The sequence of initial response, appeal response, and defense of litigation in this case consisted entirely of "We say it's exempt, we say again it's exempt, we still say it's exempt!"

The judge granted the Service's motion for a summary judgment. In doing so, he repeatedly referred to the *Hawkes* case, quoted the opinions in the *Hawkes* case, and stated that the *Hawkes* case set forth the controlling standard in the circuit for what constituted law enforcement materials.

Given the reliance placed upon *Hawkes*, it behooves us to compare *Hawkes* and *Roberts*. Hawkes asked for some *Internal Revenue Manual* materials. Roberts asked for the entire *Law Enforcement Manual*. In *Hawkes*, the court ultimately examined a small amount of material which the Service alleged to be exempt but released all of it. In *Roberts,* the court looked at no material at all but upheld the withholding of all the material, which it then believed to total 18,000 pages.

It would seem almost unbelievable that a court knowing that the controlling case involved inspection would not inspect, knowing that the Service's claims of exemption in the prior case were totally without foundation, would rely on affidavits, and knowing that the controlling case could not justify withholding a single word, would withhold 18,000 pages. But that is precisely what the court did. Moreover, in doing so, the court described the ADP handbooks as containing

> procedures for computer processing of tax returns, including, for example, information relating to the computation of the Discriminant Function System (DIF), which assigns scores to various types of returns that require more careful scrutiny by examiners; command codes that are used in processing and maintaining information in the I.R.S. master files; and procedures describing how to access and manipulate the IDRS data base.

Where did the court find an exemption for procedures for computer processing of tax returns, command codes that are used in processing and maintaining information in master files, and procedures describing how to access and manipulate a data base? There is no such exemption in the Freedom of Information Act. There was no such exemption in any prior litigation. There was no such exemption in the House Report. The investigator for the General Accounting Office did not believe there was such an exemption. The congressional staffers did not think there was such an exemption or even that there ought to be one. The judge must have been very impressed by the Service's affidavits.

The court concluded that "the material contained in the LEM is the kind of sensitive law enforcement information, disclosure of which will only serve to undermine law enforcement. As such it is protected against disclosure by the law enforcement materials exception to 5 U.S.C. 552(a)(2)(C)."

Glen L. Roberts did not appeal. That is the story of how things came together and how Internal Revenue got an exemption for its computer processing codes and related information.

The Current LEM

More recently, the Service has removed some computer processing codes from the LEM and reinserted them in the public portion of the manual in response to appeals from tax protesters. These revisions were made only to the specific chapters requested, and there has been no general overhaul of the LEM. The instructions on protecting data-processing materials which I placed in the Disclosure of Official Information handbook years ago remain in effect. The *Roberts* case continues to be the latest word on the legal status of the LEM. The public continues to assume that the construction of the LEM represented an honest effort and does not warrant attack. The second LEM remains virtually intact and continues to consist mostly of trash.

Chapter Twenty-Two

"Official Use Only"

Many years ago a respected and highly competent analyst in the Research and Planning Division arranged for the printing of a report intended for distribution within the Service. Through some unforeseen mishap, the report was printed without the designation "Official Use Only." The employee's manager became deeply upset when stocks of the printed report were received and the absence of Official Use Only was noticed. It was feared that someone might not realize the sensitivity of the report and might permit it to be released to the public.

The fears were unfounded, for these events took place at a time when no Internal Revenue Service employee would willingly have released any information to anyone. The same attitudes which would have deterred the release of the report also prompted a belief that every printed item should be designated Official Use Only. The employee was instructed to retrieve all the reports which had been distributed and hand-stamp each Official Use Only. When the number of retrieved reports was compared with the total printed, it was realized that about 100 copies were missing.

Subsequent research revealed that unknown to the issuing authorities, the missing reports had been mailed to public libraries throughout the country. The law provided that government publications, other than those determined by their issuing components to be required for official use only or for strictly adminstrative or operational purposes which have no public interest or education value, shall be made available to depositary libraries through the facilities of the Superintendent of Documents for public information. Since the report was not designated Official Use Only, it was automatically distributed to interested libraries which have been designated to serve as depositories for the preservation and dissemination of government publications.

The employee had to write to all the recipient libraries and cajole them to return the inadvertently distributed reports. Ultimately, all or almost all of the reports were returned, suitably hand-stamped and placed back into the internal distribution system. The problem had been solved, but by then, the unfortunate employee had earned a reputation as the man who failed to designate a report "Official Use Only," thereby causing its release to the public. This reputation haunted him for the rest of his career, and he became an example of what becomes of people who fail to classify documents adequately.

Several years later we received a Freedom of Information Act request for the same report. Our review showed that it was obviously not exempt, should never have been classified Official Use Only or retrieved after its initial release, contained no sensitive information, and could not be withheld from the public. The Disclosure unit was unable to obtain functional concurrence in the report's release because it was impossible to convince anyone that a report whose inadvertent distribution and subsequent retrieval had caused so much trouble did not contain highly sensitive information. Ultimately, a requester appealed the withholding of the report, and Counsel released it without any adverse consequences. Neither the tribulations nor the reputation of the poor Planning and Research analyst were warranted, nor was the lesson that it is better to classify a document and be safe than to release it and be sorry.

This story contains all the elements necessary to understand the purpose of classifying materials Official Use Only and how that classification operates. And it illustrates why for many years virtually all Service-printed materials were classified Official Use Only, although no one seems to have known what that designation meant or why it was applied.

At one time, the mania for classifying printed materials Official Use Only extended to such illogical products as warning signs posted on seized premises to caution the public against trespass on government-held property, posters adorning the walls of public-access buildings, and blank forms meant to be filled in by the public. The meaning of the classification varied from "the public shouldn't see," to "the public shouldn't use," to "the public shouldn't carry away with them," to anything at all. Even government-owned automobiles had Official Use Only on their doors, presumably intended to mean "no riders." As the Information Act began to change Service practices, it became necessary to define the meaning of Official Use Only, provide guidelines for its use, and limit its abuse.

The primary purpose for classifying a document Official Use Only is to prevent the automatic distribution to the public of printed materials which should not be subject to such distribution. The secondary purpose is to prevent the release of documents by persons who are not qualified or authorized to determine the propriety of such a release. The third purpose is to permit the rapid release of materials previously determined to be available to the public as a result of a decision not to classify them Official Use Only.

With few exceptions, the Official Use Only designation is intended for use on printed materials only. Printed materials include materials which have been reproduced by any method other than office copying machines. However, regardless of method of reproduction, printed materials do not include any materials whose originator receives and maintains control of all copies.

The Official Use Only designation does not make any document exempt from access under the Freedom of Information Act. It merely reflects an existing exemption. The true meaning of Official Use Only is that the classifying official believed at the time that the material was prepared for issuance that it was exempt from access under the Information Act. Since information may lose its sensitivity with the passage of time and since the appeal and litigation processes of the FOIA tend to broaden the definition of publicly available material, records classified Official Use Only cannot be assumed to retain an exemption indefinitely.

Any Service materials which have been printed and distributed and have not been classified Official Use Only prior to issuance have been determined to be available to the public and may be promptly released to any requester. If you have been denied access to such printed materials, it might be helpful to determine if they have actually been classified prior to issuance or if they may once have been considered to be public information not warranting classification. This may be done by requesting the Form 1767, Publication Service Requisition, which authorized printing the material. This form indicates the purpose for issuing the printed material, how it is to be distributed, and whether it is considered available to the public under the FOIA. If the Form 1767 does not support classification, such information may be of use in an appeal or litigation.

Most printed materials are subject to a continuous review process to ensure that they are current and are periodically updated and reprinted. Materials are not supposed to be automatically classified simply because their predecessors were, but such repetitions do occur. Any older printed materials or revisions of materials should always be considered suspect since they may not have been adequately considered for declassification.

There are a variety of approved methods for classifying only portions of documents Official Use Only, such as identifying protected passages with the # symbol, classifying only certain pages, or classifying only the shaded areas of a document. Printed materials which are not considered to be (a)(2) administrative staff manuals routinely made available for public inspection may still be issued classified Official Use Only as a whole, although much of the material contained may not warrant such designation. Therefore, any appeal of a denial for printed materials which have not been designated as part of the *Law Enforcement Manual* should include a request that the nonexempt portions be promptly released.

Any FOIA request for a classified document is the equivalent of a request for declassification of the document. Official Use Only documents must be reevaluated whenever requested, and that reevaluation must involve an official who has the authority to classify or declassify the record. Field offices will frequently deny access to classified National Office documents without making the necessary referral to ensure that the documents are considered for declassification. Even National Office personnel may occasionally deny access without undertaking a full review. Moreover, there is a tendency to wish to avoid releasing any part of Official Use Only material, such as the LEM, because doing so may trigger a need to redesign and reissue the entire document. The extent to which a request has resulted in the required reconsideration of the classified status of the records can be determined by requesting the history sheets which reflect the processing of the FOIA request.

Field officials are authorized to classify their own printed materials. For many years the National Office made a point of reviewing such materials on field visits, with the result that there were very few field issuances which were classified. Every once in a while, however, a manager will initiate a program to reverse the trend and overclassify field issuances. Be wary of any printed materials issued by field offices and claimed to be exempt since the field seldom has the authority to establish the types of tolerances and criteria which usually lead to classification. The major exception to this rule is Automatic Data Processing training issuances and interim instructions which are prepared in service centers on behalf of National Office functions and generally conform to the current National Office concept of what constitutes an adequate exemption.

There have been many instances in which Official Use Only has been hand-stamped on documents which do not meet the eligibility criteria established by the *Internal Revenue Manual* and have not been approved for classification by officials authorized to do so. In such cases, the Official Use Only designation is nothing more than meaningless graffiti. There is no reason to assume such documents contain exempt information, although they might. Such documents must be carefully analyzed before a disclosure determination is made. Unfortunately, once the Official Use Only designation has been applied to an undeserving document, it becomes difficult for a reviewer to overcome as a result of bureaucratic inertia.

Some control over a tendency to overclassify has been established by the requirement that disclosure specialists review any (a)(2) materials proposed for classification. This control does not extend to material which is not (a)(2), since its classification is considered a nullity having no consequence. Moreover, review by disclosure specialists does not guarantee that the material is actually exempt from release but only that it meets the National Office's current standards for exemption, which are themselves often irrelevant to any sense of reality.

Because of the tendency to overclassify, the failure to declassify promptly and the willingness to rely on a previously applied classification rather than carefully evaluate the material in response to a request, any printed material which is withheld warrants an appeal.

Chapter Twenty-Three

Training Issuances

After the Internal Management Document System, the second most valuable source of information on how the Internal Revenue Service operates are the Training Issuances. The Service provides dozens of programs designed to develop the skills and attitudes of its employees. These programs utilize hundreds of student texts, coursebooks, problems, instructor guides, and training aids. The majority of these materials are, or should be, available to the public.

Examples of some of the more popular Training Issuances currently being distributed by the reading room include texts for subjects as varied as Course 3140, Revenue Agent Basic Training Program; Course 4124, Financial Investigation Techniques; and Course 3171, Criminal Tax Trial Summary Witness Training. If your interests lie in obtaining such commonly requested items, you need merely telephone the reading room at (202) 566-3770 to inquire about the availability and cost of materials responsive to your needs.

You should keep in mind that Training Issuances are intended for teaching purposes only. They are not directives which must be followed, and they cannot be relied upon as authorization for any action. Most Training Issuances carry a disclaimer, such as "This material was designed specifically for training purposes only. Under no circumstances should the contents be used or cited as authority for setting or sustaining a technical position."

The frequency with which tax laws change and new procedures are issued results in training materials being notoriously out of date. When used by the Service, this defect is overcome by the experienced instructors assigned to present the training courses. Invariably, the instructors will begin by making pen-and-ink changes to the texts, pulling out offensive pages, or alerting their students to passages requiring revisions. Such changes cannot be noted on copies released to the public. As a result, you cannot assume that all the material received is correct and current; nor can you assume that erroneous materials are evidence that any improprieties exist since such materials are likely to be corrected before being presented to the Service's students. Nevertheless, Training Issuances are valuable resource materials.

Researching Training Issuances

The person wishing to go beyond the commonly requested materials available through the reading room will have to do some research to find what she is looking for. Each training course is identified by a four-digit number, such as 4124 for Financial Investigative Techniques. All Training Issuances which relate to the same course are identified by the same four-digit number, followed by a dash and a two-digit number. The two-digit number identifies the particular issuance, which may be one of many used for that course. Thus, Training 4124–04 is an instructor guide, whereas Training 4124–05 is the coursebook for the same course. Identifying the material wanted will usually consist of first identifying the four-digit number for the course which contains information of interest to you and then finding the two-digit number identifying the particular material wanted.

Many courses are identified in several *Internal Revenue Manual* handbooks:

IRM 0420.2: Collection, Automation, Taxpayer Service/Returns Processing Training and Development Programs Handbook

IRM 0420.3: Operations and Legal Training and Development Programs Handbook (includes Examination and Criminal Investigation Division Training)

IRM 0420.4: Servicewide Training and Development Programs Handbook (includes Disclosure Orientation Training and Illegal Tax Protester Training)

IRM 0420.6: Resources Management Training and Development Programs Handbook

IRM 0420.7: Continuing Professional Education (CPE) Program Handbook (includes all functions)

The following documents also identify courses and sometimes identify the various Training Issuances associated with each:

Document 6054: National Office Training and Development Guide

Document 6172: Training Program Index

Document 6262: ADP Training Course Catalog

Document 6314: Training Aids Catalog

Document 6398: Training Materials Catalog (best bet for identifying Examination and Criminal Investigation Training Issuances)

If you have been able to identify the four-digit course number but have not been able to identify the two-digit issuance number, you may simply request all issuances related to that course, or you may ask the National Office disclosure technician to inform you of the types of issuances (i.e., coursebook, instructor guide, problems, handouts, etc.) so that you may choose which you wish to include or eliminate from your request. If the technician does not cooperate in this approach, request all Forms 3163, Training Course Status Notice, pertaining to the course. These forms contain the titles and descriptions of all materials required for a course.

Be aware, however, that not all Training Issuances are available to the public.

Exempt Training Issuances

Training Issuances are usually printed materials, and they are subject to the procedures for classifying exempt material before it is printed, which means that they are also subject to the concept that they may continue to show an "Official Use Only" legend after they no longer warrant protection. Training Issuances therefore require examination and declassification (if appropriate) whenever they are requested.

There are three reasons for initially classifying Training Issuances. They may repeat *Law Enforcement Manual* or classified data-processing information and thus must be classified to protect the original materials. They may include original information not appearing elsewhere, which requires protection for the same reasons as law enforcement or data-processing materials. They may require classification to protect the integrity of the training process.

Instructor Guides and related materials may be classified to prevent students from obtaining advance knowledge of test questions and answers, discussion problems, and other training techniques whose effectiveness would be diminished by becoming known prior to employment by the instructor.

Training Issuances were subject to review by National Office disclosure technicians prior to classification and were seldom found to contain such extensive material requiring protection as to warrant classifying the entire issuance. Usually, only certain lines or pages were protected, and the rest was available for release to the public. Many ADP Training Issuances were prepared in the service centers and were classified by local officials acting on the recommendation of their disclosure officers. Such locally classified issuances may not have been subject to as thorough a review as that received by National Office documents and may therefore be overclassified.

IRM 0410.51 states that Exhibit 0410–5 contains a list of current materials which are restricted and are not to be released but which have not been designated Official Use Only on the materials themselves. This, of course, is in direct conflict with IRM 1272(12)32(1), which states: "Any Internal Revenue Service materials which have been printed and distributed may be assumed to be intended for public release if they have not been classified Official Use Only."

Exhibit 0410–5 contains a four-page list of such so-called Official Use Only Training Issuances, all of which pertain to ADP instructions. IRM 0410.51 and Exhibit 0410–5 have not been revised since January 30, 1981. Since ADP technology changes rapidly, all or most of these quasi-classified issuances may now be obsolete, but the existence of these manual entries provides continuing evidence of the extent of ADP materials which were once available to the public (i.e., issued without classification) and were subsequently withdrawn pursuant to the GAO comment that ADP processing codes should be protected. Chief Counsel's Disclosure Litigation Division began releasing some of the underlying LEM material in response to appeals in 1987, but this declassification effort has not yet spread to Training Issuances. Presumably, a little push could release a torrent of this material if anyone wanted it.

Training Aids

The Service uses extensive videocassettes, films, film strips, and other visual or auditory aids. The Service also has many computerized self-instructional programs. These materials are subject to the Freedom of Information Act, and many of them should be available to the public. There has not been extensive experience with arrangements for copying such materials or making them available for inspection, but these should be mere technical problems to be overcome as they are encountered.

The Service will not make available for copying or viewing any materials in which Service employees or their family members appear for fear that such persons would be identified and subject to harassment. The Service has in these cases made available a transcript so that the requester, while not permitted to view the materials, is able to know what it contained. This arrangement has been approved by a court. However, filmed presentations in which only the participants' faces were obscured are commonplace, and a serious requester willing to bear the expense might successfully pursue such a solution.

Chapter Twenty-Four

Documents and Publications

The Internal Revenue Service prints hundreds if not thousands of pamphlets, booklets, texts, tables, posters, and similar materials which contain useful information on how the Service operates. Most of these printed materials are part of what is referred to as the Publications System which is governed by IRM 1(17)00, Printing and Publication. The two major categories of printed material in the Publication System are Documents and Publications.

Documents are defined as internal-use items of an administrative-informational nature issued solely for the use of Service personnel. Because of this definition, all documents were at one time automatically classified as Official Use Only and arbitrarily withheld from the public. Today it is generally realized that information cannot be withheld from the public simply because its initial creation was motivated by an internal need. Very few documents are now classified Official Use Only, and those must be considered for declassification whenever they are requested by the public. You should be aware, however, that any item which has been designated a document was visualized as intended solely for internal use and is therefore not routinely included in public distributions.

Do not let the designation "Document" tempt you into pursuing worthless materials. Many documents are really minor items of no informational value. For instance, Document 5370 is a decalcomania, *Internal Revenue Service*, for placement on doors or windows. Document 6436 is a tag, *Do Not Unplug*. Documents 5006 and 5007 are directional arrows, pointing right and left, respectively. On the other hand, documents include such valuable reference works as Document 6743, Sources of Information from Abroad, which lists for investigators the names and addresses of official sources of public records throughout the world.

Publications are defined as public-use items which are primarily issued for distribution to the public. Naturally, publications are never classified Official Use Only and withheld from the public. Or at least almost never. There has been one schizoid publication which was issued to be distributed to the public *and* withheld from the public by an official who was able to distinguish between two types of publics, only one of which was entitled to receive the publication. Most publications are such familiar and freely distributed items as Publication 17, *Your Federal Income Tax*.

The ultimate source for information on the existence of Documents and Publications is Form 2157, Publications Status Notice, which is prepared for each publication and document in the system. A new status notice is issued whenever a new item is published or an existing item is revised, discontinued, or subject to a change in usage. The official file of status notices is maintained in the National Office, but fairly reliable sets should be available in regional offices.

More convenient sources of information on documents and publications are identified in the lists which follow. Unfortunately, in recent years the Service has not had the money for its publishing efforts necessary to keep all items current. Many documents are infrequently revised or reissued, and many older documents, while not obsolete, have become virtually unobtainable. The items listed below are those which serve as basic reference works. The serious researcher may wish to include many of them in his basic library.

Basic Documents

• Doc. 5037, Directory of Distribution Schedules: This Document serves as a guide for the distribution of Internal Management Documents, including the *Internal Revenue Manual*, the *Law Enforcement Manual* and other printed materials, and identifies the intended recipients. It is updated by Distribution Supplementary Information Listings, commonly referred to as DSILs.

• Doc. 5143, IRS Office Address Directory: Lists the street addresses and the administrative mail addresses of major IRS offices and the names and phone numbers of key officials. Frequently revised.

• Doc. 5261, Map of Internal Revenue Regions and Districts: An 11″ × 8½″ map showing which districts are part of each region. Also available as Doc. 5261A in 21″ × 16″ size.

• Doc. 5427, National Office Reports Catalog: Provides a summary of reports required by the National Office and lists reports which the National Office must submit to other organizations. More detailed information on reports can be obtained from Forms 2951, Report Approval and Cost, which is maintained by National Office. Forms for local reports may be available in regional offices.

• Doc. 6172, Training Program Index: Contains all the training programs currently in use.

• Doc. 6209, ADP and IDRS Information: A compilation of many of the codes used in master file processing in the service centers. Invaluable for deciphering many computer products. This information had been public for many years, then was swept up in the hysteria to protect ADP processing codes, and is now again available to the public. Contains much material which is still being withheld in portions of the LEM and many Training Issuances. Serious researchers should obtain a copy before it becomes secret again. Reissued annually, although many entries remain the same.

• Doc. 6314, Training Aids Catalog.

• Doc. 6372, Privacy Act of 1974, Resource Materials: Reprints the act and the governing regulations, notices of systems of records, and other related materials. Seldom updated.

• Doc. 6398, Training Materials Catalog.

• Doc. 6941, IRS Strategic Plan: Describes the plans and directions for the Service for future years. Intended to assist managers in planning their programs.

• Doc. 7008, IRS Strategic Plan: A version of the above designed for use in training programs for executives.

• Doc. 7098, Rules of Conduct: Provides the standards of behavior for Service employees, reprinted from the *Internal Revenue Manual.*

• Doc. 7130, IRS Printed Product Catalog: Lists the Forms, Documents, and Publications which are supplied to Service personnel upon request by the Centralized Inventory and Distribution Centers. Valuable because it links each Document and Publication to an *Internal Revenue Manual* instruction which established or explains it.

• Doc. 7151, IRS National Office Organizational Telephone Directory: Identifies key National Office officials by name, title, and telephone number.

Basic Publications

• Pub. 55, Annual Report of the Commissioner of Internal Revenue: A statement of the Service's accomplishments during the prior year, including statistical tables. Helpful in interpreting what the Service considers to be its most important objectives.

• Pub. 78, Cumulative List of Organizations: Provides the exact name and the general location of exempt organizations and is therefore invaluable in making requests for exempt organization returns.

• Pub. 676, Catalog of Federal Tax Forms, Form Letters and Notices: Provides a comprehensive listing and explanation of virtually every type of form required to be filed by taxpayers and the communications which the Service may issue in response. Issued annually.

• Pub. 711, Statistics of Income Publications Listing.

• Pub. 897, Publication Catalog: Identifies and explains the Publications and Documents produced by the Service. This is the major source for identifying items of interest to the requester. Although scheduled for semiannual issuance, there have been no recent editions, so that many new items are not listed.

• Pub. 1102, Uniform Issue List: Index of terms and Internal Revenue Code sections necessary for locating a variety of materials indexed under the system.

• Pub. 1118, Freedom of Information Reading Room: A handout listing the contents of the reading room.

• Pub. 1200, Catalog of Federal Tax Forms and Publications: A version of Pub. 676 designed for assisting taxpayers in ordering forms not stocked locally.

Chapter Twenty-Five

Written Determinations

The term *Written Determinations* relates to three types of documents: Private Letter Rulings, Determination Letters, and Technical Advice Memoranda, which became available to the public pursuant to section 6110 of the Internal Revenue Code in 1976.

These documents relate to the Internal Revenue Service's rulings program, the chief part of which is the Revenue Ruling. A *Revenue Ruling* is a formal interpretation prepared by the National Office of the Service for publication in the *Internal Revenue Bulletin* to provide taxpayers and Service personnel with information and guidance concerning tax matters. The chief characteristics of a Revenue Ruling are that it attempts to be responsive to every conceivable aspect of a particular set of circumstances, is intended to anticipate any relevant questions, is carefully prepared and extensively reviewed at comparatively high levels, is published, and may be relied upon by taxpayers to the extent that it applies to their affairs and Service personnel must conform to its provisions. The Revenue Ruling may be thought of as an extension of the law and regulations by which the Service attempts to apply general provisions to specific situations of fairly wide interest as it becomes aware of them.

Private Letter Rulings are somewhat similar to Revenue Rulings, but they are issued in response to a taxpayer's specific request, focus upon the circumstances provided by the taxpayer rather than attempt to be exhaustive, are generally prospective in that they apply to transactions which have not yet taken place, are issued promptly upon request, and are therefore subject to minimal review and low-level approval. They may not be relied upon by any person other than the taxpayer to whom issued, are binding upon the Service only if the taxpayer elects to attach a copy of his tax return, are not published, and have no general relevance.

Service personnel may not cite or rely upon Private Letter Rulings in the disposition of any other case. There are no provisions for the formal circulation of Private Letter Rulings within the Service. Taxpayers generally request Private Letter Rulings to provide them with guidance in activities which have not previously been the subject of any published issuance. Freuqently, the receipt of multiple requests for the issuance of Private Letter Rulings will prompt the Service to give the matter more thorough consideration, resulting in the issuance of a Revenue Ruling. Thus, Private Letter Rulings may be seen as foreshadowing Service positions subsequently taken in Revenue Rulings. Revenue Rulings may, however, take entirely different positions than might have been expected on the basis of the Private Letter Rulings which preceded them.

Determination Letters are issued by district directors in response to a taxpayer request for a determination concerning specific facts which have already taken place. They may be issued only in regard to matters subject to clearly established precedents already established by regulations, rulings, opinions, or court decisions published in the *Internal Revenue Bulletin*. While a convenience to the requesting taxpayer, they are of little interest to anyone else since they refer merely to existing public precedents.

Technical Advice Memorandums are comparable to Private Letter Rulings, except that they are not issued to taxpayers but are issued in response to a request by a district director for instructions on the treatment of a specific set of facts appearing in a taxpayer's return.

Until 1976, Private Letter Rulings, Determination Letters, and Technical Advice Memorandums were not published and would not have been released to requesters under the Freedom of Information Act. Service personnel would have assumed that these items were tax returns, or at least return information, and were highly confidential. In fact, most Service personnel would have been highly indignant if anyone had had the audacity to request access to such materials.

The Arguments for Release

Numerous arguments have been stated in favor of making all written determinations public. In an article reprinted in 1970 as Document 6062, the Chief Counsel reiterated these:

1. Publication would enable taxpayers to insist upon being treated uniformly.
2. Publication would reduce the duplication of effort which takes place within the Service as a result of the continued discussion and consideration of questions which would have been long since disposed of by published precedents.
3. Publication would permit Congress to know the manner in which the Service applies congressional mandates, thereby enabling Congress to determine intelligently the desirability or necessity of amending the Code.
4. Publication would enable Congress more effectively to hold the Commissioner responsible for the exercise of the discretionary powers which Congress has lodged in that office.
5. Reliance on unpublished materials by Service personnel would be stopped.

These or similar views were expressed in Congress from time to time. The opposing view, however, generally held sway: Publishing all rulings would in effect do away with the simple, prompt, and specific Private Letter Rulings by turning them into the slower, more carefully reviewed, more general Revenue

Rulings. But since the Service lacked the resources to increase the number of Revenue Rulings, publication would deprive the public of something they now had and provide them with little or nothing in return.

In a typical year, the Service might issue between 40,000 and 50,000 Private Letter Rulings, but publish only about 650 Revenue Rulings, so that the simple mathematics of the rulings program would support the argument that publishing or disclosing the Letter Rulings would substantially overwhelm the Service and virtually destroy the program.

Tax Analysts and Advocates

A Freedom of Information Act request was made by an organization known as Tax Analysts and Advocates for copies of a small number of Private Letter Rulings and Technical Advice Memorandums, relating to a very specific field of economic activity. This requst threw the Service into consternation not only because attempting to access these materials was tatamount to sacrilege but because Tax Analysts and Advocates was a highly respected organization. Its head, Thomas F. Field, was believed to have many good friends in the Service. There was a sort of "How could they do this to us?" reaction to the request.

Soon there were rumors that within Chief Counsel's organization, there were pro-release and antirelease factions. It was said that Tax Analysts and Advocates were making a "friendly" request at the instigation of one or another of these factions. The request was intended to provide the antirelease faction with an easy victory, thereby settling the matter once and for all; or the request was intended to destroy the rulings program; or the request was to support the pro-release faction in building their own empire. Whatever the truth of these rumors, the struggle within Chief Counsel was resolved in favor of orthodoxy. The pro-release faction, if it ever existed, collapsed. The records were withheld. In 1972, Tax Analysts and Advocates and Thomas F. Field filed suit against the Internal Revenue Service.

Section (a)(2)(B) of the Freedom of Information Act expressly requires that agencies shall make available to the public "interpretations" adopted by the agency. The Service argued that Letter Rulings are not "interpretations" because that they do not serve as precedents, and in the Service's view the statute meant precedents when it said "interpretations." this argument was based upon a statement in the ever-obliging House Report:

> An agency may not be required to make available for public inspection and copying any advisory interpretation on a specific set of facts which is requested by and addressed to a particular person, provided that such interpretation is not cited or relied upon as a precedent in the disposition of other cases.

The court, however, felt that the plain language of the statute outweighed the significance of the House Report, which was broader than the statute and conflicted with the Senate Report. Moreover, the court stated that even if the

House Report were controlling, the Service's argument would not be successful since many Letter Rulings are maintained in a file arranged by Internal Revenue Code section, the "reference file," where they served to assist in the construction of future Letter Rulings.

Curiously, prior to the effective date of the Freedom of Information Act in 1967, the "reference file" had been known as the "precedent file." Files occupying over 2,000 feet of shelf space had been laboriously stamped "Reference" in place of the prior designation "Precedent." Thus, the Internal Revenue Service had sought to avoid compliance with the (a)(2) inspection provision simply by renaming the "precedent file" the "reference file."

The court further said that rather than engage in semantic disputes whether "interpretations," "reference files," or "precedent files" were subject to the (a)(2) public-inspection requirement, the materials should be considered records available in response to a specific request, pursuant to (a)(3). In this regard, the Service claimed exemptions (b)(4), Trade Secrets and Confidential Financial Information, and (b)(3), Matters Specifically Exempted from Disclosure by Statute.

In response to the claim for (b)(4) exemption, the court stated that the Service would have to show that information in the requested documents is "independently confidential" and "not susceptible of being rendered anonymous." In response to the claim for (b)(3) exemption, the court explained at length its doctrine of the applicability of 26 U.S.C. 6103:

> The rulings and memos . . . are not returns, submitted by taxpayers, but documents generated by the agency. Those documents are, to be sure, based upon information submitted by the taxpayer. But . . . a request letter from a taxpayer voluntarily submitting information and seeking tax guidance for his own purposes is not a return within the meaning of the statute. It is only correspondence. If a taxpayer receives an adverse letter ruling, or no letter ruling, he may abandon the proposed transaction, in which event the correspondence will never become part of a "return." The fact that some information in certain correspondence might, at a later date, be included in a return does not convert the earlier correspondence into a return. Defendants argue that because the taxpayer is advised to file a copy of the ruling with his return, the ruling thereby becomes a part of the return and confidential under the statute. This is a circular and self-fulfilling rationale which cannot be accepted. Any agency would thus be able to avoid the Freedom of Information Act and public disclosure of its decisions by requiring that the parties later attach copies of the decision to otherwise confidential submissions. This is not the purpose of the Freedom of Information Act.

Finally, the Service argued that even if the materials were subject to required disclosure, the court should exercise the discretion inherent in its equitable powers and refuse to order disclosure on the grounds that it would disrupt the agency's established procedures and might mean the end of the rulings program. The court responded that once a determination is made that the materials come within the terms of the statute by which Congress required disclosure, the court has no discretion to refuse to order disclosure.

And then the court summed up its philosophy of the case:

> Finally, it is clear from the record herein that private letter rulings are in fact widely disseminated among the tax bar and taxpayers with similar interests and problems, and that the IRS is aware of this practice. Thus a body of "private law" has in fact been created which is accessible to knowledgeable tax practitioners and those able to afford their services. It is only the general public which has been denied access to the IRS' private rulings. The IRS' argument that publication would cause grave damage to its ruling system, then, is viewed by this Court as a specter having little basis in fact. Those taxpayers most likely to rely upon or challenge the rationale of letter rulings issued to others already have access to many rulings through their own efforts. Publication would simply make available to all what is now available to only a select few, and subject the rulings to public scrutiny as well. Such public availability and scrutiny are the very fundamental policies of the Freedom of Information Act. For, "one fundamental principle is that secret law is an abomination."

The Internal Revenue Service Appeals

The District Court ordered the Service to release the requested Private Letter Rulings and Technical Advice Memorandums to Tax Analysts and Advocates. In an unusually sophisticated approach, the court further ordered that if the Service wished to make any deletions, the materials would have to be submitted to the court intact, with any proposed deletions indicated and supported by a detailed written justification so that the court might determine if the proposed deletions were justified.

The Service appealed the decision on two grounds: whether the materials requested were specifically exempted from disclosure by statute and whether the court erred in holding that it did not have equitable powers to refuse to order disclosure.

In 1974, the Appeals Court decided that there was nothing in the appeal which would compel the court to alter the opinion that equitable powers to refuse to order disclosure did not exist. The Appeals Court further ruled that the Letter Rulings were not exempt but that the Technical Advice Memorandums were exempt because they depended upon information appearing on a filed return and were generated as a part of the process by which tax determinations are made. There still remained the opportunity to propose deletions from the Letter Rulings to be released.

The decision was modified in part and remanded to the District Court for further proceedings.

The Fruehauf Corporation

While the *Tax Analysts and Advocates* case was wending its way from District Court to Circuit Court and back again, the case of *Fruehauf Corporation v. Internal Revenue Service,* which involved the same classes of documents, arose.

The Fruehauf Corporation was charged with conspiracy to defraud the United States by obstructing assessment and collection of federal excise tax, to evade and defeat payment of such taxes, and to assist in preparation of false excise tax returns. Fruehauf was attempting to pursue a line of defense based upon the concept that some of the activities it was charged with were similar to acts permitted to other taxpayers in the same industry on the basis of unpublished private rulings. Consequently, during the course of pretrial discovery proceedings in this criminal case, Fruehauf sought to obtain certain rulings it believed would supply information essential to its defense.

The Service, reversing its former position that records requests pertaining to existing litigation should be pursued in discovery rather than through the Freedom of Information Act, took the position that the records were not properly subject to discovery in the criminal case but could be obtained under the Freedom of Information Act. The court in the criminal case denied the discovery motion on the theory that the information would be furnished through the Freedom of Information Act.

In a dazzling display of legalistic dexterity, the Service then withheld the records as exempt from Freedom of Information access. The Service's position appeared to be that the Information Act was the proper route of nonaccess, or you just can't get there from here.

Fruehauf brought suit, and the Service defended on the grounds that the requested Private Letter Rulings and Technical Advice Memorandums were exempt as protected by statute. The court held that the records were not exempt. Moreover, it was impressed by an argument that there was precedent that if a ruling issued to one taxpayer held that a sale or lease of an item was not subject to excise tax, the benefit of that ruling must be granted to other taxpayers making similar transactions. Thus rulings issued to one taxpayer affect and must be available to all taxpayers.

The Service appealed on the grounds that the Code precluded the release of tax returns and that even if the documents are not exempt, the court erred in failing to exercise its equitable jurisdiction to decline to issue an order compelling disclosure. The court rejected these claims and observed: "The Internal Revenue Service urges that its letter ruling program will be destroyed if the rulings are disclosed. In addition to the fact that no proof of this appears on the record, this is an argument for the legislature, not the court."

Certiorari and Legislation

On November 6, 1975, a petition for certiorari to the Supreme Court was filed in the *Fruehauf* case so that the Service might present its arguments in defense of the Private Letter Rulings and the Technical Advice Memorandums. On November 26 the District Court granted defendants' Motion for Stay of Proceedings in the *Tax Analysts and Advocates* case pending a determination by the Supreme Court on petition for certiorari in *Fruehauf* since the same issues were involved. On January 12, 1976, the Supreme Court granted certiorari, agreeing to hear the case.

The public availability of Private Letter Rulings was never to be argued before the Supreme Court, for the policy decisions on how such publicity would affect the rulings program were resolved by the Congress with the passage of the Tax Reform Act of 1976, which included a new section 6110, Public Inspection of Written Determinations.

The Service was satisfied that the availability of its written determinations was no longer subject to the vagaries of the Freedom of Information Act but would be controlled by specific, clear legislation directed exclusively to that subject. Somehow, the Service convinced itself that all it ever wanted was such special legislation rather than attempting to apply general legislation to its special circumstances. In reality, the new law contained nothing the Service wanted, and it forced the Service to go far beyond anything any court had demanded as full compliance with the Freedom of Information Act. None of the Service's arguments were recognized. There was little in the statute the Service could not have done by itself had it wanted to.

The work involved in complying with section 6110 was phenomenal, but it got done. Much of the basic labor consisted of editing existing rulings. The job was done by two or three dozen law students who worked on the project for two summers. The continuing tasks probably involved about ten staff years annually.

Section 6110 has been in effect for over a dozen years. For about ten of those years a vast collection of Private Letter Rulings, Determination Letters, and Technical Advice Memorandums, have been on the reading-room shelves. Various commercial interests ensure that these issuances receive wider circulation.

The rulings program has not collapsed. In fact, no adverse consequences of making the determinations public have appeared.

Section 6110

Section 6110 appears much like a miniature Freedom of Information Act inserted into the Internal Revenue Code. Its provisions are no easier to accept than were those the Service struggled so desperately to avoid. But because it is a part of the Code and was specifically drafted to apply to the Service alone and gives the appearance of remedying the Service's concerns, it has been taken to heart by the agency. Section 6110 is administered with dedication and has available funding, staffing, management involvement, and general acceptability far beyond that ever allotted to Freedom of Information Act processing.

Section 6110 makes available for public inspection "written determinations," which is defined to include Rulings, Determination Letters, and Technical

Advice Memorandums. The Rulings and Technical Advice Memorandums have been designated shelf materials for retention in the National Office Freedom of Information Reading Room. The Determination Letters, products of the district directors, have been designated for retention in the regional reading rooms. I have never found any Determination Letters in such reading rooms, presumably because none had actually been issued.

In addition to the written determinations, background file documents are available in response to specific requests. "Background file documents" are defined to include the request for the written determination, any written material submitted in support of the request, and any communication (written or otherwise) between the Service and persons outside the Service in connection with the determination (other than communications with the Department of Justice relating to pending civil or criminal cases or investigations) received before the issuance of the written determination. Background files documents, for section 6110 purposes, do not include internal communications, history sheets, forms, controls, drafts, or other materials which may in fact be in the background file.

Both the written determinations and the background file documents are subject to compulsory editing prior to release. The items usually deleted include the names, addresses, and other identifying details of the person to whom the determination pertains.

In addition, six categories of information similar to the Information Act exemptions must be deleted:

1. Information specifically authorized under criteria established by an executive order to be kept secret in the interest of national defense or foreign policy.

2. Information specifically exempted from disclosure by any statute other than the Internal Revenue Code which is applicable to the Service.

3. Trade secrets and commercial or financial information obtained from a person and privileged or confidential.

4. Information whose disclosure would constitute a clearly unwarranted invasion of personal privacy.

5. Information contained in or related to examination, operating, or condition reports prepared by, or on behalf of, or for use of an agency response for the regulation or supervision of financial institutions.

6. Geological and geophysical information and data, including maps, concerning wells.

Very detailed and complicated provisions exist for seeking the taxpayer's suggestions for making these deletions, and taxpayers who claim a need for more extensive deletions than the Service proposes may litigate the matter. Deletions may also be challenged by those who seek more information.

If any person other than the taxpayer or his representative communicates with the Service concerning a pending determination, the public-inspection copy of the determination will be noted, with the category of the person making the contact, such as Congressional, Department of Commerce, Department of the

Treasury, Trade Association, White House, or Educational Institution. When a determination is so marked, any person may request the release of the name of the third party making the contact, and such name will not be deleted from any background file document released. Complex provisions permit any person to petition the Tax Court or the District Court for the District of Columbia to release the identity of the recipient of such determination if the court determines that there is evidence from which one could reasonably conclude that an impropriety occurred or undue influence was exercised.

Provision is made for withholding Technical Advice Memorandums and background file documents for cases which involve civil fraud, criminal investigations, jeopardy assessments, or termination assessments until such actions have been completed. In addition, indexes are required, provisions made for resolving disputes, timeliness criteria established, and reasonable fees authorized.

All in all, section 6110 has completely resolved all issues concerning the release of written determinations. The section has been extraordinarily successful, and there have been virtually no disputes or complaints, and certainly no instances of the sort of scandalous behavior which has surrounded the administration of the Freedom of Information Act.

Success may have resulted from attention to detail, specificity, clarity and relevance. I believe, however, that the chief reason that section 6110 has been so much more successful than the Freedom of Information Act is that is was placed in the Internal Revenue Code and therefore has the attention and total commitment of the entire Service.

Making Requests

All requests for copies of Private Letter Rulings, Technical Advice Memorandums, and their background file documents must be directed to the reading room in the National Office. Requests for Determination Letters must be directed to the appropriate regional reading room. Normally, a requester would want a copy of the determination prior to requesting the background file documents to ensure that it covers what is wanted.

The easiest way to request a determination is by citing the code section which is the determination's subject matter. If all the determinations under a given code section are requested, you may receive more than expected; some may predate the time period of your interest, and many may simply repeat the same information. You may therefore ask for only the latest one, or you may ask for several within a specific time period. A request for several recent rulings which do not duplicate each other will generally be honored by reading-room personnel, although they are not required to compare the content of rulings to avoid duplication.

If you wish to avoid the risks inherent in permitting someone else to select the items considered responsive to your request, you should begin by obtaining an index, so that you may specify precisely what you want.

Written determinations are coded with a seven-digit identification number.

The first two digits represent the year, and the next two digits represent the week in which the determination was released for inspection. The last three digits represent the sequential number assigned. For example, 8823012 identifies the twelfth determination released for public inspection during the twenty-third week of 1988.

Indexes are arranged by code section and list all the determinations released in numerical order under each section. The requester may then request whatever determinations are of interest to him by their specific numbers.

The index for Current Written Determinations is issued as Pub. 1078. The index is issued every week in which determinations are released and lists all new issuances (identified by asterisks) and all issuances released during prior weeks of that quarter. Consequently, each weekly index grows larger and supersedes the prior week's index. The final weekly index of any quarter constitutes the cumulative index for that quarter. In order to have a complete index of all current written determinations, it is necessary to have all quarterly indexes issued to date plus the latest weekly index. Pub. 1078 may be requested from the reading room. If issues for prior quarters are wanted, it may be advisable to discuss what is needed with the reading-room attendant.

Written Determinations and their background file documents may be destroyed three years after the determination has been made public unless the determination was designated as a Reference Determination, which must be permanently retained. Any request for materials more than three years old should be discussed with the reading-room attendant before being submitted in writing.

The full text (less deletions) of all National Office written determinations and the weekly index are available by mail on a weekly subscription basis. The subscription service is administered by, and inquiries should be directed to

> Distribution Manager, PM:HR:F:P
> Publishing Services Branch
> Internal Revenue Service
> 1111 Constitution Avenue, N.W.
> Washington, DC 20224

Background file documents should be requested by the identification number. It may take several months to process requests for such documents, as they may require contact with the taxpayer before they may be released, unless they have been previously edited in response to another request.

Keep in mind that the term *background file documents* refers only to the limited items available under section 6110. The file will normally also contain materials which have to be evaluated pursuant to the Freedom of Information Act. Most requesters are not aware of this distinction, and it is difficult to tell which items are wanted. The Service has therefore made the assumption that every request for section 6110 background file documents is also a request for anything else that may be found in the file in the belief that most requesters want everything that might be available. This means that two separate responses will be made; one will grant all section 6110 materials in edited form, and the other will apply FOIA standards to all non–6110 items, possibly denying some. This assumption may delay the processing of the request and will add to your costs. If you do not want the non–6110 materials, your request should state that you understand the distinction between section 6110 material and non–6110 material, and want only the background file documents as defined by section 6110. Requesters may also limit their requests for background file documents to particular records, classes of records, or time frames.

Fees for services pursuant to section 6110 are revised periodically and are intended to cover the actual current costs of operations. The fee for providing copies of written determinations which are available as shelf materials in the reading room is $.15 per page. Fees for processing requests for background file documents include:

• Search Fee: $13.00 for each determination file requested.
• Deletion Fee: $2.00 for each page which must be analyzed for potential deletions.
• Duplication Fee: $.15 for each page copied, including both copies released and copies sent to the taxpayer to whom the determination pertains to permit the challenge off proposed deletions.

There are no provision for waiving fees for section 6110 materials.

Chapter Twenty-Six

Exposing Undue Influence

The provision in section 6110 for recording contacts from third parties to preclude or expose any improprieties involving undue influence was not the Service's only experience with this concept in 1976.

A general policy of disclosing third-party contacts in all types of tax cases was initiated by Commissioner Alexander that same year, but this policy was to have one of those strange "now you see it, now you don't" histories so common to Internal Revenue Service disclosure practices.

The new policy was described by the *Washington Post*'s star reporter Bob Woodward in an article which appeared on May 8, 1976. This article is worth quoting in its entirety:

IRS to Make Public "Political" Inquiries

The Internal Revenue Service yesterday announced that it will soon make public all "contacts made by federal departments and agencies and members of Congress regarding matters pending before the Service."

Meade Emory, executive assistant to IRS Commissioner Donald C. Alexander said the action was taken to reduce what he termed "political interference" with various cases and rulings pending before the IRS.

"It's designed to throw the pressure off," Emory said, adding that it was directed mainly at members of Congress. The availability of such information would "result in a diminished number of congressional inquiries," he predicted.

Emory said yesterday's announcement was not connected to any particular case although it follows by three weeks a Treasury Department investigation showing that Sen. Joseph M. Montoya (D-N.M.) who heads the Senate Committee that oversees the IRS, received favorable treatment on tax audits.

Investigators also charged that there was "improper interference by officials of the IRS national office with attempts ... to collect delinquent taxes from two taxpayers located in Sen. Montoya's home state."

According to the investigators, Montoya had sought a reversal of a decision to collect delinquent taxes in one case.

In another recent matter, Rep. Al Ulman (D-Ore), chairman of the House Ways and Means Committee, sought delays from Alexander of an audit of his own tax returns.

Alexander made the final decision on the new policy Thursday night, and the IRS spokesman said it would take several weeks before the exact procedures are developed to record and make available information on outside contacts.

There was no immediate reaction on Capitol Hill. One senior senator involved in tax legislation expressed mild astonishment at the IRS plan, but said he would have to review it before commenting in detail.

A House staff member who reviewed the IRS plan said yesterday that "it will be terribly heard [sic] to apply. It's like saying that nearly every telephone call to the IRS will be a matter of public record. I hope they don't spend all their time doing that instead of their work."

Two sources in the IRS said Alexander has been upset about criticism alleging that he has bowed to political pressure and feels this is the best way to stop it.

IRS spokesman A. James Golato disputed this, and said, "It's just a good idea that will aid sound tax administration."

The IRS spokesman had no estimate yesterday on the number of such outside contacts made to the IRS, but said, "They are numerous." Another IRS official said they run in the thousands each year.

The decision means the IRS would make public details on any future attempts to seek special audits of so-called "Enemies," as was done in 1972 by the Nixon White House.

Contacts by the White House and the Central Intelligence Agency would become public under the new policy, the IRS spokesman said.

"In such cases," according to the IRS, "the Service would make public the identity of the contracting [sic] party and the nature of the matter involved."

The IRS is prohibited by law from making public the identity of taxpayers who have matters pending before the IRS, such as tax investigations.

Nonetheless, Treasury general counsel Richard R. Albrecht said the availability of the names of those Congressmen or officials who contact the IRS would "reduce the possibility of political or improper influence."

Albrecht headed the Treasury investigation that confirmed published allegations that Montoya's tax audits were blocked for two years by Alexander and other senior IRS officials.

The IRS commissioner is responsible to the Secretary of the Treasury, the Cabinet-level department which is responsible for tax policy and collection.

An IRS spokesman said procedures are being developed to make the information on contracts [sic] available, and it was not clear if the material would be routinely released or simply be available upon request.

The decision covers contracts [sic] made by members of Congress on pending legislation, the IRS spokesman said, but it was unclear if routine inquiries by members of Congress on tax matters for their constituents will be included.

The IRS decision to make such information available to the public is unusual. Yesterday only two federal agencies could be found that do so. They are the Office of Tax Analysis in the Treasury Department and the Federal Trade Commission.

Leonard J. McEnnis, a FTC spokesman, said yesterday that the FTC initiated the procedure in 1974, and in a 14-month period FTC commissioners and staff members recorded 739 outside contracts [*sic*] on cases.

The Woodward article is the most extensive contemporary record of this incident. On May 10, the *Wall Street Journal* reported the matter in a very brief item which stressed that congressmen who "want to talk to the Internal Revenue Service . . . without a lot of people knowing about it, better call soon." The event is not listed in the index to the *New York Times* for the relevant period, so that paper may not have found it to be news fit to print.

Either the Service was voluntarily taking a revolutionary step in the direction of candid disclosure contrary to its usual nature and Commissioner Alexander was reversing his oft-expressed predilection against the release of information, or something very different was happening here.

The Woodward article made clear that firm procedures for carrying out the policy did not exist. Moreover, the policy had been announced before it was entirely clear just what would be covered. I can vouch for the fact that no procedure had been developed based upon my personal experience. In addition, I can definitely state that no disclosure personnel and no Chief Counsel attorneys involved with disclosure matters had been informed of the policy before its announcement.

The article, obviously based primarily on Service sources, states that the policy was not prompted by any specific case. For those who are not sufficiently credulous to accept the idea that an Internal Revenue Service Commissioner would implement a revolutionary program without some compelling reason, the article provides a red herring in the form of the three-week-old Treasury report on the alleged Montoya and Ulman irregularities. But no mention is made of any future event as a possible motivation for this extraordinary announcement.

The lack of internal coordination, the announcement of a policy not yet well thought out, the absence of even a draft procedure, the sudden Thursday-night decision, the Friday announcement, and the Saturday news report are not compatible with a program that is not based upon a compelling event or that is in response to a three-week-old report that dealt with incidents that had been discussed in the public press for months before.

There had to be something in the very near future that necessitated the sudden formulation of this policy. There was. On Tuesday, May 11, Commissioner Alexander appeared before the House Subcommittee on Government and Individual Rights to be questioned on the notorious Special Services operation which had improperly singled out for special treatment individuals and organizations whose ideologies conflicted with the administration's policies.

Contemporary observers were too beguiled by Commissioner Alexander's dramatic offer to consign this "outdated and useless" political file to Washington's "biggest bonfire" to suspect that the four-day-old disclosure policy was a threat intended to frighten members of the subcommittee into being soft on the Internal Revenue Service.

Representative Bella Abzug, Democrat, New York, the subcommittee chair, had introduced a bill requiring that the Service and other federal agencies notify victims of illegal surveillance, break-ins, and other improprieties of the actions taken against them. This bill was never enacted. It may be that if it had been, the Service might have retaliated against the offending congresspersons by releasing records concerning their contacts on behalf of favored taxpayers and pet projects and interpretations, and perhaps even their own tax affairs. The announced disclosure policy was sufficiently vague to permit every congressperson to imagine that it would apply to any skeleton in any closet.

Treading Water

The value of Commissioner Alexander's policy apparently lay in its announcement rather than its implementation, for nothing happened thereafter. The Service spokesperson had said that it would take several weeks before exact procedures for recording and releasing information were available. It came as a great surprise to me, therefore, that I was asked to develop those procedures within a Freedom of Information Act context after the policy had been announced. I was given no instructions as to what was wanted and no insight into the intent of the program. Apparently there were not only no exact procedures, but there was not even a rough outline of what was intended. My only guidance was the Bob Woodward article, and I therefore began work trying to develop a procedure which would be responsive to whatever it was the *Washington Post* had described.

Like all other disclosure personnel, I believed that the program as described would be clearly illegal as it would be impossible to release any meaningful information without violating the confidentiality of tax returns. I also believed that the program might border on being unconstitutional because an agency in the executive branch would be discouraging citizens from seeking the assistance of their elected representatives in the redress of their grievances. I recorded my objections to the assumed illegality of the program and proceeded to draft a procedure for carrying it out.

I assumed that most congressional contacts would concern Collection, Examination, or Criminal Intelligence actions which took place in the district offices and that the contacts would most likely involve case workers in the congresspersons' local offices rather than the congresspersons' writing to National Office. I therefore drafted a procedure which would operate primarily in the district offices. Since each state had one or more district offices, each district would be involved with a limited number of congresspersons and not be overwhelmed by this effort. I envisioned a sort of chronological collection of sanitized materials, sorted out by originating contact and maintained for public inspection by the district disclosure officer for a year or two. I thought the procedure was simple and easily workable (although illegal), although I must admit that I had paid little consideration to a National Office involvement in the program.

I was advised that there was a competing procedure being drafted elsewhere and that it apparently was preferred for implementation. I subsequently saw a draft of this procedure, which was tied into National Office correspondence controls. It put the entire project into the National Office, except for a great deal of shipping copies to the field and back. This procedure seemed to assume that the bulk of the contacts would come from congresspersons in Washington and would be addressed to National Office. My personal opinion was that this procedure was totally unworkable and seemed to do everything in the most awkward, time-consuming, and expensive way possible.

I do not know what happened to either procedure, or even if there were other procedures being considered, but months went by without anything happening. Commissioner Alexander could have invoked either procedure. Or he could have implemented something simpler to make at least a part of his program operational. He did not. His term as commissioner ended February 26, 1977, more than nine months after the breathless announcement of the revolutionary disclosure program, without any effort at implementation.

Backtracking

The Service made no further voluntary announcements concerning the disclosure of congressional contacts. A reporter for the *Wall Street Journal* refused to let the matter drop. In December 1977, a Service spokesperson explained that the Service had decided not to implement the plan on the advice of attorneys who claimed that the planned disclosures would violate the confidentiality provisions of the Internal Revenue Code as revised in 1976.

In reporting on the new announcement, the *Washington Post* stated on December 22, 1977, that

> congressional sources who participated in the drafting of the 1976 disclosure provisions said this was a ridiculous interpretation, since the IRS specifically envisioned excising any reference to specific taxpayers from the information on congressional and federal inquiries that it planned to release.
>
> However, the same sources made independent inquiries and said the new IRS decision was really made because the new leadership in the service had decided that it would be meaningless simply to release the name of a member of congress if he or she made an inquiry to the IRS about a constituent's tax problems.

Thus, within less than a year, the Service had announced a disclosure policy, escaped being subjected to a proposed new disclosure law, and withdrawn the announced policy in favor of a nondisclosure policy. Congressional sources were aware that it was not really compliance with the Internal Revenue Code that motivated nondisclosure but concern over the waste of resources. After all, we all knew that congressional contacts did not relate to any improprieties but merely reflected concern about constituents' problems. It was nice to be friends again.

Common Cause et al.

Not everyone was happy with the new accommodation. One unhappy party was the public-interest organization Common Cause. Early in 1978, Common Cause requested access to the text of the IRS disclosure procedure, all records of contacts with non–IRS personnel concerning the disclosure plan, all written reasons for not implementing the plan, and all written logs of congressional inquiries about the tax matters of third parties.

No records were released in response to this request, and Common Cause filed suit in November 1978.

I never learned whether the procedure being withheld was the one I prepared, its competitor, or some other document. However, had anyone asked me, I would have been glad to give up my copy of my proposal since I thought it was rather well done.

Information filed with the court revealed that the decision not to implement the disclosure policy was based upon 23 memorandums prepared by key Service officials expressing their opinions on how the Service should proceed. One of these memorandums was made public without the Service's consent, apparently by the originator. Oddly enough, this particular memorandum was probably the best-developed legal analysis of the issues involved and was an excellent defense of the Service's position.

The court inspected the documents at issue in camera and decided that the 22 remaining memorandums and the proposed procedure were exempt from disclosure pursuant to (b)(5) as "predecisional deliberative materials." All other documents involved were rendered meaningless by appropriate editing and therefore need not be disclosed.

Common Cause appealed the decision, but only insofar as the 22 memorandums and the proposed procedure were concerned.

Neufeld

On December 22, 1977, the same day the press reported the Service's reversal on the disclosure policy, John L. Neufeld, an assistant professor of economics at the University of North Carolina, Greensboro, requested access to documents discussing the proposed disclosure plan and to records concerning congressional contact with the IRS regarding the pending tax matters of third parties.

The Service refused to make any records available, and suit was filed. The documents discussing the proposed disclosure plan were the same 23 memorandums considered in *Common Cause*.

After some negotiating, the parties agreed that the records at issue concerning congressional contacts were to be defined as sets of correspondence, including a taxpayer's letter to his representative; a routing slip or cover letter from the representative directing the constituent's letter to the IRS; a copy of the IRS response to the taxpayer; review forms developed after the litigation began which described the correspondence, assigned a case number and indicated whether the correspondence was edited; and correspondence-control forms listing dates and a short description of the underlying matter. The issues were further limited to National Office correspondence only and to matters received from members of Congress between February 1, 1978, and June 1, 1979.

These agreements made it readily apparent that the plaintiff was interested in establishing a principle and was willing to restrict his request to materials the Service could cope with without extraordinary effort.

The court decided that the 22 internal memorandums could be withheld. It also ordered that all the letters or transmittal memorandums from members of Congress, all the IRS responses, and all the correspondence controls must be disclosed after deletion of return information. The taxpayers' letters to their representatives were not to be released, as the court decided that after the deletion of return information, they consisted only of essentially meaningless words and phrases.

Neither Professor Neufeld nor the Internal Revenue Service were satisfied with this result, and both appealed.

Appeals Argued Seriatim

The subject matter in *Common Cause* and *Neufeld* was similar, and insofar as the 22 memorandums were concerned, involved the same records. The cases had been heard in the U.S. District Court for the District of Columbia within a few months of each other. The Court of Appeals decided that the cases were to be argued seriatim, that is, one following the other, and the appellate decisions were issued together.

The court affirmed the decision to withhold the 22 memorandums and the draft disclosure procedure pursuant to (b)(5). Common Cause therefore received none of the materials for which it had filed suit. As for the correspondence requested by Neufeld, the court accepted the principle that it should be released after editing to delete return information and remanded to the District Court for reconsideration, primarily to determine the extent of release in the light of guidance as to what constituted return information.

Thus, although Common Cause and Neufeld were seeking information about the same situation, Commissioner Alexander's disclosure announcement, Common Cause was unsuccessful because it focused on the exempt internal memoranda, and Neufeld was successful because he had focused upon the nonexempt correspondence. Ultimately, analysis of the nonexempt material could have provided extensive insight into what was contained in the exempt background.

The ultimate result of *Neufeld* was that my staff spent months retrieving, analyzing, editing, and copying the congressional inquiries and IRS responses to taxpayers to be released. I instructed my lead technician to bring to my attention any item which involved a sensitive tax case, any appearance of impropriety or undue influence, any unusual congressional approach, any important taxpayer, or anything at all that might result in notoriety upon release. There was nothing. All the taxpayers were ordinary people involved with routine tax problems; all the congressional inquiries were on virtually identical form letters or constructed of pattern paragraphs. The huge accumulation of material available for public inspection as a result of this litigation was indescribably dull.

If anything at all was to be learned from the release of these records, it would have to have been that writing to your congressperson about your tax problem does not help much. Many Americans who believe that their representatives could exert influence in their behalf were to be disappointed.

In the years since the Neufeld case there have been no other attempts to access congressional or other non–IRS contacts. Perhaps this lack of interest resulted from the ordinary nature of the materials released to Professor Neufeld. One thought fascinated those of us who worked on this case. Did Professor Neufeld blow his opportunity when he agreed to limit his request to inquiries received after he made his initial request, inquiries which for the most part were written with the knowledge of his litigation and the realization that they were likely to become public? What would he have uncovered, had he insisted on receiving the existing records covered by his original request created without any suspicion that they might someday become public? It is too late to know, for all such correspondence is likely to have been destroyed in accordance with authorized records-disposition schedules.

Over the years, however, many Service officials, taxpayers, FOIA requesters, congresspersons, staffers and other government officials may have forgotten about Commissioner Alexander's policy of disclosure and its implementation by Professor Neufeld. Records of third-party contacts may not always be so dull as they were when all concerned were acutely aware of the professor's pending litigation.

A recent Supreme Court decision has eliminated the need to edit return information by deleting taxpayer identity to accommodate Freedom of Information Act requesters. It is likely that the IRS responses to the taxpayers released pursuant to *Neufeld* would not have to be made public if they were requested today. Letters and memorandums of telephone contacts from third parties would still have to be released if they were requested.

If I had reason to seek access to such materials, I would first accept the records of the inquiries. Then, if analysis showed that any seemed to imply that impropriety or undue influence existed, I would request the identity of the taxpayers involved, imitating the sequence set down in section 6110 for written determinations. The definition of *return information* is very broad, but it may not be so broad as to include the identity of the beneficiaries of undue influence on the part of friends in high places.

Chapter Twenty-Seven

Business Information

An October 13, 1987, revision to the Internal Revenue Service's Freedom of Information regulations added new business-information procedures which had not previously existed in written form.

These procedures did not pertain to the information businesses filed on their tax returns or the Service obtained in connection with the processing or investigation of tax matters, or which would be included in the Business Master File. That information was protected by the confidentiality provisions of section 6103 of the Internal Revenue Code. These procedures pertained to the information which businesses voluntarily submitted to the Service, either to assist in the performance of its duties or in connection with the contribution, sale, or rental of information, goods, or services for use in the Service's housekeeping operations.

This information would be exempt from FOIA access to the extent that it met the requirements of subsection (b)(4) as trade secrets and commercial or financial information obtained from a person and privileged or confidential. The (b)(4) exemption was intended to protect both the interests of the commercial entities which submit proprietary information to the government and the interests of the government in continuing to receive such information.

At first glance, those interests would appear to be entirely compatible, but in practice they were neither identical nor equally compelling. In many cases agencies would be either more or less eager than the submitter to defend such information. As a result, some submitters have been concerned that the government might not adequately defend their information. Reverse Freedom of Information Act suits have been filed to prevent agencies from failing to exercise the (b)(4) exemption and simply releasing information without regard to the harm that it might cause the submitter. To avoid such litigation and to be fair to the submitter, the Service has had a long-standing informal practice of seeking the advice of the submitter before making a determination on the release of such commercial information.

The *Internal Revenue Manual* provided, "Written objections received from the provider of the information are to be given considerable weight in making a decision, unless they are clearly in conflict with a legal precedent or obviously lacking merit." The new procedures were to replace the informal practices for processing requests for commercial information which might be exempt under (b)(4). The major change was to be a requirement that the submitter would be required to identify the information he believed to be confidential when he submitted it.

317

Business Information Procedures

The regulation began by stating what appeared to be a general rule: "Business information provided to the Internal Revenue Service by a business submitter shall not be disclosed pursuant to a Freedom of Information Act request except in accordance with this paragraph."

Business information was defined as "any trade secret or other financial, commercial (including research) information." Although inelegantly stated, the definition basically covered those materials which would be potentially exempt under (b)(4). The regulations then provided that under certain circumstances, the Service will provide the submitter of information requested pursuant to the FOIA with a notice advising him specifically of what had been requested.

The circumstances under which this notice is to be given will differ, depending upon whether the information was submitted to the Service before or after the regulation was published, whether the Service considers disclosure to result in harm to the submitter, how old the information is, and other factors. The key provision is that persons submitting information after the publication of the regulation are required to make a good-faith designation that the information is commercially or financially sensitive. Such a designation is valid only for requiring a notice for 10 years after submission, unless the submitter requests and provides acceptable justification for a specific notice period of greater duration.

Any voluntary submitter of commercial information who fails to make a claim of confidentiality at the time of submission is unlikely to receive any notice that his information is being sought by a requester and is therefore unlikely to have the opportunity to assist in its defense. The notice need not be given if the Service determines that the information is not to be disclosed, the information has previously been made available to the public, disclosure is required by some other statute, or the information was acquired in the course of an investigation of a possible violation of the Internal Revenue laws and notice would interfere with ongoing law enforcement proceedings.

If careful application of all the requirements of the regulation results in a notice, the submitter of the information is afforded 10 working days to provide a detailed statement of any objection to disclosure. Such a statement is to specify all the grounds for withholding any of the information, with particular attention to why the information is claimed to be a trade secret or commercial or financial information. The determining official then evaluates the submitter's arguments and makes a determination. If that determination is adverse, the submitter is advised of the reason why his objections were not sustained, the precise business information to be disclosed, and the anticipated disclosure date, which will be 10 working days after the mailing date of the decision. The requester also receives a copy of this notice.

The submitter may file suit to prevent the proposed release of the records. The requester may also file suit to compel release of the records.

Although this explanation of the regulation seems complicated, the procedure is not very different from the informal practice the National Office has carried out for many years without encountering great problems.

Contracts

Almost all of the requests the National Office has processed under the informal version of this procedure have involved contracts for the purchase of goods or services, or related records. The vast majority of those contracts have pertained to the purchase or rental of automatic data-processing equipment or software. Generally, the vendors have objected to the release of detailed pricing data, descriptions of how the various components have been put together to make a commercial "package," and details of the level of support they will provide for an operation or an installation.

Generally, the rationale given for wanting such information withheld is that there is little difference between the equipment and software that vendors can offer and little difference in the prices they are able to quote but that the competitive edge consists almost exclusively of the skill with which they can be combined. Thus, vendors are much like bartenders; they all have the same ingredients available, but the difference lies in the mixing, shaking and pouring of the drink.

The objections to release of portions of the contract were resolved by a process of negotiation, which generally satisfied both the vendor and the requester. The resulting Freedom of Information responses have neither provoked reverse litigation by the submitters nor appeals or litigation by the requesters. The results may not always have been in strict compliance with all aspects of the law, but they were satisfactory to all the involved parties.

There is some reason to doubt that the (b)(4) exemption is really applicable to the contracts which the Service makes with vendors or whether any portion of such contracts should ever be withheld from requesters. Information which may be withheld pursuant to the (b)(4) exemption must be confidential. It may be argued that any information which becomes part of a contract loses its confidentiality. A contract is an agreement binding upon the parties who sign it; it would appear that everything contained within the contract is information which is the property of both contracting parties. If the information becomes the property of both parties, either may release it, and it can hardly be considered confidential. Thus, contract information would fail the requirement that information must be confidential for the (b)(4) exemption to be valid.

It would seem inappropriate that a contract which obliges the government to pay for goods and services should be subject to an exemption which could preclude the public from knowing precisely what goods and services its taxes are paying for, at the option of the vendor who is to receive the payment. That would seem much like purchasing the proverbial pig in a poke.

Contract specialists make the argument that releasing all of the information might discourage vendors from being candid or even deter them from wanting to sell to the government, thereby reducing competition and raising costs. On the other hand, it is difficult to imagine the information-technology industry existing without doing business with the government. And it is difficult to imagine how secrecy can reduce costs, especially in view of the potential for collusion, fraud and incompetence.

The question of whether such contracts can *ever* contain (b)(4) material has not been raised to the Service by a requester. Most requesters for access to such contracts have not been members of the public interested in learning what the government is getting for its money. They have been other vendors seeking some advantage in future competition with the successful offerer. Such requesters have not attempted to question the practice of withholding some information as confidential because they might be involved as the vendor in the next contract and might then wish to avoid the release of some of their information. The practice of defending portions of the contract pursuant to (b)(4) has therefore been satisfactory to both the submitter and the requester.

If it were ever determined that contracts for the purchase of goods and services cannot contain information which is legitimately subject to the (b)(4) exemption and should be automatically available to the public, there would remain very little information in the Service's possession which might warrant the use of that exemption, and the business-information procedures would seldom be relevant.

Requesting Contracts

Copies of contracts must be requested by the contract number. The contract number may be obtained by reviewing copies of the *Commerce Business Daily*, which publishes information on contracts awarded by agencies, including the subject matter, amount, date, name and address of the vendor and the contract number.

Many contracts will ultimately be subject to modifications. The Service generally interprets a request for a contract to include all existing modifications but not to include associated correspondence which may clarify terms without altering them. A request should be as specific as possible in defining exactly what is wanted, including modifications, associated correspondence, or minutes of meetings with the vendor.

Since most requests for contracts are made by persons having a commercial interest, there may be a presumption that the fees should be computed on the basis of a commercial requester, resulting in search, duplication, and review charges, without any allowance for free search time or free duplication. Requesters who feel they do not fall in this category should be certain to include justification for being in a category warranting lower fees.

Unless you have reason to believe that the contract you wish to access is one of the few negotiated by a regional office, you may assume that contracts are maintained by and should be requested from the National Office.

The personnel servicing contracts have traditionally been slow in providing copies for disclosure processing. Invariably, my technicians have been told that there is only one person who knows where the requested file is located, and that person is always away on a field trip, presumably carrying that very contract under his arm, making it unavailable until his return. Carrying out the formal business-information procedures will add weeks to the process. A copy of a contract is unlikely to be provided in less than 90 days.

Chapter Twenty-Eight

Exempt Organization Information

Section 6104 of the Internal Revenue Code provides that certain information, including approved applications for exemption and annual information returns, are to be made available for public inspection to enable the public to scrutinize the activities of tax-exempt organizations and trusts. Congress intended that these organizations be subject to public accountability in view of their privileged tax status and because the public has a right to know the purposes for which their contributions are expended. The records which become public under section 6104 are not considered to be subject to the Freedom of Information Act since they are directly controlled by the Internal Revenue Code. The procedures under which they are released are, however, equal or superior to those available under the Freedom of Information Act and work well as they generally have the support of Service personnel.

In practice, the most frequent requesters of materials available under section 6104 appear to be writers, reporters, investigators, and persons in search of sources of grants, benefits or employment.

Applications for Exemption

Applications for exemption, filed on Form 1023 by organizations seeking exemption under section 501(c)(3), on Form 1024 by organizations seeking exemption under some other paragraph of section 501, or by letter in some cases, become available to the public when they are approved by the Service. Pending applications and denied applications are considered confidential pursuant to section 6103.

Requests for access to pending or denied applications will not be denied as the Service is prohibited from revealing that such applications exist, the doctrine being that until an application is approved, it continues to be confidential. Consequently, the response to such a request will simply state that the Service has no record of an approved application and no records which may be released exist. An application which has been approved continues to be available to the public, even though the organization may no longer be exempt.

The application available to the public includes all documents required to be filed with the application and all supporting documents voluntarily submitted with the application. Such documents may include articles of incorporation, declarations of trust, bylaws, financial statements, explanations of sources of income, explanations of activities, books, pamphlets, legal briefs, and a variety of other documents which would support the organization's claim to exemption.

For applications filed after October 31, 1976, the Service's response, including favorable Determination Letters and Technical Advice memorandums relating to approved applications, is also available. For applications filed prior to that date, the Service's response is available only to the extent that it consists of boilerplate language which reveals nothing about the organization.

Certain information may be withheld from the public. Information relating to trade secrets, patents, processes, styles of work, or apparatuses of the organization may be designated as confidential and will be withheld if the Service is satisfied with the organization's explanation of why release would be harmful. Any information whose release would have an adverse effect upon the national defense would also be withheld. However, in all the years I was involved with disclosure matters, I never encountered a single instance in which any deletions were actually made from an approved Application for Exemption or its related documentation.

Requests for approved Applications for Exemption should be addressed to the district director servicing the area of residence of the requester without regard to the location of the organization, unless the requester has actual prior knowledge of where the requested documents are filed. Requests must be in writing and should describe the materials wanted and identify the organization by name and location. Utmost care must be taken to provide the precise name of the organization, as the chief reason for failing to obtain requested applications is the use of an erroneous name. Many organizations appear to be known by names which do not accurately reflect their true legal designation and therefore do not match the names on Service records.

Applications and related documents which were filed prior to January 1, 1948, have been destroyed pursuant to congressional authorization and cannot be made available to requesters.

Statements of Exempt Status

A person may request any district director to provide a statement of the exempt status of any organization. Such statement may include the subsection and paragraph of section 501 under which the organization has been determined to be exempt and whether the organization is currently held to be exempt. If the organization is no longer exempt, the Service is prohibited from making further information available and cannot explain why it is no longer exempt or provide any information about the circumstances under which it surrendered or lost its exemption.

Information Returns

Form 990, Return of Organization Exempt from Income Tax, and Form 990-PF, Return of Private Foundation or Trust Treated as Private Foundation, are available for inspection or copying, together with any attachments which are required to be filed with those returns. The Service will also release any attachments which were received with those returns but were not required to be filed with them.

In one unusual situation, the Service decided to release Forms 990 filed by an organization which was not exempt but had nevertheless filed such returns in an apparent attempt to establish its exemption. The general doctrine was established that the Service will release anything that purports to be a releasable document without questioning its legitimacy.

In addition, information which would be deleted from an approved application, such as a trade secret, would not be withheld if the organization submitted it with its information return, and conversely, information which would be deleted from an information return, such as a list of contributors, would not be withheld if it were attached to an application for exemption.

Information which would be deleted from records subject to the Privacy Act of 1974, such as compensation, addresses, and the social security numbers of officers of the organization, would not be deleted from information returns or from approved applications or their attachments. Consequently, exempt-organization documents may sometimes be sources of information about their officers as well as the recipients of grants and other persons.

There are some exceptions to the general rule of public availability. The names and addresses of contributors will be deleted from Forms 990, but the amounts of contributions and bequests are disclosed unless such amounts could reasonably be expected to identify a contributor. I have never seen an example of an amount which could identify a contributor, and I have no idea what such an amount might be.

The names and addresses of contributors are not deleted from Forms 990-PF, with one exception. The names and addresses of contributors and the amounts of the contribution or bequest are deleted from Forms 990-PF if the contributor is not a U.S. citizen and the private foundation has since the date of its creation received at least 85 percent of its support (other than investment income) from sources outside the United States. For many years the *Internal Revenue Manual* provided that any disclosure personnel requiring assistance in determining who is a citizen or whether editing should be performed on this basis should call me. No one ever called.

Certain processing codes which the Service may sometimes stamp on the face of Forms 990 to identify delinquency penalties, payments received, and interest computations would be deleted. Such codes rarely appear. No deletions are made from Forms 990-PF.

Requests for access to information returns may be sent to the district director servicing the area of the requester's residence, regardless of the location of the organization. The regulations permit sending requests to the National Office Freedom of Information Reading Room; however, requests sent to National Office will always encounter additional delay because they must all be forwarded to field offices, as there are no returns on file in the National Office. Moreover, the research tools available in the National Office are unlikely to be as current as those in the field offices.

The shrewd requester seeking returns filed after 1980 will send his request to the service center which processes returns for the area in which the exempt organization is located. Since all requests sent to district offices require obtaining records from a service center, a wrong guess as to which service center has the records will cause no additional delay, and a right guess may save a week. However, never send a request to the Andover Service Center, which has processed no exempt-organization returns since 1982; requests involving areas which would otherwise be serviced by the Andover Service Center are processed by the Brookhaven Service Center.

When completely confused, send your request to the Philadelphia Service Center; they have extensive experience with these returns, probably have the most skilled staff, service an area which includes many of the country's major exempt organizations, and maintain a file of private-foundation returns on aperture cards.

Requests for exempt-organization information returns must specify the type of return wanted, the precise name of the organization, and the year of the return. The location of the organization should be included if known but is not required. Remember that returns cannot be made available until several months after their due date, to allow for processing and filing. Do not use general terms like "the latest return available" or "the last three years on file," since you may get returns much too old to be useful. It is far better to ask for the 1988 return and specify that if it has not been received, the 1987 return will be acceptable.

Some offices will return a request, asking the requester to specify the organization's employer identification number. There is no way that the public can know that number unless they have received a prior return. It should be researched by the employee working the request. This common error is frequently repeated because the personnel who work these cases are accustomed to obtaining copies of returns for individual taxpayers who must always supply their own social security numbers.

A 1988 General Accounting Office survey found that when the Service was provided with the correct name of the exempt organization, that is, the precise name under which the application for exemption was approved, it was able to provide 99 percent of the Forms 990 requested. If your request for returns uses the correct names and results in the receipt of substantially fewer returns without adequate explanation, you may assume that you are receiving less than adequate service, and you should make a follow-up request for further efforts.

Do not expect to receive all the attachments which are required to be filed with returns. The General Accounting Office survey found that almost half the returns received were missing one or more required attachments or schedules. The Service does not routinely follow up on such incomplete returns since it believes that a program which generates no revenue does not warrant the expenditure of resources to perfect these returns.

The interplay between sections 6103 and 6104 makes it difficult for the Service to explain the circumstances when no return has been received. If the reason for not receiving a return is that the organization need not file on the basis of one of the exceptions provided by section 6033(a)(2) of the Code, the response should say so. If the organization is not required to file because it has authority for inclusion in a group return or the return is not due because of a valid current extension of time to file or the return has been received but has not been processed, the response should say so. Unfortunately, many field offices do not make these explanations.

The Service is prohibited from saying that a return is delinquent or that an organization is under investigation. Consequently, if no return has been received, research does not show an acceptable reason for not filing, and the return appears to be delinquent, a generalized response must be made. Such a response will state that there is no record of receiving the return; however, this may be due to any of the reasons discussed above, or it may be because the return is delinquent. Whenever you receive such a generalized response, you may be reasonably certain that the return is delinquent.

Field offices will frequently respond with a simple statement that the requested return is not available. This is not an adequate response as it is virtually meaningless. You should not accept it. Service centers are required to perform considerable research to locate and obtain a copy of the return. A response which says that the return is not available can only mean that the return was not filed and the writer is afraid to make one of the required responses, the return has been filed but adequate steps to locate it have not been taken, or efforts to locate the return have been exhausted and it is considered lost. I have sometimes found that returns were checked out to a district office for examination, and the revenue agent who had the return was ignoring the service center's requests to send back a copy.

If you receive a response that a return is unavailable, request a further explanation. Ask if there is a record of receiving the return. Ask what steps have been taken to locate the return. If the ultimate answer is "We received it, but we don't know what we did with it," that ends the matter, but it is preferable to the enigmatic statement that the return is unavailable.

Responses will sometimes suggest that a further request should be made in three months or six months. Such a suggestion is valid only if the response states that the return has been received but has not been processed. Otherwise, it is merely a stalling technique. You may rest assured that in the majority of cases absolutely nothing which could possibly contribute to your receiving the requested return will take place during the months you have been asked to wait before making a further request.

If you conclude that a return is delinquent or incomplete, do not bother to ask that an investigation be made. The Service is prohibited from revealing the existence of an investigation and consequently can make no meaningful response to your request. The limited resources (if there are any resources) available for performing such investigations would be carefully scheduled to provided the maximum effect. They cannot be used in response to a request from the public.

Other Available Documents

There are several other documents available to the public pursuant to section 6104 but seldom requested.

- Form 1041-A: U.S. Information Return—Trust Accumulation of Charitable Amounts.
- Form 4720: Return of Certain Excise Taxes on Charities and Other Persons Under Chapters 41 and 42 of the Internal Revenue Code (public only when filed by foundations).
- Form 5578: Annual Certification of Racial Nondiscrimination for a Private School Exempt from Federal Income Tax.
- Form 5768: Election/Revocation of Election by an Eligible Section 501(c)(3) Organization to Make Expenditures to Influence Legislation.

Chapter Twenty-Nine

Employee Plans

Section 6104 of the Internal Revenue Code provides that certain information concerning pension, profit-sharing, and stock bonus plans may be made available to the public. Information which is not made public by section 6104 is considered to be confidential pursuant to section 6103.

General Information Available to All

Several categories of documents may be made available to any requester. These items may be requested from the National Office Freedom of Information Reading Room:

- Master and prototype plans sponsored by banks, insurance companies, trade or professional associations, or regulated investment companies.
- Prototype Individual Retirement Accounts.
- Employer-sponsored Individual Retirement Accounts.
- Nonbank trustee files.

Specific Plan Information

Information concerning specific plans is available to any requester whenever the plan has 26 or more participants. If the plan has fewer participants, availability is restricted to participants or persons who derive their right of access from a participant.

Any information which would divulge the compensation of any identified individual will be deleted from materials released. When requested by the organization and approved by the Service, any information which relates to any trade secret, patent, process, style of work, or apparatus will be withheld if disclosure would have an adverse effect on the submitting organization. In addition, information will be withheld if the Service determines that its release would adversely affect the national defense.

Information concerning specific plans is requested from the district responsible for processing the plan. If the district is unknown, requests should be submitted to the district director having jurisdiction for the area in which the requester resides. Requests should identify the name and address of the plan and its employer identification number if known. The request must describe the type of information to be provided and whether inspection or copies are desired.

Requests concerning plans with 25 or fewer participants must include a statement that the requester is a plan participant, written authorization from the participant, or an adequate explanation of the authority relied upon for access. Documentary evidence of the identity of the participant and the requester is required.

The following types of information may be released to the extent that they exist in any file:

- The application for a determination letter, if filed after September 2, 1974;
- Any documentation required to be filed with such application;
- Any supporting documentation not required, but actually filed with the application;
- Determination Letters relating to the qualification of a plan, account or annuity;
- Technical Advice Memorandums relating to the issuance of such Determination Letters;
- Technical Advice Memorandums relating to the continuing qualification of a plan, account, or annuity previously determined to be qualified, or relating to the qualification of a plan, account, or annuity for which no Determination Letter has been issued;
- Letters or documents revoking or modifying any prior favorable Determination Letter or denying the qualification of a plan, account, or annuity for which no Determination Letter has been issued;
- Determination Letters related to the exemption from tax of certain trusts or custodial accounts;
- Opinion letters relating to the acceptability of the form of any master, prototype, or other such plan or account, or notification letters issued with respect to pattern plans;
- An index of the administrative case file;
- Powers of attorney;
- Any final correspondence between the Service and the plan applicant, but not interim correspondence proposing an action and not representing a final Service position;
- Written comments and related correspondence by interested parties such as the Department of Labor or the Pension Benefit Guaranty Corporation;
- Amendments of initial qualification;
- Plans, group annuity contracts, and trust instruments;
- Supplemental data supporting the application, including statistical analyses, turnover data, coverage or allocation schedules, balance sheets, receipts and disbursement statements;
- Miscellaneous materials and correspondence relating to the application, such as specimen copies of individual life insurance contracts and formal announcements to employees.

The following forms are also available:

Form 4461: Application for Approval of Master or Prototype Defined Contribution Plan.
Form 4461A: Application for Approval of Master or Prototype Defined Benefit Plan.
Form 4646: Employee Plan Determination Record.
Form 5300: Application for Determination of Defined Benefit Plan.
Form 5301: Application for Determination of Defined Contribution Plan.
Form 5303: Application for Determination for Collectively Bargained Plan.
Form 5306: Application for Approval of Prototype or Employer Sponsored Individual Retirement Account.
Form 5307: Short Form Application for Determination for Employee Benefit Plan.
Form 5309: Application for Determination of Employee Stock Ownership Plan.
Form 5310: Application for Determination Upon Termination (Notice of Merger, Consolidation or Transfer of Plan Assets or Liabilities).
Form 5446: Public Inspection Record.

Definition of Plan Participant

For purposes of accessing the information of a plan having 25 or fewer participants, *participant* is defined as "any employee or former employee of an employer, or any member or former member of an employee organization, who is or may become eligible to receive a benefit of any type from an employee benefit plan which covers employees of such employer or members of such organization, or whose beneficiaries may be eligible to receive any such benefit."

The term *plan participant* includes:

• A current participant;
• Former employees, such as certain retired and terminated employees who have a nonforfeitable right to benefits under the plan;
• A beneficiary of a deceased former employee who is receiving benefits or entitled to receive benefits under the plan;
• The administrator, executor, or trustee of the estate of a deceased participant.

A determination that a person is a plan participant for the purpose of accessing records is not tantamount to a determination that such person is entitled to any benefits under the plan or has any interest in the plan. Persons who seek access to these records are frequently in a dispute with the administrator of the plan. It would be obviously unjust if the standard for determining access were so high that the peson who needs such records to support his argument for inclusion in the plan were to be denied. While I was running this disclosure program, I instructed my employees to be very liberal in accepting evidence of the right to access so as not to refuse any person from accessing records which might support entitlement to benefits or which might uncover impropriety in the operation of a plan. I cannot say whether that philosophy continues to govern this program.

The 5500 Series

The Form 5500 series, which includes various annual returns/reports of employee benefit plan documents, is processed by the Service and then copied onto microfiche for delivery to the Department of Labor, which makes these records available for public inspection. Requests for copies of these returns may be made to Public Disclosure, Room N-4677, U.S. Department of Labor, 200 Constitution Avenue, N.W., Washington, DC 20210.

In some cases, a return may have been processed but not yet copied on microfiche or shipped to the Department of Labor. Some requesters have been successful in obtaining copies of such returns from the service center in which they are being processed. However, there is only a narrow time frame in which such returns are processed and accessible but not yet copied and shipped. If such a return is urgently needed, call your district disclosure officer to make inquiry on the current status of processing and to ask for advice on how to proceed.

Employee Plan Master File

The Employee Plan Master File contains extensive information concerning employee plans drawn from a variety of sources. Some but not all of the information on the file is available to the public.

Extracts of the Employee Plan Master File may be purchased at a cost of $100.00 plus two cents per entity for a computer printout or $100.00 plus one cent per entity for magnetic tape. Inquiries concerning the formulation and purchase of extracts should be directed to Director, Tax Processing Systems Division, D:C:T:I, Internal Revenue Service, 1111 Constitution Avenue, N.W., Washington, DC 20224.

Chapter Thirty

One Hundred Percent Penalty Cases

Possibly the most confusing and least understood procedure used by the Internal Revenue Service is the 100 percent penalty assessment employed by the Collection Division to make individual businessmen personally liable for what are referred to as the trust-fund portions of corporate taxes. Because of this confusion, One Hundred Percent Penalty cases represent an excellent opportunity for the businessman to apply the Freedom of Information Act to obtain access to the records needed to understand what is being proposed against him and to discover how to avoid an undeserved assessment of the penalty.

Internal Revenue Code section 6672 provides, "Any person required to collect, truthfully account for, and pay over any tax imposed by this title who willfully fails to collect such tax, or truthfully account for and pay over such tax, or willfully attempts in any manner to evade or defeat any such tax or the payment thereof, shall, in addition to other penalties provided by law, be liable to a penalty equal to the amount of the tax evaded, or not collected, or not accounted for and paid over."

The most common application of this provision occurs when a corporation has employees who receive wages, a portion of which should be withheld as the employees' income taxes and the employees' share of the social security tax but the corporation does not withhold and pay to the government the full amounts due. Under the usual circumstances, a corporation which is short of cash will simply pay salaries, reduced by the amount of the taxes, thereby lowering the cost of the payroll by 20, 30 or 40 percent. The so-called withheld taxes represent a bookkeeping entry without substance, as the moneys which should be paid to the government either do not exist or have been otherwise expended. The 100 percent penalty may then be applied against the responsible officers, employees or others who failed to pay the tax.

Contrary to the name applied to this procedure, there is no attempt to penalize anyone. The objective is simply to collect the amount of tax which should initially have been paid by the corporation. This, of course, is entirely fair since the government is required to give the workers credit for these taxes even though they have never been paid. Often, refunds must be paid based upon uncollected taxes.

In order for the One Hundred Percent Penalty to be applicable, five conditions must generally be present:

1. There must be a liability for unpaid trust fund taxes due from the corporation.

2. Collection activities against the corporation must have been exhausted to the extent that there remains little likelihood of collecting from the corporation, or it must appear that failure to assert the penalty against responsible parties would endanger the ultimate collection of the tax.

3. The individual against whom the penalty is proposed must have had a duty, or the power to require someone else to collect, account for, or pay over the monies.

4. That individual must have had an opportunity to carry out his responsibilities. At the least, there must have been assets available from which the liability could have been paid. If the wages are paid but the taxes are not, funds would generally be considered to have been available. If, however, neither the wages nor the taxes are paid, that might indicate the unavailability of assets and obviate the penalty.

5. There must have been "willfulness" in failing to make the required payments. That is, the person involved, having a choice, either intentionally disregarded the law or was indifferent to its requirements.

Determining that any individual is subject to the penalty requires a study of the formal organization of the corporation, its operation in practice, and the circumstances in effect at the time of the failure to pay. This involves reference to corporate records, tax returns, canceled checks, bank signature cards, and other evidence. The rapidly changing circumstances encountered in a failing business may mean that various persons may be found to be responsible for the payment of the tax at different times and in different amounts.

Usually the responsible persons are found to be the corporate officers, but employees, board members, directors, shareholders, or others may be held liable if they are found to have had sufficient control over the disbursement of funds to have been able to direct or accomplish appropriate payment. The difficulties in these cases begin with the realization that actual conditions may have differed from the formally recorded duties for the various positions in the corporation.

A business about to go under is usually a rather chaotic affair, and it may be impossible to trace events accurately. Perhaps the officer having primary responsibility for making payments was abroad trying to raise funds to save the business. Perhaps the business was failing because the president and major shareholder was seriously ill. Perhaps the final events moved so rapidly and were so far beyond the control of the responsible officers that it was impossible for them to effect any degree of willfulness. Or the responsible persons may have made extensive efforts to comply with the law but simply failed to achieve the necessary payments. Sometimes partial payments may have been made, and questions will arise whether they covered the trust-fund portions of the tax which would have been subject to the penalty or were intended for the corporation's share of employment taxes, which would not have given rise to the penalty.

There are, therefore, many defenses and many extenuating circumstances which might affect the application of the penalty, provided the prospective taxpayer knows enough about the process to be able to raise them coherently. Frequently, the responsible persons may have had a falling-out, each relating the events to minimize his own responsibility and shift as much of the burden of liability to as many other persons as possible. Under the worst circumstances, the business may have been arranged so that an innocent and unsuspecting but loyal employee appears to be the responsible party, while the actual bosses all have some shrewdly contrived excuse.

The penalty may be assessed against several persons, but the total amount to be paid does not increase. Nor is the amount each owes divided between them. Each person responsible for the same penalty is individually liable for the total amount or whatever portion can be collected from her, with the result that those who have readily identifiable assets may pay the bulk of the penalty, while those whose assets are more difficult to locate or to restrain escape making any payment. Often, the struggle between former business associates will take on the appearance of a game of pin the tail on the donkey, the bulk of the penalty being paid by whoever failed to protect herself.

Given these circumstances, every person who may be subject to the penalty should become familiar with the rules and procedures which govern its assessment, the circumstances under which the liability arose, the information upon which the Service is basing its determinations, and the extent to which the penalty has been proposed, assessed, and collected from other responsible persons. Such information may be obtained from a cooperative, considerate revenue officer, or it may be demanded under the Freedom of Information Act.

At the least, any person against whom the penalty is proposed should immediately request copies of Chapter 700, One Hundred Percent Penalty Assessment, of IRM 57(16)0, Legal Reference Guide for Revenue Officers.

The records produced in connection with the One Hundred Percent Penalty Assessment are return information which may be accessed pursuant to 26 U.S.C. 6103. But the threshold issue in accessing such information is *whose* return information is it — that of the corporation, or that of one or more of the persons against whom the penalty is proposed, or perhaps both. To receive information, the requester must either be the taxpayer whose return information is involved, or a person entitled to receive the information upon demonstrating that she has a material interest in receiving the return information.

The Corporation Case File

Every One Hundred Percent Penalty case begins with an attempt to collect taxes from a corporation responsible for their payment. The content of such a case file consists of the returns and return information of the corporation.

Corporate returns and return information are available to any person designated by resolution of the board of directors or a similar governing body, any officer or employee of the corporation upon written request signed by any principal officer and attested to by the secretary or other officer, any bona fide shareholder of record owning 1 percent or more of the outstanding stock of the corporation, or any corporate officer authorized by the corporation in accordance with applicable state law legally to bind the corporation.

Obviously, many persons against whom the penalty is being considered could meet or arrange to meet one of the foregoing requirements, providing there has been no change in management and the requester continues to have such status with the corporation. If the corporation has been dissolved, any person authorized by applicable state law to act for the corporation may have access to the records.

These provisions, however, are primarily of benefit to the "insiders" among corporate officers, who already know how the liability arose and who was responsible for the failure to pay the tax. When the insiders try to stick the penalty on an outsider, such as a cashier, payroll clerk, or bookkeeper who had no real power, they are hardly likely to provide him or her with authority to access the corporate records.

Regardless of whether the provisions cited would yield general access to the corporate records, any person against whom the penalty is proposed may access the corporate records to the extent that the information to be released is relevant to the assessment specifically proposed against him. Any information in the corporate case file which was used or should have been used in determining that the individual should be subject to the penalty is that individual's return information, and he may access it based upon his own right. It should be noted that the information need only be relevant to the individual if it supports the proposed penalty. Information which may concern the activities of other persons would have to be released if its use would have resulted in a determination that the penalty is not applicable to the requester. An innocent party may therefore have the opportunity to find the information necessary to exonerate herself.

No access to the corporate case file can be permitted to persons who are not being considered for the penalty or who have been determined not to be subject to the penalty. If the penalty is proposed against you, your right to access the corporate records ceases when the Service makes a determination not to pursue assessment of the penalty.

The One Hundred Percent Penalty Case File

The One Hundred Percent Penalty case file consists of documents prepared or maintained to support and implement the penalty assessment. It is not the return information of the corporation, although copies of corporate records may be included in the file, and it may not be accessed by persons on the basis of their entitlement to corporate records.

The contents of the file generally constitute the return information of one, several, or all the persons subject to the penalty. Information which relates to the general operation of the business, differentiates between the duties ar.d responsibilities of the various officers and employees, or which has been used or should have been used in determining the application of the penalty is generally the return information of each person subject to the penalty. Each person has the right to access such information until a determination is made to drop the penalty against her.

Information which pertains to the personal affairs or unrelated business activities of an individual, correspondence with that individual, and records which relate only to the imposition of the penalty to that particular individual are the return information of that individual alone. They are not available to any other person. They continue to be available to the individual to whom they pertain, although the penalty may have been determined not to be applicable.

The contents of such files may have to be sorted out so that each requester would receive only the general information and whatever specifically relates to him. Editing would usually be necessary. Information whose release would interfere with tax administration would be withheld.

Report of Interview

Form 4180, Report of Interview Held with Persons Relative to Recommendation of One Hundred Percent Penalty Assessments, is available to the person whose interview is recorded, without any deletions. The forms are available to other persons being considered for the penalty after being edited to delete personal information or information whose release would interfere with tax administration. It is important that each person being considered for the penalty obtain copies of this report prepared for the interview of every other person involved. These forms contain accounts of how the business was alleged to have operated, what the person who is being interviewed claims to have done and how she interpreted her duties, what she claims other persons did or should have done, and any arguments she has raised to avoid the penalty being applied to her. You cannot adequately present your position and defend yourself from the self-serving statements of your former associates without knowing the contents of these interviews. You should also be aware that your interview will be available to them.

Persons being considered for the penalty, especially in complex businesses which involved many associates who may be found liable, should realize that the revenue officer must decide who the responsible parties were based upon the information he is able to uncover, the records available for his use, and the tall tales he is being told. The person who fails to adequately present his interests and call attention to details favorable to his position is likely to get stuck. The greatest fool of all is the person who successfully avoids contact with the revenue officer and allows the penalty determination to be made based upon what his former associates have to say about him.

Recommendation of Assessment

Form 4183, Recommendation Re One Hundred Percent Penalty Assessment; Form 2749, Request for One Hundred Percent Penalty Assessment; and

Form 5013, One Hundred Percent Penalty File Transmittal, are forms used in processing the penalty assessment. They are the return information of the individuals to whom they pertain. When they are applicable to more than one person, they must be edited so that only that information which applies to the requester is released. They are not of great interest or value since the amounts and periods of liabilities would be made available to each subject of the penalty anyhow. When several persons are involved in the same penalty, or portions of related penalties, they may be of some value, in that analysis of the deletions made may confirm the number of persons against whom the penalty was assessed and whether they were all subject to the entire penalty. This is particularly true since persons liable for the penalty are informed only of the types of persons generally considered for the penalty and whether other persons are being considered for the penalty. Such persons are not identified, and no statement is made whether the penalty is actually assessed against any other person. Thus, unless the persons subject to the penalty cooperate and share information with each other, they may not know whether each must bear the entire burden of payment alone or they may expect others to make contributions.

Taxpayer Delinquent Account Files

The TDA, or Taxpayer Delinquent Account file, which documents the efforts to collect the penalty after assessment, is the return information of the individual to whom it pertains. Each person penalized has her own TDA file, regardless of how many persons share in the same penalty. That file is not available to any other person.

In theory, amounts paid by other persons subject to the same penalty are to reflect on each TDA file as credits reducing the balance for each person subject to the penalty, although the source of such credit and how it was collected are not revealed. Taxpayers may not be advised of such reductions until the account is paid in full. Taxpayers interested in learning of such reductions to their liability may ask the revenue officer to advise them of the current payoff figure for their accounts. If this is not forthcoming, they may make a Freedom of Information request for accounting records reflecting any payments which would reduce their liability.

Taxpayers have the right to designate the account to which their payments are to be applied. At times, a taxpayer may owe a penalty for a period in which she alone was responsible and also owe a penalty for a period shared with others. Prudence would dictate that it is to her advantage to have her earliest payments applied to the account or portion of an account for which she is exclusively responsible rather than to reduce a shared liability. It is therefore necessary to keep in close touch with the revenue officer to know exactly what you owe exclusively, what you owe as a shared liability, and how your payments are being applied.

Chapter Thirty-One

Finding Loved Ones

There were 7 million stories in the Naked City, according to the popular television program of that name. But, there are 200 million stories in the Internal Revenue Service, one for each taxpayer who files a return every year. Many of these stories involve the hope of one taxpayer to find another with the help of the Service. The Service *can* help in some circumstances.

Most of the requests for help in finding loved ones come from parents trying to contact runaway adult children, but almost every combination of humanity is encountered from time to time. On one occasion we received a letter from a man who stated that in 1939 while he was in college, he met someone at a beach resort. For the next two summers he and his friend worked together as lifeguards. By the time the Japanese attack on Pearl Harbor brought the United States into World War II, both men had completed college. The writer was commissioned into the Army Air Corps. His friend entered the navy. At the end of the war, our writer married and raised a family. Forty years later, his wife and his children had long ago left him, and he was growing old alone. Suddenly he realized that the friend with whom he had shared three summers at the beach was the only person in his life he really loved. But he had not heard from his friend since 1943. Could the Internal Revenue Service help to find his friend?

He was able to provide his friend's name, the name of his college, his date of graduation, his birthdate, and the name of the ship on which he had served. He did not know his friend's social security number. We were unable to help.

A woman in Israel wrote to tell us that her husband had left her and returned to the United States. She was a religious person who lived in a religious community. Her husband had not divorced her, and she was prevented by Orthodox rules from initiating a divorce. Unless her husband divorced her, no other man in the community would court her, and she would be denied the opportunity to remarry and have children. To her, life would virtually become death. Could the Service find her husband and convince him to send her divorce papers so that she might begin again and go on living?

The woman was able to tell us her husband's name, his birthdate, the date of his return to the United States, his occupation, and many other facts. But she did not know his social security number. We were unable to help her.

A man found a German shepherd. The dog had no license or other identification, but a tattoo in his ear consisted of a nine-digit number, grouped in the familiar sequence of three, two and four digits, which identifies a social security number. We were able to reach the taxpayer who owned the dog, and soon the two were reunited.

The Service maintains a program for researching the last known address of taxpayers and forwarding a letter at the request of another person for humane reasons. The program can function only when the requester provides a social security number for the target taxpayer. Without that number, the Service cannot determine who the taxpayer is, cannot search the Individual Master File, and cannot find an address to which the letter is to be forwarded.

You may not have immediate need of this program, but it would be wise if along with the faded photograph, the pressed flower, the lock of hair, the friendship ring, the bronzed booties, and other mementos of friends, family and lovers, you would keep a record of their social security numbers.

Current tax law requires certain taxpayers to indicate their children's social security numbers on their returns. Although intended for tax-administration purposes, forcing parents to have a record of their children's social security numbers could help thousands of parents avoid a future of heartbreak and loneliness.

In order to avail yourself of the letter-forwarding service, you should write to the disclosure officer in the district office serving the area where you reside. You must explain that you wish to have a letter forwarded for humane purposes, state the name and social security number of the person you wish to contact, provide an acceptable rationale for inducing the Service to approve your request, and enclose an unsealed letter you wish forwarded. There is no charge for this service. Do not enclose an envelope for use in forwarding the letter, and do not send any stamps.

The disclosure officer will evaluate your rationale and make certain that your letter does not contain any inappropriate matters such as threats, insults, demands for funds, or illegal proposals. If the request and letter are found acceptable, a search will be made of the Individual Master File, and if the entity section contains an address for the target taxpayer, the letter will be fowarded in an Internal Revenue Service envelope. A statement will be enclosed explaining that the letter is being forwarded in accordance with current policies, that the taxpayer's address has not been divulged, that no return information has been revealed, that the Internal Revenue Service has no involvement in the matter other than forwarding the letter, and that the decision of whether to reply is entirely up to the recipient.

You will never be advised whether the Service actually located an address permitting it to mail your letter or whether the letter was received or returned as undeliverable. Occasionally the Service will receive inquiries or comments from the taxpayers to whom such letters were sent. You will not be told of such responses, and you will be given no other information concerning the outcome of your request other than that the program has been completed. Thus, you may still live with doubt. But if you are fortunate, you may soon receive a letter or telephone call from your loved one. I have seen some lovely thank-you notes from mothers who regained their daughters and from daughters who learned that you *can* go home again.

Requests to contact more than one person can be made under proper circumstances. The Service is willing to make arrangements to perform extensive operations of this nature, usually for organizations or businesses having a legitimate need. For example, if a firm learns that is operations may have threatened the health of their employees, the Service will assist the firm in contacting former employees for whom the company no longer has addresses so that they may be advised of the need to obtain medical testing or treatment or of the opportunity to file claims for available benefits.

The most important factor in making a request, whether it be a small personal request or an extensive organizational one, is properly explaining the humane reasons involved. The *Internal Revenue Manual* states that acceptable reasons include a person seeking to find a missing person to convey a message of urgent of compelling nature, such as serious illness, imminent death, or death of a close relative.

When I ran the program, we operated as romantics willing to do whatever was necessary to reunite star-crossed lovers, bring runaway children home, and restore lost pets to their masters. Each disclosure officer must evaluate requests received in accordance with her own concept of what constitutes a humane purpose.

The health and well-being of persons sought, such as those needed for medical study to detect and treat defects or illness, will generally be considered adequate justification. I approved searches to locate relatives needed to provide information necessary to establish an ill child's genetic heritage and searches seeking donors having unusual blood types.

The Service will also forward a letter seeking to advise a person of entitlement to assets. Letters have been forwarded for attorneys controlling the assets of estates, attorneys designated to represent individuals entitled to awards under a court settlement, and commercial locator services representing persons controlling the assets to be distributed. Requests involving assets require a higher degree of documentation to establish that they are genuine than personal requests since they involve a higher risk of misrepresentation. The possibility exists that a person offering the distribution of an asset may in reality be acting in pursuit of the collection of a claim against the target taxpayer.

The Service will not forward letters on behalf of creditors or others seeking payment from the recipient. The Service does not recognize a valid humane purpose in searches to construct a family tree, write a family history, establish "cousin clubs," seek recruits to societies of persons sharing a common name, originating from the same hometown, having the same birthdate, or planning reunions.

Special problems are involved in evaluating the worthiness of requests from adopted children seeking contact with biological parents since such searches may be contrary to the laws or public policies of the state in which the adoption took place. If the parent's name and social security number were obtained from the adoption agency or the search results from a need to obtain a medical history, it may meet the humane-purpose criteria.

Incompetency

There will be cases when a more drastic approach than that available through the letter-forwarding program is necessary. The Internal Revenue Code provides that if a taxpayer is legally incompetent, the applicable tax return may be disclosed to the committee, trustee, or guardian of the taxpayer's estate. Since return information is available to those persons to whom the return may be disclosed, the committee, trustee, or guardian would also generally have access to any investigatory files on the taxpayer, including investigations performed to locate a missing taxpayer.

An individual may be incompetent if he is a minor, senile, disabled, insane, or otherwise incapable of managing his own affairs. Generally, the Service will rely on state law to determine what constitutes or establishes incompetence, which may or may not involve a court order, depending upon the circumstances. State law, or in some cases common law, will also determine the identity of the committee, guardian, or trustee of the estate. Thus, control of who is to receive return information in such situations lies outside the Internal Revenue Service and outside the federal government.

There have been cases in which the parents of a missing adult offspring brought an action before a state court, arguing that the fact the individual had made no contact with anyone was indicative of his inability to manage his own affairs, warranting appointment of an officer of the court to search for the individual to assist or even rescue him. One form this may take is known as the *guardian ad litem*, or court-appointed representative. The Service has recognized such court orders as adequate to meet the Code requirements for access to returns and return information.

Anyone interested in pursuing access to returns or return information as a tool to search for missing persons should discuss their circumstances with her local disclosure officer, since state laws vary widely, before deciding on whether she requires the assistance of an attorney.

Even if the request is refused at the district level, it may be worthwhile sending copies of your request and the disclosure officer's response to National Office. I've seen several instances in which the National Office has made more liberal interpretations of the law than were made in the field.

A provision which may be of value in rare circumstances appears at 26 U.S.C. 6201(c). Any income tax assessed against a child as a result of the child's earned income which remains unpaid will for all purposes be considered as properly assessed against the parent. In other words, if your child does not pay, you must pay. As a result of this provision, the parent gains not only the child's liability but also the right to access the child's return and any relevant return information.

Decedents

The Internal Revenue Code provides that the return, and consequently the return information, of a decedent may be disclosed to the administrator, executor, or trustee of the taxpayer's estate; to any heir at law, next of kin, or beneficiary under the will; or a donee of property, provided that the heir at law, next of kin, beneficiary, or donee has a material interest which will be affected by information in the return.

For the purposes of these access provisions, a *decedent* is a person who is legally dead but not necessarily actually dead. Consequently, the decedent provisions may sometimes be helpful in locating missing persons who may yet be found among the living.

The identity and entitlement of the administrator, executor, or trustee would be established by the will or letters testamentary. The beneficiary would be named in the decedent's will. But the identity of an heir at law and of the next of kin raises questions of state law and common law which are not always readily resolved.

One problem frequently encountered and cloaked in paradox is that of the mother of an illegitimate child, allegedly the unrecognized offspring of a deceased taxpayer. The mother wishes to secure social security benefits for the child based upon the deceased father's earnings, but lacking any evidence of paternity, the benefits would be unavailable. Acceptable evidence would be established if the father had claimed the child as a dependent on his tax return. But how to get the tax return?

In some jurisdictions neither the mother nor the child may inherit from the decedent unless included in the will or legitimized in some way. Neither the mother nor the child would qualify as an heir at law, next of kin, beneficiary, or donee under state law, and consequently neither could get the return which might contain the evidence which would qualify the child for benefits. Oddly enough, an entry on the return claiming the child as a dependent, the one item which they are trying to obtain, would establish entitlement to access the return. But the rule seems to be that if the father dies in the wrong state and you do not already have the return, you can not get it. Of course, if the father filed a joint return with his wife, the mother of the illegitimate child could ask the wife to obtain the return and let her have it.

Whenever a request for a decedent's return originates from an heir at law, next of kin, beneficiary, or donee, there must also be a determination that such person has a material interest which will be affected by information contained in the return. In order to meet this requirement, the requester must elucidate his interests without knowing what information is contained in the return, thereby engaging is a sort of argument based upon supposition.

It is not entirely clear whether *material* is intended to mean "having physical substance," "substantial," "relevant," or "reasonable." The *Internal Revenue Manual* defines a *material interest* as an important interest, generally a financial interest. Since that which is described as "generally" financial is by inference also described as sometimes not financial, the only guidance which remains is that the matter should be something of consequence. The disclosure officer will view a matter as of adequate importance whenever a requester is suitably insistent upon securing his rights and unwilling to accept the first denial.

Disclosure officers have great difficulty resolving requests for the returns or return information of incompetents and decedents. They are torn between the emotional desire to satisfy often poignant requests and the need to satisfy the strict requirements of law. It is not clear how the law is to be applied, since not only will the circumstances constantly shift, but different assumptions will apply in different jurisdictions. All you can do is to make out your best case without being inhibited by a fear that your arguments may be irrelevant or inappropriate. You may be surprised to learn that you are entitled to obtain more than you expected.

Chapter Thirty-Two

Public Records

The confidentiality requirements of the Internal Revenue Code are designed to prevent returns and return information becoming available to unauthorized persons. The provisions of the code do not, however, erect a perfect barricade, and there are many ways information may legally escape to the public. The person who is desperately seeking to locate someone or who has some other reason to seriously pursue information about another person has some options which might bear fruit.

Information about a taxpayer which has become public record loses any confidential status it might once have had. That does not mean that an accidental or illegal release of information destroys its confidentiality, or that divulgence by a careless or disinterested taxpayer will destroy confidentiality. It does mean that any legitimate use by the Internal Revenue Service or any release in the course of litigation can place the formerly protected information in the public record.

Freedom of Information requesters have generally respected the rights of other taxpayers and not sought access to their returns or return information. When such requests have been made, they are uniformly denied as prohibited by statute. Such denials may not be entirely legal. Throughout my tenure as chief of the Freedom of Information operations, I lived in fear that someone would hit upon the scheme of requesting another taxpayer's Examination, Collection or Criminal Investigation file but limit that request to only those entries which on the basis of internal evidence in the file have become part of the public record or are identical to information which has become part of the public record.

I am certain that the Service would desperately resist such a request since it would create a nightmare of having to search through a file to identify and analyze the releasable items. I am not confident that such resistance would be successful.

There may even be cases in which a taxpayer requesting his own file could broaden the scope of information available to him by specifically requesting the release of every item of information which has lost its confidentiality by virtue of release to any other person.

Regardless of whether such innovative and potentially troublesome approaches would be successful, there are valuable sources of public records concerning the tax affairs of other persons.

Court Records

Taxpayers may litigate assessments proposed against them in District Courts or in the Tax Court. Taxpayers are prosecuted for criminal violations of the Internal Revenue Code in District Courts. The records of such courts, which often contain the details of these taxpayers' affairs, including copies of their returns, are available to the public. The District Court records are located throughout the country. The Tax Court case records are available for inspection at the court's Public Files Office, 400 2nd Street, NW, Washington, DC 20217.

Some Tax Court records have been turned over to the Internal Revenue Service for storage purposes. Portions of these records which were originated by the Service do not regain their confidentiality by such return. They continue to be available to the public. The request to the Service should specify that the records wanted are Tax Court files returned to the Service for storage.

Accepted Offers in Compromise

Internal Revenue Code section 6103(k)(1) provides that return information will be disclosed to the extent necessary to permit public inspection of Accepted Offers in Compromise under section 7122.

The Service may compromise any civil or criminal matter arising under the Internal Revenue laws prior to the submission of such matter to the Department of Justice for defense or prosecution. Thereafter, the Department of Justice may compromise cases that have already been referred for defense or prosecution.

Offers in Compromise may be accepted whenever there is doubt as to the legal validity of the liability or the collectibility of the tax. The taxpayer must make an offer proposing to pay some portion of the tax which avoids the necessity of further litigation or administrative enforcement action. The advantage to both parties is the avoidance of further costs in a situation where genuine doubt exists as to the ultimate outcome. It permits the taxpayer to pay less than she might have under the worst of circumstances, and permits the government to collect more than it might otherwise.

An Accepted Offer in Compromise gives rise to extensive records concerning the circumstances of the disputed tax. In the case of doubt as to collectibility of the tax, the records will contain extensive information about the taxpayer's personal affairs and financial condition, including such items as cash on hand, value of life insurance, accounts receivable, securities, real estate and personal property. Interestingly, one of the items which becomes available to the public through these records is the taxpayer's social security number.

The records to be requested are Form 7249, Abstract and Statement, and the accompanying Narrative Report. The Narrative Report is the more interesting portion of the record, as it frequently contains the juiciest details of the taxpayer's personal and financial affairs. Many disclosure officers will attempt to withhold or edit the Narrative Report, but doing so is illegal. The entire report is a public document, and it must be released. Moreover, once it comes into existence, it remains available to the public as long as a copy continues to exist.

Notices of Federal Tax Lien

Internal Revenue Code section 6321 provides that if any person liable to pay any tax neglects or refuses to pay the tax after demand, the amount (including any interest and penalty) shall be a lien in favor of the United States upon all property and rights to property, both real and personal, belonging to such person.

The lien is a charge or encumbrance upon the taxpayer's property. In order to make the lien effective against purchasers of the taxpayer's property and certain other kinds of creditors, a Notice of Federal Tax Lien has to be filed, usually in the county courthouse or hall of records. This notice and any Release of Lien are public records which indicate the taxpayer's name and address, social security number, the kind of tax, and amount of the assessment. Liens are usually filed in the jurisdiction of the taxpayer's residence, primary place of business, and any location in which he is believed to have property or other assets. Copies may be requested from the Service.

Seizure and Sale of Real Estate

The seizure and sale of property to enforce the collection of delinquent taxes involves the creation of numerous public records, including notices posted on the premises seized, newspaper advertisements announcing the sale, mailed notices announcing the sale, and Part 2 of Record 21, Record of Seizure and Sale of Real Estate. Some editions of Record 21 may require editing, as they include details not legally public. Persons who actually bid at Internal Revenue sales or who have purchased property have more extensive rights to access relevant records.

Other Litigation

A large variety of suits filed in District Courts create public records concerning tax matters and may serve as a basis for demanding the release of records in the possession of the Service. These include suits to reduce a tax claim to judgment, foreclosure of Federal Tax Lien, actions to enforce a levy, request for order to open a safe deposit box, suit to recover an erroneous refund, suits against fiduciaries, action to quiet title, suits against third parties to recover withheld taxes, suits to enforce a summons, suits to reverse a fraudulent transfer or conversion, suits to establish transferee liability, and bankruptcy proceedings.

Court records involving such matters may contain much information about the individual's affairs. They usually also contain the social security number which could be the basis of requests for other records or requests that a letter be forwarded for humane reasons.

Joint Returns

Many wives pay little attention to the information their husbands place on joint tax returns until after the divorce. Divorcees should be aware that once a joint return has been filed, it remains open to both signatory taxpayers even though they are no longer married. Both former wives and former husbands may request such returns since both are the taxpayers in such cases.

Divorced parties may also request access to joint-return information resulting from enforcement actions or investigations of tax matters which take place long after the divorce. For instance if a married couple filed a joint return in 1987 and were divorced in 1988, a Collection, Examination, or Criminal Investigation action which takes place in 1989 will generate return information based upon the joint return which continues to be available to both taxpayers. Divorced wives may thereby obtain access to information concerning the former husbands' current location and financial affairs, conveniently gathered by the government's most effective law enforcement agency. Former husbands may do the same whenever circumstances permit.

There has been at least one instance in which a former husband was more attached to an additional deduction than to his wife. For several years after a very acrimonious divorce, he continued to file joint returns which included his former wife's social security number and claimed an undeserved deduction for the wife. The Service had no way of knowing that the couple was no longer married and no way of uncovering this little fraud as the former wife did not have enough taxable income to file her own return. The wife ultimately learned of the joint returns and requested copies; when she received them, she learned all that she needed to know to increase her income substantially.

Consents

Taxpayers or persons having a legitimate material interest may designate other persons to receive copies of their returns and return information by issuing written requests for or consents to disclosure. Some recipients of such copies, such as schools considering tuition grants for the taxpayers' children, banks weighing loan applications, or local agencies evaluating eligibility for subsidized housing are likely to be under a legal obligation to protect the confidentiality of such records.

Other recipients may not be under any legal obligation to prevent a further disclosure of what they have received and may be willing to share their information with you. Prospective partners might exchange copies of their individual tax returns to ensure that each possesses the wherewithal to meet her financial obligations. Lovers contemplating prenuptial financial agreements or wishing to avoid palimony suits might exchange copies of their tax returns before they exchange vows or favors. There is no limit to the variety of situations in which a taxpayer may release information generally considered confidential and thereby make it public.

Court Orders

Courts may direct taxpayers to release copies of their returns to opponents in a variety of litigation. Sometimes the court order will include provision for maintaining confidentiality; sometimes it will not, providing more sources of information for you to approach.

Creating Opportunities

The methods mentioned for piercing the protective screen of confidentiality erected for tax returns and return information are merely the most common and the most likely to be readily applicable. There are others which may be useful but would be applicable only in rare instances. If you know something about a taxpayer and have a legitimate need to know more, a careful search of the Internal Revenue Code and the Disclosure handbook of the *Internal Revenue Manual* may reveal access methods which will be successful for you.

Chapter Thirty-Three

Learning about IRS Employees

Many Internal Revenue Service employees display a desire to remain anonymous in the performance of their public duties. The definition of the right to privacy often expands when the subject of an inquiry is a Service employee. Managers and executives are struck by a sudden sense of panic when they or their peers are the subject of a request for information. As a result, responses to requests for information about Service employees will go to great lengths to withhold what is frequently innocuous information. Sometimes a response will deny requested information identical to information the Service is actively publicizing. Sometimes a response will be virtually irrational.

Nevertheless, a great deal of information concerning Service employees is readily available to persons interested in obtaining it.

Telephone Directories

It is a well-established principle that agencies may not withhold their internal telephone directories from the public. Consequently, the directory for the National Office is offered for sale by the Superintendent of Documents, U.S. Government Printing Office, Washington, DC 20402. Directories for local offices are available from the district director or other head of the office.

The publicly available directories will not necessarily list the names of all the persons in an office, nor will they always list all the telephone numbers in use. Persons whom the Service does not wish to identify to the public are simply omitted from the directories. This creates a slight inconvenience to the users of directories within the Service, but it permits complete conformity with the requirements of the Freedom of Information Act while withholding the desired information.

Public Information Listing

The Office of Personnel Management has designated six items of information which must be made available concerning most government employees.

1. Name.
2. Present and past position titles and occupational series.

3. Present and past grades.

4. Present and past annual salary rates (including performance awards or bonuses, incentive awards, merit pay amount, meritorious or distinguished executive ranks and allowances or differentials).

5. Present and past duty stations (including room numbers, shop designations, or other identifying information regarding buildings or places of employment).

6. Position descriptions, identifications of job elements, and performance standards (but not evaluations or information inextricably intertwined with evaluations).

These six items of information were intended to permit the public to know who does what, where it is done, how it is supposed to be done, and what compensation is received for doing it.

In order to facilitate making this information available to any requester, including those who may wish the information for commercial solicitation purposes, the Service produces a Public Information Listing which contains the current aspects of the six items for most current employees. The listings are produced monthly for each office.

Three common errors occur in the use of these listings by the Service. First, it is sometimes assumed that the listing fully satisfies the responsibility to release the six items of information. It does not. The listings contain only current information, whereas the six items are considered public information going back to the beginning of an employee's career with the Service.

Second, it is sometimes assumed that the provision of earlier listings will satisfy the requirement to release historical information. It will not. The six items must be released wherever they appear in any record which is requested, unless their release would reveal information exempt in its own right, such as identifying an employee in a confidential investigation. In other words, if a requester asks for a record in which the six items appear, the entire record must be released, or the six items must be released as segregable portions which are not exempt. Some offices have withheld extensive records, claiming that the only nonexempt information has already been made available in the Public Information Listing. The National Office will not sustain such an argument on appeal.

Third, some offices have argued that since the regulations concerning employee information identify the six items as public, it may therefore be assumed that any other information is confidential. On the contrary, any information about an employee which is not included in the six items must be evaluated in accordance with Freedom of Information Act standards and unless found to be subject to an exemption, must be released. Not being included in the six items does not in itself establish that release would constitute an unwarranted invasion of privacy.

There remains one other problem with the Public Information Listing. In the form in which released, it does not include any entries for employees in the GS-1811 series (criminal investigator), such as special agents of the Criminal Investigation Division.

Special Agents

For many years information concerning special agents of the Criminal Investigation Division (CID) was considered publicly available, although I am not aware of any specific requests for such information. Any general requests for Public Information Listings or telephone directories made to district offices prior to December 1976 would have received records which included special agents, like any other employees. Although there must have been such releases, there were no adverse consequences, and no one until then had conceived any need to protect the identity of special agents. But 1976 was a year in which the increasing popularity of the Freedom of Information Act fostered a compulsion to avoid compliance with the act's requirements.

A representative of Criminal Investigation approached me with a proposal that the identity of special agents be withheld from the public by being deleted from telephone directories, employee listings, and similar compilations of information. I could see no exemption which might authorize such withholding and knew it to be in violation of the regulations governing the release of personnel information. The CID representative was unable to provide any rationale for taking such a position and could say only that some one close to his director felt very strongly about the matter. I responded that in the absence of any compelling need and any reasonably arguable legal basis, I could not support such a policy but that there was no apparent need for any immediate concern since no one seemed to be pursuing that type of information.

A month or two later, the CID representative returned with a copy of an October 6, 1976, letter which his division had coaxed out of the Bureau of Manpower Information Systems, U.S. Civil Service Commission. The relevant paragraph of the letter read:

> The public information provisions which are causing you concern stem from our regulations found in 5 CFR 294.702(a). I agree that the language in this section is not altogether clear, and for that reason we are currently in the process of revising the section to eliminate ambiguities. For example, we will indicate that the name, present and past position titles, grades, salaries, and duty stations of almost all Government employees will be information available to the public. For your present purposes, you should consider employees in undercover positions to be defined as those in the very narrow category of employees excluded from this requirement.

On the basis of this letter, Criminal Investigation proposed to withhold the identities of all special agents. But were all special agents employed in undercover positions? Certainly not. Some special agents would sometimes be in undercover assignments, but in polling the few agents that I had worked with in the National Office, I found none who had ever been in undercover assignments. How, then, could the identities of all special agents be withheld on the basis of this letter?

The rationale was quite simple. If agents who were not serving in undercover positions were identified to the public and some of those agents subsequently were placed undercover and ceased to be identified to the public, the very process of protecting their identities would serve to identify them to anyone requesting a series of listings for comparison. That seemed to me as if the solution were creating the problem!

The whole concept of protecting agents' identities seemed to make little sense, since agents are required to identify themselves to taxpayers (other than targets of covert investigations). All anyone who wanted to compile a list of agents had to do was to telephone the limited number of attorneys in any district who specialized in defending taxpayers in criminal fraud cases and ask them for the names of agents they had dealt with.

I was very uncomfortable with the thought of attempting to overcome the requirements of the Information Act and the requirements of the personnel regulations (which seemed not at all ambiguous to me) with nothing more than a chatty letter from the Bureau of Manpower Information Systems. But Disclosure had only recently become a division under the Assistant Commissioner (Compliance), and having the support of the Criminal Investigation Division might be important on other matters, so the issue seemed not to warrant argument. The solution to this dilemma was that on December 1, 1976, the text of the Civil Service Commission letter was reprinted in the Disclosure Information Digest and distributed to the field offices without comment. The digest is an informational document, not an instruction to staff, so we were not telling the field to withhold anything from anyone, merely apprising field disclosure officers of recent developments in this area. Neither the digest article nor the change in disclosure practices was noticed by the public, and no complaints or appeals were received.

Nothing more was heard on the matter of special agents' identites for almost ten years, the Criminal Investigation Division happy that they need not be released, the public indifferent to whether they were able to obtain them. The Criminal Investigation Division received a memorandum from a field office stating that they were conscientiously defending the identities whereas neighboring districts were indiscriminately releasing similar information without regard for the consequences. There was now concern that taxpayers might become aware that some districts were protecting their special agents and others were not—a state of inconsistency which could endanger the defense of this information.

Before taking any action, I sent questionnaires to all district offices to learn what was actually happening. About one-fifth of the districts claimed that they had never received any requests for employees' identities, had never considered the need for protecting special agents' identities, and made no recommendation on the matter.

More than half of the remaining districts replied that they had processed routine requests without deleting special-agent information, that this practice caused them no problem, that there were no adverse consequences, and that they could imagine no reason for withholding such information.

The balance, about one-third of all districts, stated that they had routinely deleted special-agent information but that requesters raised no objections to that practice. They felt that what they were doing was sensible, consistent with instructions, or simply what was wanted. None of these districts offered any evidence or even any speculation as to what untoward event might take place if they could no longer delete such information.

Consequently, with the exception of the one district which had raised concerns, none were really adamant about protecting special agents' identities. The National Office Criminal Investigation Division was adamant, however, and in the absence of any taxpayer interest in the matter, I decided to conform procedures to their preferences. The *Internal Revenue Manual* was revised to provide that the names of employees in the GS-1811 series (criminal investigator) must be deleted from the Public Information Listing and comparable documents. No mention was made of undercover assignments. No one objected.

Is the Criminal Investigation Division really committed to protecting the identity of special agents, especially those on undercover assignments? On July 10, 1988, the Austin *American Statesman* printed an article entitled "Money Hunter — Special Agent Tracks Crime to Its Roots." The article told how Special Agent Gary Gallman once "posed as a flashy drug peddler," once acted "the part of a shady bar owner," and once "convinced an unscrupulous businessman he was an accountant in the market to buy a legitimate business for his crooked boss."

Gallman's photograph was out of focus, but his name was mentioned 15 times! An article like this could not have appeared without the involvement of the chief of the local Criminal Investigation branch, the help of the Public Affairs officer, and the approval of the district director. Were any of them concerned about divulging Gary Gallman's identity? The article concluded: "Before agents go undercover, they have to establish an elaborate 'other identity.' ... Criminals sometimes conduct extensive background checks on agents posing as crooked businessmen or drug traffickers and kill agents whose cover has been blown."

Is the Criminal Investigation Division concerned about identifying special agents? Well, it is if you ask about them, but it is not when planting a good story publicizing their achievements.

Executive News Releases

Gathering information about the executives who actually run the Service is a far more interesting activity than merely trying to identify special agents.

To begin with, a requester may wish to obtain copies of the news releases which the Public Affairs Division issues whenever anyone is appointed to or transferred to any major executive position in the service. These news releases generally recount the individual's career progression and prior assignments of importance. But they also state the individual's age, place of origin or residence, and education, including degrees and institutions where they were earned. Until recently, the news releases included marital status and number of children. Interestingly, if information concerning such personal matters appeared in other records, such as the Official Personnel Folder, it would be withheld as an unwarranted invasion of privacy.

Financial Disclosure Statements

Persons serving as GS-16 or higher (including all members of the Senior Executive Service) are required by the Ethics in Government Act to file annual Financial Disclosure Statements on Form 278. These statements must reveal all income and sources; interests in property; purchase, sale, or exchange of property; gifts and reimbursements; liabilities; positions held; compensation in excess of $5,000 paid by one source; agreements relating to outside employment; and additional information concerning the financial data of spouse and dependent children.

Financial Disclosure Statements are maintained for six years from the date of filing, and copies are available to the public. However, a record of requesters is maintained, and it too is available to the public. The statute provides that it is unlawful for any person to obtain or use a statement for any unlawful purpose, any commercial purpose, determining a credit rating, or solicitation for charitable, political, or other purposes. However, the statements may be used by the news media and may be disseminated to the general public.

Requests for Financial Disclosure Statements may be addressed to the Administrative Assistant to the Executive Resources Board, Internal Revenue Service, 1111 Constitution Avenue, Washington, DC 20224.

Senior Executive Performance Objectives and Expectations

Each year, every member of the Senior Executive Service, including all district directors, service-center directors, assistant regional commissioners, assistant commissioners, many division directors, and other top Service executives, receives from his or her superior a Form 6419, Senior Executive Performance Objectives and Expectations. This document is designed to inform the executive of what he or she is expected to achieve in the following year and is the standard against which accomplishments or the lack thereof are to be measured.

A great deal could be learned about how the Service is managed and what it is trying to accomplish if these forms were ever to become available to the public. They could resolve, once and forever, whether employees' performance is measured by quota systems, whether the Service has a secret (possibly illegal) agenda, and whether key managers are truly expected and permitted to manage. Unfortunately, no meaningful portion of the information contained in these annual forms has ever been released. The Service has defended these Executive Expectations with a manic determination that could be justified only if their disclosure would unleash Armageddon, the final battle between good and evil heralding the end of the world.

Frank D. Ferris, the director of negotiations for the National Treasury Employees Union, requested access to the Executive Expectations for 1980–1981. The request resulted in a virtual panic among executives fearful that their Expectations would be released to the union. The Service resisted the request, and litigation resulted. On December 23, 1981, a final District Court opinion in *Ferris v. Internal Revenue Service* ordered the release of the documents, "except for those portions ... which identify specific individual employees of the IRS."

I was directed to do the editing necessary to the release of the documents and was reminded of how strongly Service executives felt about the release of these Expectations. Counsel provided me with three guidelines for making the deletions: (1) I was to take out all direct identifiers, including names, titles, and office locations. (2) I was to remove all indirect identifiers, including the names, titles and office locations of the approving and reviewing officials since it might be possible to identify the recipient of the Expectation on the basis of his being a subordinate of the issuing official. I was also to remove, as an indirect identifier, any of the text of the Expectations which referred to any matter which might be unique to a particular activity or position.

In other words, if an Expectation referred to something which only a district director would do, that information was to be deleted since it would make it obvious that the recipient was a district director. Similarly, if an Expectation differentiated between something that related to Examination, Collection, Data Processing, or any other function, that was to be deleted since it too could provide assistance in the indirect identification of the recipient. In fact, the only information which was to remain was those Expectations which could relate to anyone, anywhere. (3) I was to delete any personal information which remained which might constitute an unwarranted invasion of privacy if it were to be released. This third guideline raised a moral and legal dilemma, for the sole purpose of deleting the identifying details was to preclude an invasion of privacy. It would make no sense to delete personal information unless its release would be so traumatic as to cause the subject harm, even if it cannot be related to any identifiable person. It makes sense to delete personal information if the identity of the subject must be released, and it makes sense to delete identity if the personal information is to be released, but to attempt to delete both was the equivalent of burning the candle at both ends. Counsel advised that they thought that the court might allow withholding both identity and personal information, and we would attempt to do both. I was told that in view of the great interest that management showed in this project, the rule would be "If in doubt, take it out!"

I personally edited more than two-thirds of the Expectations while another individual did the remainder. I then reviewed all the Expectations to make absolutely certain that the editing standards had been consistently and conscientiously applied. In fact, I reviewed the entire collection of Expectations several times and thereby probably became the only person to have studied all the Expectations in great detail, doubtlessly making me the world's leading expert on the 1980–1981 Senior Executive Performance Objectives and Expectations.

At the conclusion of the editing process, all identifying information—

direct, indirect, suggestive, or deductive — had been deleted. But virtually all meaningful content had also been deleted, and the result was so skeletal as to be of no value to anyone. Despite the fact that what we proposed to release in response to the court order was little more than releasing nothing at all, we encountered continuing expressions of concern from various executives who would have preferred that we make no release whatsoever.

My review of the Expectations left me with two great concerns. The first was that I could find no information in the Expectations which if disclosed could in any way significantly impede or nullify Service actions in carrying out a responsibility or function. The second was that I could find no information whose release would constitute an unwarranted invasion of personal privacy. At best, the Expectations contained only one or two examples of any information which might be considered vaguely personal in nature. There was nothing that remotely approached an unwarranted invasion of privacy.

I explained to counsel that I was concerned that when the union received the edited documents, they would certainly notice the absence of any personal information. They would assume that we had done excessive editing (which indeed I believe we had done) and would either appeal or take some other legal action to bring the documents before the court for in-camera inspection. The court would immediately realize that there was no information whose release would result in an unwarranted invasion of privacy anywhere in these documents. The court would also realize that the documents were not exempt, that our withholding them was frivolous, that our arguments in their defense were fantasies, and that the court had been tricked. I even imagined that the court might become angry.

Counsel advised that discretion was the better part of valor and that risking the court's wrath was less threatening than advising the entire Senior Executive Service of the Service that based upon my review of the documents, we had found a way to snatch defeat from the jaws of victory.

The edited documents were duly delivered, and we waited for the union to fire the next shot. We were so convinced that we must lose these documents that telephone calls were made to all regional offices advising that in future years, Expectations were not to include any information that could not be made public, as we could not promise to defend such documents, despite the initial appearance of success.

Nothing happened. There was no appeal.

I had learned from reviewing the Expectations that district directors in the same region frequently had the same or almost the same Expectations. These instructions had not been carefully crafted to meet the developmental needs of specific individuals but tended to be boilerplate recitations. I later learned that when executives were away on other assignments, persons acting in their stead had access to the Expectations so that they might contribute to their accomplishment. Sometimes transfers or promotions occurred after midyear, and rather than issue new Expectations for a short period, the newly appointed official merely took over the prior incumbent's Expectations. Many executives shared their Expectations with their immediate staff so that all could contribute to their attainment. It was not unusual that portions of Expectations were inserted in the management Expectations of subordinates so that they too could make contributions to what appeared to be more like organizational goals than individual Expectations. None of these practices were characteristic of personal information whose release could cause an unwarranted invasion of privacy. On the contrary, the use of Executive Expectations in the Service closely resembled the use of position descriptions or instructions to staff which were required to be public.

After a time, the union requested access to the Expectations for 1981–1982. The Service offered to make the forms available in edited form as had previously been done. The union filed suit.

In December 1983 the Commissioner announced a new policy of cooperation with the union. In order to promote this policy, training classes were scheduled for managers throughout the Service. I was selected as one of the instructors for National Office managers. The two-day course was entitled "Managing Effectively in a Labor Management Environment." The thrust of the course was that labor and management had many objectives in common and should not be in conflict when cooperation could improve the Service's ability to assist the public. Too many managers opposed everything the union tried to do out of a competitive spirit that made them believe that for management to win, labor must lose. From now on, we were all to search for win-win solutions to problems, which would permit both management and labor to achieve their legitimate goals.

I received a letter of commendation in appreciation of my efforts in publicizing the win-win policy. After the presentation I suggested to my division director that we might take advantage of the win-win policy to release the Executive Expectations, which were then again in litigation. I explained that it might be far wiser to appear to be making a gesture of cooperation and amity in accordance with the Commissioner's new policy than to be cited for the arbitrary and capricious withholding of these obviously nonexempt records. The proposal was rejected. The win-win policy was not to be applied to Freedom of Information matters.

On June 20, 1984, the District Court found in favor of the Service in *National Treasury Employees Union, et al. v. Internal Revenue Service*, known in the Service as *Second Ferris*. The District Court judge observed that he was being asked to consider "the same issue . . . simply in a successive year." Another judge of the same court had given the issue "her best consideration." Therefore, he simply followed the prior decision and granted the Internal Revenue Service motion and dismissed the case.

The union appealed. The Service presented what the court referred to as a "blurred" res judicata–collateral estoppel–stare decisis argument. All of these legal terms meant more or less that once an issue had been decided, it should not be litigated in a new proceeding, that courts should adhere to decided cases.

The union argued that it had failed to realize the extent to which editing would make the documents unusable until the Service provided them, about three and a half months after the *First Ferris* decision had been rendered, which was too late to appeal. The union pointed out that the judge had not "ever actually viewed the documents" and "had to be under the mistaken impression that the documents would still be meaningful after they were sanitized." The union, however, did not claim any impropriety concerning the extent of the deletions or the manner in which they were made.

The appellate court opinion suggested that the union should have tested its belief that the district judge harbored a "mistaken impression." The court implied that instead of observing the expiration of the period for appeal, the union should have filed a "motion for relief from judgement for mistake, inadvertence, surprise, or excusable neglect."

Thus, the argument in *Second Ferris* revolved not around whether the information was indeed exempt but what the union should or should not have done in *First Ferris*. This, surely, was a strange position to take in a Freedom of Information case since it seemed completely to ignore the objective of the law to make information available to the public and to minimize the legal burden of the requester.

Stranger still, the record shows that the parties stipulated that the information deleted by the Service in *Second Ferris* was the same kind ordered deleted in *First Ferris*. Therefore, "factual differences" were "found insufficient to justify relitigating mixed question of fact and law." How could the union stipulate to anything concerning information it could not see? Neither the union nor the court, which never looked at anything, could know that the information deleted in *Second Ferris* was the same kind ordered deleted in *First Ferris* or even that the information deleted in *First Ferris* was the same kind ordered deleted in *First Ferris*. The union, like the court, knew only what the Service told it and accepted that as true and correct. But that, of course, is why management manages and labor does not.

The appellate court ruled:

> The Union and Ferris chose to pass up the opportunity they had to appeal to this court from the judgment entered in the first action. . . . There has been no change favorable to the Union in the legal climate; the FOIA requests in the two actions are identical except for the year involved; the same courts and the same procedures are implicated; no overriding public concern warrants allowing the Union to start over; and the continuing character of the Union's interest was forseeable at the time of the initial action.
>
> In sum, the Union and Ferris had a fair opportunity to present the contention they would air again; they did not avail themselves of the right to appeal from the judgment on the merits of the issue they wish to reargue.

Thereafter, the Service received a few requests every year from local union officials for the Executive Expectations of one or two district directors. The response was always precisely the same: Such a request had to be denied because its nature precluded maintaining the anonymity of the executives involved; however, if there were a request for all Expectations, they would be provided in edited form to protect the identities of the employees involved. We knew that no one would actually ask for such edited Expectations again in view of the worthless bits and pieces released in the past. We also knew that no one was ever likely to litigate such a response after the final decision in *Second Ferris* — unless, of course, some fool in the Internal Revenue Service were to change the response.

On May 12, 1987, we responded to a request from a union official for Executive Expectations for any and all Detroit District personnel. The Detroit District has long had a reputation for hard feelings between management and employees, which have been explained to me as unrelated to any specific Internal Revenue Service problem but as resulting from a strong blue-collar union ethic shared by many of our revenue officers and revenue agents in that city. Our response was carefully worded:

> This is in response to your Freedom of Information Act request for Forms 6419, Senior Executive's Performance Objectives and Expectations, as they relate to any and all Detroit District personnel.
>
> Senior Executive's Performance Objectives and Expectations are available in edited form to protect the personal privacy of the persons to whom they pertain. We cannot provide these records when a request is limited to a single district because of the small number of people involved.
>
> However, if we had a request for Forms 6419 pertaining to all District Directors and Assistant District Directors, we would be able to make those materials available. Absent such a request, we have no alternative but to deny your request pursuant to 5 USC 552(b)(6).

On May 21, 1987, I received what was tantamount to a written admonishment from my immediate superior, the director, Office of Disclosure. The relevant paragraphs read as follows:

> I have attached a copy of the memorandum . . . concerning Senior Executives' Objectives. The first two paragraphs of the memo are fine. They are responsive to the requester in telling him why we are denying his request. What I cannot understand is the third paragraph!
> *I do not understand why you put the third paragraph in the letter!* Do you realize the seriousness of this matter and what problems we have encountered in the past on this subject? Marc, did you discuss this with the specialist? Did you sign off on this memo? If so, why did you not change it? Where is your involvement in this? I also want to see the case file on this request. . . .

On May 26, 1987, I responded:

> You begin with a complaint about the handling of the request for Senior Executive Service objectives. You ask if I realize the seriousness of this matter and what problems we encountered in the past on this matter. I certainly do realize what is involved; possibly better than anyone else because I personally did most of the work which was necessary to resolve these problems in the past!
>
> You state that you approve of the first two paragraphs of the response, but you do not understand the last paragraph which extends

to the requester the opportunity to obtain edited copies of the total universe of Director and Assistant Director objectives. We cannot construct Freedom of Information Act responses on the basis of your personal likes and dislikes; we are as aware of the inconvenience of servicing the public as you are. But we are required to obey the law whether it is convenient or not.

As your chief advisor on matters pertaining to the Freedom of Information Act, let me make it as plain to you as I can. If you had signed a response to this request containing the two denial paragraphs which you like and omitting the third paragraph which you dislike, there is a very good likelihood that you would be found to be personally liable for sanctions for the arbitrary and capricious withholding of records in violation of the Freedom of Information Act.

Are you familiar with Ferris v. Internal Revenue Service? We litigated this very matter and we lost. The court ordered us to do precisely what our third paragraph offers, and our offer contains neither more nor less than is legally required. If you did not have a loyal and very knowledgeable staff, you would have been in big trouble on this one. And keep in mind, the requester in Ferris was NTEU and the requester in the case at hand is NTEU. They wouldn't have overlooked your blunder; they would have eaten you up alive.

As to where was I in this case, I was deeply involved; and so was counsel. We had quite a few concurrences on this response; a response which to us was routine, because it was consistent with clearly established precedent.

I was immediately called to the front office and given new orders by the director. I was told that in the event the union accepted my offer of sanitized Expectations, I was to reverse the established position, repudiate my offer, and refuse to give the union anything. The director said that I was out on a limb all by myself on this matter, that no one in the Service would support my releasing the sanitized Expectations, and that my friends in the union would not help me get away with this. I was advised by the director that he did not agree with the positions taken in the *Ferris* cases and that in the future I was not to offer or to release to anyone any sanitized Executive Expectations. Finally, I was ordered not to release any records whatsoever in response to a Freedom of Information Act request by the National Treasury Employees Union unless approved by higher management.

So much for the legal precedents established by the court order in *First Ferris*. So much for res judicata, collateral estoppel, stare decisis. So much for the win-win policy.

Unfortunately, the union did not take up the offer of edited Expectations, so I never had the opportunity to carry out those foolish orders. Had those orders been carried out, it would have been the biggest disclosure blunder ever made. It would have given the union cause to relitigate the availabilty of the Executive Expectations. It would probably have resulted in the release of all Executive Expectations without any deletions. And it might well have put the Service's entire Senior Executive Service on the back of the person who caused that debacle.

Merit Pay Expectations

Merit Pay Performance Appraisal Lists of Expectations, Forms 6477-A, serve a similar purpose as the Executive Expectations discussed above, except that they guide the performance of employees subject to merit-pay provisions, that is, persons in a supervisory or managerial capacity beneath the Senior Executive Service level. These Expectations are available to the public in accordance with the precedent set by *First Ferris*.

As there are far more merit-pay employees than executives, these Expectations are available in much smaller groups than the universe offered requesters of the Executive Expectations. For instance, all the managers in a single district office or in a single service center will be released as a unit.

The editing performed on merit-pay Expectations will be quite similar to that done on the Executive Expectations and would result in a similarly unusable accumulation of information if it were not that the trend in recent years has been for the Expectations to be bereft of any information that relates to an individual. Originally, considerable effort was spent in composing highly significant Expectations which were unique to each recipient, but this is no longer true. My Expectations and those of my subordinate managers for the last two or three years consisted only of the printed forms with names, dates, and approving signatures filled in. The large blank spaces provided for inserting more specific information were left blank. One might, of course, question the logic of providing each manager with annual Expectations almost all of which are always the same, but doubtlessly some regulation or statute requires it.

Position Descriptions

Position descriptions are standard formal documents which describe every position in the Service. In theory, position descriptions accurately reflect the work to be performed. An employee should be able to do and may actually be called upon to do everything in his or her position description and should not be expected to do anything beyond what is contained in the position description. Of course, position descriptions may sometimes be wildly outdated or inaccurate, but they are very valuable guides for knowing what the Service officially believes an employee should be doing.

Associated with position descriptions are job elements and performance standards, which provide further information on which tasks are considered critical. All of these documents are available to the public for all positions since they are considered characteristic of the position rather than the incumbent.

In addition, there are Annual Position Review Files, Position Management Program Files, Desk Audit Files and Classification Appeal Files, all of which involve the consideration of amendment of the position description. Such files are likely to be heavily edited as related solely to the internal personnel rules and practices of an agency and as intra-agency memorandums but may be of value in some circumstances.

Official Personnel Folder

The Official Personnel Folder is the official record of an employee's career in government service. The designated six items of information—name, present and past position titles and occupational series, salaries, grades, duty stations, and position descriptions—are routinely available to any requester.

Other items may be made available after consideration of available exemptions. For instance, it should generally be possible to obtain records of any education provided by or paid for by the agency. There are also precedents for obtaining records of prior employment for persons in certain key decision-making positions in which such employment might be considered to influence the decision-making process.

The Official Personnel Folder consists of right-side and left-side documents. The left-side documents, considered temporary, are agency records solely in control of the Internal Revenue Service. If an employee leaves the Service, left-side documents are destroyed, and the balance of the Official Personnel Folder is transferred to the Office of Personnel Management. The Service makes the initial determination and the appeal determination on left-side documents.

Right-side documents are permanent documents which are required by the Office of Personnel Management. When an employee leaves the Service, right-side documents are transferred to the Office of Personnel Management. If the employee subsequently joins another agency, the right-side documents follow to the new location. The Service will release the six designated items from the right side and deny the balance. Appeal rights for the denied records are to the Office of Personnel Management.

Since the standards for releasing records and the appeal rights differ for each side of the folder, it may be advantageous to make separate FOIA requests for left-side and right-side documents. If your appeals result in some further records being released and others being denied, it may be beneficial to send each agency copies of what the other released with a request that they release any similar records still being withheld. You may be able to take advantage of any inconsistency inherent in the right-side–left-side dichotomy.

Promotion Files

Vacancy announcements describing job openings within any office are available to the public. Each such announcement contains a vacancy-announcement number for each job offered. The vacancy-announcement number may be used to request access to the resulting promotion file.

Most of the information in a promotion file relates to the qualifications of particular applicants and would be withheld as an unwarranted invasion of privacy. A requester will receive information which shows that the file was processed in accordance with merit-promotion principles. One would, for instance, be able to tell from such a file how much competition the successful applicant had, how factors were rated, whether the procedure included interviews or tests, and similar general information.

Agency Grievance Files

Agency grievance files are maintained as a result of an employee's filing a complaint of unfair treatment by management. Such files include the complaint, documentary evidence, interview records, hearing records, examiner's recommendation, decision, statement of objections, appellate decision, and related records.

Subject to editing to avoid an unwarranted invasion of privacy or as necessary in accordance with other exemptions, grievance files will never reveal anything about the individual employees involved. They will reveal a great deal about how the office in which they arise is managed and the officials who manage it.

Equal Employment Opportunity Complaint Files

Equal employment opportunity (EEO) complaint files are created when an employee makes a complaint against the agency alleging an equal-employment violation. Such complaints are somewhat similar to grievances, except that an employee cannot pursue both a grievance and an EEO complaint on the same matter. Employees will therefore choose the arena they feel is most advantageous, except that an employee who is unable to associate himself with some group recognized to suffer discrimination will not have access to the EEO process.

Requests for access will be evaluated somewhat like a request for a grievance file; however, regulations require that a requesting member of the public must receive enough information to understand the nature of the complaint.

Ultimately, any complaint which is not resolved or dropped may be transferred to the Equal Employment Opportunity Commission or to the Merit Systems Protection Board. Consequently, after an FOIA requester has obtained whatever information is available on initial request and appeal to the Internal Revenue Service, movement of the case to another agency will allow her the opportunity to make further requests.

These files should not permit a requester to learn anything about any of the individuals involved unless they go to final administrative hearings and become public records. They can, of course, provide information about the function or office involved and how it is managed. For instance, in National Office, review of EEO files would reveal that in most years, most complaints seem to be directed at the Examination Division. In fact, I filed one myself.

Chapter Thirty-Four

Freedom from
Irrational Government

We have seen that over a period of many years the disclosure policies and practices of the Internal Revenue Service have been irrational. There have been a variety of immediate and institutional factors which have contributed to that irrationality. Irrational actions have been taken by many officials who frequently had nothing else in common and were doubtlessly unaware that they were acting in accordance with a well-established pattern. They may not even have understood the continuing consequences of their actions.

As many threads make a single fabric, all these acts have contributed to a common result. Taken as a whole, the pattern of irrational disclosure policies and practices has served to preserve an environment which will permit irrational policies and practices in the administration of tax laws. We have seen glimpses of that irrational behavior in tax administration beyond the narrow area of disclosure, although it is the subject neither of this book nor my experience. I must leave it to others to document the irrational policy decisions and irrational enforcement actions which have been commonplace in the Internal Revenue Service.

The people have a right to be free from irrational government. The Freedom of Information Act, the Privacy Act of 1974, and the disclosure provisions of the Internal Revenue Code can serve as the tools which can restore sanity to an irrational agency. But the rights these laws bestow must be better employed than has been the case.

Advocates of open government have often said that the public has a right to know. It is even more important that those responsible for administering the Service know that the public knows; and knowing, care.

Rational government can be had only when the decision makers are fully aware that the public will thoroughly examine their decisions, subject them to debate, and provide critical commentary. The decision maker can then break away from the shared assumptions prevalent in the agency and confrom her actions to the values of the society she is intended to serve.

Much can be accomplished by using the knowledge you now have to exercise the rights which every American has had since July 4, 1967, when the Freedom of Information Act went into effect. More can be accomplished if the Congress and the President would amend the act in accordance with the five proposals presented here.

The (b)(5) Proposal

Exemption (b)(5) permits the withholding of intra-agency or interagency memorandums or letters which would not be available by law to a party other than an agency in litigation with the agency. I find no fault with that exemption to the extent that it protects attorney work product and opinions and recommendations stated in preparation for litigation or enforcement actions.

The use of that exemption to protect the deliberative process in predecisional situations contributes to irrational government. The idea that government officials should not operate in a fishbowl is absolute nonsense. It serves to create the illusion that civil servants are magicians who are paid to conduct the public business in a manner which precludes the public from knowing how they perform their tricks or even why they perform their tricks.

Government should have no right to maintain the confidentiality of the ideas, opinions, suggestions, and recommendations upon which they act or do not act, since without publicizing such information, the public has no way to evaluate what prompted a policy, or even if anything prompted it. There may be occasions when important programs are launched or not launched without ideas, opinions, suggestions, or recommendations.

It does not detract from a policy for the public to learn that it has been well thought out, that opposing considerations have been evaluated, or even that some in the agency preferred an alternative. Only an idiot is truly so singleminded as not to have considered some competing course of action. Only the simplest course of action appears so perfect that it has no perceived disadvantages and its competitors no advantages whatsoever. Let us allow the public to know what was discussed and how matters were decided.

In a democracy the public should have a right to know what the deciding official and his staff knew and believed and hoped and feared. For that, exemption (b)(5) must be revised. Government awareness that it must expose its thinking process will go a long way toward ensuring that government has a thinking process.

The (b)(6) Proposal

The (b)(6) exemption permits the withholding of personnel and medical files the disclosure of which would constitute a clearly unwarranted invasion of personal privacy. I have no problem with protecting information which is truly personal and private. As a career government employee, I firmly believed that what I did before I came to work and what I did after I left work were my own affair. Had I not specialized in disclosure matters, I would never have imagined that there could be a right to privacy concerning how I performed or failed to perform my assigned duties.

It is inconceivable to me that having accepted government pay, any government employee should claim that what he does for that pay is so personal that the taxpayer's knowing it constitutes an unwarranted invasion of privacy. Yet the Internal Revenue Service, routinely and with the full blessing of the law, withholds from the public information concerning its employees' functions. I believe that exemption (b)(6) should be revised to preclude withholding information about government personnel which lacks any truly personal aspect.

Court Examination of Records

The Freedom of Information Act provides that on complaint, a court will determine whether records are to be withheld and may examine the records in camera. "May examine" also means that the court may not examine. Experience shows that the Internal Revenue Service wins cases in which the court has not examined the records and loses cases in which the court has examined the records. For a court to accept an agency's self-serving description of records instead of examining them is simply not consistent with making an independent determination. The single improvement making the Freedom of Information Act truly functional would be to require that the court must either examine the records in camera or appoint an independent expert to examine the records on behalf of the court. This proposal alone would drastically alter the Service's ability to engage in irrational government.

Disclosure Impact Statements

Every agency seems to have some body of records which can legitimately be withheld from the public. Is it, however, really necessary that the agency operate in a manner which necessitates accumulating records exempt from disclosure, exercising the available exemption, and finding no alternative process more in keeping with the objectives of open government? The Internal Revenue Service would certainly make no attempt to find an alternative, even if one were readily available.

I believe that an agency which performs the public business in a democracy should constantly strive to be as open as possible. Consequently, I propose that the Freedom of Information Act be amended to provide that whenever an agency successfully defends an identifiable category of records from public access, it be required within a reasonable period of time to publish a Disclosure Impact Statement reflecting an examination of whether it will be necessary to continue to withhold those records in the future. Such a statement should include alternatives to the collection and maintenance of the records, changes in practices to negate the need to exercise the exemption, or other alternatives to existing procedures. Possible costs or savings should be examined and weighed. It may be that the public would be willing to accept the increased costs or disadvantages resulting from a release of the information or an end to its collection.

The Disclosure Impact Statement should be published for public comments and revised in accordance with those comments, as is currently done with proposed regulations. If any member of the Congress is dissatisfied with

the final statement, he or she may request the General Accounting Office to perform an independent analysis or may propose remedial legislation.

Protecting Disclosure Officers

The Freedom of Information Act contains provisions for punishing
officials for the arbitrary and capricious withholding of records. However,
there are no provisions for defending officials who have released records or
propose to release records as required by law and then fall victim to the retribution of their agency. Unfortunately, such acts of retribution have not been uncommon. I strongly propose that the Congress fashion a safety net to protect
the grades and careers of individuals who seek to obey the law but live in constant fear of their superiors.

Your Disclosure Determination

Finally, allow me to remind you that the determination of which records
ought to be confidential and which public is entirely up to the American people,
who are free to weigh the advantages and disadvantages of disclosure law in
accordance with their beliefs and preferences.

You must determine whether you prefer secret and irrational government
or open and sane government.

You must determine how much you want to know.

Appendix I

The Freedom of Information Act
5 U.S.C. 552

As Amended

§552. Public information; agency rules, opinions, orders, records, and proceedings.

(a) Each agency shall make available to the public information as follows:

(1) Each agency shall separately state and currently publish in the Federal Register for the guidance of the public—

(A) descriptions of its central and field organization and the established places at which, the employees (and in the case of a uniformed service, the members) from whom, and the methods whereby, the public may obtain information, make submittals or requests, or obtain decisions;

(B) statements of the general course and method by which its functions are channeled and determined, including the nature and requirements of all formal and informal procedures available;

(C) rules of procedure, descriptions of forms available or the places at which forms may be obtained, and instructions as to the scope and contents of all papers, reports or examinations;

(D) substantive rules of general applicability adopted as authorized by law, and statements of general policy or interpretations of general applicability formulated and adopted by the agency; and

(E) each amendment, revision or repeal of the foregoing.

Except to the extent that a person has actual and timely notice of the terms thereof, a person may not in any manner be required to resort to, or be adversely affected by, a matter required to be published in the Federal Register and not so published. For the purpose of this paragraph, matter reasonably available to the class of persons affected thereby is deemed published in the Federal Register when incorporated by reference therein with the approval of the Director of the Federal Register.

(2) Each agency, in accordance with published rules, shall make available for public inspection and copying—

(A) final opinions, including concurring and dissenting opinions, as well as orders, made in the adjudication of cases;

(B) those statements of policy and interpretations which have been adopted by the agency and are not published in the Federal Register; and

(C) administrative staff manuals and instructions to staff that affect a member of the public;

unless the materials are promptly published and copies offered for sale. To the extent required to prevent a clearly unwarranted invasion of personal privacy, an agency may delete identifying details when it makes available or publishes an opinion, statement of policy, interpretation, or staff manual or instruction. However, in each case the justification for the deletion shall be explained fully in writing. Each agency shall also maintain and make available for public inspection and copying current indexes providing identifying information for the public as to any matter issued, adopted, or promulgated after July 4, 1967, and required by this paragraph to be made available or published. Each agency shall promptly publish, quarterly or more frequently, and distribute (by sale or otherwise) copies of each index or supplements thereto unless it determines by order published in the Federal Register that the publication would be unnecessary and impracticable, in which case the agency shall nonetheless provide copies of such index on request at a cost not to exceed the direct cost of duplication. A final order, opinion, statement of policy, interpretation, or staff manual or instruction that affects a member of the public may be relied on, used, or cited as precedent by an agency against a party other than an agency only if —

(i) it has been indexed and either made available or published as provided by this paragraph; or

(ii) the party has actual and timely notice of the terms thereof.

(3) Except with respect to the records made available under paragraphs (1) and (2) of this subsection, each agency, upon any request for records which (A) reasonably describes such records and (B) is made in accordance with published rules stating the time, place, fees (if any) and procedures to be followed, shall make the records promptly available to any person.

(4)(A)(i) In order to carry out the provisions of this section, each agency shall promulgate regulations, pursuant to notice and receipt of public comment, specifying the schedule of fees applicable to the processing of requests under this section and establishing procedures and guidelines for determining when such fees should be waived or reduced. Such schedule shall conform to the guidelines which shall be promulgated, pursuant to notice and receipt of public comment, by the Director of the Office of Management and Budget and which shall provide for a uniform schedule of fees for all agencies.

(ii) Such agency regulations shall provide that —

(I) fees shall be limited to reasonable standard charges for document search, duplication, and review, when records are requested for commercial use;

(II) fees shall be limited to reasonable standard charges for document duplication when records are not sought for commercial use and the request is made by an educational or noncommercial scientific institution, whose purpose is scholarly or scientific research; or a representative of the news media; and

(III) for any request not described in (I) or (II), fees shall be limited to reasonable standard charges for document search and duplication.

(iii) Documents shall be furnished without any charge or at a charge reduced below the fees established under clause (ii) if disclosure of the information is in the public interest because it is likely to contribute significantly public understanding of the operations or activities of the government and is not primarily in the commercial interest of the requester.

(iv) Fee schedules shall provide for the recovery of only the direct costs of search, duplication, or review. Review costs shall include only the direct costs incurred during the initial examination of a document for the purposes of determining whether the documents must be disclosed under this section and for the purposes of withholding any portions exempt from disclosure under this section. Review costs may not include any costs incurred in resolving issues of law or policy that may be raised in the course of processing a request under this section. No fee may be charged by any agency under this section—

(I) if the costs of routine collection and processing of the fee are likely to equal or exceed the amount of the fee; or

(II) for any request described in clause (ii)(II) or (III) of this subparagraph for the first two hours of search time or for the first one hundred pages of duplication.

(v) No agency may require advance payment of any fee unless the requester has previously failed to pay fees in a timely fashion, or the agency has determined that the fee will exceed $250.

(vi) Nothing in this subparagraph shall supersede fees chargeable under a statute specifically providing for setting the level of fees for particular types of records.

(vii) In any action by a requester regarding the waiver of fees under this section, the court shall determine the matter de novo: *Provided,* That the court's review of the matter shall be limited to the record before the agency.

(B) On complaint, the district court of the United States in the district in which the complainant resides, or has his principal place of business, or in which the agency records are situated, or in the District of Columbia, has jurisdiction to enjoin the agency from withholding agency records and to order the production of any agency records improperly withheld from the complainant. In such a case the court shall determine the matter de novo, and may examine the contents of such agency records in camera to determine whether such records or any part thereof shall be withheld under any of the exemptions set forth in subsection (b) of this section, and the burden is on the agency to sustain its action.

(C) Notwithstanding any other provision of law, the defendant shall serve an answer or otherwise plead to any complaint made under this subsection within thirty days after service upon the defendant of the pleading in which such complaint is made, unless the court otherwise directs for good cause shown.

(D) [Except as to cases the court considers of greater importance, proceedings before the district court, as authorized by this subsectic ı, and appeals therefrom, take precedence on the docket over all cases and shall be assigned for hearing and trial or for argument at the earliest practicable date and expediated in every way.] Repealed. Pub. L. 98-620, Title IV, 402(2), Nov. 8, 1984, 98 Stat. 3335, 3357.

(E) The court may assess against the United States reasonable attorney fees and other litigation costs reasonably incurred in any case under this section in which the complainant has substantially prevailed.

(F) Whenever the court orders the production of any agency records improperly withheld from the complainant and assesses against the United States reasonable attorney fees and other litigation costs, and the court additionally issues a written finding that the circumstances surrounding the withholding raise questions whether agency personnel acted arbitrarily or capriciously with respect to the withholding, the Special Counsel shall promptly initiate a proceeding to determine whether disciplinary action is warranted against the officer or employee who was primarily responsible for the withholding. The Special Counsel, after investigation and consideration of the evidence submitted, shall submit his findings and recommendations to the administrative authority of the agency concerned and shall send copies of the findings and recommendations to the officer or employee or his representative. The administrative authority shall take the corrective action that the Special Counsel recommends.

(G) In the event of noncompliance with the order of the court, the district court may punish for contempt the responsible employee, and in the case of a uniformed service, the responsible member.

(5) Each agency having more than one member shall maintain and make available for public inspection a record of the final votes of each member in every agency proceeding.

(6)(A) Each agency, upon any request for records made under paragraph (1), (2) or (3) of this subsection, shall—

> (i) determine within ten days (excepting Saturdays, Sundays, and legal public holidays) after the receipt of any such request whether to comply with such request and shall immediately notify the person making such request of such determination and the reasons therefor, and of the right of such person to appeal to the head of the agency any adverse determination; and
>
> (ii) make a determination with respect to any appeal within twenty days (excepting Saturdays, Sundays and legal public holidays) after the receipt of such appeal. If on appeal the denial of the request for records is in whole or in part upheld the agency shall notify the person making such request of the provisions for judicial review of that determination under paragraph (4) of this subsection.

(B) In unusual circumstances as specified in this subparagraph, the time limits prescribed in either clause (i) or clause (ii) of subparagraph (A) may be extended by written notice to the person making such request setting forth the reasons for such extension and the date on which a determination is expected to be dispatched. No such notice shall specify a date that would result in an extension for more than ten working days. As used in this subparagraph, "unusual circumstances" means, but only to the extent reasonably necessary to the proper processing of the particular request —

> (i) the need to search for and collect the requested records from field facilities or other establishments that are separate from the office processing the request;
> (ii) the need to search for, collect, and appropriately examine a voluminous amount of separate and distinct records which are demanded in a single request; or
> (iii) the need for consultation, which shall be conducted with all practicable speed, with another agency having a substantial interest in the determination of the request or among two or more components of the agency having substantial subject-matter interest therein.

(C) Any person making a request to any agency for records under paragraph (1), (2) or (3) of this subsection shall be deemed to have exhausted his administrative remedies with respect to such request if the agency fails to comply with the applicable time limit provisions of this paragraph. If the Government can show exceptional circumstances exist and that the agency is exercising due diligence in responding to the request, the court may retain jurisdiction and allow the agency additional time to complete its review of the records. Upon any determination by an agency to comply with a request for records, the records shall be made promptly available to such person making such request. Any notification of denial of any request for records under this subsection shall set forth the names and titles or positions of each person responsible for the denial of such request.

(b) This section does not apply to matters that are —

(1)(A) specifically authorized under criteria established by an Executive order to be kept secret in the interest of national defense or foreign policy and (B) are in fact properly classified pursuant to such Executive Order;

(2) related solely to the internal personnel rules and practices of an agency;

(3) specifically exempted from disclosure by statute (other than section 552b of this title), provided that such statute (A) requires that the matters be withheld from the public in such a manner as to leave no discretion on the issue, or (B) establishes particular criteria for withholding or refers to particular types of matters to be withheld;

(4) trade secrets and commercial or financial information obtained from a person and privileged or confidential;

(5) inter-agency or intra-agency memorandums or letters which would not be available by law to a party other than an agency in litigation with the agency;

(6) personnel and medical files and similar files the disclosure of which would constitute a clearly unwarranted invasion of personal privacy;

(7) records or information compiled for law enforcement purposes, but only to the extent that the production of such law enforcement records or information (A) could reasonably be expected to interfere with enforcement proceedings, (B) would deprive a person of a right to a fair trial or an impartial adjudication, (C) could reasonably be expected to constitute an unwarranted invasion of personal privacy, (D) could reasonably be expected to disclose the identity of a confidential source, including a State, local or foreign agency or authority or any private institution which furnished information on a confidential basis, and, in the case of a record or information compiled by a criminal law enforcement authority in the course of a criminal investigation or by an agency conducting a lawful national security intelligence investigation, information furnished by a confidential source, (E) would disclose techniques and procedures for law enforcement investigations or prosecutions, or would disclose guidelines for law enforcement investigations or prosecutions if such disclosure could reasonably be expected to risk circumvention of the law, or (F) could reasonably be expected to endanger the life or physical safety of any individual;

(8) contained in or related to examination, operating, or condition reports prepared by, on behalf of, or for the use of an agency responsible for the regulation or supervision of financial institutions; or

(9) geological and geophysical information and data, including maps, concerning wells.

Any reasonably segregable portion of a record shall be provided to any person requesting such record after deletion of the portions which are exempt under this subsection.

(c)(1) Whenever a request is made which involves access to records described in subsection (b)(7)(A) and—

> (A) the investigation or proceeding involves a possible violation of criminal law; and
> (B) there is reason to believe that (i) the subject of the investigation or proceeding is not aware of its pendency, and (ii) disclosure of the existence of the records could reasonably be expected to interfere with enforcement proceedings,

the agency may, during only such time as that circumstance continues, treat the records as not subject to the requirements of this section.

(2) Whenever informant records maintained by a criminal law enforcement agency under an informant's name or personal identifier are requested by a third party according to the informant's name or personal identifier, the agency may treat the records as not subject to the requirements of this section unless the informant's status as an informant has been officially confirmed.

(3) Whenever a request is made which involves access to records maintained by the Federal Bureau of Investigation pertaining to foreign intelligence or counterintelligence, or international terrorism, and the existence of the records is classified information as provided in subsection (b)(1), the Bureau may, as long as the existence of the records remains classified information, treat the records as not subject to the requirements of this section.

(d) This section does not authorize withholding of information or limit the availability of records to the public, except as specifically stated in this section. This section is not authority to withhold information from Congress.

(e) On or before March 1 of each calendar year, each agency shall submit a report covering the preceding calendar year to the Speaker of the House of Representatives and President of the Senate for referral to the appropriate committees of the Congress. The report shall include —

(1) the number of determinations made by such agency not to comply with requests for records made to such agency under subsection (a) and the reasons for each such determination;

(2) the number of appeals made by persons under subsection (a)(6), the result of such appeals, and the reason for the action upon each appeal that results in a denial of information;

(3) the names and titles or positions of each person responsible for the denial of records requested under this section, and the number of instances of participation for each;

(4) the results of each proceeding conducted pursuant to subsection (a)(4)(F), including a report of the disciplinary action taken against the officer or employee who was primarily responsible for improperly withholding records or an explanation of why disciplinary action was not taken;

(5) a copy of every rule made by such agency regarding this section;

(6) a copy of the fee schedule and the total amount of fees collected by the agency for making records available under this section; and

(7) such other information as indicates efforts to administer fully this section.

The Attorney General shall submit an annual report on or before March 1 of each calendar year which shall include for the prior calendar year a listing of the number of cases arising under this section, the exemption involved in each case, the disposition of such case, and the cost, fees, and penalties assessed under subsections (a)(4)(E), (F) and (G). Such report shall also include a description of the efforts undertaken by the Department of Justice to encourage agency compliance with this section.

(f) For purposes of this section, the term "agency" as defined in section 551(1) of this title includes any Executive department, military department, Government corporation, Government controlled corporation or other establishment in the executive branch of the Government (including the Executive Office of the President), or any independent regulatory agency.

* * * * *

Section 180 Effective Dates [not to be codified].

(a) The amendments made by section 1802 [the modification of Exemption 7 and the addition of the new subsection (c)] shall be effective on the date of enactment of this Act [October 27, 1986], and shall apply with respect to any requests for records, whether or not the request was made prior to such date, and shall apply to any civil action pending on such date.

(b)(1) The amendments made by section 1803 [the new fee and fee waiver provisions] shall be effective 180 days after the date of the enactment of this Act [April 25, 1987], except that regulations to implement such amendments shall be promulgated by such 180th day.

(2) The amendments made by section 1803 shall apply with respect to any requests for records, whether or not the request was made prior to such date, and shall apply to any civil action pending on such date, except that review charges applicable to records requested for commercial use shall not be applied by an agency to requests made before the effective date specified in paragraph (1) of this subsection or before the agency has finally issued its regulations.

Appendix II

The Privacy Act of 1974
5 U.S.C. 552a

§552a. Records maintained on individuals

(a) Definitions

For purposes of this section—
    (1) the term "agency" means agency as defined in section 552(e) of this title;
    (2) the term "individual" means a citizen of the United States or an alien lawfully admitted for permanent residence;
    (3) the term "maintain" includes maintain, collect, use or disseminate;
    (4) the term "record" means any item, collection or grouping of information about an individual that is maintained by an agency, including but not limited to, his education, financial transactions, medical history and criminal or employment history and that contains his name, or the identifying number, symbol, or other identifying particular assigned to the individual, such as a finger or voice print or a photograph;
    (5) the term "system of records" means a group of any records under the control of any agency from which information is retrieved by the name of the individual or by some identifying number, symbol, or other identifying particular assigned to the individual;
    (6) the term "statistical record" means a record in a system of records maintained for statistical research or reporting purposes only and not used in whole or in part in making any determination about an identifiable individual, except as provided by section 8 of Title 13; and
    (7) the term "routine use" means, with respect to the disclosure of a record, the use of such record for purpose which is compatible with the purpose for which it was collected.

(b) Conditions of Disclosure

No agency shall disclose any record which is contained in a system of records by any means of communication to any person, or to another agency, except pursuant to a written request by, or with the prior written consent of, the individual to whom the record pertains, unless disclosure of the record would be—

(1) to those officers and employees of the agency which maintains the record who have a need for the record in the performance of their duties;

(2) required under section 552 of this title;

(3) for a routine use as defined in subsection (a)(7) of this section and described under subsection (e)(4)(D) of this section;

(4) to the Bureau of the Census for purposes of planning or carrying out a census or survey or related activity pursuant to the provisions of Title 13;

(5) to a recipient who has provided the agency with advance adequate written assurance that the record will be used solely as a statistical research or reporting record, and the record is to be transferred in a form that is not individually identifiable;

(6) to the National Archives and Records Administration as a record which has sufficient historical or other value to warrant its continued preservation by the United States Government, or for evaluation by the Archivist of the United States or the designee of the Archivist to determine whether the record has such value;

(7) to another agency or to an instrumentality of any governmental jurisdiction within or under the control of the United States for a civil or criminal law enforcement activity if the activity is authorized by law, and if the head of the agency or instrumentality has made a written request to the agency which maintains the record specifying the particular portion desired and the law enforcement activity for which the record is sought;

(8) to a person pursuant to a showing of compelling circumstances affecting the health or safety of an individual if upon such disclosure notification is transmitted to the last known address of such individual;

(9) to either House of Congress, or, to the extent of matter within its jurisdiction, any committee or subcommittee thereof, any joint committee of Congress or subcommittee of any such joint committee;

(10) to the Comptroller General, or any of his authorized representatives, in the course of the performance of the duties of the General Accounting Office;

(11) pursuant to the order of a court of competent jurisdiction;

(12) to a consumer reporting agency in accordance with section 3711(f) of Title 31.

(c) Accounting of Certain Disclosures

Each agency, with respect to each system of records under its control shall—

(1) except for disclosures made under subsections (b)(1) or (b)(2) of this section, keep an accurate accounting of—

> (A) the date, nature, and purpose of each disclosure of a record to any person or to another agency made under subsection (b) of this section; and

(B) the name and address of the person or agency to whom the disclosure is made;

(2) retain the accounting made under paragraph (1) of this subsection for at least five years or the life of the record, whichever is longer, after the disclosure for which the accounting is made;

(3) except for disclosures made under subsection (b)(7) of this section, make the accounting made under paragraph (1) of this subsection available to the individual named in the record at his request; and

(4) inform any person or other agency about any correction or notation of dispute made by the agency in accordance with subsection (d) of this section of any record that has been disclosed to the person or agency if an accounting of the disclosure was made.

(d) Access to Records

Each agency that maintains a system of records shall—

(1) upon request by any individual to gain access to his record or to any information pertaining to him which is contained in the system, permit him and upon his requests, a person of his own choosing to accompany him, to review the record and have a copy made of all or any portion thereof in a form comprehensible to him, except that the agency may require the individual to furnish a written statement authorizing discussion of that individual's record in the accompanying person's presence;

(2) permit the individual to request amendment of a record pertaining to him and—

(A) not later than 10 days (excluding Saturdays, Sundays, and legal public holidays) after the date of receipt of such request, acknowledge in writing such receipt; and

(B) promptly, either—

(i) make any correction of any portion thereof which the individual believes is not accurate, relevant, timely or complete; or

(ii) inform the individual of its refusal to amend the record in accordance with his request, the reason for the refusal, the procedures established by the agency for the individual to request a review of that refusal by the head of the agency or an officer designated by the head of the agency, and the name and business address of that official;

(3) permit the individual who disagrees with the refusal of the agency to amend his record to request a review of such refusal, and not later than 30 days (excluding Saturdays, Sundays and legal public holidays) from the date on which the individual requests such review, complete such review and make a final determination unless, for good cause shown, the head of the agency extends such 30-day period; and if, after his review, the reviewing official also refuses to amend the record in accordance with the request, permit the individual to file with the agency a concise statement setting forth the reasons for his disagreement with the refusal of the agency, and notify the individual of

the provisions for judicial review of the reviewing official's determination under subsection (g)(1)(A) of this section;

(4) in any disclosure, containing information about which the individual has filed a statement of disagreement, occurring after the filing of the statement under paragraph (3) of this subsection, clearly note any portion of the record which is disputed and provide copies of the statement and, if the agency deems it appropriate, copies of a concise statement of the reasons of the agency for not making the amendments requested, to persons or other agencies to whom the disputed record has been disclosed; and

(5) nothing in this section shall allow an individual access to any information compiled in reasonable anticipation of a civil action or proceeding.

(e) Agency Requirements

Each agency that maintains a system of records shall—

(1) maintain in its records only such information about an individual as is relevant and necessary to accomplish a purpose of the agency required to be accomplished by statute or by executive order of the President;

(2) collection information to the greatest extent practicable directly from the subject individual when the information may result in adverse determinations about an individual's rights, benefits, and privileges under Federal programs;

(3) inform each individual whom it asks to supply information, on the form which is uses to collect the information or on a separate form that can be retained by the individual—

    (A) the authority (whether granted by statute, or by executive order of the President) which authorizes the solicitation of the information and whether disclosure of such information is mandatory or voluntary;

    (B) the principal purpose or purposes for which the information is intended to be used;

    (C) the routine uses which may be made of the information, as published pursuant to paragraph (4)(D) of this subsection; and

    (D) the effects on him, if any, of not providing all or any part of the requested information;

(4) subject to the provisions of paragraph (11) of this subsection, publish in the Federal Register upon establishment or revision a notice of the existence and character of the system of records, which notice shall include—

    (A) the name and location of the system;

    (B) the categories of individuals on whom records are maintained in the system;

    (C) the categories of records maintained in the system;

    (D) each routine use of the records contained in the system, including the categories of users and the purpose of such use;

    (E) the policies and practices of the agency regarding storage, retrievability, access controls, retention and disposal of the records;

(F) the title and business address of the agency official who is responsible for the system of records;

(G) the agency procedures whereby an individual can be notified at his request if the system of records contains a record pertaining to him;

(H) the agency procedures whereby an individual can be notified at his request how he can gain access to any record pertaining to him contained in the system of records, and how he can contest its content; and

(I) the categories of sources of records in the system;

(5) maintain all records which are used by the agency in making any determination about any individual with such accuracy, relevance, timeliness, and completeness as is reasonably necessary to assure fairness to the individual in the determination;

(6) prior to disseminating any record about an individual to any person other than an agency, unless the dissemination is made pursuant to subsection (b)(2) of this section, make reasonable efforts to assure that such records are accurate, complete, timely and relevant for agency purposes;

(7) maintain no record describing how any individual exercises rights guaranteed by the First Amendment unless expressly authorized by statute or by the individual about whom the record is maintained or unless pertinent to and within the scope of an authorized law enforcement activity;

(8) make reasonable efforts to serve notice on an individual when any record on such individual is made available to any person under compulsory legal process when such process becomes a matter of public record;

(9) establish rules of conduct for persons involved in the design, development, operation or maintenance of any system of records, or in maintaining any record, and instruct each such person with respect to such rules and the requirements of this section, including any other rules and procedures adopted pursuant to this section and the penalties for noncompliance;

(10) establish appropriate administrative, technical and physical safeguards to insure the security and confidentiality of records and to protect against any anticipated threats or hazards to their security or integrity which could result in substantial harm, embarrassment, inconvenience or unfairness to any individual on whom information is maintained; and

(11) at least 30 days prior to publication of information under paragraph (4)(D) of this subsection, publish in the Federal Register notice of any new use or intended use of the information in the system, and provide an opportunity for interested persons to submit written data, views, or arguments to the agency.

(f) Agency Rules

In order to carry out the provisions of this section, each agency that maintains a system of records shall promulgate rules, in accordance with the requirements (including general notice) of section 553 of this title, which shall —

(1) establish procedures whereby an individual can be notified in response

to his request if any system of records named by the individual contains a record pertaining to him;

(2) define reasonable times, places, and requirements for identifying an individual who requests his record or information pertaining to him before the agency shall make the record or information available to the individual;

(3) establish procedures for the disclosure to an individual upon his request of his record or information pertaining to him, including special procedure, if deemed necessary, for the disclosure to an individual of medical records, including psychological records pertaining to him;

(4) establish procedures for reviewing a request from an individual concerning the amendment of any record or information pertaining to the individual, for making a determination on the request, for an appeal within the agency of an initial adverse agency determination, and for whatever additional means may be necessary for each individual to be able to exercise fully his rights under this section; and

(5) establish fees to be charged, if any, to any individual for making copies of his record, excluding the cost of any search for and review of the record.

The Office of the Federal Register shall annually compile and publish the rules promulgated under this subsection and agency notices published under subsection (e)(4) of this section in a form available to the public at low cost.

(g)(1) Civil Remedies

Whenever any agency

(A) makes a determination under subsection (d)(3) of this section not to amend an individual's record in accordance with his request, or fails to make such review in conformity with that subsection;

(B) refuses to comply with an individual request under subsection (d)(1) of this section;

(C) fails to maintain any record concerning any individual with such accuracy, relevance, timeliness and completeness as is necessary to assure fairness in any determination relating to the qualifications, character, rights, or opportunities of, or benefits to the individual that may be made on the basis of such record, and consequently a determination is made which is adverse to the individual; or

(D) fails to comply with any other provision of this section, or any rule promulgated thereunder, in such a way as to have an adverse effect on an individual,

the individual may bring a civil action against the agency, and the district courts of the United States shall have jurisdiction in the matters under the provisions of this subsection.

(2)(A) In any suit brought under the provisions of subsection (g)(1)(A) of this section, the court may order the agency to amend the individual's record in accordance with his request or in such other way as the court may direct. In such a case the court shall determine the matter de novo.

(B) The court may assess against the United States reasonable attorney fees and other litigation costs reasonably incurred in any case under this paragraph in which the complainant has substantially prevailed.

(3)(A) In any suit brought under the provisions of subsection (g)(1)(B) of this section, the court may enjoin the agency from withholding the records and order the production to the complainant of any agency records improperly withheld from him. In such a case the court shall determine the matter de novo, and may examine the contents of any agency records in camera to determine whether the records or any portion thereof may be withheld under any of the exemptions set forth in subsection (k) of this section, and the burden is on the agency to sustain its action.

(B) The court may assess against the United States reasonable attorney fees and other litigation costs reasonably incurred in any case under this paragraph in which the complainant has substantially prevailed.

(4) In any suit brought under the provisions of subsection (g)(1)(C) or (D) of this section in which the court determines that the agency acted in a manner which was intentional or willful, the United States shall be liable to the individual in an amount equal to the sum of—

(A) actual damages sustained by the individual as a result of the refusal or failure, but in no case shall a person entitled to recovery receive less than the sum of $1,000; and
(B) the costs of the action together with reasonable attorney fees as determined by the court.

(5) An action to enforce any liability created under this section may be brought in the district court of the United States in the district in which the complainant resides, or has his principal place of business, or in which the agency records are situated, or in the District of Columbia, without regard to the amount in controversy, within two years from the date on which the cause of action arises, except that where an agency has materially and willfully misrepresented any information required under this section to be disclosed to an individual under this section, the action may be brought at any time within two years after discovery by the individual of the misrepresentation. Nothing in this section shall be construed to authorize any civil action by reason of any injury sustained as the result of a disclosure of a record prior to September 27, 1975.

(h) Rights of Legal Guardians

For the purposes of this section, the parent of any minor, or the legal guardian of any individual who has been declared to be incompetent due to physical or mental incapacity or age by a court of competent jurisdiction, may act on behalf of the individual.

(i)(1) Criminal Penalties

Any officer or employee of an agency, who by virtue of his employment or official position, has possession of, or access to, agency records which contain individually identifiable information the disclosure of which is prohibited by this section or by rules or regulations established thereunder, and who knowing that disclosure of the specific material is so prohibited, willfully discloses the material in any manner to any person or agency not entitled to receive it, shall be guilty of a misdemeanor and fined not more than $5,000.

(2) Any officer or employee of any agency who willfully maintains a system of records without meeting the notice requirements of subsection (e)(4) of this section shall be guilty of a misdemeanor and fined not more than $5,000.

(3) Any person who knowingly and willfully requests or obtains any record concerning an individual from an agency under false pretenses shall be guilty of a misdemeanor and fined not more than $5,000.

(j) General Exemptions

The head of any agency may promulgate rules, in accordance with the requirements (including general notice) of sections 553(b)(1), (2) and (3), (c), and (e) of this title, to exempt any system of records within the agency from any part of this section except subsections (b), (c)(1) and (2), (e)(4)(A) through (F), (e)(6), (7), (9), (10) and (11), and (i) if the system of records is—

(1) maintained by the Central Intelligence Agency; or

(2) maintained by an agency or component thereof which performs as its principal function any activity pertaining to the enforcement of criminal laws, including police efforts to prevent, control, or reduce crime or to apprehend criminals, and the activities of prosecutors, courts, correctional, probation, pardon, or parole authorities, and which consists of (A) information compiled for the purpose of identifying individual criminal offenders and alleged offenders and consisting only of identifying data and notations of arrests, the nature and disposition of criminal charges, sentencing, confinement, release, and parole and probation status; (B) information compiled for the purpose of a criminal investigation, including reports of informants and investigators, and associated with an identifiable individual; or (C) reports identifiable to an individual compiled at any stage of the process of enforcement of the criminal laws from arrest or indictment through release from supervision.

At the time rules are adopted under this subsection, the agency shall include in the statement required under section 553(c) of this title, the reasons why the system of records is to be exempted from a provision of this section.

(k) Specific Exemptions

The head of any agency may promulgate rules, in acccordance with the requirements (including general notice) of sections 553(b)(1), (2) and (3), (c) and (e) of this title, to exempt any system of records within the agency from subsections (c)(3), (d), (e)(1), (e)(4)(G), (H) and (I) and (f) of this section if the system of records is —

(1) subject to the provisions of section 552(b)(1) of this title;

(2) investigatory material compiled for law enforcement purposes, other than material within the scope of subsection (j)(2) of this section: *Provided, however,* That if any individual is denied any right, privilege, or benefit that he would otherwise be entitled by Federal law, or for which he would otherwise be eligible, as a result of the maintenance of such material, such material shall be provided to such individual, except to the extent that the disclosure of such material would reveal the identity of a source who furnished information to the Government under an express promise that the identity of the source would be held in confidence, or, prior to the effective date of this section, under an implied promise that the identity of the source would be held in confidence;

(3) maintained in connection with providing protective services to the President of the United States or other individuals pursuant to section 3056 of Title 18;

(4) required by statute to be maintained and used solely as statistical records;

(5) investigatory material compiled solely for the purpose of determining suitability, eligibility, or qualifications for Federal civilian employment, military service, Federal contracts, or access to classified information, but only to the extent that the disclosure of such material would reveal the identity of a source who furnished information to the Government under an express promise that the identity of the source would be held in confidence, or, prior to the effective date of this section, under an implied promise that the identity of the source would be held in confidence;

(6) testing or examination material used solely to determine individual qualifications for appointment or promotion in the Federal service the disclosure of which would compromise the objectivity or fairness of the testing or examination process; or

(7) evaluation material used to determine potential for promotion in the armed services, but only to the extent that the disclosure of such material would reveal the identity of a source who furnished information to the Government under an express promise that the identity of the source would be held in confidence, or, prior to the effective date of this section, under an implied promise that the identity of the source would be held in confidence.

At the time rules are adopted under this subsection, the agency shall include in the statement required under section 553(c) of this title, the reasons why the system of records is to be exempted from a provision of this section.

(l)(1) Archival Records

Each agency record which is accepted by the Archivist of the United States for storage, processing and servicing in accordance with section 3103 of Title 44 shall, for the purposes of this section, be considered to be maintained by the agency which deposited the record and shall be subject to the provisions of this section. The Archivist of the United States shall not disclose the record except to the agency which maintains the record, or under rules established by that agency which are not inconsistent with the provisions of this section.

(2) Each agency record pertaining to an identifiable individual which was transferred to the National Archives of the United States as a record which has sufficient historical or other value to warrant its continued preservation by the United States Government, prior to the effective date of this section, shall, for the purposes of this section, be considered to be maintained by the National Archives and shall not be subject to the provisions of this section, except that a statement generally describing such records (modeled after the requirements relating to records subject to subsections (e)(4)(A) through (G) of this section) shall be published in the Federal Register.

(3) Each agency record pertaining to an identifiable individual which is transferred to the National Archives of the United States as a record which has sufficient historical or other value to warrant its continued preservation by the United States Government, on or after the effective date of this section, shall, for the purposes of this section, be considered to be maintained by the National Archives and shall be exempt from the requirements of this section except subsections (e)(4)(A) through (G) and (e)(9) of this section.

(m) Government Contractors

(1) When an agency provides by a contract for the operation by or on behalf of the agency of a system of records to accomplish an agency function, the agency shall, consistent with its authority, cause the requirements of this section to be applied to such system. For purposes of subsection (i) of this section any such contractor and any employee of such contractor, if such contract is agreed to on or after the effective date of this section, shall be considered to be an employee of an agency.

(2) A consumer reporting agency to which a record is disclosed under section 3711(f) of Title 31 shall not be considered a contractor for the purposes of this section.

(n) Mailing Lists

An individual's name and address may not be sold or rented by an agency unless such action is specifically authorized by law. This provision shall not be construed to require the withholding of names and addresses otherwise permitted to be made public.

(o) Report on New Systems

Each agency shall provide adequate advance notice to Congress and the Office of Management and Budget of any proposal to establish or alter any system of records in order to permit an evaluation of the probable or potential effect of such proposal on the privacy and other personal or property rights of individuals or the disclosure of information relating to such individuals, and its effect on the preservation of the constitutional principles of federalism and separation of powers.

(p) Annual Report

The President shall annually submit to the Speaker of the House of Representatives and the President pro tempore of the Senate a report —

(1) describing the actions of the Director of the Office of Management and Budget pursuant to section 6 of the Privacy Act of 1974 during the preceding year;

(2) describing the exercise of individual rights of access and amendment under this section during such year;

(3) identifying changes in or additions to systems of records;

(4) containing such other information concerning administration of this section as may be necessary or useful to the Congress in reviewing the effectiveness of this section in carrying out the purposes of the Privacy Act of 1974.

(q) Effect of Other Laws

(1) No agency shall rely on any exemption contained in section 552 of this title to withhold from an individual any record which is otherwise accessible to such individual under the provisions of this section.

(2) No agency shall rely on any exemption in this section to withhold from an individual any record which is otherwise accessible to such individual under the provisions of section 552 of this title.

The following sections were originally part of the Privacy Act but were not codified:

Sec. 6 The Office of Management and Budget shall —

(1) develop guidelines and regulations for the use of agencies in implementing the provisions of section 552a of Title 5, United States Code, as added by section 3 of this Act; and

(2) provide continuing assistance to and oversight of the implementation of the provisions of such section by agencies.

Sec. 7(a)(1) It shall be unlawful for any Federal, State or local government agency to deny to any individual any right, benefit or privilege provided by law because of such individual's refusal to disclose his social security account number.

(2) the provisions of paragraph (1) of this subsection shall not apply with respect to —

(A) any disclosure which is required by Federal statute, or

(B) any disclosure of a social security number to any Federal, State or local agency maintaining a system of records in existence and operating before January 1, 1975, if such disclosure was required under statute or regulation adopted prior to such date to verify the identity of an individual.

(b) Any Federal, State or local government agency which requests an individual to disclose his social security account number shall inform that individual whether that disclosure is mandatory or voluntary, by what statutory or other authority such number is solicited, and what uses will be made of it.

Index